Global Issues

Series Editors

Jim Whitman
Wakefield, West Yorkshire, UK

Paolo D. Farah
John D. Rockefeller IV School of Policy and Politics
West Virginia University
Morgantown, WV, USA

The rapid pace of globalizing dynamics has brought in its wake a proliferation of crises, governance challenges and large-scale stresses, unprecedented in their range, seriousness and urgency. These emerging conditions and relations are variously global is their range, inclusiveness and impacts; and many of them are outpacing our legal, political and ethical systems of deliberation and control. Climate change, the ravages of contagious diseases and financial turmoil are all cases in point. Similarly, the transformative implications of new scientific and technological developments, from Big Data to gene editing, are already upon us. This book series is dedicated to providing insights into the complex interaction of human and natural systems; modes of cooperation and conflict; and the ways and degrees to which human values can be reconciled and more effectively enacted. The concentration throughout is on an integration of existing disciplines toward the clarification of political possibility as well as impending crises.

The series is published in cooperation with gLAWcal - Global Law Initiatives for Sustainable Development.

Federico Lorenzo Ramaioli

Juridical Perspectives between Islam and the West

A Tale of Two Worlds

palgrave
macmillan

Federico Lorenzo Ramaioli
Rome, Italy

ISSN 2947-8863 ISSN 2947-8871 (electronic)
ISBN 978-3-031-37843-0 ISBN 978-3-031-37844-7 (eBook)
https://doi.org/10.1007/978-3-031-37844-7

Published in cooperation with gLAWcal – Global Law Initiatives for Sustainable Development
Published in cooperation with gLAWcal – Global Law Initiatives for Sustainable Development, Essex, UK

This Palgrave Macmillan imprint is published by the registered company Springer Nature Switzerland AG.
The registered company address is: Gewerbestrasse 11, 6330 Cham, Switzerland

Paper in this product is recyclable.

"It was the best of times, it was the worst of times, it was the age of wisdom, it was the age of foolishness, it was the epoch of belief, it was the epoch of incredulity."

Charles Dickens

Law, Society, and Religion: Islam and the West

Paolo Davide Farah
Morgantown, WV, USA

While the origin of the term 'religion'[1] remains unclear, its role and prominence in structuring and shaping the relations between state and society in early civilization is undisputed.[2] Historically, religion has played, and partially still play, an important role in shaping the development of humanity whether people were believers or not. Today, some areas, such as Asia and Sub-Saharan Africa, are witnessing a drastic increase in the number of religious followers, whereas in others, religion is often portrayed as a premodern phenomenon destined to disappear in time. Its continuing relevance stems partially from the fact that some religions promise an afterlife for everyone, assuming people follow its dogma, thereby providing hope. Whether it is the eternal question of the afterlife or the meaning of life, all religions provide responses to complex and deeply philosophical questions, in turn influencing how individuals conduct their daily life and

[1] Paolo Davide Farah, Full Professor, West Virginia University, Eberly College of Arts and Sciences, John D. Rockefeller IV School of Policy and Politics; Founder and Director of the West Virginia University, Energy Justice and Just Transition Lab; Founder and Coordinator of the Eberly College Interdisciplinary Research Collaborative on Global Challenges and Local Response Initiatives; Founder, President, Director, Principal Investigator and Senior Research Fellow, at gLAWcal—Global Law Initiatives for Sustainable Development (United Kingdom). Dual PhD in International Law from Aix-Marseille University (France) and University of Milan (Italy), LLM in European Legal Studies from the College of Europe in Bruges (Belgium), Maitrise (JD) in International and European Law from Paris Ouest La Defense Nanterre University (France). Email Addresses: paolofarah@yahoo.com; paolo.farah@glawcal.org.uk.

[2] Shanjendu Nath, "Religion and Its Role in Society", in *IOSR Journal of Humanities and Social Science*, Vol. 20, Issue 11, 2015, pp. 82–83.

bringing a positive outcome for societal and human development also in marginalized populations. Throughout history, both progress and decline have been associated with religion. Religion promoted social progress, the establishment of solidarity, as well as progress in arts and sciences and overall attention for the most vulnerable parts of society. In other cases, religion disputed and questioned the role of science in human development, brought conflicts, and hindered progress. This is why, in many places and in different historical times, the targeting of religious symbols and representatives, as in the French revolution, has been a common trend. Religion has also had a difficult time defining their scope and coverage, especially when dealing with human conduct in private[3] and public life.[4]

In light of the complexity and divergence[5] of the religious landscape and its role in the progress/decline of civilization, scholars have extensively analyzed religion from a variety of perspectives. Among others, the link between religion and law has been extensively addressed in literature.[6] Some consider religion to be the opium of the masses; others see it as a way for progress[7] encouraging cooperation, including at the international level.[8] Commentators also point to the marketization and fragmentation of religion, especially in Western secular society. Still, humanity remains, in

[3] For an analysis on how religion is amongst one of the factors shaping a negative public opinion on homosexuality, see: Amy Adamczyk, *Cross-National Public Opinion about Homosexuality: Examining Attitudes across the Globe*, University of California Press, 2017, pp. 17–40.

[4] A debate is ongoing on the role of religions in public education. See generally, Steven P. Jones & Eric C. Sheffield, "The Role of Religion in 21st–Century Public Schools: Historic Perspectives on God and Goodness in the Classroom", https://files.eric.ed.gov/fulltext/EJ1047681.pdf.

[5] Akinfenwa Oluwaseun et al., "The Role of Religion in Modern Society: Masses Opium or Tool for Development: A Case Study of Saw-Mill Area, Ilorin, Kwara State, Nigeria", in *International Journal of Sociology and Anthropology*, Vol. 6, n. 1, 2014, pp. 8–17.

[6] Seyyed Mehdi Taheri, "The Role of Religion in the Development of Communities: Comparison of Protestantism, Tokugawa and Islam", in *Kom*, Vol. 5, Issue 1, 2016, pp. 37–55.

[7] Akinfenwa Oluwaseun et al., "The Role of Religion in Modern Society: Masses Opium or Tool for Development: A Case Study of Saw-Mill Area, Ilorin, Kwara State, Nigeria", in *International Journal of Sociology and Anthropology*, Vol. 6, Issue 1, 2014, pp. 8–17.

[8] Sida Partnership Forum, "The Role of Religion in Development Cooperation" (May. 2009).

many regards, under the influence of the faith despite all the contrasting developments witnessed in various fields.[9]

Law and religion are present in almost every society, where the predominance of one over the other can greatly vary, and, in some cases, they both contend for authority over the citizenry. From a historical standpoint, this resulted in a constant change in the relationship between law and religion.[10] Globalization also had a role in this regard. In some instances, globalization exacerbates differences between religions instead of encouraging mediation[11]; it seeks to fill the gap left by the diminishing role of religion in the West. Globalization also competes with religion; both are looking for ways to regulate conduct and push humanity to maintain particular worldviews. The identification of the position of religion within a secular state is debated to this day. Some tend to view and acknowledge the role of religion as fundamental to the cultivation of morality and better integration of social and cultural considerations within the international community. Others argue against such a role. Scholars in the West see the law as completely separated from religion and morality.[12] In other areas this contribution is less definite and varies based on political and social considerations. Even in predominantly Christian or Islamic nations, some countries have imposed rules limiting the influence of religion in the public sphere whereas other countries have remained either completely or partially governed and influenced by religion.[13] Even within countries where religion is held above the law, in some instances, it has been used and exploited for political goals. Similarly, in countries where religion is confined to the private and personal spheres, it still heavily influences national policy. Thus, coexistence amongst law and religion is of topical importance and has been greatly debated throughout history and

[9] J. Beyers, "The Role of Religion and Spirituality in Transforming Society", in *Acta Theologica*, Issue 32, 2021, pp. 52–69.

[10] Winnifred Fallers Sullivan, "Comparing Religions, Legally", in *Washington & Lee Law Review*, Vol. 63, 2006, pp. 913–928.

[11] Hans-Henrik Bülow et al., "The world's Major Religions Points of View on End-of-Life Decisions in the Intensive Care Unit", *in Intensive Care Medicine*, Vol. 34, Issue 3, 2008, pp. 423–430.

[12] Bryan S. Turner, "Law and Religion", in *Theory, Culture & Society*, Vol. 23, Issue 2/3, 2006.

[13] Johan D van der Vyver & M Christian Green, "Law, Religion and Human Rights in Africa: Introduction", in *African Human Rights Law Journal*, Vol. 8, Issue 2, 2008, pp. 343–350.

is key to the understanding of different cultures.[14] A great number of comparative studies emerged examining such a coexistence over the years,[15] given the impact of these relations on a national level but also for international politics.[16] Coexistence between the two in the context of the secular state also forced the judiciary to analyze and interpret religion within the legal framework of the modern state. Courts have had the difficult task of balancing rule of law and the protection of believers. Examples of tribunals that dealt with such topics include the European Court of Human Rights[17] and the Inter-American Court of Human Rights.[18] This is not an easy mission for any judge to deal with, as the final ruling will always be subject to criticism from all parties and stakeholders involved.[19]

Among the many existing religions, Islam is one of those that hold a great importance; it constitutes the world's fastest growing religion,[20] and it creates social and political rules that regulate its followers' conduct.[21] Islam, historically, played an important role in shaping major political events after its emergence and creating polities where both law and religion were intermixed, each supportive of the other.[22] As an example, empires such as the Ottomans relied on Islam to unify the nation and justify territorial expansion.[23] Islam's relevance within the political sphere varied from country to

[14] Erwin Akhverdiev & Alexander Ponomarev, "Religion as Factor in Formation of Law: Current Trends", in *SHS Web of Conferences*, Vol. 50, 2018, pp. 1–5.

[15] Russell Sandberg, *Law and Religion*, Cambridge University Press, Cambridge, 2012.

[16] Daniel O. Conkle, "Different Religions, Different Politics: Evaluating the Role of Competing Religious Traditions in American Politics and Law", in *Journal of Law and Religion*, Vol. 10, n. 1, 1993, 1–32.

[17] Effie Fokas & James T. Richardson, "The European Court of Human Rights and Minority Religions: Messages Generated and Messages received", in *Religion, State & Society*, Vol. 45, Issue 3/4, 2017, 166–173.

[18] Moncef Chaibi, "Religion and Pluralism before the Inter-American Court of Human Rights: From Individualizing Religious Freedom to Deregulating the Religious Market", in *Oxford Journal of Law and Religion*, https://doi.org/10.1093/ojlr/rwad009.

[19] Howard Kislowicz, "Judging Religion and Judges' Religions", in *Journal of Law and Religion*, Vol. 33, Issue 1, 2018, 42–60.

[20] James R. Moore, "Islam in Social Studies Education: What We Should Teach Secondary Students and Why It Matters", in *The Social Studies*, Vol. 97, n. 4, 2006, 139–144.

[21] Arthur Jeffery, "The Political Importance of Islam", in *Journal of Near Eastern Studies*, Vol. 1, Issue 4, 1942, 383.

[22] L. E. Browne, "The Development of Islam", in *The Muslim World*, Vol. 24, Issue 2, 1934, 168–177.

[23] Frederick F. Anscombe, "Islam and the Age of Ottoman Reform", in *Past & Present*, Vol. 208, Issue 1, 2010, 159–189.

country, century to century.[24] Its development took diverging paths, making Islam, rather than a monolithic entity, a multifaceted and complex religious phenomenon.[25] Particularly in the West, debate surrounds the political dimension of Islam, approaching it with worry and caution against the spread of the religion and its coexistence within secular and liberal societies.[26] Islam, as other religions, continues to serve as the principal basis for identity of its believers[27] and as a means for creating and fostering deep social trust and solidarity amongst its followers.[28] Various debates took place with regard to the place that Islam should occupy in society. In the last two decades, such debates have intensified due to terrorist attacks that have targeted Western ways of life or particular social and cultural institutions.[29] At times, there has been great confusion. Commentators have mixed up what Islam and Muslim faith are and what has nothing to do with religion or belief such as radicalization and terrorism which could happen even in any religion. Moreover, the emergence of new Islamic identities, mixing elements of Islam with Western values, as well as changing demographic and migratory patterns has also played a role in the increased attention in covering the religious landscape.

On another note, the digital revolution and the dependencies fuelled by globalization, along with advancements in new means of communication—like social media—and transportation allowed for the propagation of different ideas and ideologies, including religious ones.[30] Phenomena that, in the past, were much slower to spread and relatively enclosed within

[24] Greg Barton, "The Prospects for Islam", in *Indonesia Today: Challenges of History*, eds. Grayson J. Lloyd & Shannon L. Smith, Rowman & Littlefield Publishers, Inc. 2001, pp. 244–255.

[25] Mohammed Ayoob & Danielle Nicole Lussier, *The Many Faces of Political Islam: Religion and Politics in Muslim Societies*, University of Michigan Press, Michigan, 2020, pp. 13.

[26] For an analysis of how external factors enabled the spread of Islamism see, Mohammed Ayoob, "The Future of Political Islam: The Importance of External Variables", in *International Affairs*, Vol. 81, Issue 5, 2005, 951.

[27] Patrick D. Gaffney, "Popular Islam", in *AAPSS*, Vol. 524, Issue 1, 1992.

[28] Niclas Berggren & Christian Bjornskov, "Is the Importance of Religion in Daily Life related to Social Trust? Cross-Country and Cross-State Comparisons", in *Journal of Economic Behavior & Organization*, Vol. 80, Issue 3, 2011, pp. 459–480.

[29] Caterina Froio, "Race, Religion, or Culture? Framing Islam between Racism and Neo-Racism in the Online Network of the French Far Right", in *Perspectives on Politics*, Vol. 16, Issue 3, 2018, pp. 696–709.

[30] Ibrahim Canan, "Islam as the Religion of Peace and Tolerance", in *Terror and Suicide Attacks: An Islamic Perspective*, eds. Ergün Çapan, The Light, Inc, & Isik Yayinlar, 2004.

the boundaries of a single country or region are now increasingly being debated as part of the global conversation. Ideas and notions belonging to entirely different worldviews and philosophies are now intertwined, resulting in both an opening to find peaceful coexistence and conflict between them. Regarding the former, examples of coexistence can be found in several areas where there has been a true effort to reconcile religion with labor protections,[31] gender equality,[32] environmental protection,[33] and social justice.[34] On tensions, some scholars embrace the 'Clash of Civilizations' theory first hypothesized by Samuel Huntington, arguing that religion will fuel conflict in the medium and long term.[35] This perspective believes that such a conflict is inevitable, and instead on opening dialogue, the attention should focus on how further differences develop which makes it almost impossible to find compromises even in the short term.

The relation between Islam and the law is very complicated in modern times. This can be seen, for example, in the critique of international law by Muslim scholars through various studies and publications,[36] but it is likewise evident in the religion's positive contribution to Western public and international law as well as its influence upon it.[37] Indeed, a debate is currently taking place, arguing for the creation of synergies between the religion and existing legal frameworks such as international humanitarian

[31] Iftikhar Ahmad, "Religion and Labor: Perspective in Islam", in *Working USA: The Journal of Labor and Society*, 2011.

[32] Iman Hashim, "Reconciling Islam and Feminism", in *Gender & Development*, vol. VII, n. 1, 1999.

[33] Erhun Kula, 'Islam and Environmental Conservation' (2001) 28 Environmental Conservation 1; Andrew Chan and Md Saidul Islam, 'State, Religion, and Environmentalism: Fostering Social Cohesion and Environmental Protection in Singapore' (2015) 1 Environmental Sociology 177.

[34] Erin E Stiles, 'Contemporary Expressions of Social Justice in Islam' [2012] The Wiley-Blackwell Companion to Religion and Social Justice 153.

[35] Jody C Baumgartner, Peter L. Francia & Jonathan S. Morris, "A Clash of Civilizations? The Influence of Religion on Public Opinion of U.S. Foreign Policy in the Middle East", in *Political Research Quarterly*, Vol. 61, Issue 2, 2008.

[36] Sheikh Wahbeh al-Zuhili, "Islam and International law", in *International Review of the Red Cross*, Vol. 87, n. 858, 2005, pp. 269–283.

[37] Marcel A. Boisard, "On the Probable Influence of Islam on Western Public and International Law", in *International Journal of Middle East Studies*, Vol. 11, Issue 4, 1980, pp. 429–450.

law.[38] Under this context, new, innovative ideas and concepts, which may be beneficial to the law, have been introduced thanks to an on-going dialogue with religion.[39] In other cases, the principles and dogma of religion have clashed with liberal and secular states. This is especially the case when discussing shari'a law,[40] women's rights under the religion,[41] and immigration from developing and Global South countries and specific groups,[42] during post-colonial era.[43] This has resulted in numerous research and debate addressing these topics,[44] as many have noticed the increasing occurrence of concerns in many places and several governments globally.[45] The concept of justice is being debated in this context.[46] For instance, among many other suggestions, some have recommended the use of legislation to integrate religious communities in the West[47] and the regulation of religion through domestic legislation such as in the American system[48] or in English law.[49]

[38] James Cockayne, "Islam and International Humanitarian Law: From a Clash to a Conversation between Civilizations", in *International Review of the Red Cross*, Vol. 84, n. 847, 2002.

[39] On mental health see Georgios A. Tzeferakos & Athanasios I. Douzenis, "Islam, Mental Health and Law: A General Overview", in *Annals of General Psychiatry*, Vol. 16, 2017. For an example on environmental protection: Sayed Sikandar Shah Haneef, "Principles of Environmental Law in Islam", in *Arab Law Quarterly*, Vol. 17, 2002, pp. 241–254.

[40] Jamila Hussein, *Islam: Its Law and Society*, The Federation Press, 2011.

[41] Azizah al-Hibri, "Islam, Law and Custom: Redefining Muslim Women's Rights", in *American University Journal of International Law and Policy*, Vol. 12, Issue 1, 1997, pp. 1–44.

[42] Neil Gotanda, "The Racialization of Islam in American Law", in *The Annals of the American. Academy of Political and Social Science*, Vol. 637, Issue 1, 2011 pp. 184–195.

[43] Iza Hussin, "The Pursuit of the Perak Regalia: Islam, Law, and the Politics of Authority in the Colonial State", in *Law & Social Inquiry*, Vol. 32, Issue 3, 2007, pp. 759–788.

[44] Majid Khadduri, *War and Peace in the Law of Islam*, Johns Hopkins Press, 1955, pp. 321.

[45] Michael Humphrey, "Culturalising the Abject: Islam, Law and Moral Panic in the West", in *Australian Journal of Social Issues*, Vol. 42, Issue 1, 2007, pp. 9–25.

[46] Ahmed E. Souaiaia, *Contesting Justice: Women, Islam, Law, and Society*, State University of New York Press, 2008, pp. 195.

[47] Christian Joppke, "Europe and Islam: Alarmists, Victimists, and Integration by Law", in *West European Politics*, Vol. 37, Issue 6, 2014, pp. 1314–1335.

[48] Kathleen M. Moore, "Visible through the Veil: The Regulation of Islam in American Law", in *Sociology of Religion*, Vol. 68, Issue 3, 2007, pp. 237–251.

[49] Robin Griffith-Jones, eds. *Islam and English Law: Rights, Responsibilities and the Place of Shari'a*, Cambridge University Press, Cambridge, 2013, pp. 331.

Federico Lorenzo Ramaioli in *Juridical Perspectives Between Islam and the West: A Tale of Two Worlds* addresses all the abovementioned issues, considering them from a juridical perspective in the West. Ramaioli initially provides an overview of relations between Islam and the West explaining various notions and concepts such as *shari'a*. The book then delves into complex ideas: in this case, sovereignty and universalism after Westphalia. These terms, among others such as *ummah*, *dawla*, and transnationalism, are discussed in detail. The author then goes deeper in his analysis, providing a historical appraisal of the law during the period of the caliphate, discussing authority, personification of power, as well as external and internal legitimacy. The book then examines the topic of *Shari'a* in the West and in Islam. Based on all that, the author calls for a dialogue between different legal orders to bridge existing gaps for a more peaceful and prosperous society.

Moving to the more detailed analysis of this book, it is relevant to highlight that this book compares in detail the encounters between different juridical systems. Ramaioli draws on comparative legal theory with a particular focus on how ideas are spread and disseminated across the globe. This is even more pronounced in the mature phase of globalization. While the COVID-19 pandemic halted the international movement of people, the world is just as connected as before, at least concerning the encounter of law and diverging worldviews. Legal transplant, a central and much discussed and criticized notion in comparative law, has gained new impetus since the decolonization period and in the more mature phase of economic globalization. The suggestive metaphor, originally developed by Alan Watson, to analyze the 'pre' eminence of Roman law in shaping European civilization and their legal systems tends to interpret the juridical phenomenon as a Western-led universalization attempt. The increasing importance of non-state actors[50] in shaping and guiding legal developments, as well as the more pronounced intervention of global governance institutions, helped in considering the prominence that the law has gained latterly, as a plausible solution to address global challenges such as poverty,

[50] On the role of private corporations, see: Angelica Bonfanti (ed), *Business and Human Rights in Europe: International Law Challenges* (Routledge 2019); For an analysis of how Non-State actors are shaping and influencing the multilateral order, see Lukasz Gruszczynski and others, *The Crisis of Multilateral Legal Order: Causes, Dynamics and Implications* (Taylor & Francis 2022).

environmental degradation, and human rights.[51] Most of the time, models of laws and regulations have been imposed on Global South countries with little regard to complexities at the local level or to the fact that law is only one of the coexisting forces shaping the social fabric of a country. Ramaioli follows a different path, and rather than focusing on the, often violent, imposition of legal institutions, he is interested in how to open a dialogue between those 'two worlds' with their complementary juridical systems. This exercise, carried out with rigor and solid methodology, allows readers, both from the West and the East, to increase their understanding of the commonalities and differences between the two worlds. Ramaioli's book is centered around the need to 'avoid universalizing Western notions and constructs', and it focuses on grounding the construct of law in the social and cultural sphere. The book does not describe law as in the books on legal positivist institutions but deals with how knowledge, ideas, and discourse are shaped in a dynamic and constant manner. The book, while, strictly speaking, a title on comparative law, is much broader in its aims and goals, crossing disciplinary boundaries and highlighting the importance of establishing categories of understanding that go beyond the mere dichotomy of good versus bad. Rather than the analysis of specific legal institutions or principle of laws, Ramaioli is attentive at framing a more nuanced and philosophically oriented understanding of the theoretical underpinnings behind the legal encounter between Islam and the West. The two legal traditions are put into relation, and key notions framing the historical developments of core ideas are discussed in specific detail. The interpretative category used to do so is the concept of 'legal category'. Legal categories act in the book as the foundational stone for analysis, able to shed light on the complexities of comparing and assessing the ramifications of our reality, especially when relations between law, power, and space are in question. In reading the law as cultural multiplicity and in describing how individuals solve the intricacy of the juridical order, Ramaioli pays particular attention to context and to communities where encounters between diverging, and often not even comparable, legal systems take place. Watson's legal transplant and the René David's categories

[51] On the reforms of global governance institutions see, John N Clarke and Geoffrey R Edwards (eds), *Global Governance in the Twenty-First Century* (Palgrave Macmillan UK 2004) <http://link.springer.com/10.1057/9780230518698> accessed 26 June 2023; For an assessment of how to bridge differences in the international community see: Oliver P Richmond, *Maintaining Order, Making Peace* (Palgrave Macmillan UK 2002) <http://link.springer.com/10.1057/9780230289048> accessed 26 June 2023.

are clear examples that laws and policies in Global South countries were often labelled as non-juridical and in some cases as anti-juridical. In the famous *Traité élémentaire de droit civile compare* by René David, a mere couple of pages were dedicated to East Asia and it was pointed out the lack of 'law' to justify the brevity and scarcity of analysis. Such an approach can also be found in a wide range of initiatives and schemes carried out under the guise of global governance institutions[52] such as the World Bank, the International Monetary Fund, and private international development organizations. Legal reforms in Global South countries' judicial, political, and economic systems were carried out with the aid of the West. Priorities were to promote 'rule of law', market liberalization, and human rights and other alleged universal values of the international community.[53] With the rise of recently industrialized economies such as India, China, and Brazil, and the success of these countries in lifting people out of poverty, new models that consider local and community concerns along with global necessities and standards are being spread at the international level.[54] *Juridical Perspectives Between Islam and the West: A Tale of Two Worlds* fits within this framework and offers a much-needed perspective on how to be reflexive and attentive to local contexts in the work of legal scholars. Ramaioli, after explaining their methodological approach, begins by reviewing basic notions on *sharīʿa,* opening their analysis with the territorial dimensions of power in the two worlds. The modern state and the binding of political power to a well-defined, precise territory inhabited by a specific national population not only are the founding myth of statehood but also enable the West to uphold and structure the international community. Some resemblance of this model is often imposed as a method of

[52] Antonio Segura Serrano, *The Reform of International Economic Governance* (Routledge 2016) <https://www.taylorfrancis.com/books/9781315553603> accessed 16 July 2023.

[53] For an analysis of how resilient global politics institutions could boost human rights protection, see: Kurt Mills and David Jason Karp (eds), *Human Rights Protection in Global Politics* (Palgrave Macmillan UK 2015) <http://link.springer.com/10.1057/9781137463173> accessed 26 June 2023.

[54] For an assessment of this model in the context of China see on WTO and non-trade concerns, Paolo Davide Farah, 'Trade and Progress: The Case of China' (2016) 30 Columbia Journal of Asian Law 51; Paolo Farah and Elena Cima (eds), *China's Influence on Non-Trade Concerns in International Economic Law* (Routledge 2016); on State-Owned enterprises as a model of industrial policy and its increasing relevance in the international context, see: Paolo Davide Farah and Davide Giacomo Zoppolato, 'Public Ownership and the WTO In a Post-Covid-19 Era: From Trade Disputes To a "Social" Function' (2022) 125 *West Virginia Law Review*, pp. 644–688.

forcing change with violence on other territories and populations. Westphalian statehood is only one of the possible ways to approach relations between people, power, and space, and it is not even the longest lived. Empires, as forms of political organization, lasted much longer and, in several cases, have proven to be more accommodating and flexible to differences and in the integration of different individuals. *Ummah* as described in the *Qur'ān* is one of the different possible ways to define state-society relations and is characterized by the idea of a political community aligned with *sharī ʿa:* 'a normative dimension that defines the belonging to this communitarian idea, which ideally overcomes national borders and geographical boundaries'. Both notions are deeply political, but their founding elements could both be traced to submission to a particular political authority, described in detail in Chap. 2. The two evocative figures of Leviathan and the *Kalīfah* are seen as powerful symbolic values and used simultaneously to legitimize and personify supreme authority. Ramaioli combines historical remarks with an analysis of the social and economic development that took place in the two worlds in order to address how the West and Islam entered in diverging paths on how to legitimize political authority, the former 'based on a shared narrative whose core is the idea of institution-persona *ficta*' while the latter 'is grounded in the shared narrative of universalism, whose basis is to be found in the consensus of the community, rooted in a religious belief'. Chapter 4 progresses to the analysis of the role of human reason in the juridical sphere; that is, for Ramaioli, what really opened the apparently incompatible path amongst the two worlds: Islam is more contemplative and reflexive whereas the West is more creative-oriented. Human reason and the necessary question of the source of law affect what we intend and shape the discourse on the nature of the law, leading to the analysis in Chap. 5 of the separation between religion and the law and why, once the law is created, enforcement is needed. Repression in the West and the biopolitical state could not be as easily equated with the more all-encompassing nature of *sharī ʿa,* as it is not limited to earthly punishment and control but extending to the afterlife or the return from it. Chapter 6 highlights, with a comparative legal and historically grounded perspective, the encounter between the two worlds and the forceful imposition of the West's idea of modernity on Arab states. Constitutional momentum and the idea of 'having' a constitution transplanted by the West demonstrate how flexibility and dynamic interactions between the two worlds took place in the past and are set to be relevant for the foreseeable future.

Constitutionalism and the mutual, constantly fluctuating influence between the two worlds are described in more detail by Ramaioli in the book *Shari'a and The Constitution in Contemporary Legal Models: Two Worlds in Dialogue*.

Ramaioli's *Juridical Perspectives Between Islam and the West: A Tale of Two Worlds* is an important addition to the gLAWcal Palgrave Book Series on 'Global Issues'. gLAWcal—Global Law Initiatives for Sustainable Development is an independent non-profit research organization and think tank (http://www.glawcal.org.uk/) that attempts to shed new light on Global Issues and Non-trade Concerns through research, policy analysis, and advocacy. Non-trade Concerns include good and global governance; human rights; right to water; rights to food; social, economic, and cultural rights; labor rights; access to knowledge; public health; social welfare; consumer interests and animal welfare; climate change; energy; environmental protection and sustainable development; product safety; food safety; and security. All of these values are directly affected by the global expansion of world trade and should be upheld to balance the excesses of globalization.

The gLAWcal Palgrave book series on 'Global Issues' explores many relevant matters and provides insights into the complex interaction of human and natural systems; modes of cooperation and conflict; and the ways and degrees to which human values can be reconciled and more effectively enacted. The concentration throughout is on an integration of existing disciplines towards the clarification of political possibility as well as impending crises. The rapid pace of globalizing dynamics has brought in its wake a proliferation of crises, governance challenges and large-scale stresses, unprecedented in their range, seriousness, and urgency. These emerging conditions and relations are variously global in their range, inclusiveness, and impacts; and many of them are outpacing our legal, political, and ethical systems of deliberation and control. Climate change, the ravages of contagious diseases, and financial turmoil are all cases in point. Similarly, the transformative implications of new scientific and technological developments, from Big Data to gene editing, are already upon us. Ramaioli's book fits within the broader discussion on how to relate and engage in dialogue with divergent worldviews and transnational issues that go beyond state borders with the goal of countering the sustainability and governance crises we are facing. More dialogue and increasing encounters between seemingly unbridgeable divides and assumptions on what the law is, as well as how we understand law and society relations, are of timely importance. In a world characterized by increasing violence, conflict, and hostility, Ramaioli's suggestion to open a dialogue amongst diverging worldviews instead of merely imposing a particular set of values is not only relevant but timely and sorely needed. Only with an increased understanding of diverging assumptions and philosophies is it possible to work together to counteract challenges that are truly global in scope, impossible to solve by mere single state actors.

Professor Paolo Davide Farah

Editor-in-Chief for the gLAWcal Book Series "Global Issues" published by Palgrave Macmillan (New York/London).

West Virginia University, USA and gLAWcal – Global Law Initiatives for Sustainable Development, UK

Praise for *Juridical Perspectives Between Islam and the West*

"In this deeply thoughtful work, the author demonstrates that purportedly universal categories of legal analysis may be misleading in an understanding of Islamic law. In a work that contributes not only to Islamic studies but to the philosophy of law generally, specialists and open-minded readers will find a unique set of insights into a system of religious law that governs a quarter of the world's population and whose attributes Westerners misconstrue at their peril."

—Lawrence Rosen, *Professor of Anthropology, Princeton University*

"A comparative exploration of the triangular relationship between man as rational being, God as creator, and the legal order as a comprehensive vision for society as conceived and developed in Western and Islamic legal theory, this carefully theorized and comprehensively researched work points to differences in theoretical conceptions of legislation, the state, universalism, and the role of human reason in the elaboration of law. Carefully attentive to the specificity of terms and concepts as embedded in each tradition, Ramaioli invites the reader to engage differences in theoretical conceptions and their outcomes by bringing the systems into encounter and interaction, distinguishing and differentiating, but without giving in to clash. Original in approach and compelling in documentation, Ramaioli identifies conceptual instruments to reinterpret and rethink "law" and legal perspectives in a global context without essentializing."

—Natana J. DeLong-Bas, *Associate Professor of the Practice, Theology Department & Islamic Civilization and Societies Program, Boston College*

"The relation between faith and politics is often paradoxical, but it is not the only one. Ideologies and real facts are indeed a strange mix full of contradictions if not absurdities. Only a serious analysis of the historical events located in their theoretical and concrete contexts could indeed give us a clearer picture of what happened and seems to be happening again at the encounter of cultures and civilizations, although in different and changing conditions. The case of Islam during its fourteen centuries of life represents an interesting object of analysis, to be carried out avoiding superficial and odd shortcuts even in comparison with other political and religious traditions. This is precisely the aim of this book, in which the author carries out a comprehensive and innovative legal comparison between the "two worlds" of Islam and the West."

—Paolo Luigi Branca, *Associate Professor of Arabic Language and Literature, Catholic University of the Sacred Heart of Milan*

Contents

CHAPTER 1

Introduction: The West and Islam: Juridical Categories in a Transitional Global Scenario

1.1 A Global Space for a Global Challenge

Every civilization in history has felt the need to form and develop a precise and unique legal order,[1] characterized by the particular desire to set out rules and norms. This spontaneous regulation of the various aspects of social life cannot but illustrate a culture-specific juridical sensibility, deeply inherent to the "political" nature of the human being.[2] Evidently, it can be easily argued that a society without a certain form of legal regulation, gradually accrued and enriched along its developing path, cannot actually exist.

This is nothing less than the recurring concept expressed by the Latin formula *ubi societas, ibi jus*, whose origin, despite its use henceforth, seems to have been lost in the centuries of our ancestral past.[3] Yet, the vagueness of its origin qualifies it as a fundamental philosophical idea deeply rooted

[1] I will explain what I mean with the expression "legal order" in the paragraph dedicated to definitions and terminology. The opinions expressed in the present volume are referred exclusively to his author.

[2] The reference is clearly to Aristotle, *Politics* I, 2, 1253a2, where the Stagirite defines man as a political animal, or ζῷον πολιτικόν (*zôon politikòn*).

[3] About the substantial impossibility of identifying a precise origin for the locution, see Alessandro Levi, "Ubi societas, ibi ius", in *Saggi di teoria del diritto*, Zanichelli, Bologna 1924, p. 49.

F. L. Ramaioli, *Juridical Perspectives between Islam and the West*, Global Issues, https://doi.org/10.1007/978-3-031-37844-7_1

in our culture, indicating the universal and essential nexus between human society and the idea of law. Whenever a society grows and develops, the exigency of establishing an order characterized by a normative dimension necessarily arises. More than a legal principle, it would be appropriate to say that it represents a political and social contingency, implied in the progressive structuration of human civilizations. It is in this precise moment that a certain idea of normativity comes to life, both shaping its civilization and being shaped by it.

Regardless of the substantive content of rules and norms, the shape of a legal order greatly changes depending on the kind of social, cultural, and historical context and background from which it originates. The sense of what Herder called *Volkgeist*, as interpreted by the historical school of von Savigny,[4] is indeed something deeply affecting the juridical awareness of world history. Again, it is not simply affecting the substance of the commands imposed by the established authority on its subjects. Rather, it can be considered a meta-juridical sense of traditional and cultural heritage, influencing the following establishment of legal ideals in a given society. Law, in this respect, cannot be simply produced *ex novo* by a rational operator but is rather inherited, being deeply characterized by the philosophical and traditional customs of a community. In a given civilization, finding a certain degree of continuity is unavoidable, characterized by recurring conceptual constructs and constant normative elements. Therefore, law is neither an artificial product, nor a universal conception, but something

[4] For a selection of Herder's writings addressing the political dimension of *Volksgeist*, see Johann Gottfried Herder, *Another Philosophy of History and Selected Political Writings*, Hackett Publishing, Indianapolis 2004. With specific regard to *Volksgeist* as interpreted by the historical school, see Friedrich Carl von Savigny, *Vom Beruf unserer Zeit für Gesetzgebung und Rechtswissenschaft*, Mohr und Zimmer, Heidelberg 1814.

strictly inherent to the civilization it belongs to.[5] Again, and as Rosen has exhaustively shown, law is part of the realm of culture, and legal dynamics can be properly explained and analyzed if interpreted in this sense.[6]

Although, through the centuries, the various juridical models have been periodically subject to mutual influences due to reciprocal exchanges, there has never before been such a clear indication of juridical

[5] What is essential for this introduction, with regard to Savigny's theory and as Jhering points out, is to notice that the various conceptions of *Recht* "are not made, but become, they come forth like language and customs from out of the innermost of the life of the *Volk* and the life of the thought, without the mediation of calculation and consciousness" (Rudolf von Jhering, "Friedrich Karl von Savigny", in *Jherings Jahrbücher für die Dogmatik des bürgerlichen Rechts*, vol. V, G. Fischer, Jena 1861, pp. 364–365). See also Roger Berkowitz, *The Gift of Science. Leibniz and the modern legal tradition*, Harvard University Press, Cambridge 2005, pp. 109 ff. According to Gómez Dávila, from a more radical point of view, law is similar to language in that it is inherited by virtue of a gradual and progressive accrual of traditions and customs. In the words of the author: "The legitimate positive law is not the impossible spawn of an explicit and solemn agreement, but the historical accumulation of rules that an everyday and implicit consensus legitimizes. Men do not go to an abstract and mythical forum to agree on their rights. In the long series of centuries, men find themselves inside the law that governs them, as in the language that they speak. Law, like language, does not have a historical origin. No one invented their law or their language. Even in the Paleolithic horde, the individual was born between rules of syntax and legal rules. The first human cry reverberates between juridical structures. No one lives in a state of linguistic virginity or of juridical innocence. Law is, like language, a human construction, but it is not the intentional product of mankind. Language is a human discovery, but no man invents it" (Nicolás Gômez Dávila [1988], *De Iure*, trans. Tomàs Molina, in *Revista Nova et Vetera*, Universidad del Rosario, Bogotà, September 2017, p. 54).

[6] Understanding this point is essential to correctly frame a legal discourse dealing with different cultures and traditions, especially nowadays. Indeed, it is "no mystery that law is part of culture, but it is not uncommon for those who, by profession or context, are deeply involved in a given legal system to act as if "The Law" is quite separable from other elements of cultural life" (Lawrence Rosen, *Law as Culture. An Invitation*, Princeton University Press, Princeton 2006, p. 6).

contamination as is the case nowadays.[7] The economic and political processes of "glocalization", adopting commonly used terminology,[8] have witnessed the more and more frequent migration not only of people and capitals, but of philosophical visions and legal notions as well. Regarding this, Menski speaks of an "increasing hybridisation in locality-coloured and culture-specific forms worldwide", with legal theorists needing "to be better equipped to understand the manifold pluralities within and between legal systems as complex entities with ragged boundaries".[9] This is even truer following the progressive erosion of the political paradigm of territorial sovereignty, whose theory on law and statehood greatly influenced Western society in the post-Westphalian world. Following the eclipse of

[7] In the past centuries the world has dealt with a certain form of juridical contamination between various legal models and philosophical legal perspectives. For instance, it is possible to recall the multifaceted experience of the reception of Roman law, or the medieval legal order in which multiple normative levels coexisted in a single and comprehensive juridical framework. However, the contemporary scenario presents relevant differences, on the basis of which it is possible to argue that this transitional phase represents a sort of *unicum* in legal history. In the ancient world, the compresence and coexistence of various models was possible by virtue of a certain level of coordination, provided that the concrete application of a given law was granted by a shared criterion, being it religion, ethnicity, territory. For instance, it is possible to recall the experience of personal status law, which regulated the lives of individuals belonging to determined communities. Nowadays, we witness a new form of contamination in which different models and juridical perspectives coexist without clearly defined conceptual boundaries. For this and other reasons it is not actually possible to define, as some authors do, the present context as a form of neo-medievalism (for instance, see Jörg Friedrichs, "The Meaning of New Medievalism", in *European Journal of International Relations*, vol. VII, n. 4, December 2001, pp. 475–502). It is the case of many constitutions of the Muslim world in which a Western-derived conception of law lives along with the Islamic *sharīʿa*, being part of the same juridical text and being indistinctly enforceable in the same territory and often with respect to the same people.

[8] The English term was first used by Robert Ronaldson and then consecrated in literature by Zygmunt Bauman, who used it to underline the apparent paradox resulting from the combination of two opposite trends: globalization, intended as a force enlarging the horizon of the economic and political relations, and localization, as a force trying to root the productive processes in local realities. With regard to this, see Zygmunt Bauman, "On glocalization: or globalization for some, localization for some others", in *Thesis Eleven. Critical Theory and Historical Sociology*, vol. LIV, n. 1, August 1998, pp. 37–49.

[9] Werner F. Menski, *Comparative Law in a Global Context. The Legal Systems of Asia and Africa*, Cambridge University Press, Cambridge 2006, p. 25.

the perfect coincidence between State and law,[10] in this transitional period of our history, it is ultimately impossible to identify the overall legal order exclusively with national law as produced by the established institutions of a sovereign entity.

Today, the various conceptions of law appear to be much more complex and articulated, due to the shift in the economic and political scenario from a system fundamentally based on modern national statehood to a virtually global and a-systemic space. In this context, it is indeed the very idea of spatiality itself that is to be questioned. With the slow but inexorable loss of significance of the idea of a geographical partition exclusively delimited by national borders, due to the emergence of international entities and transnational capitalism,[11] it is inevitable that the traditional way in which the Western world conceived the juridical phenomenon would be fundamentally challenged.[12]

[10] This circumstance had already been put in light by Santi Romano in his forward-looking reflection of 1910. According to Romano, the notion of modern statehood, with its fundamental principles, was about to be put in question already at the beginning of the twentieth century because of the emergence of economic transnational entities, all of which "pursue the most disparate special aims, but all have a common character: that of grouping individuals with the criterion of their profession or, rather, of their economic interest" (see Santi Romano, "Lo Stato moderno e la sua crisi. Discorso inaugurale per l'anno accademico 1909-1910", in *Annuario*, Università di Pisa, Tipografia Vannucchi, Pisa 1910, pp. 11–40). Again, according to the Italian jurist, while overcoming this fundamental paradigm, it was necessary to understand that the conception of *jus* should incorporate not only State law—now one of the possible forms of regulation—but "every force which is effectively social, and which therefore comes to be organized", as stated in his preeminent work, Santi Romano [1918], *L'ordinamento giuridico. Studi sul concetto, le fonti e i caratteri del diritto*, Sansoni, Firenze 1967, p. 43. For a reflection of a possible future overcoming of the modern State paradigm, see Hedley Bull [1977], *The Anarchical Society. A Study of Order in World Politics*, Palgrave, Basingstoke-New York 2002, pp. 225–308.

[11] For a farsighted reflection on the intrinsically transnational nature of modern capitalism, see Norman Angell, *The Great Illusion*, G. P. Putnamn's Sons, New York-London 1913. According to the author, in "no department of human activity is internationalization so complete as in finance. The capitalist has no country" (ibid., p. 319). Cf. on the same topic, and with a focus on the post-industrial era, Phoebe Moore, *The International Political Economy of Work and Employability*, Palgrave Macmillan, New York 2010, p. 131.

[12] For a forward-looking and still topical reflection about possible evolutionary trends in the international legal order, see Richard A. Falk, "The Interplay of Westphalia and Charter Conceptions of the International Legal Order", in *The Future of the International Legal Order*, vol. I, *Trends and Patterns*, eds. Richard A. Falk, Cyril E. Black, Princeton University Press, Princeton 1969, pp. 32–72. Consider also, more recently, Rafael Domingo, *The New Global Law*, Cambridge University Press, Cambridge 2010, pp. 73–77.

If it is not likely that the national conception of law will disappear in the transition to a borderless and global (*non*)space, the juridical sciences must nevertheless identify possible new legal and philosophical trends in order to foresee the evolution of new economic and political models. To summarize, one needs to ask with which conceptual instruments it will be possible to reinterpret and rethink law in a global context in days in which the present international paradigms are about to progressively undergo relevant changes and in which, at the same time, there are no new properly theorized models to replace the current ones.

In this fast-changing scenario, characterized by the absence of fixed and dogmatic conceptions, we consequently witness a relatively free circulation of various juridical ideas and different legal models, once relegated in closed geographical spaces whose virtual borders have now been opened. Globalization,[13] from this point of view, seems to have greatly affected the legal world as well, if we consider how juridical notions progressively accrued in a given historical and social context can now, relatively easily, move to a completely different kind of society, and possibly coexist with indigenous models. It is therefore not a new idea of global legislation but rather a global circulation of different kinds of legal and philosophical constructs. As Krisch has observed, the structure of post-national law appears to be inherently pluralist,[14] thus open to the possibility of the encounter with other sensibilities.

A global juridical scenario, which inevitably lacks global juridical institutions,[15] offers at the same time opportunities and threats. On the

[13] With regard to globalization and its possible effects on legal and political theories, and as a cause of the progressive erosion of the model of the Nation-State, see Ulrich Beck, *Was ist Globalisierung? Irrtümer des Globalismus — Antworten auf Globalisierung*, Suhrkamp Verlag, Frankfurt am Main 1997, especially pp. 13–47.

[14] Cf. Nico Krisch, *Beyond Constitutionalism. The Pluralist Structure of Postnational Law*, Oxford University Press, Oxford 2010, especially pp. 3–105.

[15] So far, for structural reasons, the creation of global juridical institutions is to be considered a utopia, as well as something not desirable for its practical and political implications. It is relevant to notice that a "planetary state would set aside exclusion, making legal inclusion essential: one state, one law, one power and, of course, the threat of totalitarianism is more real and tangible than that of its predecessors. We would go from state totalitarianism to global absolutism without turning back" (Domingo, *The New Global Law, cit.*, p. 72). On the contrary, some authors still believe that the present transition will eventually lead to the development of "rules increasingly oriented towards a structuring process for a universal human society", as stated by Giuliana Ziccardi Capaldo, *The Pillars of Global Law*, Ashgate, Aldershot-Burlington 2008, especially pp. 19–92. Cf., for a political analysis, Martin Shaw, *Theory of the Global State*, Cambridge University Press, Cambridge 2000.

one hand, jurists are now given the unique opportunity to analyze and examine the effects of the encounter of legal perspectives which until now had been relatively isolated and self-sufficient. This should be regarded as a new chance to understand the dynamics of the interactions between different cultures and anthropologies, whose evolutions and outcomes are not usually predictable. On the other hand, however, attention must be paid to the possible lack of coherence in a single juridical framework—as a constitutional system, a code of legislation, a *de facto* legitimated way of ruling—incorporating trends and ideas which are not always compatible with one another. This context is the ideal one in which to develop a new approach to juridical analysis, taking the move from the discourses of legal pluralism[16] and, more recently, legal translation,[17] but overcoming their very boundaries in a broader philosophical and anthropological discourse.

Following these premises, one of the most interesting reflections to be made in this context relates to the different conceptions between two ways

[16] As well known, legal pluralism can be defined as a theory according to which the overall dimension of law cannot be resumed by the mere dimension of State law but reflects a more complicated and articulated phenomenon which comprehends a multiplicity of sources. The most important *caveat* is however related to the necessity of not grounding a reflection on a universalized and Western-derived idea of law. In this last case, the very idea of legal pluralism, notwithstanding the nominal claim to be open to broader analyses, is confined into a philosophical architecture made by Western categories. On the contrary, a real reflection on legal pluralism in a global scenario, instead of being based on substantive concepts of law, should be based on culturally oriented categories and schemes of comprehension. In this sense, and besides the already mentioned work of Menski, see Brian Z. Tamanaha, "Understanding Legal Pluralism: Past to Present, Local to Global", in *Sydney Law Review*, vol. XXX, Law Book Co. And Sydney Law School, Sydney 2008, pp. 375–411. One of the most valuable theories on legal pluralism, which correctly takes into account the various philosophical perspectives implied in the juridical reflection has been developed by Masaji Chiba, *Legal Pluralism. Toward a General Theory Through Japanese Legal Culture*, Tokai University Press, Tōkyō 1989.

[17] The concept of legal translation is particularly interesting, considering that it usually moves from a culturally oriented approach to law and might take into account all those linguistic, religious, social, and cultural elements that sometimes are ignored by other legal disciplines. Therefore, the discourse of legal translation appears to be completed and more forward looking when dealing with opposite and distant legal traditions in dialogue. While comparative legal analyses are sometimes based on the (*non*)univocal definition of legal notions, whose understanding can be biased by the author's own cultural perspective, legal translation is based on the more objective and revelatory instrument of language. Regarding this, see Le Cheng, King Kui Sin, Anne Wagner (eds.), *The Ashgate Handbook of Legal Translation*, Ashgate, Farnhma-Burlington 2014; Simone Glanert (ed.), *Comparative Law. Engaging Translation*, Routledge, London-New York 2014.

of conceiving the juridical phenomenon: the Islamic legal perspective and the Western one.

These two perspectives, reflecting two legal epistemologies and two specific ways of thinking about the relationship between God and man, and between law and society, came across one another multiple times in the course of history. However, it is in the postmodern world, and in the aforementioned transitional scenario, that they benefit from the opportunity of coexisting in the same social and legal context. In a number of countries very different historically and in terms of religious practices, such as Egypt, Saudi Arabia, and Morocco, but also in some countries of the old Europe, in an unprecedented manner we can witness the close encounter between legal visions and models of rule and justice, sometimes completing and enriching each other and other times conflicting in paradoxes whose philosophical implications require a deeper analysis.

In the last couple of decades, the contacts between civilizations have indeed intensified constantly, and so has the circulation of legal ideas. While in the twentieth century we witnessed the apogee of the affirmation of Western legal standards, such as the rule of law and the affirmation of human rights, the dawn of the twenty-first century showed new trends in the revitalization of ancient and alternative forms of juridical understanding. Islam, in the near future, cannot but represent a major cultural force in our own Western socio-political scenario, both because of the increasing migration flows of Muslim communities toward Europe and because of the new political and economic dynamics taking place in the Middle East and in African States, whose countries are constantly acquiring more importance within the international community.

Literature has already examined, in depth, the historical development and the doctrinal principles of what came to be commonly referred to as "Islamic law" or *sharīʿa*, in its various declinations and according to the different religious confessions and schools. However, something which has not yet been done in a systematic way, and could only have been conducted in the era of globalization and mass migrations, is a juridical and philosophical analysis of structural divergences and similarities of these two perspectives, in terms of their ways of conceiving law and normativity in a broader and culturally oriented sense. This analysis should not be focused on substantive aspects, but on broader philosophical and cultural constants and variables, which gradually came to define an overall juridical sensibility, whose discussion should logically precede every substantial comparison. It is only in this way that it would be possible to define the methodology of philosophically oriented and culture-specific legal comparativism and consequently outline a foundational analysis of the interactions of these two visions of the world.

According to Lyotard, postmodernity has been characterized by a substantial disbelief and incredulity in meta-narratives,[18] and it can easily be argued that meta-narratives include the juridical ones, whose most important representations in modern times have been statehood, sovereignty, and law.[19] Therefore, while overcoming postmodernity, it is now necessary to consider assuming a different approach in order to understand the deep transition occurring while facing both threats and opportunities caused by it. From this point of view, this should represent a new challenge for legal theorists and philosophers of law, as well as a potentially new field of investigation, whose outcomes are far from having been exhaustively explored.

1.2 Avoiding Universalization and Defining a New Approach: Legal Categories

As pointed out above, the globalized international system and the present age of transition impose upon law scholars a substantial shift in the theoretical paradigms used to analyze reality. In the past, we often used to consider our own juridical and philosophical outlook, proper of the Western world, as the only tool at our disposal to understand every aspect of legal models in the world.[20] However, in order to better understand the complexity of legal conceptions, especially nowadays when they are frequently engaged in peaceful dialogues, violent conflicts, challenges, and

[18] See Jean-François Lyotard, *La Condition postmoderne. Rapport sur le savoir*, éditions de Minuit, Paris 1979. For postmodernity not just as incredulity, but as fragmentation, see Robert G. Dunn, *Identity Crises. A Social Critique of Postmodernity*, University of Minnesota Press, Minneapolis-London 1998, pp. 143 ff.

[19] It should be highlighted, "the connection that the idea of State has with narrative, not only because the State, since the most ancient testimonies, innervates itself in the stories of foundation that refer to the continuity plan between myth and history, but because the State itself appears as a symbolic construction whose main purpose is the government of the temporality of men" (Andrea Tagliapietra, "Lo Stato come narrazione", in *Giornale Critico della Storia delle Idee*, year III, n. 5, Mimesis, Milan 2011, p. 3).

[20] Cf. H. Patrick Glenn, "Sustainable Diversity in Law", in *Legal Pluralism and Development. Scholars and Practitioners in Dialogue*, eds. Brian Z. Tamanaha, Caroline Sage, Michael Woolcock, Cambridge University Press, Cambridge 2012, pp. 101 ff.

confrontations, it is necessary to move "beyond Western jurisprudence"[21] and widen the spectrum of analysis. If we do not, the consequence is a quite frequent superimposition of Western legal categories upon different cultural contexts, following a process of universalization.[22]

The key concept of this passage, and of this book, is that of *legal categories*, which can be described as schemes of qualification and interpretation leading to a determined comprehension and understanding of reality.[23] A legal category is neither a substantive principle nor a positive regulation but the lens through which it is possible to understand a given phenomenon, thus properly contextualizing it and analyzing it in its overall organic location. The concept of legal category, being the way in which we comprehend and conceive normativity and its various declinations, is necessarily precedent to law as a substantial and substantive object of research; it assumes law as a wider cultural phenomenon, whose conceptual spectrum transcends its mere mechanism of functioning.[24] In a given legal order, more or less consciously, every phenomenon is inscribed in categories of comprehension, which can obviously vary depending on the context in which they come to light. They come close to Chiba's definition of the legal postulate of a country, which "is the foundation of its official and unofficial law which it also justifies and orients"[25] and takes into account Menski's consideration of the "culture-specific nature of law".[26] Legal categories define the juridical perspective of a legal order, shaping its bound-

[21] Chiba, *Legal Pluralism*, *cit.*, p. 11.

[22] Cf. Menski, *Comparative Law in a Global Context*, *cit.*, pp. 25–28. Riles speaks about a "technocratic devotion to universalism" present in Western legal theories as something potentially creating a conceptual prejudice to the definition of a really contextualized and pluralist theory of legal comparativism (Annelise Riles, "Introduction" to *Rethinking the Masters of Comparative Law*, ed. Annelise Riles, Hart Publishing, Oxford-Portland 2001, p. 18).

[23] Here I borrow a terminology used by Hans Kelsen [1960], *Pure Theory of Law*, trans. Max Knight, The Lawbook Exchange, Clark 2008, p. 3, whose position can help understanding the difference between a juridical category as a scheme of interpretation and comprehension, and a substantive norm or principle of law.

[24] It is once again worth remembering the words of Rosen according to whom "law is so inextricably entwined in culture that, for all its specialized capabilities, it may, indeed, best be seen not simply as a mechanism for attending to disputes or enforcing decisions, not solely as articulated rules or as evidence of differential power, and not even as the reification of personal values or superordinate beliefs, but as a framework for ordered relationships, an orderliness that is itself dependent on its attachment to all the other realms of its adherents' lives" (Rosen, *Law as Culture*, *cit.*, p. 7).

[25] Chiba, *Legal Pluralism*, *cit.*, p. 140.

[26] Menski, *Comparative Law in a Global Context*, *cit.*, p. 26.

aries and vivifying its outlook on the world, potentially orienting substantive contents of norms and rules, however without coinciding with them. They are fundamentally to be considered as narratives, whose beliefs are shared by a given community, and most of the time unconsciously accepted and applied over facts and events, to organize and systematize them following a predetermined order and priority. In light of what has been said, with the term universalization I intend the superimposition of certain categories over a context that would be considered alien to them. In its methodological approach, this book prescinds from the analysis of substantive aspects of legal systems but consists in the comparison of legal perspectives, defined by specific categories of comprehension.

The necessity of avoiding any conceptual universalization in such an analysis is highlighted by its consequences, which can easily substantiate in a frequent transition from theoretical aspects to substantive contents, like in the debates on global constitutionalism[27] and universal standards for human rights.[28] In order to carry out an analysis focused on divergences

[27] The present debate on global constitutionalism can be considered as an example of a universalization process, whose philosophical coherence can be regarded as questionable, even considering its political value from a neutral point of view. On this, see Christine E.J. Schwöbel, *Global Constitutionalism in International Legal Perspective*, Koninklijke, Leiden 2011; Aydin Atilgan, *Global Constitutionalism. A Socio-legal Perspective*, Springer, New York 2017.

[28] Legal and sociological literature already explored, with different conclusions, the concept of universalization of Western human rights. Assuming as a starting point the Universal Declaration of Human Rights, adopted by United Nations General Assembly on December 10, 1948, we can easily notice that the standards firstly incorporated in the Declaration have spread progressively their cultural influence throughout the world, however, with a relevant lack of universal application in certain areas of the globe. While this is an unquestionable fact, authors do not agree with regard to the causes of what can be referred to a cultural hegemony, combined with relatively poor outcomes in terms of concrete practice. Some authors state that claims over human rights application genuinely reflect universal values of dignity and tolerance, as Rhoda E. Howard-Hassmann, *In Defense of Universal Human Rights*, Polity, Cambridge 2018; cf. also Heiner Bielefeldt, " "Western" versus "Islamic" Human Rights Conceptions?: A Critique of Cultural Essentialism in the Discussion on Human Rights", in *Political Theory*, vol. XXVIII, n. 1, February 2000, pp. 90–121. Some other authors, however, argue that "human rights claims are the outcome of power relations" and that "in the current era all issues must be subordinated to imperatives of globalization" (Tony Evans, "Power, hegemony and the universalization of human rights", introduction to *Human Rights Fifty Years On. A Reappraisal*, ed. Tony Evans, Manchester University Press, Manchester-New York 1998, p. 12). In this last sense, see Samuel P. Huntington, *The Clash of Civilizations and the Remaking of World Order*, Simon & Schuster, New York 1996; Makau Mutua, *Human Rights. A Political and Cultural Critique*, University of Pennsylvania Press, Philadelphia 2002. With specific regard to the Islamic case, see Abdulaziz Sachedina, *Islam and the Challenge of Human Rights*, Oxford University Press, New York 2009.

and similarities of two juridical and philosophical visions, it is therefore necessary to discuss each element and each conception based on its *own* schemes of comprehension, having regard for the unique environment from which they originated and in which they matured. Otherwise, every comparison will never be properly contextualized, with the conceptual bias implied in depriving culture-specific notions from the background in which they have been shaped, thus missing the chance of locating them in an organic philosophical and historical framework. This necessity does not simply involve the theoretical correctness of a legal comparison, but it is also necessary for practical reasons: in a world in which intercultural exchanges have become structural, and in which legal reasoning and praxis have acquired a dimension of intrinsic pluralism, biasing this kind of analysis actually means miscomprehending how other civilizations conceive legal phenomena and normative ideals, and therefore altering the dynamics of our legal interactions.

In my opinion, the aforementioned process of conceptual universalization mainly happens for two reasons. Firstly, in a State-based system whose foundations had been laid on the paradigm of sovereignty and strictly based on the category of territoriality, we experimented with the self-sufficiency of our own philosophical and legal tradition, whose historical and political outcomes had been analyzed *within* a precise and definite spatiality, with basically no, or minor, risk of contamination from exterior elements. Secondly, the process of colonization represented the apex of the diffusion and of the imposition of Western legal models and standards as universal principles of law, practically all around the world.[29] Often, this came to legitimize the Western thought, to the present day, of reading the juridical reality of specific cultural and religious contexts without prior analysis of their philosophical traditions and anthropological views, which can only constitute the very basis for the establishment of a legal order. This is even truer if we consider, with Barzilai, that the "exploration of legal cultures has mainly been focused on countries in the Western world",[30] thus excluding from the spectrum of comparative research entire

[29] For instance, and as Chakrabarty points out, Western imperialism brought about the "universalization of the Nation-State as the most desirable form of political community" (Dipesh Chakrabarty, "L'artificio della Storia", in *Parolechiave,* n. 31*, Occidentalismi*, June 2004, p. 58).

[30] Gad Barzilai [2003], *Communities and Law. Politics and Cultures of Legal Identities*, University of Michigan Press, Ann Arbor 2006, p. 3.

worlds and visions completely alien to the foundational postulates of the Western ones.

As Fukuyama argued, in the "end of history" Western liberal democracy as a political and legal principle has been universalized and, in some way, held as a natural form of world government.[31] Consequently, we tend to use the lens of the Western legal tradition in order to understand conceptions and institutions which are fundamentally stranger to it in both nature and substance and descend from other cultural narratives and beliefs. Therefore, while examining the legal order proper of—in this case—the Muslim world, Western literature usually focused on the substantive content of what is commonly referred to as Islamic law, speaking of "State", "source", "constitution", "institution", and "law" itself.[32] All these categories, which came to maturation in our specific world following a unique path of development, are thus superimposed upon a context in which, traditionally, they had basically been nonexistent, until being imported as a foreign product during the exchanges with the Occidental world. As Wittgenstein suggested,[33] words are the essential tool to be used not just to describe reality but to give reality a certain interpretation as well. From this point of view, language is not merely descriptive but should

[31] As well known, Fukuyama considers the end of the bipolar world as the end of history and "the endpoint of mankind's ideological evolution and the universalization of Western liberal democracy as the final form of human government" (Francis Fukuyama, "The End of History?", in *The National Interest*, vol. XVI, Summer 1989, p. 3).

[32] For an in-depth and detailed scholarly study, see Javaid Rehman, *Islamic State Practices, International Law and the Threat from Terrorism. A Critique of the "Clash of Civilization in the New World Order,"* Hart Publishing, Oxford-Portland 2005, pp. 10–70. Rehman, for instance, while speaking about criminal law, constitutional law, sources of law, and others, assumes that the Islamic legal order could be in some way equalized with the Western juridical thought, without a prior contextualization of the philosophical evolutionary path of the *sharīʿa*. The same be said about Mohammad Talaat al-Ghunaimi, *The Muslim Conception of International Law and the Western Approach*, Martinus Nijhoff, The Hague 1968. The interesting work of An-Naʿim, although proposing a possible reformation of Islamic legal thought, uses in my opinion the category of statehood without a proper contextualization, referring to models and historical experiences not always coincident with one another (cf. Abdullahi Ahmed An-Naʿim, *Islam and the Secular State. Negotiating the Future of Sharīʿa*, Harvard University Press, Cambridge 2008, pp. 45–83). On the contrary, Wood expresses preliminarily all due caution in the terminological equation between *sharīʿa* and law (cf. Leonard Wood, *Islamic Legal Revival. Reception of European Law and Transformations in Islamic Legal Thought in Egypt, 1875-1952*, Oxford University Press, Oxford 2016, p. 49).

[33] "The limits of my language mean the limits of my world". Ludwig Wittgenstein [1922], *Tractatus Logico-Philosophicus*, trans. D. F. Pears, B. F. McGuinness, Routledge, London-New York 2002, p. 68.

be considered fundamentally constitutive of our outlook upon facts and history. Legal theory makes no exception and, on the contrary, is one of the fields of human knowledge in which the usage of a certain kind of language contributes in an essential way to shape an individual and unique understanding of social and political life.[34]

Therefore, speaking of "Islamic law", for instance, is not just a descriptive action but rather is to be considered as a process of qualification by which we conceptualize a phenomenon while giving it a precise reading and understanding. Thus, it cannot be a starting point in order to describe a legal conception, but, on the contrary, it is usually the resulting point of a complex—and questionable—process of Westernization of an ancient and autochthon philosophical path. Otherwise, we could incur the risk of missing the real starting point of an analysis such as this, which is considering the specific context from which we approach. Law, in this case, cannot be regarded as a content with which to fill a neutral scheme but on the contrary as a system of belief.[35] Ignoring this would result in the misunderstanding of the very object of our inquiry.[36]

[34] For instance, see Martin Stone [1995], "Focusing the Law: What Legal Interpretation is Not", in *Wittgenstein and Law*, ed. Dennis Michael Patterson, Ashgate Publishing, Farnham 2004, pp. 259–324. In the same volume consider also Brian Bix [1993], "The Application (and Mis-Application) of Wittgenstein's Rule-Following Considerations to Legal Theory", pp. 381–408.

[35] On law as a belief, see James K. Feibleman, *Justice, Law and Culture*, Martinus Nijhoff, Dordrecht-Boston-Lancaster 1985, pp. 128 ff.

[36] Again, it is possible to examine juridical literature dealing with *sharīʿa* and human rights law. Apart from the aforementioned book by Sachedina, whose analysis is properly contextualized, while examining the same topic, some other authors discuss the relationship between human rights standards and the traditional idea of Islamic normativity without a proper philosophical introduction, which should constitute an essential premise for every work about such an issue. For instance, see Nisrine Abiad, *Sharia, Muslim States and International Human Rights Treaty Obligations. A Comparative Study*, British Institute of International and Comparative Law, London 2008; Shahram Akbarzadeh, Benjamin MacQueen, "Framing the debate on Islam and human rights", in *Islam and Human Rights in Practice*, eds. Shahram Akbarzadeh, Benjamin MacQueen, Routledge, London-New York 2008, pp. 1–11; Vida Amirmokri, *L'Islam et les droits de l'homme: l'islamisme, le droit international et le modernism islamique*, Les Presses de l'Université Laval, Saint-Nicolas (Québec) 2004. For a sociological work, see Irene Oh, *The rights of God. Islam, human rights, and comparative ethics*, Georgetown University Press, Washington 2007. To summarize, we can argue that the very question of the compatibility between Islamic "law" and human rights, wherever lacking coherent and comprehensive premises, from a juridical point of view would result in a substantial nonsense. On the contrary, an author openly and consciously suggesting the answerability of the question whether *sharīʿa* is compatible with human rights standards is Dominic McGoldrick, "The compatibility of an Islamic/shariʿa law system or shariʿa rules with the European Convention on Human Rights", in *Islam and English Law. Responsibilities and the Place of Sharīʿa*, ed. Robin Griffith-Jones, Cambridge University Press, Cambridge 2013, pp. 42–71.

Nowadays, when a number of culture-specific legal traditions circulate in a virtually borderless global world in order to understand the real extent of the juridical contamination between philosophical visions, one needs to consider in which context a legal order has come into existence. With regard to the Muslim world, before making comparisons between the actual content of what should be properly called *sharīʿa* and a certain Western legislation or legal standard, it is necessary to ask ourselves a number of fundamental questions: how the different Islamic confessions and schools, in their common features, have shaped the concept of normativity; what is the role of human reason in establishing the Islamic legal order; what is the teleological perspective of the *sharīʿa*; how the Muslim legal and philosophical tradition thinks of the political organization of the community; and what is the nexus between man, God, and the legitimacy of a certain form of rule. Only after such an operation would comparisons between specific legislations or constitutional frameworks actually make sense. This book aims, therefore, to provide such a preliminary analysis.

In order to systematize the complexity of the subject and properly contextualize it in the present scenario, defining a new approach represents an unavoidable necessity. Fields of research and methodologies such as comparativism, legal pluralism, and legal translation, taken each on its own, cannot actually grasp the real extent of the reflection, in its static dimension—a description of legal visions—and its dynamic one—an analysis of the interactions between different views. Therefore, the correct approach is not to be based simply on comparing legal rules and juridical opinions but should necessarily be grounded in a categorial analysis. Legal categories, which are to be termed as structural in a juridical discourse, should then become the core of the comparison, in order to fully understand that legal constructs cannot actually exist without their being inscribed in schemes of qualification intended as shared cultural narratives.

1.3 Methodology of Research

In this book, I will focus on the analysis of some essential legal and philosophical issues, which constitute the basis for a first understanding of two worlds and two juridical visions that gradually came to shape Muslim and Western civilizations. With regard to this, it is important to understand that what is called *sharīʿa* is neither a positive legislation enforced in specific countries, nor an immutable and monolithic expression of an ancestral form of providing rules to a community. I will draw comparisons and point out differences taking into account the broader spectrum of a philosophical confrontation, as a theoretical framework within which to discuss the foundational elements of two legal orders. Each chapter of this book will therefore focus on a specific aspect of normativity, discussing how it is conceived both in the Muslim perspective and in the Western one, and shedding light on both similarities and divergences. These reflections will help to develop a new methodological approach to legal comparison, with non-secondary implications in terms of concrete legal practice.

In my first chapter, I will discuss the theoretical relationship between Islam and modern post-Westphalian statehood, with particular reference to the dimensions of sovereignty and territoriality. In particular, the Western idea of statehood and the Islamic idea of *ummah* will be taken into account in order to develop a wider discourse on how these two legal traditions conceived the relationship between community and physical spatiality, under constant tension between territorial governance and universalistic aspirations.

In the second chapter I will analyze the conception of legal and political authority, with special regard to its relationship with law. I will hold the figures of the Leviathan and of the *caliph* as iconic representations of two ways of conceiving and structuring political power, moving from them to analyze theoretical questions that help to understand how legal governance came to be progressively structured and understood. Particular attention will be devoted to the issues of personification of power and of its legitimating narratives, highlighting relevant differences between the West and Islam.

In my third chapter, I will analyze the role human reason plays in both legal orders, describing the methodology based on which it comes to define a certain legal anthropology. The Islamic and Western worlds have both assigned to reason an essential and central task in shaping their respective ways of conceiving law, however with marked divergences as to how reason is supposed to relate itself to the juridical phenomenon. From the analysis of this point, fundamental implications will necessarily follow, with special reference to issues such as the perceived origin of law, the relationship between form and substance of law, and the key figures in charge of its systematization and implementation.

The fourth chapter will be dedicated to a highly topical and debated issue: the relationship between secular and religious powers, and its legal implications. In particular, I will take into consideration the necessity of a separation between religious and temporal authorities in the legal field, both in Islam and in the West, investigating why historical and philosophical variables led to divergent and sometimes opposite outcomes. Moreover, I will discuss the particular case of criminal justice, analyzing it from a teleological perspective in order to cast light once again on the link between religion and law in both traditions.

If the previous chapters focus on theoretical analyses, from which however concrete implications follow, the fifth and final chapter will deal with more practical questions. I will focus on the historical encounters between the Western and Muslim legal traditions, contextualizing them and explaining their modalities and contingencies. Moving from this point, I will compare how both legal orders conceive the relationship between law, space, and time, and how they relate law to the ideas of bindingness and enforceability. Lastly, I will discuss the particular encounter of these two visions on the field of modern constitutionalism, as transplanted from the West to Muslim countries. Regarding this last point, I will describe various ways in which Islam and *sharīʿa* are inscribed within the constitutional frameworks of modern Muslim States.

While drawing my conclusions, I will focus on possible future perspectives, highlighting the most topical issues in order to stimulate further reflection. The challenge of integration and the sustainability of a multicultural society will indeed strictly depend on the outcomes deriving from the encounters and the clashes not necessarily between States and countries, but between cultures and civilizations. In particular, the legal dimension of intercultural dialogue, with special reference to the relationship between the West and Islam, may represent one of the main points of reflection for decades to come.

In this framework, the analysis of the interactions between Islamic and Western legal perspectives should represent a major point of interest mainly for jurists, and not only for Islamicists, scholars of religious studies, and sociologists. If the legal dimension of Islam indeed represents one of its structural elements, which happens to be more and more relevant in contemporary history, then it is necessary for legal scholarship to define and adopt a new and all-encompassing methodology to investigate the issue. This implies penetrating into a world characterized by a unique way of understanding reality, as well as a patient work of comparison between philosophical and anthropological views. Indeed, never before has the complexity of the subject required such a multidisciplinary and innovative approach in which legal philosophers and comparativists should have a major role to play.

1.4 Definitions and Terminology

In medieval Europe, following the great tradition of Scholasticism, every dispute or dissertation was necessarily preceded by an *explicatio terminorum*, in order to frame the discussion by defining in a univocal way definitions and terminology used therein.

When dealing with issues such as the legal traditions of civilizations characterized by a unique religious and historical background, it becomes a necessity to explain what will be meant by the use of a certain vocabulary. This is truer in a field such as the legal and philosophical research, where the words that are actually used reflect a precise way of interpreting and understanding facts and concepts. In this paragraph I will briefly explain the meaning of some terms that will be recurring in the following chapters.

Firstly, it is necessary to point out that with the terms *Islam* and *West* I do not refer to geographical spaces or to specific countries. Even though the Western world has been shaped by its Greek, Roman, and Christian heritages and found its most prominent and significant expression in Europe, it is to be observed that in the course of its history the boundaries of the West transcended its physical spatiality and went far beyond its initial delimitation as defined by the Semitic term *ereb*.[37] Therefore, with the Western world I refer to a specific way of conceiving of social and political life, as well as phenomena such as law and authority, justice and community, regardless of the geographical space in which these concepts ultimately took root. Analogously, I will refer to *Islam* preeminently as the way in which the Muslim tradition understands society and civilization, with specific regard to normativity. While the term *West* etymologically refers to a geographical dimension, *Islam* refers to a comprehensive system

[37] Semitic term meaning *Occident*, the place where the sun sets in, used by ancient Phoenicians to define the territories at the West of Syria. One of the possible etymologies of *Europe* links it to this term. It is interesting to note that also the word Asia derives from Phoenician *açu*, meaning morning. Etymologically speaking, both Europe and Asia derive from the same cultural milieu, denoting respectively the setting sun and the rising sun, the Occident and the Orient. Cf. Karel Blei, *Freedom of Religion and Belief. Europe's Story*, Van Gorcum, Assen 2002, p. 4.

of belief, a normative methodology, and a civilization,[38] thus devoid of an intrinsic spatial delimitation. However, it would be misleading to relegate the Western view to its spatial boundaries and the Islamic one to its religious creed, given that both perspectives deeply influence the legal conceptions of their respective civilizations. Therefore, in this book these two worlds will be analyzed and examined principally as models of thought and as systems of juridical reasoning.[39] West and Islam are here regarded as *perspectives*, that is to say, the way in which these civilizations considered certain aspects of reality such as law and justice, authority and power.

At a first glance, it could be argued that it is almost impossible to define what Western law, or Islamic law, really are. Both conceptions are indeed multifaceted and complex, varying among philosophical currents and changing along the centuries of their respective history. They are not static ideas but rather evolving and living visions of law and justice, of politics and societies, whose systematizations gradually and slowly proceed during a time span of ages. A question that may arise is therefore inherent in the very possibility of comparing not just two legal systems but two entire worlds and two ways of understanding reality, which refer to an evolving and changing scenario. Nevertheless, in order to carry out a foundational analysis of the structural elements composing these two worlds, a comparison is actually possible through the implementation of proper methodological instruments.

Although the Muslim world embraces various religious confessions and juridical schools, the path of evolution of the Islamic legal order, enriched during its history by various cultural influxes both posterior and anterior to its creation, presents a number of constant philosophical trends which

[38] Providing an exhaustive definition of Islam is as difficult—or rather impossible—as providing an exhaustive definition of *sharīʿa*. When referring to Islam as a system of belief, I do not refer to the post-Enlightenment conception of religious reduced in its scope and conceptual boundaries as a way of private spirituality. On the contrary, when I speak of a system of belief, a normative methodology, and a civilization, I intend to define it as an all-encompassing phenomenon, as it will be explained in the following chapters. As Lewis puts it, in one sense "it denotes a religion, a system of belief and worship; in the other, the civilization that grew up and flourished under the aegis of that religion" (Bernard Lewis, *The Crisis of Islam. Holy War and Unholy Terror*, Modern Library, New York 2003, p. 3).

[39] With regard to this, and with specific attention to the perceived asymmetry between the terms Europe and Islam, see the interesting reflection of Bernard Lewis, *Islam and the West*, Oxford University Press, Oxford 1993, pp. 3 ff. With reference to the usage of the same terminology, see also the historical notes of Franco Cardini [2007], *Europa e Islam. Storia di un Malinteso*, Laterza, Rome-Bari 2015, ch. 1, par. 1.

can be considered as the heritage of ancestral and atavistic categories for understating and analyzing the world. In the same way, the history of Western societies shows the progressive evolution of juridical principles deeply incardinated in the Roman and Christian heritage,[40] whose maturation and accrual witnessed a successive diversification, nevertheless maintaining a common philosophical and anthropological approach to reality. It is therefore necessary to abstract and outline the less common denominator that has been defining the Western and Muslim attitude toward normativity, intended as the constant foundations shaping the legal order of such civilizations, regardless of the progressive processes of differentiation that affected them in the course of history. In this way, it will eventually be possible to define what can be considered Western law and Islamic law in general, with regard to special legal and philosophical questions that will be dealt with in the following chapters. Needless to say, the very method of understanding and elaborating a comprehensive theory of law and rule, of justice and retribution, of governance and legitimation, represents the most important part of the philosophical reflection to be made with regard to the encounter of these two worlds.

Secondly, it is necessary to define what I mean when speaking of "legal order". With legal order, I refer to the comprehensive theoretical framework in which a given civilization organically collocates its understanding of juridical phenomena, whatever their conceptualization may be. A legal order, from this point of view, is a much broader definition than a sum of substantive norms and rules, implying a reflection on the idea of order in

[40] The Roman and Christian heritages appear to be constitutive of the Western conception of law, and although the Christian thought is to be considered eminently non-European in its origin, it is in Europe that it could innervate itself in the Greek and Roman cultural and philosophical backgrounds, laying the foundations for what will be later known as *Western world*. This point is remarkably explained by Ratzinger, according to whom "it is not surprising that Christianity, despite its origins and some significant developments in the East, finally took on its historically decisive character in Europe. We can also express this the other way around: this convergence, with the subsequent addition of the Roman heritage, created Europe and remains the foundation of what can rightly be called Europe" (Joseph A. Ratzinger [H. H. Benedict XVI], "Faith, Reason and the University. Memories and Reflections", *lectio magistralis* given at the Aula Magna of the University of Regensburg, September 12, 2006, published in *Islamic Studies*, vol. XLV, n. 4, Islamic Research Institute, International Islamic University, Islamabad 2006, p. 600).

a given civilization and on the way in which normativity is conceived.[41] Norms and rules are just a specific manifestation of a legal order, whose conception must be referred to as a philosophical way of understanding reality and society. A legal order, as already mentioned, is oriented in its perspective by legal categories.

While every civilization gradually shapes, in the course of its history, its own (perhaps peculiar) way of characterizing a legal order, the overall idea of it is in some way neutral and common to every society.[42] Therefore, while generally speaking of legal order I will refer not to a specific way of conceiving the juridical reality, but as the possibility of doing so according to a specific outlook, which can greatly vary depending on the context. As will later be explained, terms such as "law", "State", and "source" indicate a non-neutral way of understanding a juridical phenomenon, that is to say, a precisely characterized and philosophically oriented narrative. On the contrary, by "legal order" I mean the neutral idea of establishing a normative dimension for a given community or society, which will necessarily be shaped in accordance with a multiplicity of variables. Hence, the idea of legal order is the least common denominator of my analysis and the very basis from which it moves.

As stated above, in order to avoid the conceptual bias deriving from the universalization of Western legal categories, I will not use the common terminology of "Islamic law". In this way, it will be clear that the reference will not be made to a positive system of rules and norms set forth by an established authority for a determined geographical space as could be intended in a Western context. While referring to a comprehensive

[41] Romano had already observed that the idea of legal order cannot be reduced to the specific norms which may constitute it. According to the author, the concept should include, on the contrary, a reflection on the aforementioned elements of society and social order, thus giving it a comprehensive nature. (Romano, *L'ordinamento giuridico*, *cit.*, pp. 12 ff.) The jurist defines a legal order as an "institution" (ibid., p. 27 ff.), meaning by institution a comprehensive social structure or organization. Given that—as I will explain in the following chapters—the idea of institution cannot be considered as universal, but eminently Western and inscribed *in a specific* legal order, it is necessary to point out that Romano's definition of institution does not coincide with the one that will be used in this work.

[42] I agree with Frändberg while stating that "legal order is, in my opinion, a structure consisting exclusively of normative ideas." (Åke Frändberg, *The Legal Order. Studies in the Foundations of Juridical Thinking*, Springer, New York 2018, p. 25.) Regardless of his conclusions and of the aim of his work, Frändberg correctly emphasizes the neutrality of the concept "legal order", whose peculiar normative ideas can change in dependence of the historical and cultural context.

concept like the legal and cultural heritage of Islam, definitions such as "Islamic legal tradition" or "Islamic legal order" will be used instead, depending on the context. By doing so, I will refer to the philosophical perspective Islam gives to the juridical phenomenon and to the idea of normativity, while aiming at regulating the universal community of the Muslim *ummah*.[43] Coherently, with the premises of my research, these concepts will be examined as the deep legacy resulting from a precise historical experience and a given cultural background.

However, Islam being a complex, non-homogeneous, and multifaceted world,[44] it is necessary to restrict the extent of this definition as well. In my work, whenever not otherwise specified, I will refer to the Sunnī tradition, for the common structural elements found in its four primary *maḏāhib* (legal schools, sing. *maḏhab*): Ḥanafī, Mālikī, Shāfiʿī, and Ḥanbalī. As is well established, these latter four Sunnī *maḏāhib* present relevant differences in terms of legal practice; however, it is possible to identify a legal and philosophical core which is common and essential to all of them. Moreover, wherever appropriate when warranted by context, I will use the term *sharīʿa*, which will be explained further in the next paragraph. Shīʿa Islam, on the contrary, gave life to a rather different conception of legal order, as a proof of the variety of the Muslim world in all of its complexity. However, the Shīʿa perspective deserves a separate and dedicated analysis on its own and therefore will not be discussed in this book.

It is important to specify that, while analyzing the Sunnī juridical and philosophical outlook and pointing out similarities and differences with the Western view, I will not refer to laws and statutes enforced by Muslim countries in the framework of constitutional and State-based models, as established in the colonial or post-colonial era. The aim of this work is in fact that of examining the traditional outlook of the Islamic idea of normativity, whose categories and principles survived the legal and political hegemony of the West, as well as colonization and decolonization processes, until integrating themselves in the newly adopted constitutional systems.

[43] The idea of the Islamic *ummah* will be better discussed in the first chapter.

[44] For an analysis of the variety of Islam, which represents a fundamental point to understand also its legal dynamics, see Mohammed Ayoob, Danielle Nicole Lussier, *The Many Faces of Political Islam. Religion and Politics in Muslim Societies*, University of Michigan Press, Ann Arbor 2020, pp. 26–44.

By doing so, whenever it will not be possible to give to traditional notions and conceptions a proper translation, I will refer to the original Arabic terminology[45] with a brief explanation of its meaning. In this way, the deep significance of the original concepts will be maintained as much as possible, without adopting widespread yet misleading translations, which could alter the perspective implied in the definition itself. As for the Islamic conception of divinity, I will refer to the term *Allāh* in order to differentiate the Muslim philosophical and religious theorization of the divine from the Christian notion of God. Notwithstanding the common roots of the Abrahamic religions, a different terminology appears to be necessary here as a consequence of the deep differentiations in the respective ways of conceiving the Divinity and its relationship with mankind and law.

As for the Western view, analogously with what has been stated above for Islam, I will not make reference to substantive legislations of Occidental countries but to the overall philosophical theorization implied therein, intended as the structural core of Western normativity and theory of law. In describing these concepts, English terminology will be used whenever possible. However, when further specification will be needed in order to understand the ancient legacy of a philosophical vision, I will use the original Greek and Latin terms.[46]

1.5 *Preliminary Notions About* Sharīʿa

Nowadays, we can easily notice that *sharīʿa* is a recurring term, commonly used to refer to a number of different ideas and conceptions, not always in the proper way. However, *sharīʿa* is actually a complex and multifaceted concept, whose history, systematization, and interpretation represent the core of the Islamic legal perspective. However, as stated above, my book will neither focus on *sharīʿa* itself nor carry out an in-depth analysis of specific and substantive aspects of its provisions. Nevertheless, in order to pursue the object of the present inquiry it is necessary to give some brief

[45] For the romanization of the Arabic terms and to properly render them in the Latin alphabet, I will follow the ALA-LC rules. Whenever not otherwise specified, in direct quotations I will maintain the romanization as provided by the author of the excerpt, without intervening in the text. The same be said about authors' names.

[46] For instance, I will sometimes use Latin while speaking about *jus* and *lex* in order to make a fundamental distinction which cannot actually be made with the same clarity in other languages.

clarifications about what is actually to be intended with *sharīʿa*. The present paragraph does not aim to provide an exhaustive discussion about this topic or at enhancing our knowledge of it; on the contrary, these introductory notes exclusively aim at providing some preliminary fundamental notions that will be used in the following chapters.

Being something deeply rooted in an ancient and atavistic culture, it is almost impossible to give an exhaustive and univocal definition of *sharīʿa*. In literature, various authors have attempted to define the concept in different ways.[47] Abdullah Yusuf Ali has proposed a clear and concise definition in his most famous work of translation and comment of the *Qurʾān*: according to the scholar, *sharīʿa* is the "right way of religion", which "is wider than the mere formal rites and legal provisions".[48] Schacht suggests that *sharīʿa* be considered as "the epitome of Islamic thought, the most typical manifestation of the Islamic way of life, the core and kernel of Islam itself".[49] More briefly, Weiss defines the concept as "an entire way of life".[50] However, the definition given by Khadduri seems to me the most appropriate in order to understand the philosophical and legal perspective *sharīʿa* adopts: according to the author it is possible to speak about "the

[47] Analyzing the various opinions about *sharīʿa* would transcend the scope of this work. Nevertheless, it is interesting to point out the differences between the different scholarly positions regarding such a complex and articulated concept. For instance, An-Naʿim states that "Sharīʿa is the door or passageway into being Muslim and does not exhaust the possibilities of experiencing Islam. There is more to Islam than Sharīʿa, though knowing and complying with the dictates of Sharīʿa is the way to realize Islam" (An-Naʿim, *Islam and the Secular State, cit.*, p. 10). Interesting in this latter definition is the essential dimension of *sharīʿa* in order to "realize" Islam as a comprehensive ideal of life. On the other hand, Otto especially focuses on the moral aspect while describing the abstract and eternal sense of the term, describing *sharīʿa* as "God's plan for mankind consisting of His prescriptions for human behaviour" (Jan Michiel Otto, *Sharia and National Law in Muslim Countries*, Leiden University Press, Leiden 2008, p. 9). Moreover, it is worth reporting the definition proposed by Lambton, according to whom for Muslims "the foundation from which all discussion of government starts is the law of God, the *sharīʿa*. Theoretically pre-existing and eternal, it represents absolute good. It is prior to the community and the state" (Ann K. S. Lambton, *State and Government in Medieval Islam. An Introduction to the Study of Islamic Political Theory – The Jurists*, Routledge, London-New York 1981, p. xiv).

[48] Abdullah Yusuf Ali [1934], *The Meaning of the Holy Qurʾān*, Amana Publications, Beltsville 2004, XLV (*Al-Jâthiya*), 18, p. 1297, note 4756.

[49] Joseph Schacht, *An Introduction to Islamic Law*, Oxford University Press, Oxford 1964, p. 1.

[50] Bernard G. Weiss, *The Spirit of Islamic Law*, University of Georgia Press, Athens-London 1998, p. 17.

embodiment of the ideal Islamic life. It is the framework of Islam itself. For although religion describes what the ideal life should be, the road indicates the right road to follow".[51]

Discussing the etymology of the term, *sharīʿa* can simply be translated as "the path", "the straight path", or more extensively "the path leading to a watering place".[52] These translations, with particular reference to the latter, highlight a fundamental dimension of *sharīʿa*, which qualifies itself as a way to be followed, which basically involves every aspect of the life of the believer. It encompasses a moral, a social, a political, and a proper legal dimension and is therefore characterized by its comprehensiveness. The path of the *sharīʿa*, in the Muslim perspective, leads not only to justice but also to salvation: in a desert environment like the Arab peninsula, where Islam first developed and flourished, where to find water meant the very difference between life and death, and between perdition and salvation. Thus, *sharīʿa* is to be considered the righteous and straight path, which can lead the believer to water, meaning here the condition of being saved, both in this world and in the afterlife. The *Qurʾān* itself, with regard to this, addresses *sharīʿa* as the path to follow, evidently in a much broader sense than what the Western world intend while referring to law.[53]

While the Islamic *sharīʿa* is divinely originated and revealed, it is systematized and interpreted by Muslim jurists and scholars, referred to as *fuqahāʾ* (sing. *faqīh*), who play a fundamental role in the Islamic legal world. The jurists are constantly engaged in a work of interpretation and research, providing clarifications on concrete questions, as in the case of the issuance of *fatāwā* (juridical responses, sing. *fatwā*). Their main task is to translate *sharīʿa* provisions into concrete norms and rules, whose corpus is defined as *fiqh*. With *fiqh* we refer to the body of scholarly responses,

[51] Majid Khadduri [1961], "Introduction" to Muhammad ibn Idrīs al-Shāfiʿī, *al-Risāla fī Uṣūl al-Fiqh (Treatise on the Foundations of Islamic Jurisprudence)*, trans. Majid Khadduri, Islamic Texts Society, Cambridge 1997, p. 3.

[52] Ibid. Cf. Shaheen Sardar Ali, *Modern Challenges to Islamic Law*, Cambridge University Press, Cambridge 2016, pp. 23–24.

[53] "Then We put thee on the [right] Way of Religion: so follow thou that [Way], and follow not the desires of those who know not." *Qurʾān*, XLV (*Al-Jâthiya*), 18 (trans. Ali, p. 1297). While quoting the English translation of the *Qurʾān* in this work, I will refer to the aforementioned bilingual version by Abdullah Yusuf Ali. It is however important to notice that it is in some way misleading speaking of "translation": al-*Qurʾān* meaning "the recitation", and being intended as a literal revelation in the Arabic language, every translation would unavoidably result in an interpretation, thus not perfectly coherent with the original. It is not by chance that the title of Ali's version is *Meaning* of the *Qur'ān*.

interpretations, and opinions of Islamic jurists and experts, an elite class progressively systematizing a juridical vision with its conceptual instruments and philosophical constants. This later point shows how *fiqh* is neither a corpus of norms considered to be valid within a given system nor a codification in the Western sense. It is, on the contrary, a particularly complex idea that can be considered a flexible and extremely differentiated way of approaching the juridical phenomenon, mirroring the variety and the adaptability of the Islamic legal perspective. As a consequence, in the course of history, various *maḏāhib* have been established and recognized, each with its own peculiarities.[54] Nowadays, as stated above, Sunnī Islam recognizes four main legal schools, while other *maḏāhib* are to be considered extinguished or merged with other schools.[55]

The jurists put their effort to investigate the superhuman dimension of *šarīʿa*, to develop a coherent epistemic view, and therefore to shape and give form to Muslim juridical thought through their constant work in juristic hermeneutics. To do so, Muslim jurists gradually conceptualized a legal methodology referred to as *uṣūl al-fiqh*. If *fiqh* is the knowledge of *šarīʿa*, the *uṣūl* (literally, the "roots") are the instruments to achieve such knowledge and to reach a better comprehension of the divine normativity. *Šarīʿa* provisions are primarily derived from two main roots: the *Qurʾān* and the *sunnah*.

The *Qurʾān*, whose literal meaning is "recitation", is believed to be the holy text containing the divine revelation transmitted from Allāh to the Prophet Muḥammad. It represents the most important and holiest text of the Muslim world, as well as the apex of Arabic literature. It is believed that it was not merely created but "written in Heaven" and literally transmitted to the Prophet, with no secondary political and juridical

[54] See Christopher Melchert, *The Formation of the Sunni Schools of Law. 9th-10th Centuries C.E.*, Brill, Leinde-New York- Köln 1997; Ahmed Akgunduz, *Introduction to Islamic Law. Islamic Law in Theory and Practice*, Iur Press, Rotterdam 2010, pp. 147 ff.

[55] To be noted that the Ẓāhirī and Ibāḍi schools continue to exercise a certain influence in some territories and were mentioned as active in the Amman Message issued by Abdullah II of Jordan on November 9, 2004.

consequences in terms of interpretation and exegesis.[56] Although the *Qur'ān* presents just a strict minority of *suwar* (partitions of the text, sing. *sūra*) and *'āyāt* (verses, literally "signs", sing. *āya*) which contain legal provisions, it stands as the core of the Islamic *sharīʿa* together with *sunnah*.

The term *sunnah* refers to the body of traditions, teachings, practices, and customs derived from the life and words of Muḥammad, and thus recognized as holy and normative in nature, characterizing the way of life of the Muslim community. The *sunnah* is constituted by the *'aḥādīth* (sing. *ḥadīth*) of the Prophet, or written reports of its actions, words, and silent approvals, which have been transmitted according to an *isnād* (chain of transmission).[57] It can easily be noticed that, due to the millions of transmitted *'aḥādīth*, not always consistent with one another, the *sunnah* presents a fundamentally varying and articulated character, with regard to which a unique and univocal systematization is not actually possible. This latter point is evidently reflected in *sharīʿa* itself, whose theorization, elaboration, and interpretation cannot be reduced to a homogeneous and monolithic corpus of norms as it could be with a positive legislation. The multiplicity of *'aḥādīth* is also regarded as an instrument of flexibility, influencing the juristic praxis of the different schools and making Muslim legal reasoning particularly adaptive to changing circumstances.

After the *Qur'ān* and the *sunnah*, two other roots are recognized: *ijmāʿ* and *qiyās*. They are secondary roots, to which jurists may refer whenever in the *Qur'ān* or in the *sunnah* a certain juridical question is believed to be unsolved or to be dealt with in a non-univocal way.

[56] About the uncreated nature of the *Qur'ān*, see Massimo Campanini [2004], *The Qur'ān. The Basics*, trans. Oliver Leaman, Routledge, London-New York 2007, pp. 13–14, 66; Rafiq Zakaria, *Muhammad and the Quran*, Penguin Books, London 1991, pp. 88 ff. The implications deriving from the nature of the text are evident, with particular reference to its being created or not. An attempted reform was undertaken by caliph al-Ma'mūn (786–833) of the Abbasid dynasty, who attempted to introduce the doctrine of the created *Qur'ān*, even though it was soon abandoned after the death of the caliph. With regard to this latter point, see Ira M. Lapidus [1988], *A History of Islamic Societies*, Cambridge University Press, Cambridge 2014, pp. 104–105, 130, 173; Malise Ruthven [1984], *Islam in the World*, Oxford University Press, Oxford 2006, pp. 191–194.

[57] Among the extensive literature on the subject, see Yusuf al-Qaradawi, *Approaching the Sunnah. Comprehension & Controversy*, International Institute of Islamic Thought, London-Washington 2006; Mahmoud Ayoub (ed.), *Contemporary Approaches to the Qur'ān and Sunnah*, International Institute of Islamic Thought, London-Washington 2012; 'Alī Nāṣirī, *An Introduction to Hadith. History and Sources*, trans. Mansoor Limba, Miu Press, London 2013; Harald Motzk (ed.), *Hadith. Origins and Developments*, Ashgate, Farnham 2004.

The term *ijmāʿ* refers to the consensus of the Islamic community. However, there is no general agreement on the authorities who are entitled to express their opinions and thus form a consensus on a given question: especially, it is an object of debate whether the consensus should only refer to the first generations of Muslim scholars, or to Muḥammad's companions (*ṣaḥābah*), or to the Islamic jurists of certain legal schools as well.[58] Generally speaking, *ijmāʿ* finds its collocation as a root from which *sharīʿa* can be derived in a *ḥadīth*, according to which the Prophet stated that the Islamic *ummah* "will never agree upon an error".[59]

In the absence of a clear provision derived from the first three roots, it is possible to refer to *qiyās*, or analogical deduction, which is the most debated of the four aforementioned roots, due to its particularly subjective nature. In the earlier period of Islam, such a method of deduction was not really incorporated in the number of the roots, but it beneficed a later recognition,[60] however not with the same consideration among the different legal schools. In the silence of the texts and lacking consensus, by means of analogical deduction a certain question can be solved in a similar way to another one believed to be analogous in nature.

If the *uṣūl al-fiqh* can be considered as a systematic approach progressively defined by juristic scholarship, its methodology is not understood as a monolithic and univocal experience. The different schools have indeed adopted different attitudes toward the roots and their mutual interactions, and the Islamic legal discourse knows of other instruments to enrich its praxis in a considerable way. A peculiar mention is to be made for the idea of *ʿurf*, which indicates a form of knowledge based upon customary traditions. The position of *ʿurf* has been highly debated, and although the majority of jurists reject it as part of the roots, it has undoubtedly played a role in the accrual of Muslim legal understanding.[61] Other conceptual

[58] For a monographic analysis, see Ahmad Hasan, *The doctrine of ijmāʿ in Islam*, Islamic Research Institute, Islamabad 1978.

[59] For the political implications of the *ḥadīth*, see Roy P. Mottahedeh, "The Foundation of State and Society", in *Islam. The Religious and Political Life of a World Community*, ed. Marjorie Kelly, Praeger, Westport-London 1984, p. 65.

[60] Cf. Bernard G. Weiss, *The search for God's law. Islamic jurisprudence in the writings of Sayf al-Din al-Amidi*, University of Utah Press, Salt Lake City 1992, p. 633.

[61] See Ayman Shabana, *Custom in Islamic Law and Legal Theory. The Development of the Concepts of ʿUrf and ʿAdah in the Islamic Legal Tradition*, Palgrave Macmillan, New York 2010; Haim Gerber, *Islamic Law and Culture, 1600-1840*, Brill, Leiden-Boston-Köln 1999, ch. 6.

tools coming to part of this multifaceted world, which would deserve a dedicated analysis, are for instance the notions of *maṣlaḥa* (public interest) and *istiḥsān* (discretion), whose usages are once again debated and on which there has never been a shared consensus.

The core of the Islamic legal perspective is therefore represented by a constant work of juristic research, with a considerable degree of variety and complexity. If a legal issue cannot be solved in a univocal and clear way and if there is no consolidated consensus on it, the instrument by which a qualified Muslim jurist operates in order to find a solution is called *ijtihād* (literally meaning "effort"), which indicates the rational process of derivation of Islamic rules and norms from their roots. This is a central and yet complex and debated concept, essential to developing a proper Islamic legal methodology, whose comprehension is necessary to understand the dynamics of the Muslim legal tradition. If it is believed that only a qualified person may perform *ijtihād*, there is no agreement about the legitimate boundaries within which this exercise must be enclosed, both conceptually and chronologically.

These few notions, with no pretense of exhaustiveness, aim at giving an initial clarification on issues and concepts that will be recurrent in the chapters of my book in order to provide to every typology of reader an initial basis with which to properly contextualize my analyses. In the course of my book, I will come back to further illustrate some of the notions I have merely introduced here in the wider context of a culture-specific comparison that necessarily requires, at least, a basic knowledge of the Muslim world.

CHAPTER 2

Sovereignty and Universalism After Westphalia

2.1 *The State and the* Ummah*: A Premise*

Among the juridical categories, which are most frequently universalized and improperly imposed upon different cultural contexts, that of modern statehood occupies a preeminent position. Although the postmodern globalized world moves toward a substantial redefinition of its dynamics, if not toward its progressive overcoming, the present international system remains anchored to the idea of an interplay of separate and autonomous sovereignties, whose mutual interactions define an overall political paradigm. Even if its centrality and its preeminence is gradually fading, it is impossible not to consider the State as the conceptual basis of the organization of the contemporary international community and of our understanding of international law.[1]

Although usually taken as a universal idea, modern statehood can be considered as a precise and determined narrative, whose outcomes in

[1] As Pierson points out, "states do not exist in isolation. They are by their very nature part of a *system of competing states*. Frontiers might abut unclaimed territory, but borders are necessarily the dividing line between one state and another" (Christopher Pierson [1996], *The Modern State*, Routledge, London-New York 2005, p. 13). On this, with particular reference to the Nation-State in its relationship with law, see also Peter Fitzpatrick [1992], *The Mythology of Modern Law*, Routledge, London-New York 2002, pp. 111 ff.

F. L. Ramaioli, *Juridical Perspectives between Islam and the West*, Global Issues, https://doi.org/10.1007/978-3-031-37844-7_2

political and juridical terms have been the result of a precise philosophical and theoretical elaboration.[2] And, if it came to be considered as *the* dominant narrative in the progressive definition of a political spatiality in the Western world, other legal orders originally thought about political governance in radically different ways. This is the case of Islam, whose traditional tension between universalism and territoriality, especially following the spread of the Western idea of statehood, deserves a comparative and philosophically oriented analysis.

In this chapter I will therefore discuss the different conceptions regarding the relationship between individual and community, and between community and law, with particular reference to the ideas of State and *ummah*, and to the principles of territoriality and universalism.

2.2 *State and* Dawla

As pointed out above, modern statehood is not a universal conception and is not a synonym of political organization, considered from a neutral perspective. On the contrary, it is a culture-specific narrative, which finds its legitimation in a precise historical contingency. After the Peace of Augusta, and later with the Peace of Westphalia, the whole European continent had undergone a fundamental process of political reorganization through the adoption of the principle expressed in the formula *cuius regio, eius et*

[2] Harding quite effectively defines the State as "an abstraction, a piece of metaphysics" which "came to dominate political consciousness as a thing not only believed to have real existence but loved for its promise of social order and hated for its threat of coercion" (Alan Harding, *Medieval Law and the Foundations of the State*, Oxford University Press, Oxford 2001, p. v). As Böckenförde puts it, the modern State, "as well as our contemporary democratic *Rechtsstaat* and social state, is not a natural institution, but one that is deliberately created, namely created for conscious purposes. It is conceived by human beings and for human beings, for their coexistence in peace, security, and freedom. The nature of the state is determined by and its structure is formed on the basis of the purposes for which it was conceived and created" (Ernst-Wolfgang Böckenförde [1978], "The State as an Ethical State", in *Constitutional and Political Theory. Selected Writings*, vol. I, trans. Thomas Dunlap, eds. Mirjam Künkler, Tine Stein, Oxford University Press, Oxford 2017, p. 88).

religio.[3] The Protestant Reformation, challenging the legitimation of the universalistic institution of the papacy, had undermined the core of what could be considered a cultural and religious homogeneity, which constituted the very basis of medieval unity.[4] The complex medieval legal order,[5] whose supreme guarantors had been the emperor and the pope as representatives of Christ on earth, was unable to survive the deep social and spiritual rift brought about by Martin Luther's theses. This rift could be considered not only the cultural product of a historical process but also a geographical division of the once-united Christendom.[6] From this division, the idea of modern statehood would gradually emerge[7] and be coherently conceptualized by the theory of the social contract and by authors such as Jean Bodin and, most of all, Thomas Hobbes with his *Leviathan*. The abandonment of the idea of a Christian universalism, with a *monarchia mundi* and a universal empire, had marked the transition to the idea of territoriality.

These historical and social conditions can be considered as decisive. The State, as the product of a specific vision of world, law, and society, could only have developed in the framework of late medieval Europe, with

[3] Falk defines the Westphalian system as "the classical framework of legal constraint postulated to regulate a highly decentralized world of sovereign states" yielding "a permissive, voluntaristic system of law stressing matters of the allocation of competence among sovereign states" (Falk, *The Interplay of Westphalia and Charter Conceptions*, *cit.*, p. 32). With regard to this, cf. Stéphane Beaulac, *The power of language in the making of international law. The word sovereignty in Bodin and Vattel and the myth of Westphalia*, Martinus Nijhoff Publishers, Leiden-Boston 2004, pp. 71–101. For an analysis of the religious foreign policy after Westphalia, deeply linked to the new political system, see Andrew C. Thompson, "After Westphalia: Remodeling a Religious Foreign Policy", in *War and religion after Westphalia, 1648–1713*, ed. David Onnekink, Ashgate Publishing, Farnham-Burlington 2009, pp. 47–68.

[4] For a comprehensive historical analysis of this period, see Mark Greengrass, *Christendom Destroyed. Europe 1517-1648*, Penguin Books, London 2014.

[5] A fundamental text to understand the complexity of the medieval legal order is Paolo Grossi [1995], *L'ordine giuridico medievale*, Laterza, Rome-Bari 2004 By the same author, see Grossi [2007], *A History of European Law*, trans. Laurence Hooper, Wiley-Blackwell, Chichester 2010, pp. 1–38.

[6] For a complete analysis of the transition from the medieval political system to territorial statehood, with particular attention to the transition from a hierarchical and vertical to an anarchical and horizontal architecture, cf. Jeremy Larkins, *From Hierarchy to Anarchy. Territory and Politics Before Westphalia*, Palgrave Macmillan, New York-Basingstoke 2010.

[7] Among the various authors analyzing the birth of the modern State, see Thomas Ertman, *Birth of the Leviathan. Building States and Regimes in Medieval and Early Modern Europe*, Cambridge University Press, Cambridge 1997. Consider also the already mentioned work of Harding.

a crucial contribution given by the religious wars which broke out across the continent.[8] The theoretical and political framework in which the idea of modern statehood rose and flourished is deeply rooted in Western thought, history, and contingencies, to the point that Schmitt addressed this form of legal order *in fieri*, from the Middle Ages to the modern State, as *jus publicum europaeum*.[9] Therefore, as every specific juridical conception, it has to be considered as a legacy deeply inherent to a given cultural context.

From Europe, the notion of modern statehood progressively spread and became a political paradigm whose efficacy in governing and administering justice was considered as undisputed. Its adoption beyond the Western world has indeed greatly contributed to make the Western tradition as "the paramount source of perceptions of law worldwide",[10] with the acceptance of the structural elements of modern statehood as something stably acquired by the internal legal discourse. European colonization represented the decisive force in imposing this intellectual construct, once again intended as a narrative concerning law and society, in lands in which it had been basically nonexistent. From a juridical point of view, one of the most important consequences of the colonization of Muslim countries was the transposition of the idea of statehood into an Islamic cultural context. It was not simply a redefinition of internal political dynamics or the establishment of a different form of political governance. On the contrary, it was the transplantation of the very conceptual basis on which the Western world had conceived law and power in relation to spatiality. As is evident, the implications were enormous, both from a theoretical and from a practical point of view. Since then, the worldwide affirmation of modern statehood as a shared and mutually accepted narrative bore traces

[8] According to Casanova, distinguishing however between early modern absolutist States and contemporary pluralistic States, "the so-called 'religious wars' could also more appropriately be called the wars of early modern European state formation" (José Casanova, "Religion Challenging the Myth of Secular Democracy", in *Religion in the 21st Century. Challenges and Transformations*, eds. Lisbet Christoffersen, Hans Raun Iversen, Hanne Petersen, Margit Warburg, Ashgate, Farnham-Burlington 2010, p. 25). This position concerning the State as a cultural and juridical product emerged from the European religious wars is shared, among others, by Böckenförde, *The State as an Ethical State*, *cit.*, p. 89.

[9] Cf. Carl Schmitt [1950], *Der Nomos der Erde im Völkerrecht des Jus Publicum Europaeum*, Duncker & Humblot, Berlin 1974, pp. 111–186.

[10] John O. Haley, *Law's Political Foundations. Rivers, Rifles, Rice, and Religion*, Edward Elgar, Cheltenham-Northampton 2016, p. 128.

so deep that even after the colonial period, Muslim countries retained it without putting it into question.

However, given the culture-specific nature of the concept, its simple transplant so into such a different context of cultural and legal backgrounds could evidently result in incoherence.[11] The very terminology of "Islamic State" tends to be misleading, implicitly merging two perspectives that are not always consistent with one another, without a proper analysis of the structural elements of both views. This kind of discussion can only begin from an etymological and linguistic premise.

The Arabic term commonly used for State, *dawla*, has been adopted with this specific signification only as a consequence of the importation of the idea of statehood from the Western world. Originally, since the early Abbasid era, it was used with the meaning of "period of rule" or extensively as "dynasty".[12] As evident having regard to the etymological origin of the term, denoting something wandering, moving, or turning,[13] *dawla* had been a word conceived to point out the cyclical element of the alternance in power of rulers. Therefore, while it can actually indicate a caliphal dynasty without a conceptual denaturation of its original meaning, the posterior translation of *dawla* into State appears to be the object of the imposition of a Western philosophical idea, which is to be considered structurally different. While *dawla*, pointing at the turning of the ruling eras and of the dynasties, has a fundamentally dynamic dimension, on the contrary the idea of State, appearing to be grounded in its geographical delimitation, is to be considered substantially static. The etymology of State, in fact, comes from the Latin past participle *status*, which can be translated as "that which has been",[14] with an evident shift from the Islamic outlook focusing on the dynamic dimension of authority to the stable and static dimension of a territorial conception of power. Moreover, while the lexicon commonly used to define the State and its pertinences points to the idea of stableness and fixity, starting from the very term

[11] With regard to this, see the reflections of Bassam Tibi, "The simultaneity of unsimultaneous: old tribes and imposed Nation-States in the modern Middle East", in *Tribes and States Formation in the Middle East*, eds. Philip Khoury, Joseph Kostiner, University of California Press, Berkeley 1990, pp. 127–152.

[12] See Patricia Crone, *God's Rule. Government and Islam*, Columbia University Press, New York 2004, p. 4.

[13] Cf. Franz Rosenthal, "Dawla" (voice), in *The Encyclopaedia of Islam*, vol. II, eds. Bernard Lewis, Charles Pellat, Joseph Franz Schacht, Brill, Leiden 1965, pp. 177–178.

[14] For a philosophical *excursus* on the etymology of "State", see Michael Herzfeld, *Cultural Intimacy. Social Poetics in the Nation-State*, Routledge, New York-London 2005, p. 73.

status, the Muslim lexicons referring to political society and juridical reality, such as *imām* and *sharīʿa*, "are all derived from roots to do with travelling and roads"[15] thus mirroring the desertic and dynamic reality of pre-Islamic Arabia.

This etymological premise helps when attempting to grasp some of the structural elements characterizing the Western and Islamic views about political and social organizations, which will be further examined in the following paragraphs. The dynamic nature of the Arabic *dawla*, in particular, appears to be significant in highlighting the fluidity of the political theory of the Islamic discourse about power and government, while the static nature of the Western *status* highlights an outlook on spatiality that deeply influenced the Occidental conceptions of law and its structural limits.

2.3 Structural Elements of the State Narrative in the West

Once again, when discussing fundamental social issues, such as the compatibility between the Islamic religious principles on social organization and Western legal standards such as human rights, we incur the risk of skipping a preliminary analysis on the compatibility between the structural elements of Islamic thought and modern statehood that we usually—and improperly—take for granted. Some authors, despite the great accuracy of their works, when examining the possible evolution of the legal systems of the Muslim world, miss the opportunity of highlighting similarities and differences between Islam as a way of conceiving the world, and the concept of statehood, as a scheme of comprehension of authority and law.[16] In order to understand this point, it is necessary to point out three structural features of modern statehood: sovereignty, territoriality, and social contract.

[15] Crone, *God's rule*, *cit.*, p. 21.

[16] For an example, see An-Naʿim, *Islam and the Secular State, cit.*, especially pp. 45–83. An-Naʿim, in his well-documented work, takes the distances from an abstract conception of Islam, considering on the contrary the concrete practice of faith by Muslims; by doing so, however, he tends to assume the State as a sort of natural form of government and rule. The author, in any case, correctly emphasizes territoriality as a characteristic of post-Westphalian systems (ibid., pp. 30 ff.). For a different point of view, although similar in taking modern statehood as a sort of universal philosophical construct, see Sherman A. Jackson, *Islamic Law and the State. The Constitutional Jurisprudence of Shihāb al-Dīn al-Qarāfī*, Brill, Leiden-New York-Köln 1996, especially pp. 185–224. On the contrary, the aforementioned volume of Patricia Crone (*God's rule, cit.*) appears to be properly contextualized from a juridical and philosophical perspective in that it highlights the divergences in conceiving determined juridical constructs between Islam and the Western world.

The definitions we can give to the concept of sovereignty are various and depend on the interpretation and evolution of this idea, according to the thought of authors such as Bodin,[17] Jellinek,[18] Schmitt,[19] Kantorowicz,[20] and others. In a concise but rather exhaustive way, we could describe sovereignty as "the right to exercise supreme authority within a territory".[21] From this point of view, and from a factual perspective, the Leviathan-State embodies the authority, which retains a power with respect to which there is no other superior power[22]; as the Latins used to say, an authority *superiorem non recognoscens*, intimately linked to the notion of a superior

[17] "Maiestie or Soveraigntieis the most high, absolute, and perpetual power over the citisens and subiects in a Commonweale: which the Latinscal *Maiestatem*, the Greeks *akraexousia*, *kurion arche*, and *kurion politeuma*; the Italians *Segnoria*, and the Hebrewes *tomechshévet*, that is to say, the greatest power to command." Jean Bodin [1576], *The Six Bookes of a Commonweal*, I, trans. Richard Knolles, Harvard University Press, Cambridge 1962, p. 84.

[18] Jellinek defines sovereignty as an "originary power to rule". See Georg Jellinek [1900], *Allgemeine Staatslehre*, Verlag von Julius Springer, Berlin 1929, p. 180–181.

[19] According to Schmitt, as well known, sovereign is he who decide on the state of exception: therefore, it is only in the state of exception that the core of the discussion about sovereignty is properly understood. From this point of view, sovereignty could be comprehended only through the idea of sovereign: "Although he stands outside the normally valid legal system, he nevertheless belongs to it, for it is he who must decide whether the constitution needs to be suspended in its entirety. All tendencies of modem constitutional development point toward eliminating the sovereign in this sense." See Carl Schmitt [1922], *Political Theology. Four Chapters on the Concept of Sovereignty*, transl. George Schwab, Massachusetts Institute of Technology, Cambridge 1985, pp. 5–15.

[20] For a historical perspective analyzing the medieval situation with regard to what will be later known as sovereignty, see Ernst H. Kantorowicz, *The King's Two Bodies. A Study in Medieval Political Theology*, Princeton University Press, Princeton 1957.

[21] Robert Paul Wolff [1970], *In Defense of Anarchism*, University of California Press, Berkeley-Los Angeles-London 1998, p. 5.

[22] It is important to recall the Hobbesian definition of the State through the image of the Leviathan: "one person, of whose acts a great multitude, by mutual covenants one with another, have made themselves every one the author, to the end he may use the strength and means of them all as he shall think expedient for their peace and common defence. And he that carryeth this person is called sovereign, and said to have sovereign power; and every one besides, his subject." Thomas Hobbes, *Leviathan, or the Matter, Form, & Power of a Common-wealth Ecclesiasticall & Civill*, for Andrew Crooke, at the Green Dragonin St. Pauls Church-yard, London 1651, ch. 17. For Schmitt's commentary on the theory of Hobbes concerning the birth of the State, see Carl Schmitt, *Der Leviathan in der Staatslehre des Thomas Hobbes. Sinn und Fehlschlag eines politischen Symbols*, Hanseatische Verlagsanstalt, Hamburg 1938, ch. 3.

and ultimate use of physical force.[23] This latter point transcends the concrete organization within the State itself, that is to say, the historical manifestations and the actual shapes the exercise of power assumes in a given context. Whether a State adopts a democratic or a totalitarian form of government, it does not influence the perspective of its sovereignty, intended once again as the effective possibility to exercise a supreme and ultimate power.

This supreme power, however, must be exercised exclusively within a spatially limited territory,[24] beyond which the Leviathan loses all its sovereign rights. While the medieval *Respublica Christiana* adopted a fundamentally universalistic perspective, the transition to modern statehood witnessed the fragmentation of a potentially global scenario into self-sufficient and autonomous sovereignties. Here, borders assume the central role of delimiting and defining different States, constituting ontologically separate and theoretically equal entities, which on this basis engage in mutual relationships and consequently define an international system. This point is evident from an iconographical observation: the Hobbesian Leviathan, supreme symbol of the modern State, is sometimes represented as a giant monarch or as a biblical monster.[25] It features, therefore, a physical and concrete form in contrast to the medieval institutions of empire and papacy, whose metaphysical dimension can be considered preeminent with respect to their contingent and physical embodiments.[26] With regard to this, it is the very physicality of the Leviathan to constitute the immanent limit to its ultimate power: the

[23] As Weber suggests, "one can define the modern state only in terms of the specific means peculiar to it, as to every political association, namely, the use of physical force" (Max Weber [1919], "Politics as vocation", in *From Max Weber. Essays in sociology*, Routledge London 1970, p. 78). For a detailed analysis on the force of law, see Frederick Schauer, *The Force of Law*, Harvard University Press, Cambridge 2015. With regard to this, Poscher moves from the position of Schauer and suggests that the force to which the State's monopoly refers is not a legitimate or legal force, but on the contrary a superior or ultimate force, because in order "to transform potentially violent social conflicts into legal ones, the law must be capable of overpowering any other force" (Cf. Ralf Poscher, "The ultimate force of the law: on the essence and precariousness of the monopoly on legitimate force", in *Ratio Juris*, vol. XXVII, n. 3, 2016, pp. 311–322).

[24] Cf. Pierson, *The Modern State, cit.*, pp. 12–14; Larkins, *From Hierarchy to Anarchy, cit.*, pp. 17–52.

[25] For a commentary on the representations of the Leviathan, see Schmitt, *Der Leviathan, cit.*, ch. 1.

[26] I will come back to this point in the next chapter, discussing the idea of *persona ficta*.

physical and finite body of the Leviathan corresponds to the necessarily spatial dimension of the State. In this context, sovereignty is indeed inseparable from its territorial dimension, becoming the concrete field in which the sovereign power can be exercised.

As for the third point, the social contract's theory[27] can be defined as the conceptual basis for the concrete existence of a sovereign power in a given territory. For the purpose of this research, it is necessary to highlight that the social contract, being ideally stipulated between consociates in order to avoid the insurgence of the state of nature, has a fundamentally horizontal dimension, being the idea "which redefines the horizontal bonds between members of the same society as a civic bond".[28] Regardless of the narratives on authority and legitimation of power adopted in every State, the horizontal dimension of the social contract represents a logical and tacit premise for the theoretical elaboration of the notion of sovereignty, which surges from a horizontal basis and consequently builds a pyramidal structure of power, just as the Leviathan emerges from the state of nature.[29]

[27] This position is common to the major authors sharing the contractualist position, as Grotius, Locke, Rousseau, Pufendorf, and of course Hobbes. For an analysis of the different positions among contractualists, see Wolfgang Kersting, *Vertragstheorien. Kontraktualistische Theorien in der Politikwissenschaft*, Kohlhammer, Stuttgart 2016. With reference to Hobbes' position, it is to be observed that the social contract "is the consequence of an infinity of pacts between individuals. The sovereign simply reaps the benefit without being himself a party, which gives him unequalled power: he is not bound by contractual obligations" (François Héran, "A few thoughts on the concept of social contract and equity between generations", preface to *Ages, Generations and the Social Contract. The Demographic Challenges Facing the Welfare State*, eds. Jacques Véron, Sophie Pennec, Jacques Légaré, Springer, Dordrecth 2007, p. xiii).

[28] Héran, *A few thoughts on the concept of social contract, cit.*, p. xiii.

[29] Böckenförde exhaustively highlights the purposes for which the State has been created, defining the State as an "entity of peace", a "decision-making entity", as well as an "entity of power". In his words: "In political disputes and in the political power struggle within the state as well, no friend-enemy grouping occurs, one that includes the willingness to use physical violence; instead, all disagreements remain at a level of intensity that does not fracture the integration into the shared order of peace. This entity of peace as a structural characteristic of state order is not given by nature. As a look at European constitutional history shows, it had to be wrested from a multitude of contrary forces, not least from the religio-political clashes of the confessional civil wars" (Böckenförde, *The State as an Ethical State, cit.*, p. 89).

These three points represent the structural characteristics of the Western narrative on modern statehood, considered as the main product of modernity aimed at regulating social coexistence and politically internal and external relationships. The Western world therefore shaped its theories of modern law, it being national or international, taking into account these three elements, with particular reference to the binominal sovereignty-territoriality, which came to define prerogatives and limits of political authorities. In the monist theories, which were predominant until relatively recent times,[30] law could only come from the State, as the ultimate source of sovereignty. Overcoming strict legal monism, State law continues to be perceived as one among the prevalent form of regulations, with the idea of sovereignty still considered as the main source of legal legitimacy. In this context, law is not simply a space-dependent phenomenon but is structurally limited by the borders of the State. Legal validity comes therefore to be measured based on a spatial delimitation, whose extension basically coincided with the State's territoriality. Indeed, these points outline a conceptual framework, almost unescapable in the modern era, within which to inscribe institutions and legal constructs, and consequently to shape a determined vision of law and community.

2.4 *Universalism in Islam:* Sharīʿa *and* Ummah

If the Western world witnessed the progressive affirmation of the paradigm of modern statehood, with special reference to the idea of territorial sovereignty, the Muslim world outlined a form of political governance based on deeply different criteria. Since the beginning of its history, Islam has indeed assumed an intrinsically and essentially universalistic perspective, whose survival has been challenged by the widespread diffusion of Western concepts and notions, with special regard to the dimension of territoriality. However, and notwithstanding its loss of actual political relevance in a State-based international scenario, the idea of Islamic

[30] For a dedicated monograph on legal monism, see Paul Gragl, *Legal Monism. Law, Philosophy, and Politics*, Oxford University Press, Oxford 2018. For a reflection on legal monism in the broader discourse of legal pluralism, see Brian Z. Tamanaha, *Legal Pluralism Explained. History, Theory, Consequences*, Oxford University Press, Oxford 2021, pp. 52–54.

universalism still represents a constant narrative influencing the juridical perspective of the Muslim world and deserves a deeper look. To do so, and to relate it with the three aforementioned elements constituting modern statehood, it can be examined from a political, religious, and juridical point of view.

From a political point of view, Islamic universalism has been shaped from the very beginning of the Islamic era and is deeply linked to the cultural views on community and politics of the Arabian Peninsula, by the time in which Muḥammad started his predication. In this context, which had been characterized by a fundamentally clan-based organization, social and political relations were based on the bond of blood. The perspectives on social life and political activity were thus based on belonging to a certain clan or on the descendance from a certain blood line. The Arabian Peninsula, from this point of view, appeared as a fragmented reality in which the cooperation between clans had to be considered as something essential in order to ensure the preservation of stableness and peace, and in which the bond of blood was still an unescapable characteristic of social organization. Moreover, the Arabian clans were not the only social and ethnic groups which were present in the pre-Muḥammadan society. Especially in Medina, a relevant presence was constituted by Jewish clans and by migrants.[31] The core of the social revolution brought about by Muḥammad's predication can be considered a shift in considering the constituting element defining the unifying dimension of a community: from the bond of blood to the bond of faith.[32] In order to overcome the ethnic and clan-based divisions historically present in the Peninsula, the new Islamic doctrine introduced the idea of a political community whose cohesion would have been granted by the adherence to a new belief and to the acceptance of a new and comprehensive idea of normativity, overcoming every difference in terms of ethnicity, clan, or land of origin. From this peculiar intuition, further strengthened and enshrined by the

[31] With regard to this, see David Norcliffe, *Islam. Faith and Practice*, Sussex Academic Press, Portland 1999, pp. 16–19.

[32] See Henry Siegman, "The state and the individual in Sunni Islam", in *The Muslim World*, vol. LIV. n. 1, 1964, p. 14.

covenant of Medina (*dustūr al-Madīnah*[33]) of AD 622, the Islamic *ummah* was born.[34]

From a religious point of view, it is worth saying that the universalistic structure of the Islamic political and legal order finds a justification in the doctrine of the creation of life by Allāh. The *Qur'ān* [35] expresses the idea of a pre-human condition in which all souls are created by Allāh and express an oath of loyalty and obedience to him as their Lord.[36] As evidenced, the doctrine of creation presents a fundamental difference from Jewish and Christian beliefs on the same subject, from two main points of view: on the one hand, in the holy book of Islam the creation of the soul

[33] The Arabic term *dustūr* is commonly translated as "constitution", and the definition of the covenant as "constitution of Medina" is somehow recurrent. As it will be explained in Chap. 5 of this book, I do not adopt this terminology to differentiate it from modern constitutionalism, for which the term *dustūr* is nowadays widely used. I prefer therefore to speak about a covenant of Medina (*mīthāq al-Madīnah*).

[34] Cf. Lambton, *State and Government in Medieval Islam, cit.*, pp. 13 ff; Abdullah Saeed, "The Nature and Purpose of the Community (Ummah) in the Qur'ān", in *The Community of Believers. Christian and Muslim Perspectives*, eds. Lucinda Mosher, David Marshall, Georgetown University Press, Washington 2015, pp. 15–28. In Black's words, Muḥammad "adapted ideas current in the Middle East. He gave a rationale for seeing the Arabs as the chosen people, and giving them a mission to convert or conquer the world. He enabled them to achieve the transition simultaneously from polytheism to monotheism and from tribalism to nationhood to internationalism. [...] In revolt against the étatiste Roman and Persian empires, Islam developed a stateless praxis" (Anthony Black [2001], *The History of Islamic Political Thought. From the Prophet to the Present*, Edinburgh University Press, Edinburgh 2011, p. 10). It is important to observe, with Mathewson Denny, that "The umma is not a governmental idea in the administrative sense; rather it is the totality of Muslims in the worlds upholding the Sharīʿa however they can" (Frederick Mathewson Denny [1994], *An Introduction to Islam*, Routledge, London-New York 2016, p. 201). However, with regard to this last position it is necessary to clarify that the *ummah* cannot be considered as the expression of a government as intended in the Western world, especially in the framework of modern statehood, but can be undoubtedly considered as a political community. From this point of view, the *ummah* is not—and could never be—a State but a comprehensive community sharing at least the structural elements of a common idea of justice, power, and law, regardless of the differences between the various currents of Sunnīsm.

[35] *Qur'ān*, VII, 172, with comment in the edition by Abdullah Yusuf Ali at p. 395.

[36] About the covenant between Allāh and the souls, see Tosun Bayrak Al Jerrahi, *The Name and the Named. The Divine Attributes of God*, Fons Vitae, Louisville 2000, p. 203. For a more radical view on the same subject, but still interesting on the issue of Islamic pre-creation, see Abu Ameenah Bilal Philips, *The Fundamentals of Tawheed (Islamic Monotheism)*, International Islamic Publishing House, Riyadh 2005, pp. 61–67.

and the creation of the body are conceptually separated; on the other hand, at the same time Allāh creates all the souls throughout human history, and these latter declare their loyalty to him. The implications in terms of free will and, most of all, in terms of conception of history are evident: while the Christian idea of history finds its basis on a linear eschatological doctrine, in Islam we could conclude that history is to be considered as circular, where all the souls are created loyal to Allāh, and thus Muslim, and in which all of the incarnated souls should then return to Allāh. Hence, it is not actually possible to speak of a conversion to the Islamic religion because it should be considered instead as a "return" to Islam[37] and to the oath of alliance stipulated between the Divinity and humanity before the creation of Adam.[38] The theorization of a pre-human condition in which we can witness a religious ideal unity of all the souls in Islam perfectly explains how this universalistic claim can be considered structurally inherent to Islamic thought.

From a juridical point of view, the legal dimension of Islam necessarily follows the same conceptual path. The Islamic *sharīʿa* is to be considered as the straight path to follow and as a way of life ideally encompassing every aspect of human existence. Therefore, *sharīʿa* is thus conceived as intrinsically incompatible with the legal concept of a State's *border* defining a spatial delimitation for the validity and efficacy of norms and legal concepts. Being the "way" given by the Divinity and to be followed by the *ummah*, it can only mirror its universalistic character. Its

[37] To be noticed that in Islam "conversion is not the acceptance of a new religion, but a return to the original religion: the Qur'ān suggests that everyone is born a Muslim, or rather that the natural state or *fitrah* of the human being is a state of submission (*islam*) to God. Someone who converts to Islam in a sense remembers her original religion and returns to it. Some English- speaking Muslims prefer the term 'reversion' to conversion; others, particularly some African Americans, use the term "transition" to describe the process of coming to identify religiously as Muslims" (Oliver Leaman, Kecia Ali, *Islam. The Key Concepts*, Routledge, London-New York 2008, p. 22).

[38] With regard to this, it is interesting to examine the concept of *fiṭrah*, that is to say that original and innate mark which in the Islamic vision can be seen as a reminiscence of humanity's pre-creational covenant with Allāh. As al-Faruqi argues, *fiṭrah* can be seen as "*religio naturalis*" or "the first presuppositions of human religiosity". See Ismail Raji al-Faruqi, *Islam and Other Faiths*, ed. Ataullah Siddiqui, The Islamic Foundation and the International Institute for Islamic Thought, Herndon 1998, pp. 138 ff.

comprehensiveness is reflected by its being at the same time a spiritual, moral, political, and social phenomenon, whose normative nature encompasses all of its dimensions. The common acknowledgment of being subject to *sharīʿa* is solely capable of creating not just a spiritual bond between individuals regardless of their geographical collocation, but of founding a political community.[39] If the unifying and universalizing element of the *ummah* is Islam, *sharīʿa* is its distinguishing mark, a normative dimension that defines belonging to this communitarian idea, which ideally overcomes national borders and geographical boundaries.

Despite the divergences among Islamic scholars and the differentiated praxis in enforcing *sharīʿa* in different territories,[40] what is to be considered here is the ideal and abstract dimension of its universalistic perspective, greatly affecting the political and social theorization in the Islamic world. The Islamic legal order does not recognize a limited efficacy to a normative act depending on the territory where this act is to be enforced:

[39] From this point of view, *sharīʿa* could be considered both as a religious and as a secular normative ideal. The distinction between spiritual and temporal power in the West and in Islam will be discussed in Chap. 4.

[40] The legal practice with regard to this point may vary according to the *maḏhab*. It is debated if *sharīʿa* provisions may be effectively implemented also in the territories of *dār al-ḥarb*, bearing consequences once the believer has returned to *dār al-Islām*. From the resolution of this issue descends, for instance, the possibility of punishing someone for an illicit act previously committed in *dār al-ḥarb*. Another possibility is that an illicit act committed outside of the Muslim lands, where *sharīʿa* is not enforceable, bears consequences only in front of the divinity. For an example of this divergence of opinions, see Khaled Abou El Fadl, "Striking the Balance: Islamic Legal Discourses on Muslim Minorities", in *Muslims on the Americanization Path?*, eds. Yvonne Yazbeck Haddad, John L. Esposito, Oxford University Press, Oxford 2000, pp. 56–57. Some of the concepts mentioned in this note will be furtherly developed and analyzed in the course of this book.

a provision of *sharīʿa*, thus derived from the will of Allāh, is maintained as universally valid, regardless of any territorial issue.[41]

Juridically speaking, the Muslim world traditionally recognizes a form of spatial delimitation which once again can be considered a fundamental alternative to the idea of territoriality as has prevailed in the West. From this point of view, *dār al-Islām* (the house of Islam) represents the territories where the practice of Islam is free, and where *sharīʿa* can be enforced, while *dār al-ḥarb* (the house of war) represents the territories where the Muslim practice, including its normative dimension, is not tolerated or finds obstacles to its complete enforcement.[42] With the adoption of the Western models based on national statehood in almost every part of the globe, these distinctions, which belong to the traditional juridical lexicon of the Islamic legal tradition, are to be considered basically a historical legacy. Nevertheless, they are relevant in order to understand the deeply different theorization of the relationship between normativity and

[41] It is possible to quote the famous Islamic scholar ibn ʿĀshūr: "It is a necessary part of Islamic knowledge that the Sharīʿah came as a universal law requiring the adherence of all human beings. Since it is the last revealed law, it is inevitably applicable to the whole of humankind everywhere on earth until the end of the world" (Muhammad al-Ṭāhir ibn ʿĀshūr [1946], *Treatise on Maqasid al-Shariah*, trans. Mohamed el-Tahir el-Mesawi, The International Institute of Islamic Thought, London-Washington 2013, p. 134). Moreover, as Zifcak observes, "where law is regarded as the legal expression of divine will, no such territorial boundaries can be recognized. The law has a universal, theological foundation which is incapable of containment by geography. On an Islamic view, localities are important, not because they are the source of law but rather because they are its object" (Spencer Zifcak, "Western and Islamic Conceptions of the Rule of Law", in *Islam Beyond Conflict. Indonesian Islam and Western Political Theory*, eds. Azyumardi Azra, Wayne Hudson, Ashgate Publishing, Aldershot-Burlington 2008, p. 36). Cf. Jasser Auda, "Realizing the Maqasid in the Sharīʿah", in *The Objectives of Islamic Law. The Promises and Challenges of the Maqasid al-Sharīʿah*, eds. Idris Nassery, Rumee Ahmed, Muna Tatari, Rowman & Littlefield, Lanham-London 2018, pp. 49–50. Moreover, as Vikør concisely explains, "Islamic law is not, in its nature, linked to any particular territory or state, it is linked to man's nature as a believer, someone who must follow God's commandments" (Knut S. Vikør, *Between God and the Sultan. A History of Islamic Law*, Oxford University Press, Oxford 2005, p. 280).

[42] See Siegman, *The state and the individual in Sunni Islam, cit.*, p. 14. For a comprehensive analysis, see Johannes Bork, *Zum Konstrukt von dār al-islām und dār al-ḥarb. Die zeitgenössische Rezeption eines Konzepts des klassischen islamischen Rechts*, De Gruyter, Berlin-Boston 2020. For a collection of texts dealing with *dār al-Islām* and *dār al-ḥarb*, see Giovanna Calasso, Giuliano Lancioni (eds.), *Dār al-islām / dār al-ḥarb. Territories, People, Identities*, Brill, Leiden-Boston 2017. A third distinction is represented by *dār al-ṣulḥ* (the house of treaty), designating the territories and the population with which the ummah has concluded a peace treaty.

geographical spatiality in Islam. While in the Western world the border separates two entities entitled with a sovereign right and legitimacy to enforce their own legislation, the distinction between *dār al-Islām* and *dār al-ḥarb* refers to the descriptive plan of pragmatical recognition.

Assuming as a basis for our analysis the dichotomy *Sein-Sollen*, we can argue that from the beginning of its history, the Western State has had a fundamentally prescriptive nature, where its territoriality separates it from a different sovereignty where its regulations and laws are not considered valid in that they lose their ultimate source of legitimacy.[43] On the contrary, the Islamic bipartition of *dār al-Islām* and *dār al-ḥarb* presents a descriptive nature in that it describes from a factual point of view the lands subjected to Islamic rule and the lands in which the practice of Islam is not entirely free. Here, the source of the theoretical validity of legal principles is not put into question,[44] but only the possibility or the opportunity of their implementation. Therefore, although this distinction expresses a spatial delimitation, it is not susceptible to undermining or questioning the universalistic approach of the Islamic legal vision, where *sharīʿa* is regarded as potentially valid in every place and in every time,[45] preexisting every sort of earthly boundary.

To summarize, in order to point out a fundamental distinction between the binomials *ummah-sharīʿa* and statehood-law in the post-Westphalian context, we may say that *sharīʿa* represents a universalistic conception of life and reality, transcending the boundaries of the strictly legal field, and not being limited in its enforcement by a given territory or by belonging

[43] Here I speak of prescriptive nature because of the legal pretense of the State of being an ordering power, which is entitled of deciding on how things *should be* ordained *(Sollen)* in its sovereign space of action. This characteristic is even more evident at the beginning of the Westphalian international system, where the religious separation between Catholics and Protestants is to be identified with the originating necessity at the basis of the State narrative.

[44] In present times, the dichotomy *dār al-ḥarb-dār al-Islām* is to be considered factually overcome by the progressive imposition of the State system. However, it is still important to understand it as a deep cultural heritage and a factual confirmation of the universalistic approach of the Islamic legal vision. In order to examine the concept from a contemporary point of view, see Sarah Albrecht, *Dār al-Islām Revisited. Territoriality in Contemporary Islamic Legal Discourse on Muslims in the West*, Brill, Leiden-Boston 2008.

[45] As al-Shāfiʿī stated, "There is no difference between *dār al-ḥarb* and *dār al-Islām* as to the laws that God has decreed to his people". Al-Shāfiʿī, *al-Umm*, vol. VII, pp. 354, cit. in Albrecht, *Dār al-Islām Revisited, cit.*, p. 77. It is to be observed, however, that the Ḥanafī legal school considers that certain provisions may not be applied outside *dār al-Islām* (ibid., pp. 75–84).

to an ethnic community.[46] It represents the embodiment of the bond of loyalty and submission between Allāh and the *ummah*, which expresses its obedience through following prescribed rituals and legal rules in organizing social and personal life. As is evident, the idea of social contract at the basis of modern statehood is totally absent in such a cultural context. In order to draw a parallelism, however, it can be said that while the Hobbesian State is based upon a contractual scheme, the bond between Allāh and the *ummah* is based upon a covenant as the expression of an oath of submission.[47] While, as already mentioned, the social contract theory appears to have a fundamentally horizontal nature in the relationship between the consociates, the covenant between Allāh and the *ummah* can only present an eminent vertical nature, being based on a revelation from above and on the submission to such a revelation.

[46] Bouzenita correctly points out that it is actually impossible to define *sharīʿa* as a personal or a territorial norm, because these very definitions find no counterparts in the Islamic legal discourse. The Islamic territory, from this point of view, is "not represented by determined frontiers and a clearly shaped territory. The modern territorial nation state which is considered as a legal subject of international law is defined by a theory of three elements, i.e. consists of the state's territory, its people and authority. But this definition cannot be applied to the self-definition of the Islamic state, as it is inherent in the classical legal literature. The frontiers of the Islamic state are, due to the division of the world between the two *dār* which has to be overcome, not consistent but subject to change" (Anke Iman Bouzenita, "The Siyar – An Islamic Law of Nations?", in *Asian Journal of Social Science*, vol. XXXV, n. 1, March 2007, p. 43).

[47] When proposing a social contract-like scheme for the Muslim community, Mustafa Cerić correctly addresses the actual bond between the *ummah* and Allāh as a covenant, "as well as a commitment of man toward God imposed by God and accepted by man as it is written in the Qur'ān" (Mustafa Cerić, *Toward a Muslim Social Contract in Europe*, The Association of Muslim Social Scientists (UK)-The City Circle, Richmond 2008, p. 6). In this work, I use the word covenant as well, in order to make a fundamental distinction with the Western idea of social contract, having regard to their respective dimensional natures (horizontal-vertical). As it will be pointed out in the next chapter, a sort of contractual scheme was indeed used to discipline the bond of personal loyalty between a subject and a political ruler, but once again on a merely personal basis.

2.5 Conclusions: Transnationalism, Universalism, Territoriality

These few elements help to outline a preliminary overview of some major conceptual divergences between Islam and the Western world in conceiving social and political organization, with non-secondary juridical implications that will be explained further in the following chapters.

The State and the *ummah* are considered two eminently political figures,[48] both being at the core of the political life of a precise vision of the world and yet irredeemably separated by a reverse theorization of their structural and constituting elements: while ideally the State comes into existence as a consequence of a contract between consociates for pragmatical reasons, the *ummah* comes to life as a response to a covenant with divinity, embodied by the voluntary submission to a preexistent normative order; while the law of the State embodies the exercise of absolute power over a given territory, *sharīʿa* draws a path to be followed by a universal community. To summarize, if the theory of the State follows the scheme horizontal contract-territorial law, the Islamic traditions follow a reverse path: vertical covenant-universalistic normativity.

From a historical point of view, the developing path of the ideas of Muslim *ummah* and Western statehood can again be considered as reversed. The State is the final philosophical and juridical outcome of the acknowledgment of the irreversible dissolution of medieval unity, after the collapse of the idea of the *Respublica Christiana*, thus with the aim and the necessity of dividing an ideally universalistic political body. On the contrary, the *ummah* is a concept which gives a response to the divisions between clans and ethnicity in the Arabian Peninsula, characterized by a multiplicity of religions, languages, and traditions, in order to build a cultural and religious unity under obedience to a universal rule.

Referring to the universalistic nature of the Islamic legal view, it should be noted that in literature the description of *sharīʿa* as a "transnational law" and of the *ummah* as a "transnational community" is something

[48] Both the State and the *ummah* are political subjects, although the political dimension of both greatly varies in its theorization depending on their constituting elements. Therefore, the modern State founds its political nature on precise elements such as territoriality and sovereignty, while the Islamic *ummah* on a completely different understanding of social cohesion, as derived from a universal spiritual vocation that nevertheless creates a political unity through the common acknowledgment of a normative ideal.

recurrent.[49] This definition, however, tends to be quite misleading as for the aforementioned relationship between *sharīʿa* and the Nation-State system of the modern period.

Indeed, the term "transnational" characterizes something overcoming national borders while at the same time admitting their actual existence and factually acknowledging them as a juridical reality. From this point of view, we can describe capitalism as being fundamentally transnational in its nature or Catholic canon law as being a form of transnational regulation. Necessarily, transnational phenomena admit the existence of Nation-States, and consequently coexist with them, although along different plans of interaction. We can conclude by saying that transnational is something operating in an overall system in which the concept of Nation-State, and thus of territoriality, is something acquired, just like the possibility of transcending it by operating at a different level. When referring to *sharīʿa*, it is not actually possible to define it as transnational because in that specific juridical and philosophical context the very theorization of Nation and State is something to be considered basically alien, as previously observed. Therefore, it would be more proper to define it as universally conceived or, in order to report it in Western terminology, as *a*-national, that is to say, a phenomenon which lacks a national dimension and which is to be considered self-sufficient with its own conceptualization of spatiality. With regard to this, *sharīʿa* does not simply transcend the national borders and the territoriality of modern States, but prescinds from them and predates them. The substantial non-recognition of territoriality should not be reconducted only to the aforementioned historical contingencies, but from a philosophical point of view, it can be considered as the coherent consequence mirroring the rejection of the bond of blood in favor of the bond of faith, which once again cannot be limited by territorial boundaries.

However, it could be observed here that the universalistic aspiration of *sharīʿa* is an ideal perspective which, in practical terms, had to face the various challenges of internal divisions and doctrinal fragmentations. From this point of view, the great schism which led to the separation between Sunnī and Shīʿa Islam can be held as an example of how an ideal aspiration

[49] For instance, *ex mult.*, see Ina Merdjanova, *Rediscovering the Umma. Muslims in the Balkans between Nationalism and Transnationalism*, Oxford University Press, Oxford 2013, pp. 54–59; Jorgen S. Nielsen, "Transnational Islam and the Integration of Islam in Europe", in *Muslim Networks and Transnational Communities in and Across Europe*, eds. Stefano Allievi, Jorgen S. Nielsen, Brill, Leiden 2003, pp. 28–52.

to universal unity can ultimately meet the concrete obstacles of political rivalry and religious dissidence. Another example, as already mentioned, is the contamination by Western legal models which, mostly in the colonial period, progressively spread throughout the Muslim world, establishing a new and rival way of ruling and administering justice. Nevertheless, as for this research, what should be considered here is the philosophical perspective by which the Islamic tradition considers and understands the juridical phenomenon, regardless of the historical outcome resulting from the concrete contingencies. What should be noted, again, is that *sharīʿa*, although practically incapable of doctrinal unity and universal enforcement, aspires in its theorization to universalism and to the rejection of the principle of territoriality.

In order to achieve a better understanding of this point, however, it is necessary to discuss in detail the conception of authority in Islam and in the Western political tradition, and its relationship with the legal order.

CHAPTER 3

The Leviathan and the Caliph Between Authority and Law

3.1 Premise

When analyzing the concept of political authority from the Islamic perspective, it must be observed that supreme and absolute authority belongs to Allāh alone, and from the Divinity it is uniquely derived.[1] This form of authority is not to be intended as sovereignty, as theorized in Western thought, but as a metaphysical authority over creation and souls and in a wider perspective over existence itself, where Allāh is the only creator and "sustainer of the worlds".[2]

[1] As Maududi argued: "The basic principle of Islam is that human beings must, individually and collectively, surrender all rights of overlordship, legislation, and exercise of authority over others. No one should be allowed to pass orders or make commands *on his own right* and no one ought to accept the obligation to carry out such commands and obey such orders. None is entitled to make laws on his own authority and none is obliged to abide by them. This right vets in Allāh alone" (Sayyid Abdul A'la Maududi [1976], "The Political Theory of Islam", in *Contemporary Debates in Islam. An Anthology of Modernist and Fundamentalist Thought*, eds. Mansoor Moaddel, Kamran Talattof, Palgrave Macmillan, New York-Basingstoke 2000, p. 270).

[2] *Qur'ān*, 1, 2.

F. L. Ramaioli, *Juridical Perspectives between Islam and the West*, Global Issues, https://doi.org/10.1007/978-3-031-37844-7_3

As for the concrete exercise of power, Islamic thought does not require a particular institutional architecture to be adopted by the *ummah*,[3] as an analysis of the evolutionary stages of the Islamic community through the centuries easily illustrates. Therefore, power can be held and concretely exercised by a number of figures, vesting different roles, which underwent progressive evolutions during history: the Muslim political community has thus assisted in the rise to power of kings (*mulūk*), sultans (*salāṭīn*), commanders (*umarāʾ*), and other forms of local governors, depending on the concrete historical contingencies and on the political currents of the time. Theoretically, and given the inexistence of prefixed and necessarily prescribed forms of political power, the Islamic community could be ruled in accordance with any type of governance, from autocracy and despotism to a shared form of decision-making power based on consultation,[4] provided that the rules of *sharīʿa* are respected and its ultimate goals pursued.

As it will be explained in further detail, in Islam *how* power is exercised is basically more important than *who* comes to exercise it. In other words, even in cases of non-optimal ways of governing, the supreme imperative is seeking "the most suitable means to realize the normative *ethos* of Islam".[5] Based on this preliminary observation, I will examine in this chapter the

[3] As Mathewson Denny points out, the *sharīʿa* "precedes the caliphate or any other form of Islamic government that could be developed. That is, there is no prescribed form of Muslim government, either in the Qur'ān or the Sunna; there are only guidelines and principles that can be followed as Muslim peoples do their best to order society wherever they may be" (Frederick Mathewson Denny [1994], *An Introduction to Islam*, Routledge, London-New York 2016, p. 201).

[4] Ideally, as it has been argued in the contemporary debate, this flexibility is very adaptive and could range from despotism to democracy. Clearly, with the terms despotism and democracy I do not refer to the figures of power experienced by the Western world, thus precisely characterized by elements inherent to the European philosophical and legal history. I use these terms only to point out the great flexibility of the Islamic political theory, which could be adapted to fit a great range of forms and practices. For instance, the autocratic rule could be justified by the idea of vicariate as inherent to the caliphal power, while a democratic idea of a shared decision-making process could be grounded on the concept of *shūrā* (consultation). An example in classical Islam is provided by the political thought of al-Ghazālī, according to whom consultation was a mandatory principle for all the Muslim rulers. For an analysis on the ties between al-Ghazālī's view and the idea of democracy, see Mohammed Moussa, *Politics of the Islamic Tradition. The Thought of Muhammad al-Ghazali*, Routledge, London-New York 2016, pp. 105–108.

[5] Moussa, *Politics of the Islamic Tradition, cit.*, p. 106.

major theoretical divergences between the Islamic and Western perspectives on the exercise of power and its relationship with the juridical phenomenon, having particular regard to the symbolic figures of the caliph and the Leviathan.

3.2 *The* Khalīfah *and the Factual Idea of Islamic Power*

Given the universalistic aspiration of the Islamic vision, we can easily observe that the concrete exercise of power in the Muslim world, at least in principle, should be reconducted to a wider perspective, that is to say, to the common observation and enforcement of *sharīʿa*. The fragmentation of the Islamic political spectrum should not be understood as an abdication from the universalistic idea but as the consequence of the lack of a political model universally accepted in Muslim discourse and directly derived from the classic roots of the legal tradition. Consequently, without a formal political and doctrinal unity, and without a recognized and *de facto* legitimated central authority, the spontaneous harmony and concord of different and sometimes rival local powers would not be possible.

The only figure which actually mirrors the universalism of *sharīʿa*, and possibly serves as a comprehensive political framework in which to inscribe a coordinated guidance of the *ummah*, is represented by the caliph, whose rule, however, should not be maintained as mandatory in Islamic legal and political thought. The origin of the term *khalīfah* can be traced back to the *Qur'ān*,[6] where it is stated that Allāh told the angels that he would establish a vicar, a successor (*khalīfah*) on earth. Therefore, the term caliph can be translated simply as "someone who stands in place of another", a vicar, the representative of Muḥammad—and later of Allāh— in this world.

[6] "Behold, thy Lord said to the angels: "I will create a viceregent on earth". They said: "Wilt Thou place therein one who will make mischief therein and shed blood?—Whilst we do celebrate Thy praises and glorify Thy holy (name)?" He said: "I know what ye know not."" *Qur'ān*, 2, 30, trans Abdullah Yusuf Ali [1934], *The Meaning of the Holy Qur'ān*, Amana Publications, Beltsville 2004, p. 24. Another reference to the term *khalīfah* in the holy book of Islam is made in *Qur'ān*, 38, 26, trans. Ali, *cit.*, p. 1166, where the title of vicar is given to David. It is worth noting that Ali translates the term *khalīfah* as "viceregent". In my work I will use the term "vicar" in order to point out the fundamental character of the caliphal role, that is to say, the representativeness of someone else.

Although the term is mentioned in the scriptural text, it is not expressly stated that the concept of vicariate should be interpreted as a political form of government or as a universalistic political architecture; in the same way, no explanation is given for the concrete characterization of the caliphal way of ruling, its prerogatives, or its formalization. The substantial lack of details in the primary source of Islamic revealed knowledge is particularly indicative, if we consider how its first establishment actually responded to the pragmatic exigency of giving the *ummah* a unitary representation after Muḥammad's death. In the Muslim tradition, the role of the caliph is never dogmatically theorized in a univocal way, and in order to grasp the essential elements of this notion, we should refer to the historical development of the figure and, most of all, to doctrinal and scholarly works. In this context, the caliph comes to be the representative of Prophet, vesting the authority in the name of Allāh, and is granted the title of *ʾamīr al-muʾminīn* or "commander of the believers".[7] It is interesting to note, with regard to this, that the title refers to the believers considered in a universalistic way, thus potentially not limitedly to the Muslims alone. On the contrary, the title of *amīr al-muslimīn*, translatable as "commander of the Muslims" and first adopted by the Almoravids in dependence of the Abbasid caliphate, shows a minor conceptual extension than its caliphal counterpart, purposely conceived to be a universal and all-embracing title.[8] The caliph is considered as the representative of the believers on earth, regardless of their geographical collocation, with a marked emphasis on universalistic representation, for their activity, and on consultation

[7] Cf. Yusra Khanam, "Amir al-Mu'minin" (voice), in *Islam. A Worldwide Encyclopedia*, ed. Cenap Çakmak, Abc-Clio, Santa Barbara 2017, pp. 131–132.

[8] The title of *amīr al-muslimīn* was adopted by the Almoravids by the time in which they recognized the caliphal prerogatives of the Abbasid rule. Their rule has been described as "sub-caliphate" (Clifford Edmund Bosworth, "Laḳab" (voice), in *The Encyclopaedia of Islam*, eds. Clifford Edmund Bosworth, Emeri Johannes van Donzel, Charles Pellat, vol. V, ns. 87–88, Brill, Leiden 1982, p. 626). However, given the universal nature of the caliphal rule, at least in principle, the definition of sub-caliphate would result paradoxical in that it would subordinate a power that in principle considers itself as the highest on earth on another equal power.

(*shūrā*), for their appointment.[9] On this basis, the caliphate can be defined as the supreme political authority in the Muslim tradition, whose doctrinal elaboration fulfills the concrete needs and necessities of the Islamic community in its first decades, with particular attention to its unitary guidance and political leadership.[10]

Sunnī history can be divided into four main caliphal periods. After the death of the Prophet, a decade after the Hegira (*hijrah*), a caliph was elected among the closest of his companions, and Abū Bakr ascended to the supreme authority of the *ummah*. After him, 'Umar, 'Uthman and 'Alì followed in assuring the Islamic community a unitary leadership, in force of the close relationship which had tied all of them to Muḥammad. This period, from 632 to 661 AD, is commonly referred to as the era of the four "rightly guided" (*rāshidūn*) caliphs.[11] In these years, the caliphal figure represented the supreme political, military, and religious authority and was a *de facto* physical expression of the *ummah* of the believers.[12] After the first four caliphs, the Umayyad dynasty rose to power, starting the era of a new caliphate (661–750 AD).[13] During this period, Damascus was chosen as the capital city of the new administration instead of Medina, and

[9] The idea of consultation is central in the appointment of a Muslim ruler, although, as already mentioned, a parallelism between the Islamic idea of *shūrā* and the Western idea of democracy could be too audacious and culturally decontextualized. Moreover, it is necessary to notice that, lacking a univocal way of conceiving role and prerogatives of the caliph, a univocal way of appointing one has never been theorized either. On this concept, see Roswitha Badry, "Consultation" (voice), in *The Princeton Encyclopedia of Islamic Political Thought*, ed. Gerhard Bowering, Princeton University Press, Princeton 2016, pp. 116–117. Historically, the principle of *shūrā* dates back to the appointment of the third caliph, ʿUthmān, by a committee established by the second caliph 'Umar. On this, see Wilferd Madelung [1997], *The Succession to Muḥammad. A Study of the Early Caliphate*, Cambridge University Press, Cambridge 2001, pp. 57–77.

[10] For an overall analysis on the mai doctrinal positions on the caliphate, see Mona Hassan, *Longing for the Lost Caliphate. A Transregional History*, Princeton University Press, Princeton 2016, pp. 98–141.

[11] For a detailed and comprehensive historical account of this period, see Madelung, *The Succession to Muḥammad*, *cit.*

[12] With regard to the religious authority of the caliph, it is necessary to remember that this aspect underwent relevant evolutions during the centuries and in dependence of the various dynasties. The extension and pervasiveness of the spiritual influence of the caliph is still debated. See Patricia Crone, Martin Hinds [1986], *God's Caliph. Religious Authority in the First Centuries of Islam*, Cambridge University Press, Cambridge 2003.

[13] See G. R Hawting [1986], *The First Dynasty of Islam. The Umayyad Caliphate, AD 661-750*, Routledge, London-New York 2000.

the conception of the caliphate underwent important modifications: first of all, the supreme magistrate of Islam ceased to be elected and ascended to power for hereditary and dynastical succession,[14] and the official title changed from ***khalīfah rasūl Allāh*** (vicar of the messenger of Allāh) to ***khalīfah Allāh*** (vicar of Allāh).[15] After the fall of the Umayyads, a new dynasty emerged, starting the experience of the Abbasid caliphate, which exercised supreme rule over the ***ummah*** until 1258, when the Mongol conquest ended their dominion.[16] With the Abbasids, the capital was moved to Baghdad, and the caliphate experimented with alternate phases of expanded and limited interference in the spiritual affairs of Islam.[17] In 1517 a new caliphate was born, with the formal assumption of the title of caliph by the Ottoman sultan Selim I, based in Istanbul.[18] This represented a major shift in the history of the caliphate, for two main reasons; firstly, the Turkish Ottoman rule was the first one coming from a non-Arab dynasty[19]; secondly, the Ottoman sultanate came to resemble more

[14] The hereditary character of the caliphal authority modified the conception of the vicariate, in some way giving it features of an earthly monarchy. With regard to this, the Shīʿa authorities criticized the asserted secularization of the caliphate, on the basis of the hereditarily nature of the title. Cf. Jonathan Porter Berkey, *The Formation of Islam. Religion and Society in the Near East, 600-1800*, Cambridge University Press, Cambridge 2003, pp. 78 ff.

[15] Cf. Crone, Hinds, *God's Caliph, cit.*, pp. 4–12.

[16] With regard to the Abbasid caliphate, see Amira K. Bennison, *The Great Caliphs. The Golden Age of the ʿAbbasid Empire*, I.B. Tauris, London-New York 2009; Hugh Kennedy [1981], *The Early Abbasid Caliphate. A Political History*, Routledge, London-New York 2015.

[17] With regard to maximum expansion of the spiritual and religious prerogatives of the Abbasid caliphate, with the already mentioned rule of al-Maʾmūn, see Ira M. Lapidus [1988], *A History of Islamic Societies*, Cambridge University Press, Cambridge 2014., pp. 172–173. On the subsequent limitation of the religious influence of the Abbasids, see Majid Fakhry, "Philosophy and Theology: from the Eighth Century C.E. to the present", in *The Oxford History of Islam*, ed. John L. Esposito, Oxford University Press, Oxford 1999, pp. 279–280.

[18] The formal assumption of the title marks the beginning of a new caliphal era. It is worth mentioning, however, that it is only in 1774 that the sultan will use the title of caliph in an official document, in the Küçük Qaynarce treaty stipulated between the Ottomans and the Russian Empire. See Philip K. Hitti, *History of the Arabs*, MacMillan, New York 1949, p. 705; Hassan, *Longing for the Lost Caliphate, cit.*, pp. 145–156.

[19] Sultan Selim I, who ascended to the throne in 1512, was actually the first non-Arab ruler to ideally unify the ***ummah*** under a caliphate. Cf. Kenneth W. Morgan [1958], *Islam, the Straight Path. Islam Interpreted by Muslims,* Motilal Banarsidass Publishing, Delhi 1993, pp. 256 ff.; Radhey Shyam Chaurasia, *History of Middle East*, Atlantic Publishers & Distributors, Delhi 2005, pp. 13–14.

and more a temporal kingdom, while the title of caliph continued to represent a powerful spiritual symbol of the ideal unity of the Muslim community, although substantially deprived of political power.[20] The Ottoman caliphate lasted until 1924, a few years after the suppression of the sultanate by the secular Republic of Turkey, and can be considered the last major caliphal experience in Sunnī Islam.

Apart from these four experiences, it is possible to recall other Sunnī caliphal dynasties, like the Berber dynasty of the Almohadas, the Abbasid pseudo-caliphate under the Mamluk rule based in Cairo, and the Umayyad Spanish caliphate of Cordova,[21] in al-Andalus. It is worth mentioning the Shīʿa caliphal experience of the Fatimids of Egypt as well, although in this case it would be more appropriate to speak about an *imām* rather than about a caliph.[22]

Having regard for this historical background, it is evident how a proper theorization of the institute of the caliphate does not proceed from the traditional roots of law, but from the philosophical and political thoughts of classical Muslim scholars, depending on concrete political necessities. Throughout history the caliphate underwent significant modifications for

[20] Cf. Caroline Finkel, *Osman's Dream. The Story of the Ottoman Empire, 1300-1923*, John Murray Publishers, London 2005, ch. 15. For the spiritual element in the Ottoman experience, with particular attention to the rule of Abdulhamin, see Azmi Özcan, *Pan-Islamism. Indian Muslims, the Ottomans and Britain, 1877-1924*, Brill, Leiden 1997, pp. 48–54. For an in-depth analysis of the relationship between the Ottomans and the idea of caliphate, see Hüseyin Yılmaz, *Caliphate Redefined. The Mystical Turn in Ottoman Political Thought*, Princeton University Press, Princeton 2018, especially pp. 181–276.

[21] The Umayyad dynasty survived in the Islamic Andalusian dominion and conducted an autonomous policy from the Abbasid caliphate. However, even in ideal terms, the universal representation of the *ummah* of the believers can be considered rather doubtful, due to the rival Abbasid power and its objective predominance in terms of representativeness. The Andalusian rule can be however considered as an interesting experience, especially for the flourishing of arts, culture, and philosophy in its territories. With regard to this, see William Montgomery Watt [1965], *A History of Islamic Spain*, Edinburgh University Press, Edinburgh 2001, pp. 30–57.

[22] See Yaacov Lev, *State and Society in Fatimid Egypt*, Brill, Leiden 1991; Farhad Daftary, Shainool Jiwa (eds.), *The Fatimid Caliphate. Diversity of Traditions*, I.B. Tauris, London-New York 2018. In Shīʿa Islam, it is more appropriate to speak about *imām* instead of caliph, because of the radically different conception of the imamate in Shīʿa tradition and thought, as well as the different theorization of a religious hierarchy, basically inexistent in the Sunnī world. However, the analysis of this aspect falls outside the scope of this work.

its spiritual prerogatives, the supreme representation of the believers, the actual authority over the overall Muslim community, and the requisites for ascending to power. In order to understand its progressive conceptualization, we should refer to various authors, like Abū l-Hasan al-Māwardī (972–1058) and later on Ibn Taimīya (1263–1328), whose theories, however, are not always concordant in defining the requisites and aims for the establishment of the supreme vicariate in the *ummah*. In particular, al-Māwardī, with his work *al-Aḥkām al-sulṭāniyya*,[23] is the author of the most complete and exhaustive scholarly systematization of the theory of the caliphate[24] while pragmatically attempting to legitimate the Abbasid rule which came to be menaced by the growing factual power of the Buwaihid emirs and by the Shīʿa Fatimids. It is worth noticing, with regard to this, that every definition of the competences of the caliph can be regarded as a rationalization of the concrete history of the Muslim community in a given time, with a posterior justification of the precedent political events of a certain faction.[25] From this point of view, and given the limited references on institutional and political governance in the main roots of law, it is possible to argue that every theory related to political authority, its legitimation, and its relationship with the law should be regarded as fundamentally rising from a praxis. Therefore, the Islamic

[23] For an English translation of al-Mawardi's work, see Abū l-Hasan al-Māwardī [XI c.], *Al-Aḥkām as-Sulṭaniyyah. The laws of Islamic governance*, trans. Asadullah Yate, Ta-Ha Publishers, London 1996.

[24] Cf. M. A. Muqtedar Khan, "The Islamic State", in *Encyclopedia of Government and Politics*, eds. Mary Hawkesworth, Maurice Kogan, vol. I, Routledge, London-New York 1992, pp. 269–270; Nur Kibraev, "The Political and Legal Culture of Medieval Islam", in *Values in Islamic Culture and the Experience of History. Russian Philosophical Studies*, eds. Nur Kirabaev, Yuriy Pochta, vol. I, Council for Research in Values and Philosophy, Washington 2002, pp. 148–150; Erwin Isak Jakob Rosenthal, *Political Thought in Medieval Islam*, Cambridge University Press, Cambridge 1958, pp. 27 ff.; Henri Laoust, "La pensée et l'action politique d'al-Mâwardî", in *Revue des Etudes Islamiques*, n. XXXVI, Paris 1968, pp. 11–92.

[25] Cf. Hamilton Alexander Rosskeen Gibb [1937], "Al-Mâwardî's theory of the Khilâfah", in *Studies on the Civilization of Islam*, eds. Stanford J. Shaw, William R. Polk, Princeton University Press, Princeton 1982, p. 162.

political theory on authority, with all of its juridical implications, is considered an orthopraxis, instead of an orthodoxy.[26]

Notwithstanding this, it is possible to identify some structural features of the different theories on authority in Islam, whose characters are in some way recurring among the various classical scholars. While analyzing this point, it is necessary to focus on the juridical implications of the conception of political authority and how it differs from the Western outlook. In doing so, three main points of reflections emerge: first, the relationship between authority and law; second, the idea of personification of power; and third, the idea of legitimation of power.

3.3 Authority and Law

With regard to the binomial authority-law, it is worth recalling the Western conception, once again in the framework of the paradigm of the modern State. Assuming that the supreme authority in a given territory is exercised by the State-Leviathan,[27] as a symbol of a self-sufficient sovereign power, we can easily argue that the law[28] can be considered an instrument of the established power aimed at pursuing its goals and its own survival. According to Hobbes, the Leviathan, which is not subjected to laws, imposes its own regulations and norms upon the subjects, in order to craft

[26] As Branca argues, the conception of power and authority in the Islamic thought is to be conceived as orthopraxis because every theorization and systematization of the subject by the Islamic scholarship cannot but follow a concrete praxis, which had been established in order to respond to pragmatical exigencies of the community, in the silence of *sharīʿa*. See Paolo Branca, "Pouvoir de iure et pouvoir de facto dans la pensée polique islamique classique", in *Authority, Privacy and Public Order in Islam*, proceedings of the 22nd Congress of the Union Européen des Arabisants et Islamisants, Peeters Publishers & Department of Oriental Studies Bondgenotenlaan, Leuven 2006, pp. 29–40. The definition is also used by Ayman Shabana, *Custom in Islamic Law and Legal Theory. The Development of the Concepts of ʿUrf and ʿAdah in the Islamic Legal Tradition*, Palgrave Macmillan, New York 2010, p. 3.

[27] Once again, it is worth remembering that we are not referring to the specific forms of government, such as absolutism and democracy. With the expression State-Leviathan we are referring to the conception of sovereignty, according to the structural elements as analyzed in the previous chapter, and regardless of the concrete institutional configuration of the established power within the borders of the State.

[28] In this sub-paragraph, I will refer to law and preeminently State law, although, as stated in my introduction, the dimension of State law does not preempt the field of law considered in its entirety. However, in order to infer from various perspectives an overall and comprehensive vision belonging to the Western legal conception, the example of State law in the sovereignty-based discourse is particularly relevant.

order from chaos. The legal dimension of this order, as theorized by the model of the State, is regarded as substantially functional and instrumental to the aim authority pursues.[29] Therefore, law comes substantially from authority, as stated in the famous Hobbesian formula ***auctoritas, non veritas, facit legem***,[30] just as in Hobbes' vision *jus* does not come from ***iustum*** but from ***iussum***, a command by the authority. Böckenförde synthetizes this position by defining the State by necessity as a "decision-making entity", which creates regulations and norms to preserve itself and to

[29] As Hobbes states, "men, for the attaining of peace and conservation of themselves thereby, have made an artificial man, which we call a Commonwealth; so also have they made artificial chains, called civil laws, which they themselves, by mutual covenants, have fastened at one end to the lips of that man, or assembly, to whom they have given the sovereign power, and at the other to their own ears. These bonds, in their own nature but weak, may nevertheless be made to hold, by the danger, though not by the difficulty of breaking them" (Thomas Hobbes, *Leviathan, or the Matter, Form, & Power of a Common-wealth Ecclesiasticall & Civill*, for Andrew Crooke, at the Green Dragonin St. Pauls Church-yard, London 1651, p. 130). Regarding the Hobbesian vision and its relationship with State law, in particular in Schmitt's understanding, it is worth noticing that "the sovereign should express his judgement through a system of positive law, since the determinate content of positive law preempts disputes arising as to what law is, and so preserves the peace. Once order is established in this way, individuals can enjoy their liberty, which is the area of freedom given to them by the silence of the law" (David Dyzenhaus, "Why Carl Schmitt?", introduction to *Law as Politics. Carl Schmitt's Critique of Liberalism*, ed. David Dyzenhaus, Duke University Press, Durham 1998, p. 6).

[30] This is particularly evident in the following excerpt from the *Leviathan*: "The legislator in all Commonwealths is only the sovereign, be he one man, as in a monarchy, or one assembly of men, as in a democracy or aristocracy. For the legislator is he that maketh the law. And the Commonwealth only prescribes and commandeth the observation of those rules which we call law: therefore the Commonwealth is the legislator. But the Commonwealth is no person, nor has capacity to do anything but by the representative, that is, the sovereign; and therefore the sovereign is the sole legislator" (Hobbes, *Leviathan, cit.*, p. 163).

pursue its goals.[31] From this point of view, while the established order and the avoidance of the state of nature represent the end and the supreme aim toward which the entire model is theorized, the law represents the medium to pursue that end. Following this path, we can also assume that the State, intended as a narrative discourse pursuing the establishment of an order, represents the end and the law represents its preeminent instrument of action. The teleological perspective of the State as a final aim in the life of the consociates is properly theorized by Hegel, according to whom the State can be considered as the very embodiment of an ἦθος (*ethos*),[32] and the ultimate horizon in which the life of the individual finds its complete realization. In Schmitt's theory concerning the sovereign power as the authority which can decide upon the state of exception, the instrumental nature of the law is particularly evident as well: from this perspective, it is the will of the sovereign, pursuing his own self-conservation, which comes

[31] Cfr. Ernst-Wolfgang Böckenförde [1978], "The State as an Ethical State", in *Constitutional and Political Theory. Selected Writings*, vol. I, trans. Thomas Dunlap, eds. Mirjam Künkler, Tine Stein, Oxford University Press, Oxford 2017., pp. 88–90. This is true even with regard to the highest normative act of a legal system: a constitution. Even the constitution does not *create* the State, establishing its institutions, but *is created* by it: "It can be said of every organized state, including a democratic one, that the state is not created and constituted as an entity of power, decision- making, and peace by the legal constitution, but that it precedes the constitution" (E. W. Böckenförde [1997], "The Concept and Problems of the Constitutional State", in *Constitutional and Political Theory, cit.*, p. 148). In this excerpt, the author correctly takes the distance from those conceptions according to which a constitution is the original act through which a State comes into existence, before which nothing exists of the followingly established legal order. These views may be acceptable within a specific political narrative and in determined democratic contexts, but from a juridical point of view they do not constitute a comprehensive and far-reaching theory of the constitutional State.

[32] Hegel reverses the terms of the discourse, explaining why the State should not be considered as instrumental to the life and needs of the individuals: "The state is the actuality of the ethical Idea [...] If the state is confused with civil society and its determination is equated with the security and protection of property and personal freedom, the interest of individuals [*der Einzehzen*] as such becomes the ultimate end for which they are united; it also follows from this that membership of the state is an optional matter.—But the relationship of the state to the individual [*Individuum*] is of quite a different kind. Since the state is objective spirit, it is only through being a member of the state that the individual [*Individuum*] himself has objectivity, truth, and ethical life" (Georg Wilhelm Friedrich Hegel [1821], *Elements of the Philosophy of Right*, trans. H. B. Nisbet, ed. Allen W. Wood, Cambridge University Press, Cambridge 2003, pp. 275–276).

to be the source of law, deciding when to derogate to the previously established procedures and regulations.[33]

Notwithstanding the progressive evolutions of the theory regarding the State, we can conclude that in an international order which is still based on the paradigm of territorial sovereignty, although subject to progressive questioning, the conception of law intended as instrumental with respect to a sovereign power is unchanged and represents something acquired from Western juridical doctrine. In spite of the physiological differentiations internal to the Western conception of law and State, such as the divergences between legal positivists and normative cognitivists, the understanding of State law as being instrumental to the order granted by the political authority seems to be stably acquired and basically unquestioned.

In the Muslim tradition, on the contrary, the philosophical relationship between authority and law follows a fundamentally reversed path. Despite the aforementioned divergences between the various Muslim classical scholars, in the Islamic traditional discourse about political power an unquestioned point is the conception of ***sharīʿa*** as the end toward which every power must be exercised.[34] The very aim of authority in Islam is thus to be considered the enforcement of ***sharīʿa***, that is to say, the guidance of the ***ummah*** in "the path" given by Allāh to mankind. From this perspective, ***sharīʿa*** "is not merely an integral part of Islam, but is its ***raison d'être***.

[33] Regarding the sovereign, as Schmitt argues, "He decides whether there is an extreme emergency as well as what must be done to eliminate it. Although he stands outside the normally valid legal system, he nevertheless belongs to it, for it is he who must decide whether the constitution needs to be suspended in its entirety. [...] All law is "situational law." The sovereign produces and guarantees the situation in its totality. He has the monopoly over this last decision. Therein resides the essence of the state's sovereignty, which must be juristically defined correctly, not as the monopoly to coerce or to rule, but as the monopoly to decide" (Carl Schmitt [1922], *Political Theology. Four Chapters on the Concept of Sovereignty*, transl. George Schwab, Massachusetts Institute of Technology, Cambridge 1985, pp. 7–13).

[34] Hallaq admirably synthetizes this point by drawing a comparison between the attitudes of Western and Islamic jurists with respect to political power: "Although it is commonplace for the Western lawyer or jurist to view the state as a body wielding and exercising legal authority, such a view is neither obvious nor normative for his Muslim counterparts, and even less obvious by far to the Muslim masses around the world" (Wael B. Hallaq, "Juristic Authority vs. State Power: the Legal Crises of Modern Islam", in *Journal of Law and Religion*, vol. XIX, n. 2, 2003–2004, p. 243).

That is, Islam was communicated to Muhammad for the purpose of revealing Sharia, which is the vehicle of a Muslim's salvation".[35]

It is here where the main differentiation between the conceptions of Leviathan and caliph relies: ideally speaking, the State expresses its authority through the law in order to guarantee the equilibrium descending from the self-preservation of its power, while the caliph—or every supreme authority in the Muslim world—serves the functional objective of safeguarding the *sharīʿa* and administering justice accordingly.[36] To summarize in the Western post-Westphalian tradition the establishing and conservation of a historically contextualized sovereign authority represents the end, and the law is to be considered as its instrument; in the Muslim perspective the end is to be identified with *sharīʿa*, and political authority is conceived as an instrument to pursue that end. Pragmatically speaking, in the Western tradition, law serves power while in the Islamic it is power which serves the cause of *sharīʿa*.[37] From this point of view, as Makdisi and other authors argue, with regard to Islam it is correct to speak

[35] Glenn L. Roberts, *Islamic Human Rights and International Law*, Dissertation.com, Boca Raton 2007, p. 13. Cf. Patricia Crone, *God's Rule. Government and Islam*, Columbia University Press, New York 2004, p. 292.

[36] According to Lambton "in Islam the law precedes the state, which exists for the sole purpose of maintaining and enforcing the law" (Ann K. S. Lambton, *State and Government in Medieval Islam. An Introduction to the Study of Islamic Political Theory – The Jurists*, Routledge, London-New York 1981, p. xv).

[37] As Coulson argues: "The elaboration of the law is seen by Islamic orthodoxy as a process of scholastic endeavour completely independent of historical or sociological influences. Once discovered, therefore, the law could not be subject to historical exegesis, in the sense that its terms could he regarded as applicable only to the particular circumstances of society at a given point in time. Moreover, the law was of necessity basically immutable; for Muhammad was the last of the prophets, and after his death there could be no further communication of the divine will to man. Law, therefore, does not grow out of, and is not moulded by, society as is the case with Western systems. Human thought, unaided, cannot discern the true values and standards of conduct; such knowledge can only be attained through divine revelation, and acts are good or evil exclusively because God has attributed this quality to them. In the Islamic concept, law precedes and moulds society; to its eternally valid dictates the structure of State and society must, ideally, conform" (Noel James Coulson, *A History of Islamic Law*, Edinburgh University Press, Edinburgh 1964, p. 85).

about nomocentrism.[38] Paraphrasing Moussa with regard to the thought of al-Ghazālī (1058–1111), in Islam history jurisprudence "provided the tools, content and experience of negotiating the Muslim past, present and future".[39] This is particularly evident with reference to the Arabic term *dīn*, used to denote Islam as a faith and as a religion, but sharing an etymology linked with its Aramaic and Hebrew counterparts, however this time with the meaning of law.[40] The same term *dīn* has been variously translated in the course of European history, again in meaningful ways. The first to have utilized the term *religio* to refer to *dīn* was cardinal Nicholas of Cusa (1401–1464) in relatively recent times, while in precedence the term was translated by medieval commentators with other words, including *lex*.[41] However, the same Nicholas of Cusa described the *Qur'ān* as "liber legis Arabum",[42] therefore assigning to it a prevalently juridical nature, in spite of the small number of verses with an actual legal

[38] Makdisi suggests that Islam be considered not only nomocentric but also nomocratic (see George Makdisi, "Hanbali Islam", in *Studies on Islam*, ed. Merlin L. Swarz, Oxford University Press, Oxford 1981, p. 264). Dahlén speaks of nomocentrism as well, at such an extent that to "discuss law was therefore as essential to premodern Islam as the discussion of theology in medieval Christianity" (Ashk P. Dahlén, *Islamic Law, Epistemology and Modernity. Legal Philosophy in Contemporary Iran*, Routledge, London-New York 2003, p. 39). Hallaq, in turn, highlights the preeminence of the legal professions in Islam by terming as difficult "to conceive of, much less write, the social, cultural and legal history of the Muslim world without due attention to the central role the legists played in it. In fact, there is little Islamic history to be written without Islam's legal profession and its contribution to its own civilization" (Hallaq, *Juristic Authority vs. State Power*, *cit.*, p. 246).

[39] Moussa, *Politics of the Islamic Tradition, cit.*, p. 100.

[40] See Bernard Lewis, *Islam and the West*, Oxford University Press, Oxford 1993, p. 3.

[41] Cf. Reinhold Glei, Stefan Reichmuth, "Religion between Last Judgement, law and faith: Koranic dīn and its rendering in Latin translations of the Koran", in *Religion*, vol. XLII, n. 2, April 2012, pp. 247–271. On the same point, see also Pin Valkenberg, "Una Religio in Rituum Varietate: Religious Pluralism, the Qur'an, and Nicholas of Cusa", in *Nicholas of Cusa and Islam. Polemic and Dialogue in the Late Middle Ages*, eds. Christopher Levy, Rita George-Tvrtković, Donald Duclow, Brill, Leiden-Boston 2014, pp. 46–47.

[42] "Est liber legis Arabum Alkoranus ob praeceptorum collectionem atque Alfurkanus ob discretam capitulorum separationem nominatus." Nicholas of Cusa [1461], "Cribratio Alkorani", in *Nicolai de Cusa opera omnia* vol. VIII, *Cribratio Alkorani. Edidit commentarisque illustravit Ludovicus Hagemann*, Felix Meier Verlag, Hamburg 1986, p. 21. The expression is recurrent and comes to relevance also in the following important passage: "Alia autem, quae in ipso libro continentur, quaedam aiunt probationes illius fidei, quaedam vero leges Arabum, quas secundum librum illum creduli Arabes servare tenentur, si deo, quem colunt, oboedire et in eius gratia persistere volunt et iuxta merita felicem assequi in paradiso remunerationem" (ibid., p. 26).

content. These particulars exhaustively shed light on the structural dimension that the normative element acquires in Islam, to the point of being considered a single and inseparable unity with it.

Consequently, this latter point can also be examined on the basis of a logical *consecutio*. In the State model, based on the social contract theory, the establishing of political authority is logically antecedent to the establishing of State law. Even before the theorization of the State system, we can argue that in the famous formula *ubi societas, ibi jus*, the binomial law-society is based on a precise *consecutio*, where *societas*, representing the political element, precedes *jus*, that is to say, its legal dimension. In the Islamic perspective, on the contrary, the immutable and eternal *sharīʿa* can only come before the establishment of every human authority. *Sharīʿa*, being the path that has been laid by Allāh and consequently revealed to mankind, is considered a logical antecedent to the establishment of human authority on earth, this latter being a caliphal rule, a kingdom, a sultanate, or every other form of government adopted in the Islamic political tradition.[43] In other words, *sharīʿa*, in its eternal form, which is thought to be conceived *in mente Dei*, preexists the *ummah* and consequently precedes and orients every form of political power.

Regarding this, it is necessary to distinguish between the historical development of the Islamic political community and Islam as a system of thought. When discussing the preexistence of the legal dimension with respect to the political element in Islam, I do not refer to the historical experience of the formation of the *ummah* and the establishment of the first caliphal rules. With regard to this latter point, on the contrary, we could argue that the path of evolution in Islam was the opposite, with the rise to power of Muḥammad and his companions preceding the

[43] In his work on political Islam, Ayubi expresses this concept clearly: "Legislation is not really a function of the State, for the (divine) law precedes the State and is not one of its products. The legal process is confined to deducing detailed rules and judgments from the broader tenets of the sharīʿa" (Nazih N. Ayubi [1991], *Political Islam. Religion and Politics in the Arab World*, Routledge, London-New York 2005, p. 17). Once again, cf. Lambton, *State and Government in Medieval Islam, cit.*, p. xv. Khadduri expresses a similar position: "In Islamic legal theory the law precedes society and is considered to be as eternal as God" (Majid Khadduri [1961], "Introduction" to Muhammad ibn Idrīs al-Shāfiʿī, *al-Risāla fī Uṣūl al-Fiqh (Treatise on the Foundations of Islamic Jurisprudence)*, trans. Majid Khadduri, Islamic Texts Society, Cambridge 1997, p. v).

systematization of a *sharīʿa*-based legal system.[44] While speaking about the preexistence of *sharīʿa*, I refer to the Islamic perspective by which the juridical phenomenon can be understood in a given civilization: in this framework, and as already noted, *sharīʿa* comes before human authority because it is human authority which is created to safeguard the observation of *sharīʿa*.

The nexus between political authority and *sharīʿa*, with the former being instrumental in pursuing the observance of the latter, is exhaustively highlighted in the works of various classical Islamic authors. Al-Māwardī, for instance, and despite his pragmatical intent of legitimating the Abbasid rule, underlines the instrumental role of power while explaining the case of the usurpation of the caliphal authority. According to al-Māwardī, in the case of usurpation it is necessary to distinguish: if the usurper defends Islam and enforces *sharīʿa*, then he should be followed, while if he transgresses these obligations, he should be rapidly overthrown.[45] As evident from this position, according to al-Māwardī the most important thing in Islamic authority is not related to who comes to exercise factual power but is fundamentally inherent to the very aim toward which power is exercised. With reference to the extreme case of usurpation and factual coercion of the caliphal rule, it is necessary to distinguish whether the usurper acts in order to serve the cause of Islam and its normative ideals, or acts contrarily to this aim. An intervention to restore the factual power of the caliph is required only in the latter case: therefore, it can be argued that the real usurpation does not refer to the authority but actually to the goals pursued by it.

[44] With regard to the later systematization of *sharīʿa*, and to the pre-Islamic influences on it examined and contextualized from a historical point of view, see Knut S. Vikør, "The origins of the sharia", in *The Ashgate Research Companion to Islamic Law*, eds. Rudolph Peters, Peri Bearman, Ashgate, Farnham-Burlington 2014, pp. 13–26.

[45] "This does not exclude him from Imamate and it does not impair the validity of his governance, but the actions of the person who has taken over his affairs should be investigated: if they are in accordance with the judgements of the deen and according to the requirements of justice, he may be allowed to remain in order that the Imamate may continue to function and its rulings be executed, lest the affairs of the deen be interrupted and the Ummah is corrupted. If however, his actions are outside the rule of the deen and the requirements of justice, he may not tolerate his actions and he must seek the help of another in order to overcome him and put an end to his dominance". Al-Māwardī, *Al-Aḥkām as-Sulṭaniyyah, cit.*, p. 34. *Dīn*, meaning in this case religious faith or, in a broader sense, the Islamic religion.

The preeminent role of the *sharīʿa* as a criterion of orientation in establishing and preserving political authority is underlined by al-Ḥaramayn al-Juwaynī (1028–1085) as well.[46] It is relevant to note that his disciple al-Ghazālī shared this conception,[47] conceiving political authority as an instrument to serve the cause of *sharīʿa*. The author, following the same reasoning, states that even in the absence of the majorly accepted requisites for the caliphate, the better choice is to accept that the caliphal authority exists in a factual way in order not to "let the people live in sin".[48] The Ḥanbalī jurist Ibn Taimīya shares the same conclusion while emphasizing the guiding role of the *sharīʿa* and while explicitly stating that every political power is established only to guarantee its observance.[49] Authors like Ibn Taimīya are usually considered to be strictly for the enforcing of Islamic provisions; however, when it comes to political authority, the flexibility shown in their conceptions reflects the instrumental vision of power,[50] and the teleological perspective on authority, whose principal reason for being is the guidance of the *ummah* in observing the *sharīʿa*. Power comes therefore to be a ductile instrument, capable of rapidly adapting to the concrete circumstances to pursue a determinate goal.

The aforementioned authors, while greatly diverging in theorizing the requisites of a supreme political authority, agree to the consideration of *sharīʿa* as the aim toward which power is granted and exercised. According to Siegman, along the centuries to be caliph basically came to mean to be a ruler who "recognized the universality of the *sharīʿah* and did not interfere with its operation".[51]

The lack of a unitary and comprehensive political theory in Islamic classical thought, and the variety of possible forms of government which have been experimented with by the Muslim community along its history, only serves to confirm the preeminence of *sharīʿa* over the establishment of a

[46] See Lambton, *State and Government in Medieval Islam, cit.*, pp. 104 ff.

[47] Cf. Leonard Binder, "Al-Ghazâlî's Theory of Islamic Government", in *The Muslim World*, vol. XLV, n. 3, 1955, pp. 229–241.

[48] Abū Ḥāmid al-Ghazâlî', *al-Iqtisâd fî-l-i`tiqâd*, cit. in Branca, *Pouvoir de iure et pouvoir de facto dans la pensée polique islamique classique, cit.*, p. 36.

[49] See Branca, *Pouvoir de iure et pouvoir de facto dans la pensée polique islamique classique, cit.*, pp. 38–39.

[50] About Ibn Taimīya's political thought, see Henri Laoust, *Essai sur les doctrines sociales et politiques de Takî-d-Dîn Ahmad b. Taimîya*, IFAO, Cairo 1939.

[51] Henry Siegman, "The state and the individual in Sunni Islam", in *The Muslim World*, vol. LIV, n. 1, 1964, p. 19.

certain, and certainly legitimated, political form of authority. According to the necessities of the *ummah*, even the supreme caliphate, as observed, can be easily sacrificed in order to grant the enforcement of *sharīʿa* in the territories of Islam. From this point of view, we can conclude by saying that "all Islamic thought, including the political, has but one overriding goal: living a life according to the will of Allah, as revealed for all time to the Prophet and recorded in the Qur'ān and Tradition".[52] In a broader sense, and consequently, it should be observed that "political authority is embodied, not in a ruler or in a cleric, but in sharia".[53]

The inversion of plans with respect to the Western conception of authority is evident: while in the West the ruler sets forth the rules to be followed by the consociated, according to the Islamic tradition the theoretically preexisting rules of *sharīʿa* are served by the ruler, whose main goal is to have them observed by the *ummah*. The present point should not be considered the mere outcome of historical contingencies related to the rise in power of the caliphal dynasties and their consequent fall, but mainly as a matter of philosophical and juridical elaboration, whose practical implications greatly affect the dynamics of the Islamic political and legal discourse, as will be explained in the following chapters.

3.4 Personification of Power in the West

Having discussed the instrumental role of power with respect to the observance of *sharīʿa*, a second fundamental point in the present analysis is constituted by the idea of personification of power in the Islamic and Western views.

In the Western legal tradition, the personification of power could be considered an exception to the general idea of impersonal authority, in a context in which the institutional dimension prevails over its human embodiment and over the physical manifestation of its *pro tempore* occupant. A separation between authority and power, as it will be seen, is therefore structural in the Western political discourse. This is certainly truer in the framework of the modern State, but with deeper observation it is possible to recognize a similar conception of impersonal authority even in the pre-Westphalian period.

[52] Ibid., p. 14.

[53] Natalie Goldstein, *Religion and the State*, Facts on File, New York 2010, p. 41.

Having regard for the medieval legal order, we can argue that the two universalistic institutions, the papacy and empire, vested a substantially preeminent metaphysical and impersonal dimension in which the personal element is basically considered secondary and transient in respect to the supreme authority of the institution. This comes as a consequence of a proper and rather univocal theorization of the two institutions, with particular reference to their legitimation and to the dynamics of their selection and succession. The laws regulating the elections of emperors and popes, aimed at preventing fractures and violent contrasts in the succession to the throne, suggest the idea of a supreme power whose preeminent attribution is to be transmitted according to a legitimate line of succession, where the person exercising it is considered a relative and historical manifestation of an ideally everlasting figure of power.[54] The ritual dimension of authority, especially regarding enthronement ceremonies, exemplifies once again the transmission of power from one ruler to another, where the personal element can only be as transitory as human life is, and where the institutional role, with its shared idea of legitimacy, on the contrary is permanent and preeminent. However, this doesn't mean that the personality of the ruler did not affect the concrete dynamics of power in a given context; however, personality almost never transformed into the personification of power.

From this point of view, it is possible to say that the medieval juridical order was eminently based upon institutions rather than individuals. This conclusion is also suggested by the political terminology, with a clear prevalence of abstract figures denoting attributions of power rather than individuals: *auctoritas* and *potestas*, *imperium*, and *seacerdotium*[55] are all terms that do not refer to individuals but to abstract attributions. The medieval political discourse was indeed largely based on the idea of legitimacy

[54] With regard to the papacy and the prevalence of its institutional dimension over the personal element, it is worth to remember the words of Caspar, according to whom "über den einzelnen Päpsten steht die Institution, das Papst*tum*, als der historische Organismus, welcher der eigentliche Inhalt und Gegenstand der Papsgeschicthe ist (above the individual popes stands the institution, the papacy, as the historical organism, which is the actual content and subject of the papal history)" (Erich Caspar, *Geschichte des Papsttums von den Anfängen bis zur Höhe der Weltherrschaft*, vol. I, Mohr Verlag, Tübingen 1930–1933, p. 266).

[55] In Chap. 4 I will analyze the ideas of *imperium* and *sacerdotium* in light of the separation between a spiritual and a temporal authority in the Western world.

which, as will be shown, may in this case be described as a substantial coincidence between the physical person and an abstract figure of authority.

Notwithstanding the historical disputes and concrete controversies over the respective attributions, empire and papacy embodied the supreme legal framework in which the various organs of the same order could be inscribed: consequently, the medieval order could not exist without its institutional dimension, which served as supreme guarantee for its overall functioning. This prevalence of the binomial authority-institution over the binomial power-individual opens to the possibility of a theorical separation between the ruler, considered as a physical person, and his institutional role, considered as the stable safeguard of an order established through time: a famous example is constituted by the only apparent paradox of Dante's belonging to the papal faction of the Guelfs, denoting a political judgment over an institution, and his personal hatred for pope Boniface VIII, resulting in an adversity for an individual.[56] Following this perspective, the dimensions of authority (*auctoritas*) and power (*potestas*) physiologically coincide in the person of the legitimated ruler, but this identification is by no means to be regarded as necessary or ineludible.[57]

[56] With regard to the papacy, the distinction between the individual pope, as vicar of Christ, and the papal institution, as the office of the vicariate of Christ, or between *sede* and *sedens*, see Michael Wilks [1963], *The Problem of Sovereignty in the Later Middle Ages. The Papal Monarchy with Augustinus Triumphus and the Publicists*, Cambridge University Press, Cambridge 2008, pp. 362 ff. The same distinction can be made with regard to the imperial institution as well. "Although the idea of the emperor, his *persona ficta*, is unassailable, the actually existing emperor, his *persona actuale*, can indeed be attacked without serious eschatological consequences" (Erik Ringmar [1996], *Identity, Interest and Action. A Cultural Explanation of Sweden's Intervention in the Thirty Years War*, Cambridge University Press, Cambridge 2007, p. 169).

[57] The differentiation between *auctoritas* and *potestas*, which is particularly relevant in the juridical theorization of the medieval papacy, cannot be exhaustively examined in this work. However, this reference is particularly useful to point out the theoretical separation between impersonal authority and personalized power. The actual coincidence of the two dimensions represents the physiological phase of the overall political theory of the medieval Christendom, while their separation is inherent to a pathological phase, which however does not put in question the premises of the philosophical system upon which Christendom was built. For an overall analysis of the concepts of *auctoritas* and *potestas*, with their possible separation, see Giorgio Agamben [2003], *State of Exception*, trans. Kevin Attell, The University of Chicago Press, Chicago-London 2005, pp. 74–88; Rasmus Ugilt, *Giorgio Agamben. Political Philosophy*, Humanities-Ebook, Penrith 2014, pp. 79 ff. See also Juan Fernando Segovia, "Schmitt y Álvaro d'Ors. Una inspiración ad modum recipientis", in *Fuego y Raya*, n. 11, December 2016, p. 11.

In the Western tradition, the separation between the institutional dimension of authority and the factual exercise of power can be considered as a concrete possibility and as a major consequence of the impersonal character of authority.

With regard to the Western and Christian ideas of kingship, both in the Middle Ages and in early modern times, it is possible to argue that the automatism of succession, whose dynamics are set forth in precise laws and regulations, does not only serve a political purpose, that is avoiding conflict,[58] but shows an essential philosophical trend: it is in the moment of succession, and in its automatism, that the transitory immanency of the individual-ruler communicates with the ideally eternal and transcendent dimension of the authority rule. It is exactly in the passage of sovereign power from one king to another that the transient manifestation of the ruler vanishes and the abstract and supreme conception of impersonal authority rises, in order to seek another historical form in which it manifests itself. Consequently, the personification of power, whose apex seems to be touched in the figure of the king, proves itself to be an illusion in the moment of the transmission of power, in which the personal element is indeed revealed to be impermanent, in opposition to the everlasting and impersonal idea of authority.[59]

This conception follows the institutional dimension of political authority—that is to say, the prevalence of an institution over the physical person who exercises power—that has been present in the Western view since the Roman civilization. However, a proper juridical theorization of this institutional and impersonal dimension is consequent to the emergence of the notion of *persona ficta*, which would later give birth to the modern idea of legal and corporate personhood. The notion of *persona ficta* was

[58] Cf. Yves-Marie Bercé, "Succession et Vacance", in *Les Monarchies*, ed. Yves-Marie Bercé, Presses Universitaires de France, Paris 2015, pt. 3, ch. 4.

[59] The famous French formula *le roi est mort, vive le roi*, as commented by Chateaubriand, explains the deep meaning of the distinction between the king, as an individual ruler, and the idea of kingship, as an institution and a figure of authority. "The King is dead! Will the Monarchy dissolve? Has the rage of the Heaven struck again down on France? Where to flee? Where to hide in front of terror and tyranny? Cry, Frenchmen! You have lost the King who saved you, the King who gave you peace; the King who set you free. But do not tremble at all for your destiny; the King is dead, but the King lives. The King is dead, long live the King! It is the cry of the old Monarchy; it is the cry of the new Monarchy as well. A double political principle is reaffirmed in this acclamation of joy and sorrow: the inheritance of the sovereign family, and the immortality of the State" (François-René de Chateaubriand [1824], "Le roi est mort: vive le roi!", in *Oeuvres*, vol. IV, Dufour et Mulat, Paris 1852, p. 243).

elaborated in medieval canon law, especially thanks to the work of Sinibaldo de' Fieschi (c. 1195–1254), the future pope Innocent IV, and appears to be inseparably linked to the Christian cultural and juridical legacy of medieval Europe. Considered to be an innovation with respect to Roman law, which never knew such a definition, the idea of legal personality takes the move from saint Paul's definition of the Catholic church as *corpus mysticum* and serves the cause of the newly established religious entities such as monasteries and orders, legally separating the intellectual creation of the fictional *persona* from the individuals contained by it.[60] The birth of the idea in this context should not be considered casual: as Grossi suggests, canon law, moving from a Roman heritage and assimilating the Catholic experience of the *corpus mysticum*, was the ideal field in which the conception of the *persona ficta* could rise, due to its preeminent capacity for separation between the practical questions and the theorization of abstract legal notions.[61] As Kantorowicz points out, even before the birth of the modern State, the notion of legal personality, as developed by canonists, greatly influenced the conceptions of lay power as well, through the usage of the idea of fictional legal personality to the temporal *imperium*.[62] Thus, the impersonality of power, and the virtual separation between the institutional dimension of authority and the individuals playing political roles can be considered as something structurally acquired by the medieval order and later on by the modern era.

With the theorization of the modern State, the impersonality of power indeed appears even more evident. As Hobbes underlines, the Leviathan is figuratively to be considered as an "artificial man",[63] or a great machine, and not as an individual. Although geographically delimitated by its spatial

[60] See the historical reconstruction of Costantino Matteo Fabris, *La natura della persona giuridica nell'ordinamento canonico. Profili generali e particolari. Il caso della Caritas internationalis*, Giappichelli, Turin 2018, pp. 11–19.

[61] See Paolo Grossi [1995], *L'ordine giuridico medievale*, Laterza, Rome-Bari 2004, pp. 219–222.

[62] See Ernst H. Kantorowicz, *The King's Two Bodies. A Study in Medieval Political Theology*, Princeton University Press, Princeton 1957, pp. 207 ff.

[63] "For by art is created that great Leviathan called a Commonwealth, or State (in Latin, *Civitas*), which is but an artificial man, though of greater stature and strength than the natural, for whose protection and defence it was intended; and in which the sovereignty is an artificial soul, as giving life and motion to the whole body". Hobbes, *Leviathan*, *cit.*, p. 7.

dimension and by its boundaries, the body of the Leviathan is not the body of an individual, but, as in the early representations, a fictional character composed of the multitude of individuals of the State.[64] The body of the Leviathan is thus a collective body, as collective is the intentionality expressed by it.[65] From this point of view, it is crucial to distinguish between the political doctrine of absolutism and the legal construction of the State, in which, as Hobbes observes, the concrete organization of powers inside the sovereign space is irrelevant. Having regard for this, the sovereign power could be exercised through an absolutist monarchy or through an elected assembly in a democratic regime or by an aristocracy, without any major difference in the external theorization of sovereignty.[66] It is precisely in this point, in Hobbes' indifference for the organization of internal powers, that the impersonality of the Leviathan is revealed: in the Hobbesian system, no individual is really indispensable. Even in Rousseau's understanding of sovereignty, the sovereign is actually considered to be

[64] "Representation by fiction is not misrepresentation. This last point is politically crucial because the state itself is a *persona ficta*: an artificial person who is also a natural nonperson. Beyond inanimate bodies, irrational animate bodies, and purely imaginary things, Hobbes listed a further category of *persona ficta*, of which the state is Hobbes's most important example: a sundry array of individual bodies, a "Multitude of men", who may by fiction be represented as a single, corporate 'Body Politique'." Arash Abizadeh, "The Representation of Hobbesian Sovereignty: Leviathan as Mythology", in *Hobbes Today. Insights for the 21st Century*, ed. S. A. Lloyd, Cambridge University Press, Cambridge 2013, p. 133.

[65] The representation of the Leviathan as a collective body composed by many individuals offers the chance to understand Hobbes' position as an example of collective intentionality, which influenced the sociological sciences on the theory of action. On the Hobbesian theory in the discourse on collective intentionality, see Philip Pettit, "Corporate agency: the lesson of the discursive dilemma", in *The Routledge Handbook of Collective Intentionality*, eds. Marija Jankovic, Kirk Ludwig, Routledge, London-New York 2018, pp. 252 ff.

[66] "When the representative is one man, then is the Commonwealth a monarchy; when an assembly of all that will come together, then it is a democracy, or popular Commonwealth; when an assembly of a part only, then it is called an aristocracy". Hobbes, *Leviathan, cit.*, p. 114.

the people, an impersonal unity which is actually entitled to the exercise of ultimate power.[67]

The idea of *Führerprinzip*, which animated the totalitarian regimes of the twentieth century, by substantially theorizing the coincidence between authority and the physical person of the leader, proved to be an exception to the general trend of impersonality of power of the Western political tradition.[68] It is worth noting, with regard to this, that often this personification of ultimate power and its reduction to the figure of the leader overcame and transcended the very political and legal paradigm of the modern State while founding a social and rather mystical civil cult, an example of which was constituted by Hitlerism. This exceptional trend of personifying power proved however to be the actual limit of such regimes, which never elaborated a structural way of transmitting authority after the dismissal of the charismatic leader.

With the exceptions of the aforementioned totalitarian experiences, which should be considered in their peculiarity and differentiations as well, it is possible to say that the Western legal and political tradition showed a major trend in recognizing the impersonality of power and

[67]With regard to this, Krabbe defines Rousseau's theory on political authority as the "authority of an impersonal power". See Hugo Krabbe, *The Modern Idea of the State*, Martinus Nijhoff, The Hague 1922, pp. 28 ff. The definition of "impersonal power of a people" in describing Rousseau's theory is also used by James Miller, *Rousseau. Dreamer of Democracy*, Yale University Press, New Haven-London 1984 p. 120. It is to be noticed, however, that in Krabbe and in Miller the impersonality of power is mainly referred to the internal organization of the powers of the State and not to the overall conception of non-personified political power in the Western legal tradition, as in this work. Such a definition is nevertheless significant to point out the even greater character of the non-personification of authority in this political and historical context.

[68]I define totalitarian conceptions of leadership as generally an exception in Western political tradition, considering two factors. Firstly, the fact that totalitarian political experiences occupied a relatively short time span in Western history. Secondly, and most importantly, the fact that the idea of personified power, deeply rooted in the *Führerprinzip*, is to be referred only to the experiences where the institutional dimension of authority is overcome by the personal element. This latter overcoming happened actually very rarely, if we consider that most forms of autocracies could be actually considered as authoritarian, but not as properly totalitarian, given the endurance of a certain form of institutionalism. While examining the differences between authoritarian and totalitarian regimes, Linz analyzes personal rule and personified power as well, referring to this idea with the term *caudillismo*, with particular attention to the South American experiences. With regard to this latter point, see Juan J. Linz, *Totalitarian and Authoritarian Regimes*, Lynne Rienner Publishers, Boulder-London 2000, especially pp. 143–158.

authority, notwithstanding the different forms of government it has experimented with. Liberal democracy, as adopted by the majority of the Western countries after World War II, responded to the historical necessity of providing the respective peoples with real forms of political representation, by preventing individuals from gaining excessive amounts of power without proper instruments of checks and balances; therefore, it substantially granted the theorization of an impersonal and neutral form of authority, that is to say, an authority exercised through the mediation of elective and collegial organs.[69]

In an international system which is still based on the State paradigm, although in its crises, it is not possible to prescind from considering the State as a *persona ficta*, whose authority is exercised through individuals, but does not coincide with them. As already observed about the instrumental role of the law with respect to authority, it is possible to conclude that in the Western experience, individuals are in a certain way instrumental to the exercise of authority, whatever its scope and theorization in a given historical and social context may be.

3.5 Personification of Power in Islam

Dissimilarly to what has been observed with reference to the Western perspective, in the Islamic tradition the conception of power is considered eminently personified.

First of all, it should be noted that in Islamic traditional thought there is no such philosophical construct as the *persona ficta*, as elaborated in the European canonistic science. This happened for historical reasons and for the extremely different context in which the two legal perspectives have come to maturation. As already seen, and in spite of its theorization of an

[69] It is interesting to notice, with regard to this, that the assumed characters of neutrality and impersonality of liberal democracy actually pushed some theorists, such as Fukuyama, to argue that the world would eventually embrace this ultimate form of government in the "end of history". It is the impersonal—and thus allegedly non-arbitrary—nature of liberal democracy that persuaded so many that this would eventually be considered as the final form of political rule of global society. See Michael J. White, *Partisan or Neutral? The Futility of Public Political Theory*, Rowman & Littlefield, Lanham 1997, pp. 28 ff., while, for Fukuyama's position on democracy and apart from his already mentioned article, see Francis Fukuyama, *The End of History and the Last Man*, The Free Press, New York 1992.

eternal juridical dimension *in mente Dei*, the systematization of *sharīʿa*, and the progressive distinction between the various legal schools, responded to the historical necessity of giving answers to practical needs of the newly established *ummah*.[70] Given a substantially different role of human reason in the process of formation of a rather stable corpus of provisions in what would be known as *fiqh*,[71] in the Islamic legal discourse abstract concepts and notions were not to develop as in medieval Europe, where on the contrary the flourishing of Scholasticism and canonistic sciences gave a fundamental impulse to processes of juridical speculation and abstraction.[72] The relevant differences in the temporal and cultural contingencies of medieval Christendom and early Islamic Arabia, and therefore the lack in Islamic legal thought of a concept such as the *persona ficta*, brought about fundamental consequences with regard to the understanding of the relationship between the idea of rule, intended as a figure of authority, and the idea of ruler, intended as an individual.

In the Islamic tradition, the only source of authority is identified with the divinity and is thus metaphysical, metahistorical, and fundamentally transcendent.[73] Without the theoretical construct of legal personality, the interposition and the mediation of an impersonal institution, which could virtually separate the dimension of authority from the personality of the

[70] As Ercanbrack states, "Islamic law is not concerned with the abstraction of general principles and systemic logic. Rather the sharia illustrates a casuistic approach to the law that eventually gave rise to an elaborated superstructure of rules" (Jonathan G. Ercanbrack, *The Transformation of Islamic Law in Global Financial Markets*, Cambridge University Press, Cambridge 2015, p. 32).

[71] A dedicated paragraph in Chap. 3 will be dedicated to the issue of the role of human reason between *sharīʿa* and *fiqh*.

[72] On the absence of the notion of *persona ficta* in the Islamic legal discourse, see Sandy Lamalle, "Multilevel Translation Analysis of a Key Legal Concept: Persona Juris and Legal Pluralism", in *The Ashgate Handbook of Legal Translation*, eds. Le Cheng, King Kui Sin, Anne Wagner, Ashgate, Farnham-Burlington 2014, pp. 307–308.

[73] As Crone observes, and as it will be repeated in the following paragraphs, "Divine government has always been and always will be, and it must necessarily manifest itself as government on earth [...] Without recognition of God's sole government there could be no proper relations among people, only tyranny or anarchy, with all the bloodshed, arbitrariness, and immorality that both implied" (Crone, *God's rule*, *cit.*, pp. 6–7).

ruler, are actually not possible.[74] The figure of the institution, intended as a center of authority which however does not coincide with who exercises *pro tempore* this authority, is thus to be considered alien from the Islamic discourse. The eminent figures exercising power in the Muslim traditional political and juridical framework, such as caliphs, emirs, and sultans, are not to be considered as institutions, as conceived by the Western world, but firstly as individuals.[75] Power, in this context, is eminently personified, and the institutional dimension is totally absorbed by the personal element, without any neutral and impersonal mediation between the source of (divine) authority and the individual-ruler exercising power. As Crone observes, in their traditional perspective the Muslims "saw themselves as governed by persons rather than institutions and would speak of a ruler, such as a caliph (*khalifa*) or king (*malik*)",[76] instead of an abstract figure of authority.

This assertion is once again proven by the political terminology concretely used, which in the Islamic discourse tends to refer to individuals rather than to their abstract attributions. While in the Western tradition the political discourse revolved around concepts such as *auctoritas* and *potestas*, the Muslim legal tradition reflects the factuality and fluicity of its political theory by using a far more concrete terminology. As already observed, the term *khalīfah* refers to "someone who stands in place of another", emphasizing the individuality of the subject acting as vicar. The abstract idea of "vicariate" might be deduced only through examination of its concrete actions, and not *vice versa*—attributing to the vicar the preexisting functions of an abstract "vicariate"—as would be the case in

[74] As von Grunebaum noticed, in principle "authority and power are not separated. The principle of authority and the resultant power are personified in the caliph (or the supreme *imam*). But God has not delegated any of his power to man. God alone governs even though he will do so through a human ruler. Whether this ruler has been appointed or elected, or has merely usurped his position by force, his authority results from direct investiture by God, for God's authority is the only true authority even *in temporalibus*" (Gustave Edmund von Grunebaum, *Modern Islam. The Search for Cultural Identity*, University of California Press, Berkeley-Los Angeles 1962, p. 49).

[75] To be noted that "the law is declared and given effect not through impersonal institutions such as a secular parliament, but rather through a more personalized form of religious leadership, taking a quasi-judicial form, whose task is not to make law but rather to interpret it" (Spencer Zifcak, "Western and Islamic Conceptions of the Rule of Law", in *Islam Beyond Conflict. Indonesian Islam and Western Political Theory*, eds. Azyumardi Azra, Wayne Hudson, Ashgate Publishing, Aldershot-Burlington 200, p. 35).

[76] Crone, *God's Rule, cit.*, p. 3.

medieval Christendom. Even the word defining the dominions of the highest Islamic magistrate, *khilāfah*—usually translated as "caliphate"—refers more to the act of serving as a vicar of someone else than to the—often not clearly defined—competences and prerogatives of the leader intended as an institution. The same can be said of *sulṭān*, from Aramaic *šulṭānā*, which means factual power, intended more as "strength" than as *potestas*, therefore with a marked material connotation, whose final significance can only be grasped when put in action by an individual. The sultan, from this perspective, is he who factually exercises power and who dominates determined lands (*salṭanah*). The same conclusion could be drawn with the terms *malik* and *ʾamīr* in their respective meanings, with little to no variations on the philosophical perspective implied in the use of such a terminology. As *dawla*, commonly translated as State, originally referred to the changing dynasties of the rulers, the term *dustūr*, widely used in modern States to define the constitution, was originally used to denote the individual exercising political power and giving orders, and came latterly to denote rules, regulations, and also standards and criteria of conduct.[77] However, this does not mean that abstract terminology in Islam does not exist, but with reference to power and authority the practical connotation of the terms implies a fundamentally personified vision of the exercise of governing and administering justice. Even the widely used term *imām*, designating a Muslim community leader, eminently refers to an individual, as the etymology suggests: the *imām* is "he who stands in front of others" and he who leads the community in prayer, pragmatically denoting the activity of an individual.[78] Although a term referring to the office of the *imām* does exist (*imāmah*),[79] the preeminence is once again given to the individual, provided the inexistence of univocally theorized theories of

[77] Cf. Ami Ayalon, *Language and Change in the Arab Middle East. The Evolution of Modern Arabic Political Discourse*, Oxford University Press, Oxford 1987, pp. 94–96.

[78] "The word "Imam" itself means "to stand in front of" in Arabic, referring to placement of the Imam in front of the worshippers during prayer. In principle, every Muslim can act as an Imam, but the most worthy to lead people in prayer is the one who is most versed in the Qur'an. […] The term Imam is fluid. Imams are not like the clergy in Christianity and often have more diffuse, varied and informal roles" G. Hussein Rassool, *Islamic Counselling. An Introduction to Theory and Practice*, Routledge, London-New York 2016, pp. 253–254. Of course, in this work I am referring exclusively to the use of the term Sunnī Islam, provided that in Shīʿa Islam it may acquire a completely different meaning.

[79] The term refers to the act of "he who stands in front", thus referring once again to an act proper of an individual, as in the case of the caliph intended as someone who stands in the place of another.

legitimation based on the abstract notion of *institution*. In the absence of a properly theorized idea of legal personality, theoretically separated from the physical person of the ruler, the abstract figure of power is destined to disappear with the disappearance of the ruler as an individual.

Therefore, not only the concept of (modern) statehood remains alien to the Islamic legal and political discourse until its contamination with the Western world, but the piece of abstraction we commonly call "institution", which represents the outcome of a process of philosophical and legal construction coming from medieval Christendom, is considered absent in the Muslim outlook on political power. From this point of view, in the Islamic tradition it is possible to speak about caliphs, sultans, and emirs as individual rulers, while the respective ideas of caliphate, sultanate, and emirate are far more fluid and ethereal, sometimes representing the projection of the institutional dimension of the Western *persona ficta* upon a Muslim context, whose path of development has been substantially different.

It could be observed, following this reasoning, that the personification of power in the Muslim tradition leads to what we can call "privatization" of power, which is conceived of as absorbed by the private person of the ruler, who, in the lack of an institutional dimension reconducting power to the public sphere, can ultimately dispose of it as he pleases.[80] A relevant argument for this point is given by al-Māwardī himself: while discussing the designation of a successor by the caliph, the author uses the sale contractual scheme, thus eminently private, to draw an analogy with the transfer of power between a caliph and his designated successor.[81] Moreover, the oath of allegiance traditionally pledged to a caliph or to a Muslim leader was called *bayʿah*, originally referred to the act of selling and to the act of shaking hands between buyer and seller following an economic transaction, mirroring once again the relevance of commerce and trading

[80] On the issue of "privatization of power" in the Islamic conception of caliphate, see Abderraouf Boulaabi, *Islam et pouvoir. Les finalités de la Charia et la légitimité du pouvoir*, L'Harmattan, Paris 2005, p. 34. Roy talks about a "contractual" power in Sunnī Islam, showing an eminently private nature. In his words: "Power is contractual, not because of the will of the people but because it is contingent; the sultan or the emir takes power by force and keeps it by a more or less explicit contract with the ulema (as long as he defends Islam abroad and advocates sharia domestically he is legitimate)" (Oliver Roy [2005], *Secularism Confronts Islam*, trans. George Holoch, Columbia University Press, New York 2007, p. 55).

[81] For the use of the contractual scheme to discipline the caliphate, see al-Māwardī, *Al-Aḥkām as-Sulṭaniyyah, cit.*, pp. 10–36.

in early Muslim societies. Hence, not just the succession in power, but also the submission to it was considered through the contractual scheme as interpreted by the tribal and merchant communities of Arabia.[82] Again, when discussing the establishment of *wulāt* (governors, sing. *wālī*) and *umarāʾ* (commanders, sing. *ʾamīr*), al-Māwardī contemplates the possibility of legitimating a dominion simply acquired by virtue of military conquest, thus based on the pragmatical exercise of "private" power as an element definitely prevailing over any legalistic discourse.[83]

The actual fluidity in the understanding of political theory in the Islamic tradition, as it has already been noted, mirrors exactly the absence of a comprehensive theory on institutional legitimation, due to the aforementioned impossibility of conceiving abstract institutions and separating them from the persons concretely exercising power. As for the profile of succession in power, even after the end of the initial period of the *rāshidūn* caliphs, the automatism of succession laws of Western monarchies[84] is far

[82] This point is well expressed by Islamic celebrated historian Ibn Khaldūn (1332–1406) in his *Muqaddimah*: "It should be known that the *bayʿah* (oath of allegiance) is a contract to render obedience. It is as though the person who renders the oath of allegiance made a contract with his amir, to the effect that he surrenders supervision of his own affairs and those of the Muslims to him and that he will not contest his authority and that he will obey him by (executing) all the duties with which he might be charged, whether agreeable or disagreeable. When people rendered the oath of allegiance to the amir and concluded the contract, they put their hands into his hand to confirm the contract. This was considered to be something like the action of buyer and seller (after concluding a bargain)" (Ibn Khaldūn [1377], *The Muqaddimah. An Introduction to History*, trans. Franz Rosenthal, ed. N. J. Dawood, Princeton University Press, Princeton-Oxford 2005, p. 166). On this point, with special reference to the contractual scheme considered in this case as "the exchange of commitments of fidelity to prescribed rules by a leader and by followers", see Hossein Askari, "Economic Development in Islam", in *Economic Development and Islamic Finance*, eds. Zamir Iqbal, Abbas Mirakhor, The World Bank, Washington 2013, p. 162.

[83] Cf. Al-Māwardī, *Al-Aḥkām as-Sulṭaniyyah, cit.*, pp. 53–56. This peculiar form of establishing a ruler is commonly known in literature as "emirate by seizure" (as in the case of Eltigani Abdulqadir Hamid, "Al-Mawardi's Theory of State: Some Ignored Dimensions", in *American Journal of Islamic Social Sciences*, vol. XVIII, n. 4, Fall 2001, pp. 9–10).

[84] It is interesting to notice with regard to this that in Western monarchies the institution continues to virtually exist even in the absence of the physical person of the king, for instance, in periods of *interregnum*. This is particularly evident in elective monarchies, such as the papacy, where the period of the *sede vacante* is properly theorized and does not cause the abolition of the institution, which on the contrary must be everlasting and perpetual. In the Islamic view, as the positions of the aforementioned classical authors suggest, it is not possible to speak about a caliphal institution actually existing without a caliph concretely exercising its powers.

from being fully theorized in Islamic political doctrines, where the flexibility in the methods of succession and election responds to the needs of the preservation of the community and to the observance of the *sharīʿa*, as a ductile instrument responds to its goal.

For instance, the various theories on caliphal rule appear to be shaped by the concrete contingencies of the ruling dynasties, and even there the supreme power in the *ummah* presents rather undefined characteristics and attributions, modeled on the basis of pragmatical exigencies and guided by the necessity of following and enforcing *sharīʿa*. Usually, political theorists would not write texts on abstract theorizations of power and authority, but rather manuals of conduct for caliphs and rulers, often addressing specific individuals. In these texts, the author usually focuses on two elements, both regarding the ruler in his individuality: the ideal features of the personality of the ruler, and the aims toward which his power must be necessarily exercised. This is the case, for instance, of Ibn al-Muqaffaʿ (d. 756) and Abū Yūsuf (731–798), whose works[85] present a great attention to the personal characteristics of the ruler instead of being concerned with the legitimacy of the institution or with its theorization as an abstract figure transcending the individual in charge. Later on, al-Māwardī himself, who can be considered one of the greatest political thinkers of classical Islam, in his already mentioned work on the way of governing explicitly focused on the personal characteristics of the ruler, including his health, at the point of asserting that, in the case of two candidates of equal merit, the ultimate criterion of choice is based on what the *ummah* most needs in that given moment and with regard to the concrete characteristics of the candidates.[86] Many years after him, al-Ghazālī would focus on the personal qualities and vices of the ruler to base his thought on the necessity of rebelling against tyranny, a recurring ideal in Islam. From this point of view, al-Ghazālī takes as an example of despotism and

[85] For an analysis of the political thought of these two authors with particular reference to the caliphs, see Lambton, *State and Government in Medieval Islam, cit.*, pp. 43 ff.

[86] "If two people fulfil equally the conditions of Imamate [...] If one of them is more knowledgeable and the other more courageous then attention should be paid to the situation at the time of making the choice: if there is a greater need for the quality of courage because of expansion of the border fortresses or the spread of injustice and tyranny, then the more courageous person would have the most right to the Imamate; if, however; there was a greater need for excellence in knowledge to ensure the tranquility of the masses or because of the existence of the people of innovation then the one with more knowledge is more eligible." Al-Māwardī, *Al-Aḥkām as-Sulṭaniyyah, cit.*, p. 14.

tyranny the Qur'ānic figure of the Pharaoh of Egypt, observing that the *ummah*, in this case, has the duty of rebelling against an oppressive and defective ruler,[87] regardless of any possible idea of legitimacy.

It should not be forgotten, in this perspective, that despite the contingencies of Islamic history, the Muslim political ideal acknowledges a special preference for a unique guide, intended as an individual, for a universal *ummah*, intended as a community of individuals.[88] Once again, this is not considered as the conceptualization of an institution whose existence transcends the single individuals in charge of it, but as the pragmatic necessity of appointing a single ruler in order to prevent personal rivalries from damaging the Muslim concord and the ultimate goals of Islamic rule. For instance, al-Jāḥiẓ (781-868-9) is quite explicit in stating that it is not right "that the government of Muslims according to the dictates of reason, firmness and prudence should be entrusted to more than one person",[89] where all the attention is drawn to the person exercising power.

To summarize, in the Muslim perspective political power belongs to a person, rather than belonging to an institution, with relevant implications in terms of relationships between rulers and community (*ummah*).

The aforementioned relationship will thus be based on the pursuit by the individual-ruler of the aims which are inherent to power as conceived in the Islamic framework, that is to say—mainly—the defense of Islam and the enforcement of *sharīʿa* as the path divinely revealed to mankind. The extreme consequence of what has been said necessarily leads to the apparent tautology of stating that an individual, in order to be a Muslim ruler, needs to be a *good* Muslim ruler. If this latter proposition may sound obvious, it should not be forgotten that the extremely practical and flexible theories on political authority in Muslim thought respond to a precise way of conceiving power. Just as authority is absorbed by the individual concretely exercising power, so power is absorbed by the very aim toward which it is exercised.[90] Any ruler is seen as automatically losing his

[87] See Moussa, *Politics of the Islamic Tradition, cit.*, pp. 104–105.

[88] On the reasons of this preference and on other opinions on it, see Crone, *God's rule, cit.*, pp. 272–276.

[89] Cit. in Lambton, *State and Government in Medieval Islam, cit.*, p. 59.

[90] See Charles Le Gai Eaton, *Islam and the Destiny of Man*, State University of New York Press, Albany 1985, pp. 164–165.

authority whenever his power deviates from the aim toward which it had been given to him, without any legal formality that, on the contrary, would be considered as absolutely necessary in a Western context such as medieval Europe.[91] Every authority is thus an authority *sub condicione*, where the condition points at the ultimate goal of power, deviating from which would necessarily cause the duty of the *ummah* to rebel.[92] Following this view, any dissertation on authority and power cannot possibly survive the disappearance of the physical person embodying it. In other words, with the disappearance of the ruler, the idea of its office cannot survive in the abstract, and new forms of power, best fitting the concrete situation, would ultimately rise. Therefore, it is possible to draw an intimate and immediate nexus between the three elements, in which the previous one is absorbed by the following one: the ruler as an individual in a position of authority, authority as power toward a certain end, and this end being identified with the way of Allāh for mankind.

What is fundamentally absent, with respect to the Western tradition, is the institutional and impersonal dimension of authority, which would in some way break the direct and immediate nexus between the three aforementioned elements of ruler, power, and *sharīʿa*. The idea of institution would indeed represent a mediation, an element juxtaposing itself between authority and power, eventually leading to a possible and theoretical separation between these two concepts. However, without the mediation of the institutional element, the relationship between ruler, power, and law is

[91] Here, I refer, for instance, to the deposition of emperors and popes, which had to be necessarily justified and legitimized by proper juridical conditions.

[92] Once again, it is useful to refer to the work of al-Māwardī, with particular reference to the qualities and the prerogatives of the caliph. According to the author, the *ummah* has the duty to obey the caliph at the condition that the caliph fulfills his own duties as supreme ruler. It is then to be considered an absolute obedience at the condition of fulfilling the purpose of authority, or in al-Māwardī's words, "as long as his state does not change" (al-Māwardī, *Al-Aḥkām as-Sulṭaniyyah*, *cit.*, p. 29). In his theories, the author does not deal with obedience to the abstract figure of the caliphate but to the individual caliph, who, in order to claim obedience, must simply be a good caliph (ibid., pp. 28–30). A very similar principle had been previously expressed by political and religious polemist and author al-Jāḥiẓ: the *ummah* must obey its ruler in every way, but this obedience, although being absolute in principle, is somehow conditioned to the ruler's accomplishment of his duties; otherwise, the *ummah* has not a right but a duty of resisting (cf. Lambton, *State and Government in Medieval Islam, cit.*, pp. 63–64).

considered an immediate and direct one, mirroring the immediate relationship between Allāh as a transcendent divinity and the community of believers.[93]

The most relevant implication of the absence of the institutional dimension in the conception of Islamic power is the virtual impossibility of elaborating a comprehensive and univocal theory on legitimation of power. While every legitimacy comes from Allāh—an undisputed point in every Islamic doctrine—the real question is how this legitimation can be understood and comprehended by man, and therefore inscribed into a stable theorical framework. From this point of view, it is possible to argue that the extreme fluidity of Islamic political theory follows the objective difficulty in establishing a univocal vision on political and juridical legitimation.

3.6 Legitimacy and Legitimation of Power

When dealing with the issue of legitimation of power in the Western and Islamic perspectives, it is necessary to distinguish between two different dimensions of legitimacy: the external dimension and the internal dimension.

[93] In Sunnī Islam the absence of a hierarchical organization of religious authority, which on the contrary characterizes Catholicism and Shīʿa Islam, reflects the immediate (*non*-mediate) nature of the relationship between Allāh and the *ummah*. While in Catholicism the event of the incarnation establishes Christ as the human-divine mediator between heaven and earth, and while in Shīʿa Islam the *imām* is regarded as a supreme leader operating a mediation between Allāh and the community, in Sunnī traditions the relationship between the divinity and the believers is to be considered substantially immediate. As Ezzati states, the "absence of priesthood and ecclesiastical orders in Islam is associated with Islamic theology. Islam means submission to God and Muslims are submitted to the authority of Allah only. Submission to God does not need any mediation or mediator" (Abu-Fazl Ezzati, *The Spread of Islam. The Contributing Factors*, Islamic College for Advanced Studies Press, London 2002, p. 132). Al-Jibouri is even more direct, stating that "Christianity considers Jesus as a mediator between man and God. Christians pray "in the name of our Lord, Jesus Christ", appealing to God through him. Islam recognizes no mediator between man and God: "everyone can be in direct contact with God and actually does so when he performs his prayers" (Yasin T. al-Jibouri, *Allah. The Concept of God in Islam*, vol. I, AuthorHouse, Bloomington 2012, p. 444).

3.6.1 External Legitimacy

In a State-based international system, with external legitimacy I refer to the conditions by which a State, as an international actor, might be considered legitimate according to shared international rules and standards. This concept is eminently factual, given that, in spite of more recent idealist views,[94] a State power might be considered internationally legitimate whenever it factually exercises ultimate and unchallenged authority in a given territory, whatever the nature of its claim over such a territory may be—being it occupation, war, and so on—and whatever its internal

[94] Some authors tend to consider the concept of external legitimation not as the coherent and factual outcome of a system that is still based on sovereignty and territoriality, thus shaped in their image, but as the idealistic aspiration toward a global form of governance. Therefore, while the aforementioned view on legitimation is traditionally based on the pragmatically exigency of the States to legitimate themselves in the framework of an international system where the use of force is unavoidably the *ultima ratio regum*, according to these views legitimation does not respond to a pragmatical and factual need, but it *should* have a substantial content. Wheatley, for instance, aims at demonstrating that the concept of democratic legitimation "developed at the level of the state can be applied to international law, broadly defined to include the inter-state system of public international law and new forms of international governance by international organizations and non-state actors". (Steven Wheatley, *The Democratic Legitimacy of International Law*, Hart Publishing, Oxford-Portland 2010, p. 1.) However, by giving to legitimacy a positive and substantially non-neutral characterization in terms of moral values, these opinions tend to necessarily transcend the most rigorous field of law and approach the most mutable field of politics. If democracy can easily be considered as a diffuse legitimating narrative *within* a certain international subject, it cannot be considered as an *external* way of legitimating international actors, for three main reasons: firstly, because of the absence of a super-national and super-State entity originally entitled of the use of force and therefore because of the absence of an external control; secondly, because of the lack of neutrality and objectivity in considering a non-univocal and multifaceted political concept such as democracy as the distinguishing element between legitimate and non-legitimate international actors; lastly, because these opinions tend to consider what reality *should* be like according to certain values, thus adopting a prescriptive and non-descriptive approach, which can be easily considered as biased *ab origine*. As a major voice discussing the possibility of a world democratic republic, it is worth remembering Jürgen Habermas, "The Constitutionalization of International Law and the Legitimation Problems of a Constitution for World", trans. Ciaran Cronin, in *Constellations*, vol XV, n. 4, 2008, pp. 444–455.

organization may be—being it a democracy, autocracy, and so on.[95] As is evident, this process of (self-)legitimation appears fundamentally to be a Western juridical construct, belonging to the modern era and being consequent to the establishment of the Westphalian international system. This kind of legitimacy basically coincides with the concrete exercise of sovereignty.

In the Islamic tradition there can be no concept of external legitimacy of power, given that the very reference to an "external" dimension means the recognition of an overall system composed by different and separate sovereignties, a vision considered alien to the Islamic legal view. The traditional universalism of the *ummah* cannot coincide, necessarily, with Western spatial delimitations and partitions characterizing the international system of the modern era, in which an international actor might be considered legitimate by external parties, which share its own vision of sovereignty and territoriality.

[95] It is important to distinguish between external legitimation, which is a juridical concept belonging to the field of international public law, and recognition by the international community, which is a political concept. In the State system, as previously pointed out, external legitimacy is to be considered essentially as a synonym to factual sovereignty, therefore a sort of self-legitimation through the concrete control of the territory. Political recognition should not be considered as a constitutive element of legitimation belonging to a completely different discourse and responding to substantially different exigences. While in the past decades the two concepts were far more closer than today, in the present time the distinction between the two is necessary: this need of distinguishing arises because of the spreading of opinions according to which the international community, usually through international organizations such as the United Nations, would be entitled of a pervasive power of recognition of States on the basis of far-reaching criteria regarding the domestic jurisdiction and the internal organization of power, among which the democratic principle represents nowadays a fundamental condition to achieve international recognition. This view might lead to confusion between legal legitimacy and political recognition, and again between external and internal legitimacy, not to mention the problems inherent to the violation of the long-standing principle of domestic jurisdiction. Buchanan, for instance, proposes a justice-based and moral theory of recognition, which ends to be identified with legal legitimacy, with an actual confusion between the two concepts in the idea of "recognitional legitimation". Cf. Allen Buchanan, *Justice, Legitimacy, and Self-Determination. Moral Foundations for International Law*, Oxford University Press, Oxford-New York 2004, pp. 233–330.

3.6.2 *Internal Legitimacy: Normative and Descriptive Dimensions*

With regard to internal legitimacy, I in turn distinguish two dimensions in which this concept can be intended: a normative and a descriptive dimension.

On a normative level, it is necessary to focus on the source legitimizing every authority, thus able to communicate normative power directly to a legitimate subject. In this sense, the Western tradition does not recognize, in the course of its history, a single normative source of legitimacy, passing from divine legitimation to national and popular legitimation. In the Islamic tradition, on the contrary and as already mentioned, the only normative source of legitimacy is Allāh alone, the transcendent divinity in whose name every power is validly legitimized. This point is fundamentally shared by every school or current in Sunnī Islam, and therefore can be considered as univocal and undoubtable. The real question, once again, is epistemological: if the normative source of legitimacy is univocally acknowledged, how can mankind understand it? Again, if the source of legitimacy is identified with the divinity, how is it possible for men to comprehend the process of legitimation? In the Islamic view, this point is far more complex and fluid, involving what can be referred to as descriptive dimension of legitimation.

With descriptive dimension of legitimation, I refer to the religious, historical, or political narratives by which political authorities legitimate their own rule with respect to their subjects. This issue is clearly more controversial and multifaceted, and it is not necessarily limited to the State construct but dates back to the most archaic political and legal theories of mankind. Any political rule has felt the unavoidable necessity to elaborate a narrative and create a political mythology in order to enshrine its legitimacy. Given the narratological nature of this peculiar and essential concept in any political discourse, as Max Weber argued, it is possible to agree upon its definition as the "willingness to submit to an order" which "always in some sense implies a belief in the legitimate *authority* of the source imposing it".[96]This kind of legitimation, therefore, is considered

[96] Max Weber [1922], *The Theory of Social and Economic Organization*, trans. A. M. Henderson, Talcott Parsons, ed. Talcott Parsons, The Free Press-The Falcon Wing's Press, Glencoe 1964, p. 132. On the different types of legitimation according to Weber, see Max Weber [1922], "Die drei reinen Typen der legitimen Herrschaft", in *Gesammelte Aufsätze zur Wissenchaftslehre*, Verlag von J. C. B. Mohr (Paul Siebeck), Tübingen 1988, pp. 475–488.

preeminently as the "reference to beliefs shared by both dominant and subordinate".[97]

In the Western world, the political and juridical discourse resolved the issue of the legitimation of power in multiple ways, depending on the philosophical elaboration which has been given to fundamental concepts such as authority, power, and law. With Weber[98] again, it is possible to say that the conception of a divinely legitimated power, or founded on the sanctity of tradition, is the most archaic and the most ancestral we could find in the history of mankind, with respect to which the Western world makes no exception. The classical Greek and Roman world had already legitimated juridical rules and political decisions with responses from oracles and haruspices, and from this point of view, it is particularly interesting to note the same etymological origin of the Latin terms *jus* and *Jovis*, common to the ancient act of swearing, *jovestod*,[99] as a trace of the sacredness of the conception of political authority as divinely legitimated. Rome herself was founded on the sanctity of the *pomerium*, which represented the sacred border in which Roman authority was circumscribed and on which the blood of Remus sealed in the tragedy of fratricide the birth—or re-birth—of the West.[100] However, if the classical world, with particular regard to the Greek world, referred to the vague and yet pervasive concept of νόμος (*nomos*) in order to express a hidden and veiled sacredness of law and authority, with the advent of Christianity and its conception of Revelation, the Western idea of divine legitimation was to acquire a new shape. Following Saint Paul's statement according to which *non est enim potestas*

[97] David Beetham, *The Legitimation of Power*, Macmillan, London 1991, p. 16.

[98] Cf. Weber, *The Theory of Social and Economic Organization*, *cit.*, p. 131.

[99] Cf. Olìs Robleda, s.j., "La costante evoluzione dell'antico sistema giuridico romano: principi invocati per legittimare le diverse fasi evolutive", in *Ortodossia e revisionismo. Studio interdisciplinare su processi di legittimazione*, Università Gregoriana Editrice, Roma 1974, pp. 26–28. For other possible etymologies, see Reginaldo M. Pizzorni, *La filosofia del diritto secondo S. Tommaso d'Aquino*, Edizioni Studio Domenicano, Bologna 2003, pp. 25–27.

[100] The killing of Remus, caused by the violation of the *pomerium* and thus of the sanctity of the spatial delimitation of Roman political authority, is related by Livy, *Ab Urbe Condita*, I, 7. For a concise but exhaustive comment on the sanctity of the idea of *limes*, with important implications on the issue of legitimation of political authority, see Jost Trier, "Zaun und Mannring", in *Beiträge zur Geschichte der deutschen Sprache und Literatur*, vol. LXVI, Halle 1942, pp. 232–264; Régis Debray, *Éloge des Frontières*, Gallimard, Paris 2010, ch. 1.

nisi a Deo,[101] the Christian world shaped its narrative on legitimacy on the basis of a divinely designated authority, whose competences were to be divided between spiritual and temporal institutions, both legitimated by God. If a religiously based legitimacy appears to be the most archaic and most pervasive in the Western ancient world, rooted as it is in the Christianized Roman Empire and accepted even after the creation of modern statehood, the most recent can be considered the democratic form of legitimation. As well known and notwithstanding its relatively recent success, democratic legitimation is not considered a philosophically new idea, since its origins can be traced back to ancient Greece, especially to Aristotle's view on the organization of the πόλις (*polis*) and to the republican experience of ancient Rome, although with the necessary differentiations.

From the view on divine right up to the perspective of representative democracy, it can be easily argued that the theories of legitimation in the Western legal discourse changed greatly depending on historical contexts and philosophical visions. This is a logical and coherent consequence of the aforementioned necessity inherent to legitimation, conceived as a narrative that must be shared by both rulers and the ruled, in order to create a stable basis for the concrete exercise of power. Therefore, from this perspective legitimation can be seen as the process of progressive construction of a narrative to be shared by the authority and the consociates.[102]

With the affirmation of the juridical construct of the *persona ficta*, regardless of the various theories of legitimation progressively elaborated in the Western world, a structural and common feature can be identified. Thanks to the instrument of legal personhood, seen as a lens through which examining the interactions between legitimate authority and society, it can be argued that in the Western view legitimation is always the process of adherence of an individual to a predetermined impersonal institution. Whatever the legitimating narrative may be, the core concept of Western legitimation relies on constituting a link between the individual and the institution, by virtue of which the former adheres to the latter,

[101] "Let every person be subordinate to the higher authorities, for there is no authority except from God, and those that exist have been established by God. Therefore, whoever resists authority opposes what God has appointed, and those who oppose it will bring judgment upon themselves". *Rom* 13, 1–2 (trans. *New American Bible*).

[102] Again, in Beetham's words, "without a minimum of the appropriate beliefs defined above being shared between the dominant and the subordinate, and indeed among the subordinate themselves, there can be no basis on which justifications for the rules of power can find a purchase" (Beetham, *The Legitimation of Power, cit.*, p. 17).

however without confusion between the two. Therefore, the convergence of the individual and the institution represents what can be called legitimate authority, while their divergence leads to a crisis of legitimacy, whose original order must be reestablished, or alternatively, replaced by another legitimating narrative. This scheme can be considered valid for the divine legitimation of the great European monarchies of the past, where the immanent person of the king was to adhere to the impersonal dimension of kingship by virtue of his belonging to a dynasty legitimated by divine right, and for the modern democratic republics, where the individual comes to be a part of a collective institutional body by virtue of popular choice.

As previously seen, in the Islamic view there is no univocal political conception as the one on legitimation as conceived of by the Western world, with the aforementioned characteristics. The issue of internal (descriptive) legitimation was solved in the history of Sunnī Islam in multiple ways, from the consensus of the community in the time of the four *rāshidūn* caliphs to the dynastic succession in the following caliphal rules.[103] However, Islamic political theory, in the course of the centuries, proved to be flexible and perfectly able to adapt to the concrete circumstances of a certain social and political context. If the Western vision on legitimation presupposes a shared belief, which should be universally accepted by both the ruled and the rulers, thus implying a sort of fixity in a given time, in the Islamic thinking the political theory appears on the contrary to be pragmatically shaped by the concrete exigences of the *ummah* and of the preservation of *sharīʿa*.[104] Moreover, the lack of the idea of legal personality, latterly imported from the West, leads to the virtual impossibility of developing a theory of legitimation similar to the one

[103] Cf. Boulaabi, *Islam et pouvoir, cit.*, especially pp. 17–35.

[104] Gibb explains Islamic flexibility when it comes to political thought by recalling al-Māwardī's principles, according to which "Necessity dispenses with stipulations that are impossible to fulfill" and "fear of injury to public interests justifies a relaxation of conditions". Gibb observes that this extreme flexibility, whose aim is to affirm the supremacy of *sharīʿa* in problematic historical circumstances, shows the theorical premises for the overcoming of the caliphal rule it wants to preserve. According to Gibb "Necessity and expediency may indeed be respectable principles, but only when they are not invoked to justify disregard of the law" (Hamilton Alexander Rosskeen Gibb [1962], *Studies on the Civilization of Islam*, Princeton University Press, Princeton 1982, p. 164).

previously examined. On the contrary, recognizing a ruler as legitimate acquires in Islam a completely different meaning with regard for what happened—and happens—in the Western world: in Islam, legitimacy does not attain to institutions on the basis of comprehensive political theories but rather relies on individuals and, therefore, on a direct relationship between ruler and community, concretely shaped by contingencies and personal qualities. Evidence of this is provided by the previously mentioned oath of allegiance (*bayʿah*) pledged to a leader by the community, with special attention to the *bayʿah* pledged to the caliph as the representative of the *ummah*. Although variously ritualized along the eras of Muslim history, the *bayʿah* symbolizes the handshake between buyer and seller, thus the (private) agreement reached by two parties, regardless of fixed and preexisting rules, but on the exclusive basis of their commitment.[105] As the caliph rose to power because of his factual commitment to fulfill his duties, like defending Islam and enforcing *sharīʿa*, the community pledged allegiance to him not on the basis of abstract schemes of legitimation but on the basis of the concrete and pragmatic acceptance of his leadership as an individual, considered able to achieve the goals of the community. It should not be forgotten that the *bayʿah*, whose semantic significance dates back however to ancient ages, was assumed as a stable political act following the allegiance pledged twice to Muḥammad in ʿAqaba,[106] prior to any form of systematization of a *sharīʿa*-based system, but on the exclusive basis of a bond of personal fidelity. The factual nature of political power in Islam is therefore mirrored by the expression of the fidelity of the community, which in turn is modeled on factual and pragmatic considerations, directly binding a leader and his subjects.

Considering what has already been said concerning authority and law in Islam and to *sharīʿa* as the supreme aim of the ruler, we can conclude noticing that internal legitimation in Islam is considered eminently factual and pragmatically conceived in order to shape itself to the needs of its

[105] On the oath of allegiance and its nature, consider the already mentioned opinion of Ibn Khaldūn, *The Muqaddimah*, *cit.*, pp. 166–167.

[106] On the two meetings of ʿAqaba, see Richard A. Gabriel, *Muhammad. Islam's First Great General*, University of Oklahoma Press, Norman 2007, pp. 60–61.

ultimate goal.[107] Because of its factual nature, the construction of a shared narrative among the consociates about legitimacy is not actually even necessary, given the overall conception of power as instrumental to the legal order and not *vice versa*. In the lack of a comprehensive and shared political theory, the legitimation of power in Islam is more of a self-legitimation, whose structural element is once again the concrete eligibility to pursue a determinate goal. To sum up, while for the West legitimacy refers to the initial conditions by which power can be exercised, in Islam it refers to the final aim for which it is factually maintained.

3.6.3 Conclusive Remarks on Legitimation

Once again, in order to grasp the real distinguishing element between Islam and the West with regard to legitimation, it is necessary to reverse the terms of the Western perspective. I argued that in the Western view the idea of external legitimation shows, in a State-based system, a factual nature, while internal descriptive legitimation is based on a shared narrative whose core is the idea of institution-*persona ficta*. In the Islamic view, on the contrary, the relationship between the *ummah* and the external world, despite the impossibility of being properly considered as legitimation, is grounded in the shared narrative of universalism, whose basis is found in the consensus of the community, rooted in a religious belief. Islamic universalism, a utopist ideal never fully realized by the *ummah*, far from being self-legitimating by the force of its immanent factuality, is fundamentally a shared belief. Internal legitimation, on the other hand, is univocally theorized as a normative dimension but extremely fluid in its descriptive nature: in this latter sense, it is the result of a factual auto-affirmation of a personified power in pursuing a predetermined divinely

[107] Clément notes that "this absence of delimited boundaries between concepts that we consider primordial implies that nothing, or almost nothing, distinguishes ethics from law. [...] This undoubtedly explains the necessarily arbitrary or despotic nature of Muslim power" (François Clément, *Pouvoir et légitimité en Espagne musulmane à l'époque des Taifas (V-XI siècle)*, L'Harmattan, Paris 1997, p. 22).

revealed goal, which in this case basically coincides with the defense of the *ummah* and the enforcement of *sharīʿa*.[108]

Evidentially, from a sociological point of view, legitimation itself appears to be an eminently Western concept whose categories of thought and analysis can barely be juxtaposed with a different cultural context. However, if we are to find structural elements defining what we would call legitimation in the two universes—West and Islam—we should conclude that the two perspectives follow a reverse path of reasoning and development. While with the exterior world the West has adopted a factual approach of self-legitimation of the sovereign State *superiorem non recognoscens*, Islam adopted the idea of universalism on the basis of a shared religious belief. Again, and with regard to the interior dimension, while the West conceived legitimation as a shared narrative based on the coincidence between individual and institution, Islam adopted a factual approach to political authority, where the aim toward which power is exercised is to be considered prevalent over the eventuality of elaborating a stable political theory defining univocal legitimating conditions.

[108] It is particularly relevant to recall Ibn Khaldūn's criticism of the gradual shift from the supremacy of *sharīʿa*, considered the end toward which the caliphal rule should tend, to autocracy in the late Umayyad and Abbasid periods, that is to say, the ruling for merely political or personal purposes. Political legitimacy, from this perspective, is once again tied to the supreme aim of the ruler: the enforcement and preservation of *sharīʿa*. To summarize, when the rulers forget about the very aim toward which power must be exercised, and for which power is given, dynasties fall. For the position of Ibn Khaldūn on this issue, see Muḥammad Maḥmūd Rabīʿ, *The Political Theory of Ibn Khaldun*, Brill, Leiden 1967, pp. 93–100. With regard to the same question, and as Moussa notes, when "Muslim rulers fail to apply the objectives of the Sharīʿah, and by extension justice, it is inevitable for decline to take place within a civilization" (Moussa, *Politics of the Islamic Tradition, cit.*, pp. 52–53). Another example is certainly Ibn Taimīya, who uses the expression *al-siyāsa al-shar'iyya*, that Anjum translates with "Islamic politics", but that in a non-literary but exhaustive sense should be translated more appropriately as "governance based on *sharīʿa*", as Masud does. According to Ibn Taimīya legitimacy is not a legalistic or formal concept but a substantial one that must be anchored on the observance and enforcement of *sharīʿa*. As Anjum states, Ibn Taimīya intends to "furnish a feasible model of substantive legitimacy (as opposed to legalistic or formal legitimacy) to both the rulers and their political activity on the basis of the *Sharīʿa*" (Ovamir Anjum, *Politics, Law, and Community in Islamic Thought. The Taymiyyan Moment*, Cambridge University Press, Cambridge 2012, p. 30). As Masud explains, according to the aforementioned author "the ruler must abide by the Islamic law. As long as he does so, the people should obey him because, according to Ibn Taimīya, the political authority has no legitimacy if the ruler does not abide by the divine law" (Muhammad Khalid Masud, "The changing concepts of caliphate. Social construction of Sharīʿa and the question of ethics", in *New Directions in Islamic Thought. Exploring Reform and Muslim Tradition*, eds. Kari Vogt, Lena Larsen, Christian Moe, I.B. Tauris, London-New York 2009, p. 193).

CHAPTER 4

Law, *Sharīʿa*, and Human Reason

4.1 Premise

Notwithstanding the focus of the major legal literature on more substantive aspects of the Islamic legal world, one of the most important points in comparing the Islamic and Western perspectives is the different roles that human reason plays in the respective legal orders.

Reason represents the universal character that defines humanity in all its civilizations and culture, and the distinguishing mark of the human race all over the world. Nevertheless, the role every civilization gives to the instrument of reason, as well as a coherent theorization of its function, is something deeply rooted in the cultural background of peoples and societies, in given historical and social contexts. If reason is the extraordinary element that characterizes mankind from ancestral ages up to the present, without any distinction of space and time, the conceptualization of its role marks relevant and important differences between civilizations and can only represent a major philosophical point of interest. This is particularly evident with regard to the juridical discourse, where crucial issues such as justice and retribution, rule and coercion, coexistence and social regulation call for a preliminary analysis on the nexus between reason and law.

This fundamental issue might be considered as a pre-juridical question, inherent to a wider anthropological reflection, which however deeply

F. L. Ramaioli, *Juridical Perspectives between Islam and the West*, Global Issues, https://doi.org/10.1007/978-3-031-37844-7_4

affects concepts such as authority, normativity, and legislation in a given society.[1] Once again, when dealing with the role that human reason plays with regard to the conceptualization and the systematization of juridical phenomena, it is necessary to avoid universalizing Western notions and constructs. Consequently, it is necessary to avoid taking for granted the endpoints of a complex process of juridical construction and elaboration, which developed over centuries and which is necessarily grounded in a precise cultural background. The theorization of the human element of reason as a primary agent in creating law, or *vice versa* its confinement to a contemplative role of a superhuman dimension, brings about legal implications that are definitely worth considering.

When analyzing the different ways in which human reason interacts with and shapes the juridical discourse, respectively, in the Western and in the Islamic perspectives, I will discuss four major points of interest, which will help in grasping the core of a complex reflection, whose importance usually seems to be underestimated.

Firstly, I will focus on the idea of creation and its possible legal implications. Secondly, I will analyze the role of reason in conceptualizing the idea of normativity in the Western conception of law, both before and after the modern era, and in systematizing a *sharīʿa*-based system, with particular regard to the concepts of *fiqh* and *qānūn*. Thirdly, I will examine the nexus between a certain use of reason and the ideas of promulgation and codification, in the broader discourse on form and substance of law. Lastly, I will examine the peculiar role which reason plays in theorizing what is understood as the primary origin of the juridical phenomenon, with particular reference to the Western and modern idea of *source*, and to the Islamic conception of *uṣūl* (root).

By doing so, it will be possible to properly highlight what is considered as a major structural difference in understanding law in the Western and

[1] As Tymieniecka points out, every investigation of human reason, carried out by means of reason itself, necessarily ends up being an investigation concerning "not the mind per se, human reasoning and rational powers, but reality, life, world and the *role* of the mind in the unity of living beings" (Anna-Teresa Tymieniecka, "Toward the Manifestation of Reason in the Edifice of Life", in *Manifestations of Reason. Life, Historicity, Culture*, part 2, *Phenomenology in the Adriatic Countries*, ed. Anna-Teresa Tymieniecka, Springer Science-Business Media, Dordrecht 1993, p. xi). Therefore, even my analysis will focus on the role of reason in conceiving and systematizing a legal order, with major consequences on the comprehension of society and justice.

Islamic legal traditions, underlining a crucial issue whose implications are considered as deeply affecting the respective juridical systems, in the past and in the contemporary era as well.

4.2 Preliminary Considerations About Law and Creation

A juridical reflection on the role of reason between Islam and the West cannot be considered exhaustively complete without a preliminary introduction on the nexus between law and creation in these specific cultural contexts. Human rationality can interact with the concept of law in a number of different ways: it can interpret it, it can understand it, it can explain it, and it can *create* it. This latter point, evidently the most relevant in the present reflection, is not to be taken for granted, although in the Western context it is usually assumed that a certain creative role of reason in the activity of lawmaking is a sort of universal idea. It is the idea of creation, in fact, that represents a nexus between law and reason, and can consequently highlight this crucial relationship and allow us to read it in a new light: the act of creation can be regarded as the most radical activity of reason in interacting with law, in this case with a constitutive nature. If reason is legitimated to *create*, then creating law is considered a logical consequence of the activity of the ruler, by which social reality and political architecture can be established and shaped. *Vice versa*, if reason comes to play a completely different role in understanding and elaborating the act of creation, in all of its aspects and meanings, the juridical and political implications will be radically different.

The idea of creation is necessarily linked to the various religious and ancestral beliefs and mythological accounts about the world and mankind coming into existence. The act of creation is indeed present, to various extents, in the majority of ancient cosmogonies and foundation myths, from the East to the West, and is linked to the most intimate questions man has been asking himself across the ages. Depending on the tenure of these narratives, the understanding of the interaction between the divine, the earth, men, and the act of creation can greatly vary, with relevant consequences in terms of social and political organization. In particular, the Judeo-Christian vision, which deeply influenced the West and ultimately contributed to constituting what is now commonly referred to as "Western world", and the Islamic vision represent two opposite ways of giving a determined significance to the act of creation and to the legitimacy of mankind to participate in it.

As for the Western perspective, as mentioned, the Judeo-Christian thought represents the main influence in determining the relationship between man and creation, and consequently between man and the production of law. In Genesis, God not only constitutes man as possessor and guardian of all creatures but also entitles him with the right to give names to all things.[2] In the Judaic culture, as is well known, the power of imposing names hides the power of possessing and controlling things, thus an eminently *creative* power.[3] It should not be forgotten that men, in the biblical account of the Tower of Babel,[4] lost their concord with the loss of a unique language, as retribution for their hubris. In a broader sense and as highlighted in the famous legend of the Golem,[5] the word symbolizes the most powerful instrument of possession, to the point of being able to give life and death. In the Judaic culture, the mysterious and undetectable name of God represents the most sacred of words, and the only one that cannot be spoken, because nobody would ever be able to control God in his transcendence. It is worth remembering, with regard to the advent of the Christian era, that the incarnation of Christ is described in the Gospel

[2] "So out of the ground the LORD God formed every animal of the field and every bird of the air, and brought them to the man to see what he would call them; and whatever the man called every living creature, that was its name. The man gave names to all cattle, and to the birds of the air, and to every animal of the field; but for the man there was not found a helper as his partner". *Genesis*, II, 19–20 (trans. *The New American Bible*, ed. United States Conference of Catholic Bishops, Washington 2002).

[3] On the creative power of the word in the Judeo-Christian culture, see Whitney Shiner, *Proclaiming the Gospel. First-Century Performance of Mark*, Trinity Press International, Harrisburg 2003, pp. 191–192. It is worth recalling the words of Schepis, according to whom in the "Hebrew paradigm the importance of the word (*dabar*) is central. The existential, cultural and political heritage of a nomadic people is rooted in it. The *dabar*, unlike the *logos* that clarifies thought in the demonstration of concepts, is a limit-place, coexistence of contradictions, of blurred meanings; it is not a point of arrival, but a starting point" (Maria Felicia Schepis, *Colui che ride. Per una ricreazione dello spazio politico*, Franco Angeli, Milan 2011, pp. 107–108). Moreover, while explaining the crucial role of symbols, Alleau underlines the importance of language, because it is by naming objects and creatures that man gives them significance and meaning, in what the author refers to as *logosphere*. Cf. René Alleau [1976], *La scienza dei simboli. Contributo allo studio dei principi e dei metodi della simbolica*, Sansoni, Florence 1983, p. 166.

[4] Cf. *Genesis*, XI, 1–9.

[5] Cf. Geoffrey W. Dennis, *The Encyclopedia of Jewish Myth, Magic and Mysticism*, Llewellyn Publications, Woodbury 2007, pp. 110–111.

according to saint John as the incarnation of the λόγος (*Logos*), the Word of God coming into this physical world, and which is considered as the beginning of everything. According to John, in fact, in the beginning "was the Word, and the Word was with God, and the Word was God".[6] The word, from this perspective, is vested with the divine power of creation, and the word, with which man has been gifted, represents a way in which man participates in the creative power of God, from the act of imposing names to creation.

According to this vision, it can be argued that man is a co-creator along with God in the eschatological vision of salvation.[7] Therefore, God's command to men and women to populate the earth and to multiplicate is nothing less than a command to create and spread life, thus once again participating in the act of creation, which can be seen as continuous and continuative. As Dante poetically but exhaustively stated in his *Commedia*, the double role of men, as creatures and creators, is particularly evident in the figure of the Virgin Mary, at the same time "Virgin Mother, daughter of thy Son",[8] at the same time creature of God and creator of the life of God in the world.[9] The Greek term by which the Virgin is known, Θεοτόκος (*Theotókos*), commonly translated as "God-bearer" or in a broader and non-literary sense "Mother of God", shows in its etymological root the act of generating and creating life (τόκος, parturition), just like the

[6] *The Gospel according to John*, I, 1 (trans. *The New American Bible*, *cit.*). It is worth mentioning the Stoic idea of the λόγος σπερματικος (*Logos spermatikòs*), or *ratio seminalis*, which was later reinterpreted and incorporated by Christian theology, emphasizing the creative power of the λόγος and its "seeds" in human reason. See Maryanne Cline Horowitz, *Seeds of Virtue and Knowledge*, Princeton University Press, Princeton 1998, p. 49.

[7] According to Bertocci, "God is the creator of co-creators, for man does not create outright - that is, the very possibilities of creation. But man is co-creator with God; and God is implicated in the creations, the good and the bad creation of man. Likewise, man as co-creator with God has to accept the consequences of the order within which God must work if man's creativity is to exist at all" (Peter A. Bertocci [1970], *The Person God Is*, Routledge, London 2002, p. 312).

[8] "Vergine madre, figlia del tuo figlio". Dante [c. 1321], *Paradiso*, XXXIII, 1. The English translation comes from *Divine Comedy*, *Paradiso*, trans. Henry Wadsworth Longfellow, Ticknor and Fields, Boston 1867, p. 217.

[9] "Tu se' colei che l'umana natura / nobilitasti sì, che 'l suo fattore / non disdegnò di farsi sua fattura", Ibid., XXXIII, 4–6. "Thou art the one who such nobility / To human nature gave, that its Creator / Did not disdain to make himself its creature". *Paradiso*, trans. Longfellow, *cit.*, p. 217.

equivalent Latin term *Deìpara*, which is composed from the term *parĕre*, with the same meaning.[10]

The creative power of man, in the Western world, is testified by the rise of the visual arts as well. With the definitive fall of iconoclasm in ancient times, Western art came to be characterized by the focus on the human figure, both in painting and sculpture, coherently with its Christian influences and with its Roman and Greek reminiscences. The artistic representation of nature, man, and God himself embodies the visual expression of the legitimation of the human reason to create and fully participate in the divine act of creation.[11]

This point has relevant juridical implications, if we consider that one of the creative activities of man might regard the production of law. As creation is mirrored by the reproduction of the human figure as an expression of art, in the same way it is reflected in the act of regulating human society. This form of regulation can be verily expressed and understood, and is not necessarily linked to a positivized idea of law, but is however grounded in the conception that man is entitled with the faculty of establishing rules to common and social life. The possibility of creating law, and consequently of shaping society accordingly, was followed by the establishing of the role of the legislator, however named and whatever the role assigned to him. In ancient Rome, the legal order was originally shaped and conceived not just as civil law but also as praetorian law, according to the Latin phrase *da mihi factum, dabo tibi jus*, with human reason enabled to elaborate rules

[10] For the contextualization and meaning of the term *Theotókos*, see Frederic M. Jelly, o.p., *Madonna. Mary in the Catholic Tradition*, Wipf and Stock Publishers, Eugene 1986, pp. 90–99.

[11] While this point appears more evidently in visual arts, the philosophical traces of this conception can be found even in literary production, with special regard to the notions of *fantasy* and *fantastic*, which greatly developed in the Western world. In his academic production on literary criticism, Tolkien describes the artistic act in the genre of fantasy as "sub-creation". According to the author, who is implicitly referring to the Western and Christian tradition, the human faculty of shaping new worlds in artistic forms reflects the very nature of man, to be considered both as a creature and as a (co-)creator. "Fantasy remains a human right: we make in our measure and in our derivative mode, because we are made: and not only made, but made in the image and likeness of a Maker". John R. R. Tolkien [1947], "On Fairy-Stories", in *The Monsters and the Critics and Other Essays*, ed. Christopher Tolkien, Harper Collins, London 1997, pp. 139 ff., 145.

and norms from concrete situations, both when legislating and when adjudicating. With the transition to the imperial era, the Roman emperor came to be regarded not just as a keeper of the legal order but as a supreme legislator as well, somehow mirroring the legislating function of the Roman kings as authors of the mythical *leges regiae*.[12] While the comprehensive concept of *jus* was conceived as a bridge in some way unifying heaven and earth, given its originally sacred function, the instrument of the *lex* symbolized the concrete possibility for human beings to actively participate in the legal order with their own decisions. This is even more evident with the Christianization of the empire. While in the Judaic tradition, with the era of the judges and later on with the kings of Israel, the patriarchs and the sovereigns are considered more as lawgivers, as Moses, and as guardians of the law, as Salomon, the Christian belief would deeply change this perspective. With the advent of the Christian era, the two main political and religious authorities, popes and emperors, were seen as the supreme legislators of the medieval world, granted the right of regulating society and legislating in the matters of respective competence.[13] With his *Corpus Juris Civilis* and with his work of juridical systematization, Justinian became the legislator of the empire par excellence, establishing

[12] The system of the sources of law in Roman time was rather complex and multifaceted, with various changes taking place over the various phases of the life of Rome. However, it is possible to recognize a *fil rouge* in the acknowledgment of men's power in creating regulations. Cicero, Gaius, and Justinian list three main sources of law, every one of which referred to humanmade rules and norms: legislation, resolutions of the Senate, and edicts of the magistrates. From the second century A.D. it is possible to add imperial enactment as a source of law, following the acquirement of a *de facto* legislative power by the Caesars. For an in-depth analysis of the makers of Roman law in the framework of the sources, see O. F. Robinson [1997], *The Sources of Roman Law. Problems and Methods for Ancient Historians*, Routledge, London-New York 2006, ch. 1; Paul du Plessis [1994], *Borkowski's Textbook on Roman Law*, Oxford University Press, Oxford 2010, pp. 27–62.

[13] While popes and emperors were undoubtedly enabled with the juridical faculty of creating law, this legislating function is not to be interpreted in the modern or contemporary sense. As Grossi observes with regard to temporal power, the legislative production of early medieval legislators heavily relied on customs, with the political authority manifesting the *lex non scripta* of custom with a *lex scripta* (see Paolo Grossi [2007], *A History of European Law*, trans. Laurence Hooper, Wiley-Blackwell, Chichester 2010, pp. 13–14).

an order that would leave fundamental traces up to the modern era.[14] Even the medieval monastic rules, which are not comparable to legal norms[15] but which undoubtedly have a relevant role in the development of a juridical system,[16] reflect the idea that man can regulate common life and social practice and be considered as the author of such regulations as in the case of the founders of great monastic orders. In the new Christian era, following the incarnation and the new covenant between God and mankind, Christ legislator[17] was mirrored in this function by human authority, both temporal and spiritual.

In the Western tradition, deeply affected by the aforementioned influences, the act of creation is thus considered as something inherent to the human personality, whose rationality represents the main instrument by which man, created in God's image, continues the creative activity of the divinity.[18] Lawmaking, being one of the most relevant activities in which human creativity and rational effort come to play a preeminent role, is

[14] The compilation of the *Corpus Juris* constituted the very basis of Western law for centuries, at the point of being considered as the major achievement of the reign of Justinian, who is even generously praised by Dante in his *Paradiso* (*canto* VI) for it. From this point of view, "the writing of the *Corpus Juris Civilis* expressed Justinian's obedience to his divine call to rule Christendom after God's design. The emperor, under God, was the font of justice. And, while the emperor's will was law, he was yet under the law, for the law granted him his authority. His rule must reflect God's perfect justice" (Craig A. Stern, "Justinian: Lieutenant for Christ, Legislator for Christendom", in *Regent University Law Review*, vol. XI, n. 1, 1998–1999, p. 157). With regard to what will be noted on the Islamic perspective, it is interesting to notice that in Islam the legislating function of the transcendent divinity prevents human authorities—even the highest—from being legislators, while in the Christian perspective it may be said that authorities exercise a legislative function because so does Christ, as mediator between heaven and earth.

[15] On the nature of monastic rules and on their relationship with the law, see the well-known work of Giorgio Agamben [2011], *The Highest Poverty. Monastic Rules and Form-of-Life*, trans. Adam Kotsko, Stanford University Press, Stanford 2013., especially pp. 28–47.

[16] See James Q. Whitman [2006], "Comparative Law and Religion", in *The Oxford Handbook of Comparative Law*, eds. Mathias Reimann, Reinhard Zimmermann, Oxford University Press, Oxford 2019, p. 751.

[17] On Christ as *legislator* the thought of John Mair is particularly important. On this point, see J. H. Burns, *The True Law of Kingship. Concepts of Monarchy in Early-modern Scotland*, Clarendon Press, Oxford 1996, p. 49.

[18] As it has been observed, "the likeness of God seen in man is a precondition for revelation because it institutes a compatibility between divine Logos and human logos. Man is a creator and a poet as long as he resembles God, or, precisely speaking, Christ" (Bogumil Jarmulak, "Theology of Beauty in Evdokimov", in *The Glory of Kings. A Festschrift in Honor of James B. Jordan*, eds. Peter J. Leithart, John Barach, Pickwick Publications, Eugene 2011, p. 277).

regarded as a structural element in Western legal perspective, where the figure of the legislator, along with the judge,[19] has always been a capstone in every juridical system.[20]

In the Islamic vision, on the contrary, the act of creation is strictly reserved for the divinity alone and cannot be delegated to man under any circumstance. The Islamic divinity, conceived as one and unique on the basis of the *tawḥīd* (monotheistic principle), is considered as transcendent and infinitely distant in his omnipotence. From this point of view, Allāh is seen as the only possible creator, as expressly stated by the *Qur'ān*,[21] while man, as a creature, is beneficiary of the creationary act of the divinity, without taking active part in it. This is evident from the various attributes of the divinity, such as the "creator", the "originator", the "fashioner of shapes", or "the maker",[22] which underline Allāh's exclusive prerogative of creating.

In the idea of Islamic creation and cosmology, as already mentioned, the divinity initially creates all the souls that would ever exist in the world, with a substantial shift in the conception of history. As a consequence, and

[19] The importance of the judicial power and its role in the respective legal orders will be discussed in a paragraph dedicated to the idea of enforceability, in Chap. 5.

[20] It is worth considering the position of Thomas Paine, who expressly pointed out the correlation between the *homo creator*, or *homo faber*, being created in God's image and thus participating to his creative activity and lawmaking. Man's activity as a creator, according to the author, cannot but be reflected in his activity as a lawmaker. With regard to this, see Jack Fruchtman jr., *The political philosophy of Thomas Paine*, The Johns Hopkins University Press, Baltimore 2009, pp. 47–55.

[21] Allāh is described in the holy text of Islam as "the Creator of all things" (VI, 102; XIII, 16; XXXIX, 62; XL, 62) and "the Creator of the heavens and the earth" (XIV, 10; XXXIX, 46; XLII, 11). The divinity, when addressing directly man with regard to the human seed, testifies his faith in his creative power, by asking: "Is it ye who create it, or are We the Creators?" (LVI, 59). In the known dispute against the so-called associators (*mushrikūn*), who associate Allāh in his omnipotence to other beings and therefore put in question the *tawḥīd*, the *Qur'ān* states: "Do they indeed ascribe to Him as partners things that can create nothing, but are themselves created?" (VII, 191). This latter point is particularly significant because the act of creating is regarded as the real distinguishing characteristic of the divinity, while the idols associated to Allāh are to be considered as his creatures, thus fundamentally deprived from the divine power of creating. The aforementioned excerpts follow the translation of Ali, respectively, at pp. 324, 592, 1198, 606, 1194, 1248, 1414, 400.

[22] "In relation to the acts of creation, He is styled as *al-Khaliq* (Creator); *al Bari'* (maker of soul); *al-Mufawwir* (Fashioner of shapes) and *al-Badi'* (wonderful originator)". Muḥammad 'Azīz Aḥmad, *The Nature of Islamic Political Theory*, Ma'aref, Karachi 1975, p. 96. Cf. Yasin T. al-Jibouri, *Allah. The Concept of God in Islam*, vol. I, AuthorHouse, Bloomington 2012, p. 216.

necessarily, man cannot vest the role of creator with regard to the generation of human life, following the biblical command to multiplicate and populate the earth, in consideration of the fact that the decision whether to create every single life had already been taken by Allāh. The power to create is thus remitted to the divinity alone,[23] to whom it is not possible to "associate" anything and anybody. Again, the power to create distinguishes the real and transcendent divinity from the preexisting and powerless idols of the pre-Islamic world, to such an extent as to be considered as an exclusive prerogative of Allāh.

Evidence about the impossibility for man to be considered a creator can be found in the Islamic narrative on the creation of Adam: unlike in the biblical account, in the *Qur'ān* Adam cannot name the creatures of the earth, but on the contrary, it is Allāh who imposes names upon them and then reveals them to Adam.[24] It is a detail that is definitely worth considering, as it shows that in the Islamic vision man does not participate in the creative power of God but benefits from it and contemplates it.

In the field of artistic expression, the strict prohibition to represent the image of God, and the reluctance or the hostility toward the representation of human figures, is a coherent consequence of the theorization of the impossibility of man to participate to the creative power of Allāh.[25] Creating images may be interpreted as granting human intellect the right

[23] Cf. Nidhal Guessoum, *Islam's Quantum Question. Reconciling Muslim Tradition and Modern Science*, I.B. Tauris, London-New York 2011, pp. 42–44.

[24] "And He taught Adam the names of all things; then He placed them before the angels, and said: 'Tell Me the names of these if ye are right.' They said: 'Glory to Thee: of knowledge we have none, save what Thou hast taught us. In truth it is Thou who art perfect in knowledge and wisdom.' He said: 'O Adam! tell them their names.' When he had told them, Allah said: 'Did I not tell you that I know the secrets of heaven and earth, and I know what ye reveal and what ye conceal?'" *Qur'ān*, II, 31–33, trans. Abdullah Yusuf Ali [1934], *The Meaning of the Holy Qur'ān*, Amana Publications, Beltsville 2004, pp. 24–25. This excerpt is particularly significant because of the exclusiveness of the power of naming things, which is not shared with man as in the corresponding biblical version but seen here as something inherent to the transcendent nature of God, to whom nothing and nobody can be associated or compared.

[25] The prohibition of representing Allāh follows the affirmation of the total transcendence of the divinity, which cannot be limited by any plastic representation or intellectual exhaustive comprehension. As for the human figure, the *Qur'ān* does not explicitly forbid its artistic reproductions, but for the aforementioned reasons and because of what is related in some *'aḥādīth*, depicting human imagery is discouraged when not forbidden. On the complex issue of the relationship between Islam and images, see Titus Burckhardt, *L'art de l'Islam. Langage et Signification*, Sindbad, Paris 1985, pp. 65–77.

to being properly called a creator, thus associating man to God. Creating images, moreover, may intensify the risk of creating idols, whose cult could be rival to the cult of Allāh. Therefore, the approach of Islam to the human figure responds to a double exigence: on the one hand, man cannot be associated with the divinity in his creative activity, and on the other hand, representing human figures may lead to idolatry. Islamic traditional aniconism, although changing depending on time and religious currents, led to the development of a different aesthetic, based on the sanctity of empty spaces, like in mosques, in architecture, and in graphic ornaments like arabesques. The flourishing of the art of Islamic calligraphy, whose florid expressions prevent the artist from depicting plastic representations of the human image, represents one the most evident signals of a conception that goes far beyond the artistic field and that is deeply inherent to the philosophical elaboration of the Islamic culture.[26] This does not however mean that in Islam the role of man is somehow less relevant: in Islam, man is a researcher and a contemplator, someone in constant quest for an everlasting truth in the way of his life.

What has just been observed leads to important consequences in the legal field as well, because, as Weiss suggests, "God's sovereignty derives from his status as a creator and requires no further justification beyond sheer creatorship. The ultimate power in the universe is the power to create, and that is possessed by God alone".[27] In this scenario in which Allāh is the only creator, it can only follow "by an inexorable monotheistic logic that he is the only one to whom mankind must first turn as a source of law".[28] In the Islamic vision, Allāh is the only lawmaker and lawgiver, while man can be, depending on circumstances, an interpreter or an administrator, a researcher or an enforcer, but definitely not a legislator. In

[26] As Schuon argues, the Islamic restriction on the human images, "by eliminating certain creative possibilities, intensified others, the more so since it was accompanied by the express permission to represent plants; hence, the capital importance of arabesques, and of geometrical and botanical decorative motifs" (Frithjof Schuon, "Islamic art", in *Voices of Islam. Voices of art, beauty, and science*, vol. IV, ed. Vincent J. Cornell, Praeger, Westport-London 2007, p. 1). On Islamic aniconism, see also Hunt Janin, *The Pursuit of Learning in the Islamic World, 610-2003*, McFarland & Company, Jefferson-London 2006, pp. 184 ff. For an analysis of the relationship between Islamic and Judaic aniconism, see the classic text of Tryggve N. D. Mettinger, *No Graven Image? Israelite Aniconism in Its Ancient Near Eastern Context*, Almqvist & Wiksell International, Stockholm 1995, pp. 69–80.

[27] Bernard G. Weiss, *The Spirit of Islamic Law*, University of Georgia Press, Athens-London 1998, p. 24.

[28] Ibid.

the opposite case, man himself would challenge the divinity in his exclusive power to create, in a specific field on which Islamic nomocentrism built a relevant part of its religious, philosophical, and social architecture: the field of *sharīʿa* and of juridical sciences.

Therefore, in order to understand a major divergence between the Western and Islamic legal conceptions, it is necessary to analyze the role of reason in lawmaking, with a specific reference to the power to *create* legal norms.

4.3 *Law*, Sharīʿa, Qānūn: *A Question of Reason*

4.3.1 Law and Reason in the West

The analysis of the role played by human reason in conceiving the juridical phenomenon involves a number of different disciplines and doctrines, and can be regarded as an essential philosophical question, examined in order to understand the structural elements of a given legal conception. Ultimately, it is this issue that shapes characters and limits of the juridical vision of a civilization.

In order to understand the way in which the Western world conceptualized, during the course of its history, the relationship between law and reason, it is necessary to start from the ancient Greek and Roman contexts. In the classical world, it is possible to discover a superhuman and non-revealed juridical dimension, ancestrally linked to the religious beliefs in the heathen gods and in a profound sense of cosmic order.[29] The Greek term κόσμος (*kosmos*) means order and shows the same etymological root of the verb κοσμέω (*kosmeo*), underlining the inextricable nexus between reality and the necessity of an order.[30] The legal dimension of this order is what is commonly referred to as νόμος (*nomos*), in the broadest sense of its meaning, which represents a supreme level of regulation whose provisions are not revealed to the knowledge of men but difficultly intuited by the work of omens and oracles, which sometimes disclose a ray of mysterious

[29] See Donald R. Kelly, *The Human Measure. Social Thought in the Western Legal Tradition*, Harvard University Press, Cambridge-London 1990, pp. 17–20.

[30] Cf. Paul Cartledge, *Ancient Greek Political Thought in Practice*, Cambridge University Press, Cambridge 2009, pp. 41–42.

and superior light.[31] However, this does not prevent the establishment of a human and rational level of regulation, granted by the authority of the legislators,[32] starting with Draco and his written code of laws for Athens. This human level of regulation was usually called νόμος as well, from which νόμισμα (*nomisma*), money,[33] and οἰκονομία (*oikonomiā*), economy (literally "rule of the household"),[34] derived. Mirroring the broader dichotomy between νόμος and φύσις (*physis*),[35] these two juridical plans are not always concordant. Therefore, the real existential tragedy of men, from this point of view, consists of the perception of the possible divergence between the cosmic order and the human law, and by the virtual impossibility of their perfect coincidence and reconciliation, whose cathartic tension is admirably expressed by tragedies such as Sophocles' Antigone.[36]

In light of this, the Greek world assigns not just a contemplative role to reason but an active role as well, a role that consists of elaborating a human and autonomous level of law, whose correspondence to the mysterious

[31] It is not to be forgotten that the Greek word μυστήριον (*mystērion*) does not simply refer to an unknown object but to a revealed secret, that is to say to something unknown but that is in some way detectable. The word also refers to ancient cults of initiation, where sectarian rituals served the purpose of introducing the new candidate into a new knowledge. Moreover, it is not to be forgotten that μυστήριον, properly reinterpreted, was used to refer to the Christian Sacraments as well. On its meaning in the initiation rituals, see David Torevell, *Liturgy and the Beauty of the Unknown. Another Place*, Routledge, London-New York 2007, ch. 5.

[32] With regard to the legislators as individuals concretely operating on norms, especially in the thought of Aristotle, see Dario Ventura, *Giustizia e costituzione in Aristotele*, Franco Angeli, Milan 2009, pp. 80–81, 105–117.

[33] This latter term is relevant because, as the Philosopher explains in *Nicomachean Ethics* (V, 1133b 1), its derivation from νόμος stresses the human rational and conventional element in establishing it and giving it significance and value.

[34] Another possible translation is "household management", furtherly emphasizing the normative dimension of the Greek suffix *-nomiā*, denoting something inherent not just to the domain of God but to the concrete managerial skills of humans as well. On this term and on its possible meanings and usages, see Giorgio Agamben, *Il Regno e la Gloria Per una Genealogia Teologica dell'Economia e del Governo*, Neri Pozza, Milan 2007, pp. 31–64.

[35] On the νόμος-φύσις discourse from a juridical point of view, see Carl Joachim Friedrich [1958], *The Philosophy of Law in Historical Perspective*, The University of Chicago Press, Chicago-London 1963, pp. 13 ff.

[36] For the juridical implications in the tragedy of Antigone, see François Ost, *Raconter la loi. Aux surces de l'imaginaire juridique*, Odile Jacob, Paris 2004, pp. 162–203; Giovanni Magrì, "Giustizia", in *Luoghi della filosofia del diritto. Idee, strutture, mutamenti*, ed. Bruno Montanari, Giappichelli, Turin 2012, pp. 70–76.

and hidden principles of the νόμος charges it with a relevant political and moral responsibility. Aristotle pointed out the nexus between law and reason, by stating that for, in particular law, it should be understood that the "written law in accordance with which a state is administered",[37] consecrating with its famous phrase, "law is understanding without desire",[38] the union between law and reason.

In the Roman world, the great distinction is made between the broader concept of *jus*, denoting the overall legal order as shaped and conceived by Rome from ancestral times, and the concept of *lex*, as a precise instrument with a precise characterization. According to Gaius, *lex est quod populus iubet atque constituit*,[39] identifying the original element of the law in the rational will of men, while even the idea of a natural law, which is common to all men, is based on *naturalis ratio*.[40] Even more clearly, Cicero states that *lex* is nothing other than *recta ratio*, which is regarded as a common feature of men and gods, who could be considered as associates to the rational production of laws.[41] Therefore, in the Roman view, reason plays a major role in constructing and defining the juridical architecture of the ancient world, entrusting to human rationality the considerable task—not to be taken for granted—of *making* laws and *producing* norms.

With the advent of Christianity, the superhuman and divine dimension that characterized the νόμος came to be revealed in the incarnated λόγος (*Logos*), the person of Jesus Christ. The very term λόγος, as expressed in the previously mentioned prologue of saint John's Gospel, recalls a supreme rationality, which came to communicate itself to mankind through the historical event of the incarnation, thus acquiring a physical,

[37] Aristotle, *Rhetoric* 1373b (trans. John Henry Freese, William Heineman publisher, London 1926, p. 107).

[38] Aristotle, *Politics*, III, 1287a.32 (trans. C. D. C. Reeve, Hackett Publishing Company, Indianapolis-Cambridge 1998, p. 97).

[39] Gaius, *Gai Institutionum Commentarii Quattuor*, I, 3.

[40] Ibid., I, 1.

[41] "Est igitur, quoniam nihil est ratione melius, eaque <est> et in homine et in deo, prima homini cum deo rationis societas. Inter quos autem ratio, inter eosdem etiam recta ratio [et] communis est: quae cum sit lex, lege quoque consociati homines cum dis putandi sumus". ("And therefore, since there is nothing better than reason, and it is found both in humans and in god, reason forms the first bond between human and god. And those who share reason also share right reason; and since that is law, we humans must be considered to be closely allied to gods by law".) Marcus Tullius Cicero [c. 52 BCE], *De Legibus*, I, 23, English excerpt from *On the Commonwealth and On the Laws*, ed. James E. G. Zetzel, Cambridge University Press, Cambridge 1999, p. 113.

and consequently detectable, nature. In the Christian world, with special regard to medieval Europe, Christ as mediator between heaven and earth constitutes a bridge between the rationality of God and the rationality of men, with the latter participating with the former, with Christ representing the joining link between humanity and the divine.

In early medieval Europe, this consideration for human reason is evident in the progressive systematization of the law of barbarian populations, as in the case of the Edict of Rothari of AD 643, in which the authority of the Lombard king enacts a written regulation marking it with its authorship. From a theoretical point of view, in the following centuries, this point was made clearer. In the scholarly debate about the law, the issue regarding human reason, and more in general the role of man within the legal order, becomes central. As it has already been observed, medieval society is one in which multiple levels of orders coexist and live together, ideally constituting a universal harmony. Among these various levels, man can establish his own norms to regulate society, acting as a rational being and concretely intervening in the shaping of the legal order. The involvement of man in the production of laws and regulations is more or less explicitly acknowledged by relevant authors, such as saint Thomas Aquinas and Duns Scotus. In the debate between Scotus and Aquinas, the former considers God's will to be the ultimate source of law,[42] while Thomas considers it to be God's reason. In spite of the concrete theological and anthropological consequences of the two stances, both positions do not preclude the possibility for men to be authors of an autonomous level of regulation, distinct from God's. Scotus, for instance, acknowledges the possibility of the law being "in the agent's power, so that the law is correct only because the agent has established it",[43] and that is a case both applicable to God's laws and to man's own regulations. From this point of view, human law is simply defined as "law of the king",[44] almost taking for granted not just its existence but also its legitimacy. Regardless of the

[42] On this point, see Etienne Gilson, *John Duns Scotus. Introduction to His Fundamental Positions*, trans. James Colbert, T&T Clark, London-New York 2019, pp. 479 ff. In the words of Duns Scotus, "some general laws that dictate correctly are pre-established by the divine will, and not indeed by the divine intellect as it precedes an act of the divine will" (John Duns Scotus [c. 1300–1308], *Ordinatio* I, d. 44, q. un., translation from, *Selected Writings on Ethics*, trans. Thomas Williams, Oxford University Press, Oxford 2017, p. 96).

[43] Duns Scotus, *Ordinatio* I, d. 44, q. un., trans. from *Selected Writings on Ethics*, *cit.*, p. 96.

[44] Id, *Ordinatio* IV, d. 15, q. 2, n. 80, trans from ibid., p. 272.

substantive contents of the rules man gives to society—that is, their potential contrariety to God's laws—this represents once again the admission of man being effectively an active part in the establishment of a legal order.

In this context, Scholasticism came to be a major philosophical current theorizing the use of reason in understating God, thanks to a new reading of ancient and classical philosophy, with special regard to Aristotle. The juridical implications, as evident, are enormous. Thomas Aquinas, while theorizing four normative dimensions, recognized the role of human reason in elaborating and producing law, with reference to the earthly dimension of *lex humana*.[45] According to Aquinas, law "is an ordination of reason for the common good by one who has the care of the community, and promulgated".[46] Reason, in this perspective, is not simply charged with detecting the traces of a superhuman order but plays a creative role in what can be regarded as the *production* of law. The act of promulgation, regarded by St. Thomas as necessary and constitutive of human law, represents the necessary consequence of a conception in which legislative production belongs to man, who elaborates on it and then seals it with a legitimizing act. Therefore, it is man who appears to be charged with the

[45] Saint Thomas addresses this issue in his treatise on law in *Summa Theologiae* [1265–1274], where he states that "law is a rule and measure of acts that induces persons to act or refrain from acting. For law [Lat.: *lex*] is derived from binding [Lat.: *ligare*] because law obliges persons to act. And the rule and measure of human acts is reason, which is the primary source of human acts, as is evident from what I have said before. For it belongs to reason to order us to our end, which is the primary source regarding our prospective action, as the Philosopher says. And the source in any kind of thing is the measure and rule of that kind of thing (e.g., units in numbers and first movements in movements). And so we conclude that law belongs to reason" (Thomas Aquinas [1265–1274], *Summa Theologiae*, I-II, q. 90, art. 1). Thomas remarks the point, highlighting that "law in the strict sense primarily and chiefly regards ordaining things for the common good. But ordaining things for the common good belongs either to the whole people or to persons acting in the name of the whole people. And so lawmaking belongs either to the whole people or to a public personage who has the care of the whole people. For also in all other matters, ordaining things for ends belongs to those to whom the ends belong" (*Summa Theologiae*, I-II, q. 90, art. 3). The translations come from *Treatise on Law*, trans. Richard J. Regan, Hackett Publishing Company, Indianapolis-Cambridge 2000, pp. 1, 4–5. For a commentary on the Aquinas' conception of the nexus law-reason, see Brendan F. Brown, "The Influence of St. Thomas Aquinas on Jurisprudence", in *The Catholic Lawyer*, vol. III, n. 4, art. 11, Queens, Autumn 1957, pp. 356–364.

[46] "Et sic ex quatuor praedictis potest colligi definitio legis, quae nihil est aliud quam quaedam rationis ordinatio ad bonum commune, ab eo qui curam communitatis habet, promulgata". Thomas Aquinas, *Summa Theologiae*, I-II, q. 90, art. 4. The translation comes from *Treatise on Law*, *cit.*, p. 6.

burden of *creating* a system of law in accordance with the Christian revelation and with the superhuman dimensions of *lex æterna*, *lex divina*, and *lex naturalis*. This does not imply a positivization of the legal system, which constitutes a much later phenomenon, but on the contrary implies the involvement of man, as a rational actor, in establishing a legal order in which the agent is not simply an executor but also an author.

This responsibility, together with the Christian conception of free will, fundamentally constitutes an autonomous space for human rationality in producing law, which can follow God's teaching, but in any case needs to pass through human elaboration, and be authored by the means of human reason.[47] Here, reason does not simply derive legal provisions from a superior and given divine-based law but is legitimated in creating an autonomous form of legislation.[48] In this context, pre-Christian Roman law was incorporated in the organic medieval corpus of the *jus commune*, as an expression of perfect and functional juridical rationality, once again anchoring the two dimensions of law and reason, with reason being considered as a constituting element of law.

After the dissolution of the medieval unity and with the rupture of the concord of the Catholic Powers, the conception of law underwent a relevant shift; nevertheless, it maintained itself fundamentally unaltered with regard to the nexus between law and reason. With the artificial "machine" of the modern State or the "artificial man" borrowing a Hobbesian

[47] Stating that human reason actively participates to the reason of God doesn't mean that the rationality of men simply derives his prerogatives from the divine one, but that human reason is *per se* legitimated to develop an autonomous narrative. With regard to law, and as exhaustively explained by Coughlin, "Thomas held that positive law based on human reason participates in the divine law present in the mind of God" (John J. Coughlin, *Law, Person, and Community. Philosophical, Theological, and Comparative Perspectives on Canon Law*, Oxford University Press, New York 2012, p. 65).

[48] It is interesting to compare this point to Thomas' view on determinism. As it has been observed, according to the Aquinas, "Nature has laws, and God is their source; they are created and furnished with things. The determinism of laws is providential" (Patrick Halligan [1988], "The Environmental Policy of Saint Thomas Aquinas", in *Aquinas and Modern Law*, eds. Richard O. Brooks, James Bernard Murphy, Routledge, London-New York 2016, p. 497). Similarly, man is created in God's image, and his rationality is capable not just of understanding but also of establishing an autonomous level of law, determined by its condition as a rational creature. However, given man's free will, determinism cannot be accepted at the point of depriving man of its capacity of regulating society, with all the consequences this implies. On the Aquinas' view on determinism and free will, see James F. Keenan, s.j., *Goodness and Rightness in Thomas Aquinas's Summa Theologiae*, Georgetown University Press, Washington 1992, pp. 45 ff.

imaginary, the complexity of the multilevel legal order that characterized medieval Europe was basically absorbed by the unitary sovereignty of the Leviathan, unique and ultimate source of law. Once again, in the State-based political model law is conceived as a product of human reason, anchored to the will of the sovereign, as an expression of its volitional rationality. In this context, what the sovereign commands becomes law, with a relevant simplification with respect to the medieval order but with the maintenance of the link between law and human reason.

Even with regard to the conception of natural law, whose origin is identified in nature, thus in a trans-human dimension, law is theorized as being based on rationality. Even natural law, in fact, needs a human author to elaborate and construct a system of laws, although inspired by natural principles. With regard to this, it should not be forgotten what Grotius stated, defining law as *dicatmen rectae rationis*,[49] thus eminently inherent to the rational sphere of the human intellect.

In the following centuries, the Western conception of law changed considerably with reference to various issues, such as judicial interpretation and the legal monopoly of the State in producing law. However, that the juridical phenomenon belonged to the domain of human rationality represented a constant element in the progressive legal elaboration which characterized the West in its modern era.

The aforementioned conception, which binds law to rationality, does not mean that the production of Western law has not been influenced by superhuman inspirations and religious influxes. During the centuries of its history, the West has shaped its juridical corpus of normative rules and acts in accordance with ancestral cultural elements and persistent religious beliefs, such as its Christian and Roman heritages, which deeply influenced the Occidental juridical discourse. However, this persistence of influences and inspirations does not put into question the entitlement of human reason in producing and elaborating law, whatever the punctual content of a given legislation. It is necessary, with regard to this point, to distinguish between the substantive content of legal provisions and the perceived

[49] Hugo Grotius [1625], *De jure belli ac pacis libri tres,* I, 1, X. According to Grotius, "Natural right is the rule and dictate of right reason, shewing the moral deformity or moral necessity there is in any act, according to its suitableness or unsuitableness to a reasonable nature, and consequently, that such an act is either forbid or commanded by God, the author of nature". The translation comes from *The Rights of War and Peace*, trans. Jean Barbeyrac, ed. Richard Tuck, Liberty Fund, Indianapolis 2005, pp. 150–151.

origin of normativity in a certain conception. Catholic canon law, for instance, represents the most evident example of a religious-based legislation, whose production is however demanded by the rationality of human legislators, and is not conceived as a divinely written corpus of norms and rules, although inspired by religious dictamens.[50] The mediation of the human element, which in the Christian view mirrors the mediation of Christ, is indeed constitutive of law, whatever the source of its inspiration.[51]

A structural element of the Western conception of law, therefore, is the entitlement of human rationality of the responsibility of producing and organizing law, which is not considered as something whose exclusive and distinguishing origin is to be researched elsewhere. To summarize, and as Sir Coke stated, "reason is the life of the law", while law "is the perfection of reason".[52]

4.3.2 Reason, *Sharīʿa*, and *Fiqh* in Islam

In the Islamic legal conception, reason is given a relevant role to play, which is however very different in respect to the role it plays in the Western view. In Islam, the role of human reason is considered neither creative nor productive but eminently deductive. Jurist hermeneutics indeed acquires a central importance in the Islamic world, far greater than in other legal order. In order to examine this latter point, it is once again necessary to

[50] With regard to this it is worth remembering that the very nature of Catholic canon law "reflects the nature of the Church: *it is truly human* because the Church is a human community; *it has an affinity with the divine* because it is an integral part of the Church as sacrament. In the law itself, human prudence blends with divine wisdom in a close union but without confusion. This complex nature gives to canon law its incarnation character" (Ladislas M. Orsy, s.j., "Theology and Canon Law", in *New Commentary on the Code of Canon Law*, eds. John P. Beal, James A. Coriden, Thomas J. Green, Paulist Press, New York-Mahwah 2000, p. 2).

[51] The concept of Christ as mediator between the reason of man and the reason of God, although not specifically referred to the legal field, has been exhaustively approached by Ratzinger in his reflection on Christian faith and reason. According to Ratzinger, "the faith of the Church has always insisted that between God and us, between his eternal Creator Spirit and our created reason there exists a real analogy" (Joseph A. Ratzinger [H. H. Benedict XVI], "Faith, Reason and the University Memories and Reflections", *lectio magistralis* given at the Aula Magna of the University of Regensburg, September 12th, 2006, published in *Islamic Studies*, vol. XLV, n. 4, Islamic Research Institute, International Islamic University, Islamabad 2006, p. 599).

[52] Edward Coke [1628], *The First Part of the Institutes of the Laws of England*, vol. I, J. & W. T. Clarke *et al.*, London 1832, p. 97b.

distinguish between *sharīʿa* and *fiqh*, of whom a distinction has already been mentioned in the premises of this book.

Sharīʿa, in its divine origin and conception, is ideally to be considered transcendent, immutable,[53] and metahistorical. With the last qualification I refer to the fact that *sharīʿa* embodies an idea of normativity that is established exclusively by the divinity and thus collocated in a conceptual dimension beyond human history and beyond space and time. From this point of view, it transcends the borders of the concrete human experience and cannot be considered "incarnated" in history just as the *Verbum Dei* of the Christian world. This peculiar conception of normativity refers to what Allāh forbids, commands, suggests, and belongs to the sphere of the divine will, which can never be completely known to men, except by the means of the Muḥammadan revelation. Human reason, necessarily, does not play any role in the creation of *sharīʿa*, which is entirely conceived of by Allāh in his transcendence, and is totally absorbed by the divinity. In the Sunnī perspective, the absence of human mediation between men and God is reflected in the juridical discourse: there can be no mediation of reason in *creating* law while detecting the signs of a superior good, because *sharīʿa*, as supreme normativity, has already been set forth by Allāh in the dimension of eternity.[54]

Human reason, on the contrary, plays an essential role with regard to *fiqh*, which is, as already said, the corpus of provisions and opinions

[53] The qualifications of *sharīʿa* as being transcendent and immutable are shared by Salim as well (Arskal Salim, *Challenging the Secular State. The Islamization of Law in Modern Indonesia*, University of Hawai'i Press, Honolulu 2008, p. 12). However, while his definition of *fiqh* as mutable is entirely sharable, the qualification of the same concept as temporal can be misleading, for the reasons that will be explained in the next chapter of this book.

[54] The exclusive authorship of Allāh in creating and establishing the "laws" of *sharīʿa* is common to Shīʿa Islam as well, notwithstanding its different approach to human mediation. With regard to Allāh being the only origin of law from the perspective of Shīʿa, it is possible to recall the words of Ayatollah Khomeini, who stated that "in Islam the legislative power and competence to establish laws belongs exclusively to God Almighty. The Sacred Legislator of Islam is the sole legislative power. No one has the right to legislate and no law may be executed except the law of the Divine Legislator". Ruhollah Khomeini [1970], *Islamic Government. Governance of the Jurist*, trans. Hamid Algar, The Institute of Compilation and Publication of Imam Khomeini's Works, Tehran 2002, p. 53. Moreover, it is worth noting that in Islam "there is no authority – person or assembly [personal or institutional] invested with the power to create a juridical norm; in fact, not even to simply modify a rule [which is] in force since ten centuries. The idea of law, in its Western sense is unknown here" (Y. Linant De Bellefonds, "The Formal Sources of Islamic Law", trans. M. Khalid Mas'ud, in *Islamic Studies*, vol. XV, n. 3, Autumn 1976, p. 189).

descending from *sharīʿa* and derived from the various "roots", as recognized by the major Sunnī legal schools. In order to simplify, it is possible to state that *fiqh* is the way in which the eternal and immutable *sharīʿa* is understood,[55] and then transposed by juridical interpreters into concrete norms and rules, and translated from the divine transcendence, in which *sharīʿa* is originated, into the concrete reality, in which it is applied. While Allāh creates law, the jurist understands it.[56] The Muslim jurists, as shown by the etymology of their Arabic name (*fuqahā*), are "those who comprehend" and represent indeed an élite class in charge of systematizing a legal order based on the idea of deductive comprehension. As Hallaq points out, "legal practitioners and jurists constituted likewise an *epistemic* community, which was systematically engaged on a hermeneutical level".[57] In this context, the roots of *fiqh* represent the means by which concrete rules of conduct are provided in this complex process of legal derivation.[58]

[55] As it has been stated, "Sharia is the law itself whereas *fiqh* is the knowledge of that law" (Niaz A. Shah, *Islamic Law and the Law of Armed Conflict. The Conflict in Pakistan*, Routledge, London-New York 2011, pp. 12–13).

[56] Vogel remarkably synthetizes this point, stating that "law is perfect but humans are not. Mankind struggles to learn the sharīʿa from the Qur'an and sunna" (Frank E. Vogel, *Islamic Law and Legal System. Studies of Saudi Arabia*, Brill, Leiden-Boston-Köln 2000, p. 4).

[57] Wael B. Hallaq, "Can Shariʿa Be Restored?", in *Islamic Law and the Challenges of Modernity*, eds. Yvonne Yazbeck Haddad, Barbara Freyer Stowasser, AltaMira Press, Walnut Creek 2004, p. 41.

[58] It could be argued that the process by which *fiqh* is derived is actually a process of law-making and legislative production. However, in the Islamic view, the only origin of law is to be considered Allāh and the only straight path to follow the *sharīʿa*. While from a practical point of view we can state that elaborating *fiqh* means producing *jus*, it is not equivalent to creating *lex*. In my work, I will focus on the Islamic perspective of the juridical phenomenon, that is to say how the Islamic tradition conceived its idea of normativity to shape a comprehensive legal order. The point is highlighted by Khadduri, according to whom *fiqh* represented the answer to the practical need of other rules and norms that were not contained in the *Qur'ān*, however without contradicting the premises of Allāh as the sole legislator. The necessity of bringing about further juridical responses to the pragmatical exigences of the community, therefore, did not cause the introduction of a human and autonomous level of legislation, but the elaboration of *fiqh*, with the aforementioned philosophical implications, which could not be considered as a contradiction to the divine authorship of law (on this, see Majid Khadduri [1955], "International Law", in *Law in the Middle East*, vol. I, *Origin and Development of Islamic Law*, eds. Majid Khadduri, Herbert J. Liebesny, The Lawbook Exchange, Clark 2009, p. 352). Therefore, and precisely for the different theorization of human reason in its relationship with the legal order, any conceptual equation between *fiqh* and (Western) law (for instance, Salim, *Challenging the Secular State*, *cit.*, p. 12) is not sharable.

Consequently, while *sharīʿa* never differs depending on space and time, *fiqh* can considerably vary between *maḏāhib* and jurists. For instance, it is worth remembering that while the *Qur'ān* and *sunnah* are unanimously recognized as roots of *fiqh*, thus ideally universally accepted, the composition of *sunnah* as for the authenticity of the various *ʾaḥādīth* is highly debated, with a consequent and considerable variation in the rules derived from it. Again, as mentioned, there is no unanimity in the Sunnī *maḏāhib* as for the extent at which *ijmāʿ* (consensus) and *qiyās* (analogical deduction) can be accepted and practiced, while the incorporation of *ʿurf* (custom) is even more controversial. These tools provide great flexibility to a normative world that is basically juristic in its epistemological work of constant research and that flourished in variety and richness, with no univocal definition as for its contents.

This being said, the role human reason plays in the Islamic legal order differs significantly from the role it plays in the West. While in the Western conception the role of reason is creative, thus entitled to produce and create law, in the science of Islamic *fiqh* the role of reason is deductive.

In the conception of Islamic normativity, human rationality is not legitimated to *produce* legal provisions, while, in the juridical field, it is entitled to *derive* concrete rules from a normative dimension—*sharīʿa*—whose divine author lies beyond historical and physical reality. Therefore, it is not a process by which jurists grasp the traces of a divine and universal good and consequently elaborate and produce law, such as in the classic Western world, neither is it the process of legislation that characterized State-based systems: rather, it is a derivative process,[59] in which the jurist deduces, and

[59] In the words of al-Shāfiʿī, in summarizing the roots and the attitude of human reason toward them: "Certain traditions have come from the Apostle on these matters for which there are no specific texts in the Qur'an, but the Apostle has specified on God's behalf the meaning intended by Him, while the Muslims provided a number of derivative rules on which the Apostle laid down no specific sunna" (Muhammad ibn Idrīs al-Shāfiʿī, *al-Risāla fī Uṣūl al-Fiqh (Treatise on the Foundations of Islamic Jurisprudence)*, trans. Majid Khadduri, Islamic Texts Society, Cambridge 1997, p. 149). For a comprehensive analysis on the process of derivation of legal norms from the sources, see Serdar Kurnaz, *Methoden zur Normderivation im islamischen Recht. Eine Rekonstruktion der Methoden zur Interpretation autoritativer textueller Quellen bei ausgewählten islamischen Rechtsschulen*, EB Verlag, Berlin 2016.

not produces, and in which the jurist understands, and does not create. Hence, the roots of *fiqh* represent the tools with which the jurist operates in order to accomplish the course of his rational derivation, by which it is possible to derive the known from the unknown.

The rational effort of the qualified interpreter[60] is *ijtihād*, whose conception can actually aid in grasping the effective role of reason in the Muslim legal discourse. *Ijtihād* is a concept that refers to independent reasoning,[61] which cannot be actuated in the presence of other authoritative and exhaustive means of derivation of concrete provisions, such as the *Qur'ān* and *sunnah*. From this point of view, *ijtihād* is an instrument at the disposal of the jurist, but as any instrument, *ijtihād* tends to an end, which in this case is identified with the comprehension of *sharīʿa*. Therefore, *ijtihād* has to be regarded as the major expression of human reason in the Islamic tradition: reason, in this case, makes an effort in determining what can be derived from the will of Allāh, and, in the case of

[60] I specify here *qualified* interpreter, because the performance of this rational effort presupposes the ability of performing it correctly, thus a certain knowledge in the Islamic legal field. However, in classical Islam the debate was particularly vivid as for who could be considered entitled to the right of exercising *ijtihād*. On this last point, see Taha Jabir Al-Alwani, *Issues in Contemporary Islamic Thought*, The International Institute of Islamic Thought, London-Washington 2005, pp. 102–106.

[61] It should be noted that, following Schacht's pioneering opinion, in literature a recurring statement is that "the gates of *ijtihād* are closed" since the tenth century, due to the number of legal opinions produced in the past and to the non-necessity to give innovative and different interpretations to cases that are to be considered already solved. For an in-depth analysis on this concept, see Joseph Schacht, *An Introduction to Islamic Law*, Oxford University Press, Oxford 1964, pp. 69–75; Intisar A. Rabb, "Ijtihād" (voice), in *The Oxford Encyclopedia of the Modern Islamic World*, vol. II, ed. John L. Esposito, Oxford University Press, Oxford 1995, pp. 179 ff.; more briefly, see Cyril Glassé [1989], *The New Encyclopedia of Islam*, Altamira Press, Walnut Creek-London 2002, p. 209. The view regarding the closure of the gates of *ijtihād* has been however challenged by some scholars such as Hallaq (Wael B. Hallaq, "Was the Gate of Ijtihad Closed?", in *International Journal of Middle East Studies*, vol. XVI, n. 1, March 1984, pp. 3–41). In contemporary societies, liberal thinkers refer to *ijtihād* to justify evolutive interpretations and innovative conceptions, even in the interactions between *sharīʿa* and the constitutional State. On the use of *ijtihād* in the contemporary Muslim contexts as an instrument of legal innovation, see the work of L. Ali Khan, Hisham M. Ramadan, *Contemporary Ijtihad. Limits and Controversies*, Edinburgh University Press, Edinburgh 2011, especially pp. 80 ff.

necessity, in filling gaps and investigating his silence.[62] Obviously, this operation charges the interpreter with a relevant amount of responsibility,[63] in that exercising *ijtihād* improperly may eventually lead to a concrete *creation* of legal norms, thus exercising something that is exclusively a divine prerogative. This necessarily implies a constant swinging between opposite choices, following the opinions of the predecessors or, on the contrary, opening the way to new interpretations.[64] This responsibilization of the interpreter is also mirrored in the case of misjudgment, where human reason mediates between divine will and its concrete application.[65] Therefore, *ijtihād* cannot be considered an autonomous power to create law but as the tendency of reason to systematize legal provisions from a superhuman dimension. Human reason, in the exercise of *ijtihād*, is not enabled to act freely according to its own discretion but on the contrary must follow the guidance of the divine revelation, thus referring to specific indications and evidence.[66]

[62] This rational effort cannot be applied in the presence of a clear provision present in the *Qur'ān* or in the *sunnah* but represents a possible resource only in case of silence of the main roots. Therefore, an essential dimension of *ijtihād* relies in its usage aimed at understanding an unknown object, which only Allāh knows. Thus, the extremely close relationship between *ijtihād* and analogy emerges. Again, in the words of al-Shāfiʿī "one is under an obligation to exercise ijtihad only in the search for an unknown object. If one does so, he would be right by doing what he was obligated to do. This is right for him on the basis of the literal meaning [of the text]; only God knows the implicit meaning" (al-Shāfiʿī, *al-Risāla*, *cit.*, p. 300).

[63] For a reflection on proper and improper use of *ijtihād*, see Said Shabbar, *Ijtihad and Renewal*, The International Institute of Islamic Thought, London-Washington 2008, p. 11. While not anybody is considered entitled of engaging in *ijtihād*, the Islamic legal tradition usually regards positively a jurist performing *ijtihād* in good faith, although coming to wrong legal conclusions. This last position, however, is not univocally recognized.

[64] Regarding this, the concepts of *muʿāraḍa* (opposition, contradiction) and *tarǧīḥ* (consideration, measurement) are emblematic, highlighting the juristic necessity of adapting the rational effort to a changing reality. On this last point, see Ulrich Rebstock, "Abwägen als Entscheidungshilfe in den „uṣūl al-fiqh". Die Anfänge der „tarǧīḥ"-Methode bei al-Ǧaṣṣāṣ", in *Der Islam. Zeitschrift für Geschichte und Kultur des islamischen Orients*, vol. LXXX, n. 1, 2003, pp. 110–121.

[65] On this specific case, see the exhaustive work of Ulrich Rebstock, "A Qāḍī's Errors", in *Islamic Law and Society*, vol. VI, n. 1, 1999, pp. 1–37.

[66] Reason is considered here to be a gift from Allāh but once again aimed at understanding an objective reality from a subjective viewpoint and not at creating new rules and norms in the absence of indications. To summarize, "God, Glorified and Praised be He, has endowed men with reason by which they can distinguish between differing viewpoints, and He guides them to the truth either by [explicit] texts or by indications [on the strength of which they exercise ijtihad]" (al-Shāfiʿī, *al-Risāla, cit.*, p. 302).

Every instrument that can potentially be considered a vehicle of legal change and innovation, such as the notions of *istiḥsān* (discretion)[67] or *maṣlaḥa* (public interest),[68] is destined to represent a source of debate and controversy, challenging the ideal principle according to which the jurist can reach knowledge of a normative preexisting content, however without altering it. Such a controversy, necessarily, "centers on whether or not the human intellect is able to discern *maṣlaḥah* without concrete textual indication (*dalīl*) in the revealed sources",[69] therefore highlighting a

[67] Literally meaning "considering something good", *istiḥsān* refers to a juridical operation by which a Muslim jurist, in the understanding of *sharīʿa*, chooses a (derivative) rule among various possibilities, departing from previously derived rules and even against the principle of analogical deduction. As evident, it represents a particular use of human reason, in which the subjective judgment is particularly involved. Therefore, this possibility is considered something to deal with in an extremely cautious way, avoiding the risk of expressing "creative" positions not supported by any evidence in the roots of *fiqh*. The exercise of *istiḥsān*, aside from the various positions admitting or rejecting it, aims in any case at understanding the superior reality of *sharīʿa*, thus not *producing* law as in the Western perspective. Notwithstanding the flexibility of this idea, some classical jurists, like al-Shāfiʿī himself, expressed extremely critical positions about the use of *istiḥsān*, considering it like being wandering without a guidance: "ijtihad should not be exercised except for a specific object, and the object must be something definite that can be determined by means of evidence or resemblance to an established object. Thus, it should be clear that it is unlawful for anyone to exercise istihsan whenever it is not called for by a narrative, whether the narrative is a text of the Qur'an or a sunna, by virtue of which an [unknown] object is sought" (al-Shāfiʿī, *al-Risāla*, *cit.*, p. 304). For a monographic study on this concept, see Saim Kayadibi, *Istiḥsan. The Doctrine of Juristic Preference in Islamic Law*, Islamic Book Trust, Kuala Lumpur 2010, especially pp. 30–33, 57 ff. On this concept as an innovative instrument in the Islamic legal tradition, with a marked character of flexibility, see Haim Gerber, *Islamic Law and Culture, 1600–1840*, Brill, Leiden-Boston-Köln 1999, pp. 92–104. In literature, *istiḥsān* has sometimes been compared to equity (cf. Rakesh Kumar Singh, *Textbook on Muslim Law*, Universal Law Publishing, New Delhi 2011, p. 41); however, Makdisi correctly puts in light the inconsistency of this equation, based on the inexistence in the Islamic legal tradition of concepts such as natural law, on whose ground the idea of equity has been built (see John Makdisi, "Legal Logic and Equity in Islamic Law", in *The American Journal of Comparative Law*, vol. XXXIII, n 1, Winter 1985, pp. 63–92). Somehow close to the concept of *istiḥsān* are the controversial concepts of *istiṣlāḥ*, based on the idea of public interest (*maṣlaḥa*), and *istidlāl*, based on juridical inference. However, and notwithstanding their importance, the analysis of these instruments of comprehension, and of the debates surrounding their possible use, falls outside of the scope of this work.

[68] For a dedicated analysis, see Felicitas Opwis, *Maṣlaḥa and the Purpose of the Law. Islamic Discourse on Legal Change from the 4th/10th to 8th/14th Century*, Brill, Leiden 2010.

[69] Jonathan G. Ercanbrack, *The Transformation of Islamic Law in Global Financial Markets*, Cambridge University Press, Cambridge 2015, p. 35.

permanent and recurring tension in the Islamic legal conception, that is to say: the tension between the foundational principles of the legal order, involving a certain vision of legal anthropology, and the concrete necessities of change and innovations that are inevitably experimented with by an evolving society.

4.3.3 The Case of *Qānūn* Between Islam and the West

With the progressive enlargement of the *ummah* of the believers and with the spread of the Islamic community from the Arabian Peninsula toward Europe, Asia, and Africa, the necessity of structuring a certain level of earthly regulation gradually emerged as an ineludible exigency. It was evident that all the complexity of governing an extended community that incorporated preexisting cultures and civilizations could not factually be reduced to the process of deriving provisions from the superhuman level of the *sharīʿa* by means of the roots of *fiqh*. For instance, it was necessary to establish taxes and tributes in the conquered territories, as well as face the challenges deriving from the economic and political administration of a *de facto* multicultural empire.[70] Therefore, a certain and further level of regulation, in response to the concrete and mutating needs of the community, appeared to be necessary. However, given the complex legal order shaped by the Islamic society, divine in its origin but earthly in its systematization, the initial premises of the nature of *sharīʿa* and the role of man could not be eluded. In order to answer this pragmatical need the concept of *qānūn* was elaborated.

Qānūn refers to a human level of political regulation[71] by means of which a Muslim ruler carried out the administration of the community in domains not covered by the *sharīʿa* and its consequent legal opinions and rules.[72] This sort of administrative level of regulation, which came to

[70] Cf. Sami Zubaida, *Law and Power in the Islamic World*, I.B. Tauris, New York 2003, pp. 107 ff.

[71] Heyd's definition of this concept, that is to say a "law of human origin", highlights the distinction between it and *sharīʿa* with specific regard to its origin, rather than to its substantial content. See Uriel Heyd, "Ḳānūn and Sharīʿa in old Ottoman criminal justice", in *Proceedings*, vol. III, n. 1, Israel Academy of Sciences and Humanities, Jerusalem 1967, pp. 9–10.

[72] See Boğaç A. Ergene, "Qanun and Sharia", in *The Ashgate Research Companion to Islamic Law*, eds. Rudolph Peters, Peri Bearman, Ashgate, Farnham-Burlington 2014, p. 109–122.

discipline areas such as taxation and criminal repression, constituted a kind of parallel regulatory level, whose characters resemble the features of Western law, with particular regard to the role of human rationality. Especially in the Ottoman empire, it introduced a kind of inequal legal dualism: *qānūn* could never be in contrast with *sharīʿa* and could never be concurrent with it in the same fields of application on an equal stance. This particular form of regulation is indeed to be considered as a manmade law, elaborated by the political authority and belonging to the field of administrative discretion, however circumscribed to fields where the sciences of *fiqh* did not provide answers. Based on this, the conceptual equivalent of law in a Muslim context is not *sharīʿa*, nor can it be *fiqh*, but, with all due approximation, it could be *qānūn*.

The original and constituent element of *qānūn* belongs therefore to the sphere of rationality, while the origin of *sharīʿa* is to be identified with the will of the divinity. Nowadays, while *sharīʿa* is still present in a great number of Muslim legal systems,[73] the original understanding of *qānūn* was abandoned and substantially replaced by secular laws and regulations as imported from the Western world. However, traces of the conceptual distinction between the two ideas are still visible in some legal systems, where the formal legislative acts of the sovereign power cannot be properly named as law—with consideration for the traditional impossibility for the Islamic ruler to create law—but rather as decree or ordonnance,[74] just as the old *qānūn* could not be equated to *sharīʿa*.

The introduction of *qānūn* does not actually invalidate what has been said with regard to the deductive role of human reason with respect to the systematization of *sharīʿa* and its translation into concrete rules and

[73] I will come back to this point in Chap. 5, providing an overview of the various ways in which *sharīʿa* can be incorporated in contemporary constitutional systems.

[74] The most relevant case is the Saudi legal system, where the equivalents of Western laws are called *niẓām* (pl. *ʾanẓima*), because the very basis of Saudi legal model is said to be the Islamic *sharīʿa*, as stated in its *de facto* constitution, known as Basic Law of Governance (1992). Therefore, the Saudi system cannot enact properly nominated laws, but only royal decrees, considered to be administrative acts somehow conceptually comparable to the ancient *qānūn* in its relationship with *sharīʿa*. The same be said about the already mentioned Saudi Basic Law, which is a form of supreme *niẓām*, but cannot be considered as a constitution. A similar situation is present in the sultanate of Oman, with regard to the royal decrees functioning as laws, however without being addressed to as such.

norms. Even if it seems an apparent paradox, the parallel system of *qānūn* does not contradict the theorization of a deductive and derivative role of reason for three main reasons.

Firstly, from a historical point of view, the introduction of the concept of *qānūn* as a corpus of regulations is subsequent to the initial establishment of the *ummah* and to the progressive systematization of *sharīʿa*. The idea of a human regulation was first present in the early Abbasid period is some limited fields but was greatly accrued only after the Mongol conquest of Baghdad of 1258 and within the framework of the subsequent Turkish rule. The idea of *qānūn*, consequently, acquired a particular significance in the Ottoman sultanate, to such an extent that the Sultan Suleiman I (1494–1566) came to be known as *kanunî sultan*, for his extensive use of this kind of instrument. This represents fundamentally a part of the process of progressive transformation of the Ottoman empire into an increasingly earthly kingdom, due to the relationships with Western and non-Muslim Powers and the progressive contamination with alien juridical and political systems.[75] The concept has two main influences: on the one hand, the influence of pre-Islamic nomad populations, especially Mongols and Turks,[76] and, on the other hand, the legacy of Roman law, whose memory was still present and vivid at Constantinople after the Ottoman conquest of 1453.[77] Therefore, the idea of *qānūn* can be regarded, as for its origin, as a non-Muslim product, which was later incorporated into the Ottoman legal system. It is possible to argue, therefore,

[75]The same could be said with regard to the State-based political paradigm and a factual abandonment of the universalistic inspiration which characterized the *ummah* of the believers, notwithstanding the formal preservation of the universal idea of the caliphate up to 1924.

[76]See Ergene, *Qanun and Sharia, cit.*, pp. 109–110.

[77]With reference to the Roman element in *qānūn*, Peters correctly points out that its distinctive dimension, in opposition to *sharīʿa*, relied on the fact that the "emperor's will was one of the 'roots' of Roman law – the primary one in its latest stages of development". The author continues by highlighting that "the Ottoman sultans from Mehmed II onward did not hesitate to make such enactments, not, as they understood it, in contradiction of the sharia, but as its implementation" (Francis Edward Peters, *The Monotheists. Jews, Christians, and Muslims in Conflict and Competition*, vol. II, *The Words and Will of God*, Princeton University Press, Princeton-Oxford 2003, p. 122). An-Na'im describes eighteenth-century *qānūn* as "enacted state law [...] under European influence" (Abdullahi Ahmed An-Naʿim, *Islam and the Secular State. Negotiating the Future of Sharīʿa*, Harvard University Press, Cambridge 2008, p. 183).

that *qānūn* is not really to be considered part of the Islamic legal tradition if not for its later assimilation. More properly, it is a part of the legal framework that characterized Islamic territories, by the time in which the exclusiveness of the Islamic legal view was starting to fade out and be integrated by Occidental juridical elements. The pragmatical assimilation of *qānūn* represented a first legal contamination between the Islamic autochthonous legal view and a non-Muslim (or pre-Muslim) concept initially imported and later on incorporated by Ottoman rulers.[78] The same path was later followed by the incorporation of the Western ideas of law, State, and constitution, consequently to the processes of colonization and decolonization of Muslim territories, although it is reasonable to argue that this latter form of juridical contamination was significantly more intrusive and far-reaching.[79] The expansion of *qānūn* as a Turco-Mongol and Byzantine legacy can be regarded as a rather exhaustive signal that, in the Islamic legal vision, the ruler had been substantially deprived of the power to legislate, due to the peculiar conceptualization of the role of reason in the process of interpreting and elaborating law, with the necessity to find an answer to this essential issue outside the borders of traditional Islamic thought.[80]

Secondly, from a philosophical point of view, *qānūn* cannot be considered as an alternative form of "Islamic law". The etymology of the word comes from the Byzantine Greek κανών (*kanōn*), the origin of the Western

[78] "The systematic usage of *kanun*, along with *Sharīʿa*, by the Ottomans reflected a long tradition of state authority as the lawmaker, which can be traced back to the pre-Islamic Turkish culture that some historians argue underlies Turkey's modern secularism". An-Na'im, *Islam and the Secular State, cit.*, p. 190.

[79] Mallat suggests that the use of this rather new form of manmade legislation represented a precursor to the process of Westernization of the Ottoman empire and a first importation of Western legal elements in the Muslim juridical discourse. With regard to this, see Chibli Mallat, *Introduction to Middle Eastern Law*, Oxford University Press, Oxford-New York 2007, p. 121. On the contamination between the Ottoman legal system and the Western juridical tradition, in the context of the latest period of the sultanate, An-Na'im, *Islam and the Secular State, cit.*, pp. 191–196.

[80] As Ergene points out, the introduction of *qānūn* by the Muslim leaders was not derived from the Islamic legal vision but on the contrary represented a response to a pragmatic necessity. In the words of the author: "According to Islamic jurisprudence, canonical standards [...] regulate the entirety of public and private life. Thus, technically, political leaders do not possess any legislative authority but are responsible solely for enforcing the divine will as reflected in jurisprudential principles. In reality, however, Muslim rulers and their representatives often played important roles in shaping fiscal, administrative, and penal regulations. It is these legislative activities that constitute the basis of qanun legislation" (Ergene, *Qanun and Sharia, cit.*, p. 109).

word “canon”. The term, presumably imported by the Arabs following the Muslim conquest of Egypt and Syria, shows again a foreign and pre-Islamic origin, recalling the Byzantine legal tradition.[81] The original meaning of the term did not even refer to law but simply to the idea of measurement, with an eminently non-juridical significance. Its Greek origin, with its elaboration following an individual path of development, is once again significant in highlighting the non-Islamic nature of the concept, although subsequently reimagined to be implemented in Muslim societies. The formal distinction between the real and original Islamic idea of normativity—*sharīʿa* and *fiqh*—and the foreign concept of *qānūn* only serve to confirm that in the Islamic legal discourse, reason has a fundamentally deductive role, while human authorities cannot be properly considered as legislators. The expediency of the introduction of *qānūn* underlines the exigency of establishing a formal distinction between Islamic normativity, whose characteristics have already been mentioned, and other forms of secondary regulation, whose theorization must necessarily follow a different path of reasoning. Once again, it is possible to argue that *qānūn* found application in Islamic territories, but not as a form of Islamic normativity such as *sharīʿa*, which has to be regarded both as constitutive of the Islamic vision and constituted by it: while *qānūn* can exist autonomously in non-Muslim contexts, representing an instrument latterly introduced for pragmatic purposes in a given administrative and political body, there cannot be *sharīʿa* outside the domain of Islam and there cannot be Islam without *sharīʿa*. If qānūn is a contingent element adopted for practical reasons, *sharīʿa* is a structural dimension of Islam.

Thirdly, from a Muslim perspective the idea of *qānūn* is not perceived as juridical in nature, and its theorization is considered as alien to the legal field.[82] The juridical sciences in Islam are indeed circumscribed to the area of *sharīʿa* and the ways in which provisions and rules can be derived from it, and later applied in concrete cases. Conversely, *qānūn* represents the

[81] See Leonard Wood, “Legislation as an instrument of Islamic law”, in *The Oxford Handbook of Islamic Law*, eds. Anver M. Emon, Rumee Ahmed, Oxford University Press, Oxford 2018, p. 553.

[82] As in the case of caliphs’ authority in legal matters, see Nimrod Hurvitz, “The contribution of early Islamic rulers to adjudication and legislation: the case of the mazalim tribunals”, in *Law and Empire. Ideas, Practices, Actors*, eds. Jeroen Duindam, Jill Harries, Caroline Humfress, Nimrod Hurvitz, Koninklijke Brill, Leiden 2013, pp. 135 ff.

concrete way in which political authorities regulated society to satisfy the most basic needs of the community, however without interfering with what was really perceived as normative in its nature—*sharīʿa*.[83] An equation between *qānūn* and Western law, although potentially correct when having regard to the constitutive elements to the two concepts, should however take into account the profound difference of the context and, above all, the different perception of these two phenomena in their respective originating cultures. While the West delimited the field of what it perceived as juridical according to its own criteria, the Islamic world did the same from its own specific perspective. As a result, the two delimitations of what is considered as inherent to the legal order are not superimposable, and the idea of *qānūn* falls outside of the Islamic legal conception. On the contrary, and given its later incorporation into the Islamic discourse, it was absorbed by the dimension of political governance (*siyāsa*).[84] Emanating from the political power, it acquired the function of an administrative regulatory faculty, subsidiary in nature to *sharīʿa*, and covering distinct and separate ambits of competences. It was enforced in specific political courts, which were once again not perceived as properly juridical tribunals, as were the *sharīʿa* courts presided by a *qāḍī*.[85] In spite of its progressive evolution into a wider and more incisive corpus of *de facto* legislation, especially in late-Ottoman times, the conceptual framework in which *qānūn* is located is indicative of its theoretical role in Islamic society.

[83] The distinction between manmade regulations, intended as mere political and administrative tools, and *sharīʿa*, intended an expression of the supreme Islamic normativity, is described by March as a pragmatic distinction of competences between jurists and rulers. On this, see Andrew F. March, "Modern Islamic Conceptions of Sovereignty in Comparative Perspective", in *The Oxford Handbook of Comparative Political Theory*, eds. Leigh K. Jenco, Murad Idris, Megan C. Thomas, Oxford University Press, Oxford 2020, pp. 549–551.

[84] Analyzing the contemporary legal system is Saudi Arabia, this point is highlighted by Frank E. Vogel, "Saudi Arabia. Public, Civil, and Individual Shariʿa in Law and Politics", in *Shariʿa Politics. Islamic Law and Society in the Modern World*, ed. Robert W. Hefner, Indiana University Press, Bloomington-Indianapolis 2011, p. 58. March describes *qānūn* as *siyāsa* law, highlighting its political nature (March, *Modern Islamic Conceptions of Sovereignty, cit.*, p. 550).

[85] Cf. Knut S. Vikør, "Muslim Subjects and the Rights of God", in *The Crisis of Citizenship in the Arab World*, eds. Roel Mejer, Nils A. Butenschøn, Brill, Leiden-Boston 2017, pp. 281–282.

4.3.4 Conclusive Remarks About Law, *Sharīʿa,* and Reason

Following what has been said so far, two main distinctions can be made between the Western and the Islamic legal traditions with regard to the role of reason.

Firstly, in the Islamic legal perspective human rationality is not entitled to produce law and is never perceived as constitutive of an idea of normativity. Consequently, in the Muslim juridical discourse there is no autonomous space for human reason that can serve the active elaboration of an earthly law, which is to be considered fundamentally distinct from a divinely established normative ideal.[86] On the contrary, in the Western conception there has always been an autonomous sphere of juridical elaboration entrusted to men, whose relationship with the idea of a superior good constituted the core of the legal reflection of the ancient world. The ancestral drama of the West relied on the possibility of a disjunction between a divine and superior *bonum* and human laws and rules, which may differ from their ideal inspirations due to the responsibility entrusted to human reason in regulating reality. On the contrary, in the Islamic vision this possibility is ideally inexistent: due to the derivative and deductive process of *fiqh*, what can happen is a misleading outcome in the said derivation from *sharīʿa*, while a disjunction between the law of God and the law of men is prevented *ab origine*, given the inexistence of an autonomous level of regulation.

Secondly, and as a consequence, it should be noted that in Islam there are figures such as jurists (*fuqahā*), experts (*ʿulamāʾ*), judges (*qadah*), and legal interpreters (*muftī*), but the figure of the legislator is actually nonexistent. The jurists and the experts provide doctrinal opinions on juridical matters, and the judges give application to legal provision as derived by the means of the roots of *fiqh*, while there is no such earthly authority that is entitled to legislate. The juridical operators of Islam may rule upon

[86] As Eaton argues, man "is by definition a knower and by destiny a chooser; but, in the Islamic view, he does not have the capacity to make laws for the conduct of society. The belief that God is the sole Legislator flows directly from the Muslim confession of faith, *lā ilāha illa ʾLlāh*, which, in this context, can be interpreted as meaning 'there is no legislator but the Legislator'. The message embodied in the Qurān – and the laws derived from it and from the *Sunnah* of the Prophet – bind the community together; no exterior pressure is required to make this binding effective" (Charles Le Gai Eaton, *Islam and the Destiny of Man*, State University of New York Press, Albany 1985, pp. 163–164).

concrete cases, mediate, release opinions, and issue *fatāwā*, like in the case of the *muftī*. The very etymology of the word *fatwā* comes from *fata*, which has preserved the semantic meaning of clarification or explanation,[87] thus deprived of an original and creative legislating power. The act of legislation, and consequently the creation of law, is an exclusive pertinence of Allāh, who gives to mankind the "straight path" of *sharīʿa*, which is to be regarded as already complete in itself and not needing any further level of innovative or creative legislation.[88] What *sharīʿa* needs, on the contrary, is to be "translated" into concrete juridical opinions to be applied to single cases, thus to descend from heaven to the domain of reality. As evident, it is not possible to speak about the act of legislating, but, on the contrary, it is necessary to speak about the act of deducting, clarifying, interpreting, and enforcing.

Even the caliph, as the supreme political authority of the Muslim tradition, is not invested with the power to legislate and to create laws. On the contrary, the caliph has to be regarded as a guardian[89] and as an

[87] See Muhammad Khalid Masud, "Fatwā. Concepts of Fatwā", in *The Oxford Encyclopedia of the Modern Islamic World*, *cit.*, p. 8.

[88] It is interesting to consider what Hallaq suggests about the cultural context of the Near East at the time of the rise of Islam, in which the faculty to legislate had been previously attributed to gods. In the words of the author: "It was most natural in this Near Easter milieu for a god to legislate. And it was equally natural that both the Prophet and the Qurān should have taken this tradition for granted. […] In the Qurān, and for Muhammad and the vast majority of people who lived then and long afterwards, God, every god, legislated. The question was which god was the true god, the True Law-giver" (Wael B. Hallaq [2009]. "Groundwork of the moral law: a new look at the Qurān and the genesis of sharīʿa", in *Islamic Legal Theory*, vol. I, ed. Mashood A. Baderin, Routledge, London 2014, ch. 4, par. 5). In the words of Crone, "As the ruler of the universe, God issued laws. Adam had received a set of them; so had later prophets, most recently Muhammad, whose version was final. Living in accordance with God's law was the essence of religion. In the early centuries it was practically all there was to religion" (Patricia Crone, *God's Rule. Government and Islam*, Columbia University Press, New York 2004, p. 8). Crone suggests that the exclusive attribution of the legislative power to Allāh finds a reason in the absence in Islam of the concept of natural law inscribed in men's conscience, provided that only the divinity can freely assign moral value to actions, and in the acknowledgment of the lack of sufficient intellectual resources in human beings to enact just laws with respect to *sharīʿa* (ibid., pp. 263–266).

[89] In medieval Christendom, monarchs were also considered as custodians and guardians of the legal order, as well as supreme *iudices* of the community, but at the same time they could enact new regulations, and were therefore vested with a legislating faculty, to ordain society and to regulate social life. This last prerogative is absent in the caliphal world, except with reference to the already mentioned concept of *qānūn*.

enforcer, or as an administrator, but not as a legislator.[90] The same, with all the necessary distinctions, could be said for the other political roles of the Islamic tradition, such as sultans and kings. With the progressive Westernization of the legal systems of the Muslim world, the juristic hermeneutics left room for lawmaking activity, thus marking the transition from the comprehension of a preexisting level of normativity to the production of an earthly one. In light of this, it is not by chance that this passage represented "the most important phenomenon of modem legal reform, one that signified simultaneously the eternal loss of epistemic authority and the dawning of the much-abhorred authority of the state".[91]

[90]The caliph ruled over the *ummah* without any formal legislative power. In order to answer the basic needs of the community, the caliph took care of the administrative issues, which, by that time and in that specific context, were not regarded as law at all and therefore were not considered as a part of the juridical conception of Islam. The legal prerogatives of the caliph are to be considered executive but never legislative. Hurvitz explains that the legislative activities of the caliphs in the administrative field were not perceived by Islamic legal literature and should be considered as a *de facto* legislating activity. For the aim of this work, I focus here on the Islamic view, according to which the caliph could not be considered a legislator, notwithstanding its administrative prerogatives that today could be considered part of a branch of (Western) law. Taking this into consideration, however, would result once again in a forced imposition of Western juridical categories upon a Muslim context. Cf. Hurvitz, *The contribution of early Islamic rulers*, *cit.*, pp.135 ff. One the non-legislative nature of the caliphal authority, it is necessary to recall the words of Hallaq, according to whom the caliphate "was by no means a distinct or a comprehensive source of law. No edicts regulating law are known to have come down from caliphs, no constitutions, and certainly no legal codes of any kind. Even when no class of legal specialists had yet appeared, neither the caliphs nor their viziers or provincial governors made any effort to control or appropriate the sphere of law, which was largely customary and Quranic" (Wael B. Hallaq, *An introduction to Islamic Law*, Cambridge University Press, Cambridge 2009, pp. 39–40). Crone and Hinds seem to disagree with the aforementioned position, stating that the caliphs, in the field of adjudication, could be regarded as a source of holy law (Patricia Crone, Martin Hinds [1986], *God's Caliph. Religious Authority in the First Centuries of Islam*, Cambridge University Press, Cambridge 2003, pp. 43–57). In this position, however, the conception of law implicitly reflects the Western idea, while the consideration of Hurvitz seems more convincing having regard to the specific context.

[91]Wael B. Hallaq, "Juristic Authority vs. State Power: the Legal Crises of Modern Islam", in *Journal of Law and Religion*, vol. XIX, n. 2, 2003–2004, p. 258.

While discussing and comparing the way in which the juridical phenomenon has been conceived in Islam and in the West, the role of reason represents therefore a fundamental issue, and properly analyzing this aspect may help to understand the necessary implications in terms of systematization and elaboration of a coherent legal and political system, starting from given premises.

4.4 *Law and* Sharīʿa *Between Form and Substance*

4.4.1 Form and Substance in the West

The debate on what should be considered the truest and most authentic nature of law, and on the possible prevalence of its formal or substantial element, has characterized the Western juridical discourse for centuries. As is well known, authors like Carl Schmitt and Hans Kelsen passionately debated on this specific point, elaborating meaningful and comprehensive theories of law in form or substance. For instance, Schmitt's decisionism transcended the mere formal aspect of juridical conceptualization, going as far as stating that the core essence of law relies in the will of the sovereign. On the contrary, according to Kelsen's *Pure Theory of Law* the validity of a normative act should be investigated on the basis of its formally belonging to a procedural system of legislative production.[92] Regardless of the merit of these positions, it can easily be argued that the discussion on form and substance of law is a crucial part of the Western juridical

[92] The views of Kelsen and Schmitt on this fundamental issue that have been mentioned above fall outside the aim of my work and won't be analyzed in detail here. However, on Kelsen's legal formalism it is possible to see Gustav Bergmann, Lewis Zerby, "The Formalism in Kelsen's Pure Theory of Law", in *Ethics*, vol. LV, n. 2, January 1945, pp. 110–130, as well as Jean d'Aspremont, *Formalism and the Sources of International Law. A Theory of the Ascertainments of Legal Rules*, Oxford University Press, Oxford 2011, pp. 48–51. On Schmitt's position on this matter, see Paul Hirst, "Carl Schmitt's Decisionism", in *Telos*, vol. VII, n. 72, July 1987, pp. 15–26, as well as Martin Loughlin, "Politonomy", in *The Oxford Handbook of Carl Schmitt*, eds. Jens Meierhenrich, Oliver Simons, Oxford University Press, Oxford 2016, pp. 570–591. On the debate between Kelsen and Schmitt in the context of Weimar constitutionalism, see Lars Vinx, *The Guardian of the Constitution. Hans Kelsen and Carl Schmitt on the Limits of Constitutional Law*, Cambridge University Press, Cambridge 2015.

perspective. Moving from the theorization of the distinction between form and matter, dating back to Aristotle's hylomorphism,[93] the West has shaped its view of legal phenomena on juridical categories such as form, substance, and procedures, and cannot prescind from them in understanding juridical realities.

Two consequences necessarily follow. Firstly, it is possible to state that form and substance, with all their various declinations, represent two essential elements of the way in which the Western tradition structured the idea of law, which in some way cannot be understood without at least an embryonal and initial approach to form and substance. Secondly, starting from the aforementioned premise, it is possible to hypothesize at least a theoretical separation and non-coincidence of the two dimensions, with the first not adhering to the latter, with a consequent discrepancy between what law formally is and what law substantially should be.[94] Following the previously mentioned tragedy of Antigone, the discordance between the factuality of law and the ideal dimension of it—being it divine or human—mirrors a possible irreconcilability between heaven and earth, or between justice and power, which represented a major cathartic reflection for the Western world in many stages of its history.

In the Western view, the theoretical possibility of conceiving law in form and substance, and then of virtually separating these two dimensions, is a consequence of understanding law as being a fundamentally human activity and a product of human rationality. Regardless of the specificities inherent to what should be intended by law, the human authorship of it necessarily calls for a distinctive mark by which it would be possible to

[93] See John Lawrence Hill, *After the Natural Law. How the Classical Worldview Supports Our Modern Moral and Political Values*, Ignatius Press, San Francisco 2006, pp. 40–45.

[94] For an exhaustive reflection about form and substance of law, see Robert S. Summers, *Form and Function in a Legal System. A General Study*, Cambridge University Press, Cambridge 2006. As Summers suggests, the distinction between form and substance dates back to Aristotle and the ancient Greeks (ibid., pp. 134, 159 ff.), and can be thus considered as a Western legal conception, regardless of the various theories about it. About Summer's position on the matter, see Philip Soper, "On the Relation between Form and Substance in Law", in *Ratio Juris*, vol. XX, n. 1, March 2007, pp. 56–65.

identify a certain act as law and organize it in a functional way.[95] This process of identification responds to two different necessities. On the one hand, it is necessary in order to ascribe a certain act to the specific sphere of the law, thus isolating a single act belonging to general human behavior and assigning to it a shared normative significance. This aspect attains an objective reflection about *what* is to be considered as law among the various products of human rationality and what is concretely eligible to produce legal effects. On the other hand, it is necessary to trace back the origin of a normative act to the legitimate authority, which in a given legal system is entitled to produce law. This second aspect attains the subjective dimension of law and follows what has been said about legitimation of power, thus regarding the reflection about *who* is legitimated to legislate.[96]

As Jhering observed, just like the effigies of kings and emperors on ancient coins represented a visible sign of the imputability of currency to the legitimate authority, thus marking their authenticity and attributing value to a specific object once again on the basis of a shared narrative, in the Western legal discourse law needs to be identified for its objective and subjective dimensions by a distinctive and univocal mark, which represents its form.[97] Therefore, it is possible to argue that the form of law refers to the exterior conditions by which a determined act is recognized as law both by rulers and ruled, and as ascribable to the legitimate lawmakers. While the form of law is a rather static concept, its dynamic evolution, attaining to the act of legislating and lawmaking in a given society, is represented by legislative

[95] Implicitly referring to the Western conception of law, Summers grasps the functional meaning of form in legal phenomena. According to the author, "form is highly important in practical terms. Without the requisite forms, legal phenomena could not even exist. We could not have legislatures, courts, statutory rules and other species of law, interpretive methodologies, sanctions and the like. Those phenomena consist of more than non-formal elements. Forms are required to define and organize these phenomena, non-formal elements and all, into functional wholes" (Robert S. Summers, "On Giving Legal Form its Due. A Study in Legal Theory", in *Proceedings of the 21st IVR World Congress*, Lund (Sweden), August 12th–17th, 2003, part 2, *Law and Practice*, eds. Svein Eng, Franz Steiner Verlag, Stuttgart 2005, p. 118). The tacit premise of Summers, however, is that law is a product of human rationality and has therefore to be organized from a functional and practical perspective.

[96] Summers, in his aforementioned monography, explicitly refers to the role of form in identifying legal phenomena both from an objective and from a subjective point of view. See Summers, *Form and Function in a Legal System*, *cit.*, p. 134.

[97] Jhering observes that form is to a related object what "the mark of the mint is to coniage" (Rudolf von Jhering [1852–1865], *Geist des römischen Rechts: auf den verschiedenen Stufen seiner Entwicklung*, Scienta Verlag, Aalen 1933, p. 494).

procedures. The establishment of defined procedures according to which creating and enacting norms and regulations is thus to be regarded as the response to the exigency of both ruling classes and subordinates of recognizing specific products of rationality as legally binding.[98] As a consequence of the imputability of legal production to the human rational sphere, the theorization of form and procedure of law is the coherent outcome of Western juridical thought, which moves from an essential and tacit premise: not every product of human reason is to be considered as law, with the logic and consequent exigency of circumscribing the scope of the juridical field by the means of determined forms and procedures.

Following the classical tradition and adopting the categories of form and substance, Aquinas deals with the necessity of recognizing in a univocal way what, among human acts and commands, is to be considered as law. He resolves the matter on form and procedure by referring to the idea of *promulgatio*. Notwithstanding the successive elaboration of the juridical sciences on the concept of promulgation, with *promulgatio* Saint Thomas means the formal act by which it is universally knowable that a specific rational command comes from a legitimate authority and is eligible to legally bind the consociates to its dispositions.[99] The observation of St. Thomas is eminently practical and answers the pragmatic necessity of having a disposition of human law known by all the subjects who have to observe it. Therefore, the issue of promulgation refers uniquely to man-made law, while natural law, according to Thomas, is originally inscribed in man's mind by God at the act of creation.[100] Once again, this view strengthens the nexus that links law to human rationality and identifies it as the primary origin of the necessity of forms and procedures in enacting laws.

Once again, the Western legal discourse has focused on which extent the form of law could be considered as a constitutive dimension of it and

[98] Cf. Gernot Biehler, *Procedures in International Law*, Springer, Berlin-Heidelberg 2008, pp. 61–62. It is worth noticing that, as in Summers, when analyzing the international legal system Biehler moves from the tacit premise of the validity of Western juridical and philosophical categories, such as the distinction between form and matter expressed by the Philosopher in *Physics*. Therefore, this view should be termed as a Western conception, which cannot be superimposed on other cultural contexts.

[99] In the words of the Aquinas, "laws are imposed on others as rules and measures, as I have said. But rules and measures are imposed by being applied to those ruled and measured. And so laws, in order to oblige persons, as is proper to law, need to be applied to those who are to be ruled by the laws. But the promulgation leading them to knowledge achieves such application. And so promulgation is necessary for laws to be in force" (Thomas Aquinas, *Summa Theologiae*, I-II, q. 90, art. 4, trans. *Treatise on Law*, *cit.*, p. 6).

[100] Ibid., art. 4, resp. to obj. 1.

on which forms and procedures could be regarded as most functional to the pursuit of a certain goal, but it never prescinded from taking into account a formal and a procedural dimension of law. Once again, this aspect recalls the Draconian laws of Athens at the end of the seventh century B.C.,[101] where the physical act of engraving the laws on tablets fulfilled the necessity of giving them a visible form. We can conclude, from a Western point of view, that law needs to be recognized by consociates by referring to a formal mark of identification and to be produced along predetermined procedures.

4.4.2 Form and Substance in Islam

In the Islamic legal view, the necessity of establishing certain procedures for lawmaking is not perceived,[102] given that *sharīʿa*, conceived as the supreme Muslim normativity, is not a manmade legislation but a product of a transcendent divinity. Consequently, the two aforementioned exigencies calling for a virtual distinction between form and substance can only fall, along with the initial premise of the imputability of law to human rationality. The overall conception of normativity is therefore resumed in its origin, which does not need any mark of distinction in order to be knowable or considered to be in force. If the juridical sphere represents one of the possible fields of human activity, thus calling for specific procedures and forms, in the Muslim view the act of legislating and creating law is proper of the divinity in its transcendent essence, to such an extent that every word of the Islamic revelation can potentially represent the issuing of a juridical principle.[103]

[101] Cf. Aristotle, *The Athenian Constitution*, pars. 4–5.

[102] In literature, attention must be paid as for what is intended by Islamic procedural law. Usually, with this term authors refer to the Western-based legal procedures in force in the States of the Muslim world and not of a procedural aspect in Islamic legal tradition. Therefore, it is common to find articles and texts dealing with forms and procedures of courts enforcing *sharīʿa* or on *sharīʿa*-based family law in modern States, but it is unlikely to find literature on what can be properly termed as form and procedure of *sharīʿa*. This latter point is a consequence of what I will explain in this paragraph.

[103] I use the word *potentially* because this is true in principle, although from a practical point of view, as evident, not all of the verses of the *Qur'ān* are eligible to be transposed in rules of conducts. Indeed, and having regard to their substantive content, a strict minority of verses of the Islamic holy book are inherent to legal matters, although every verse is perceived as vested with the highest authority being directly revealed by the divinity. On this, see Abdullah Saeed, *Interpreting the Qur'ān. Towards a Contemporary Approach*, Routledge, London-New York 2006, pp. 65–66.

In Islam, the necessity of establishing forms and procedures may arise not at the time of legal production as in the West but in two following moments: when subsuming and deducing legal rules from *sharīʿa* (*fiqh*[104]) and when enforcing and applying them.[105] What is basically unknown, therefore, is the exigency of a formal and procedural dimension inherent to the *constitution* of the juridical phenomenon. This latter point would imply that law descends from the reciprocal recognition of the consociates, both rulers and ruled, who set forth a number of norms and procedures regarding production and recognition of laws. In the Islamic discourse, *sharīʿa* is reveled from above, and the task of men, from this perspective, is to investigate and research it based on a work of juristic hermeneutics. The idea of normativity implied in *sharīʿa* is thus eminently immediate, given that, apart from the methods of deduction and interpretation, no formal or procedural mediation is required in order to make a certain act binding by force of law. What is necessary is the acknowledgment of the jurists of its preexisting and self-sufficient normative nature.

To summarize, there is not a human act such as promulgation or enactment, which would serve the aim of making law knowable and ascribable to its author. From this perspective, it is not the form of law that identifies it as descending from a certain source of authority and that marks it as eligible to bind its subjects to its prescriptions. On the contrary, it is its provenience to identify it as *sharīʿa*, and it is its authorship that marks it as part of the supreme Islamic normativity, once derived according to the necessary instrument of legal practice. Once again, the question is eminently epistemological, revolving around the necessity of detecting Allāh's

[104] With regard to *fiqh* and to its roots, it is important to notice that the process of derivation of *sharīʿa* is in no way to be regarded as constitutive of it. As it will be later shown, the human participation in the Islamic legal order regards essentially the act of deriving and deducing concrete provisions from *sharīʿa*: therefore, it is to be considered as a recognizing and declaratory activity, and by no means a legislating—thus constituting—act. This is a fundamental point because of its immediate consequence: no formal or procedural requirement is necessary for what is to be termed as a mere recognition, declaration, deduction of a norm that has already been laid down before the birth of man. I will examine in further detail the issue of *fiqh* and its roots in the next paragraph.

[105] Legal procedures in enforcing *sharīʿa*-derived provisions are particularly evident in the field of criminal law, as observed by Mohamed Seli El-Awa, "Confession and other methods of evidence in Islamic procedural jurisprudence", in *Criminal Justice in Islam. Judicial Procedure in the Sharīʿa*, eds. Muhammad Abdel Haleem, Adel Omar Sherif, Kate Daniels, I.B. Tauris, London-New York 2003, pp. 111–130.

will, especially in case of silence of the textual sources. The Islamic view, therefore, does not theorize the necessity of legislative procedures, but the exigency of instruments of hermeneutical derivation of normative rules from *sharīʿa*, and the need of rules of enforcement. Evidently, the distinction is obvious: while in the West the ideas of form and procedures are in some way constitutive of law at the moment of its creation, in Islam it is not possible to speak about rules of legal production but of methods of legal deduction instead.[106]

Concepts such as promulgation, or codification, are to be considered as exclusively belonging to the Western legal and philosophical thought, as a consequence of its theorization of the relationship between law and reason, and between form and substance. With specific regard to codification, this is particularly evident when we consider that the most important codifications of the West are culturally linked to the name of their compilators or to the political authorities that have commissioned them. It is not by chance that the French Civil Code of 1804, which served as basis for many other European codes, came to be commonly known worldwide as *Code Napoléon*. The very idea of codification, as a product of the Enlightenment, follows the attempt by man to juridically regulate society as a whole, with an ideal—and utopist—pretense of exhaustivity and completeness, and with the clear indication of man, as a rational being, as the author of the law and the regulator of society.[107]

[106] In analyzing contemporary legal systems in the Muslim world, with mostly Western-based institutions, Baderin correctly underlines that the traditional concept of Islamic "law" does not deal with procedural aspects but with substantive rules. Again, the author suggests that in this context it is not possible to properly speak about procedures, but it would be appropriate to speak about methods. See Mashood A. Baderin [2006], "Effective legal representation in "Sharīʿah" courts as a means of addressing human rights concerns in the Islamic criminal justice system of Muslim States", in *Issues in Islamic Law*, vol. II, ed. Mashood A. Baderin, Routledge, London-New York 2016, p. 417.

[107] Cf. Heinz Mohnhaupt, "The object of interpretation: legislation and competing normative sources of law in Europe during the 16th and 18th centuries", in *Interpretation of Law in the Age of Enlightenment. From the Rule of the King to the Rule of Law*, eds. Yasutomo Morigiwa, Michael Stolleis, Jean-Louis Halperin, Springer, Heidelberg-London-New York 2011, pp. 88–89. On the authorship of law, it is to be noted that the "advocates of codification shared the conviction of the natural law lawyers – as they themselves also often were – that man was capable of formulating a legal system that was complete, consistent, clear and comprehensible to all" (Randall Lesaffer [2009], *European Legal History. A Cultural and Political Perspective*, trans. Jan Arriens, Cambridge University Press, Cambridge 2012, p. 453).

In the Muslim tradition, the idea of codification can only be in contrast with the perspective of *sharīʿa*, whose author, as previously seen, is not man. Necessarily, *sharīʿa* cannot be codified,[108] because codification would result in its limitation and would result in binding the divine will to human juridical schemes, instead of these latter being bound by it.[109] Codifying *sharīʿa* would also mean limiting the constant work of the jurists, which represents the core of Muslim legal practice and an instrument of adaptability of it through time. If not *sharīʿa*, what can actually be collected in compilatory works is *fiqh*, as the result of human comprehension. However, given the nature of *fiqh*, its collections may result in a compilatory and doctrinal work, but not in a codification as intended in the West. In fact, if codifications may be considered as the systematization of human legislative production, the works of *fiqh* can be regarded as collections of legal opinions, thus a work *about* the law and not the law itself. Indeed, these compilatory volumes may make the complex work of the Muslim jurists easier, but by no means can they be considered as definitively binding in nature by their own authority. In the Islamic legal discourse, the concept of *taqlīd* designates the act of adhering to someone else's judgment, which is considered lawful in principle, but which in no case can be pushed to the limit of acknowledging force of law to human opinions considered *per se*, and not as interpretations of a superior reality.[110]

It is relevant to notice, with regard to this, that the first real attempts of codification in the Muslim world date back to the second half of the

[108] As Dahlén concisely observes, while "Islamic law possesses a normative and established structure, it nevertheless resists codification of any kind as a potential unfolding of the revealed sources" (Ashk P. Dahlén, *Islamic Law, Epistemology and Modernity. Legal Philosophy in Contemporary Iran*, Routledge, London-New York 2003, p. 51).

[109] This is particularly true with reference to the historical process of Westernization of Islamic legal systems following European colonization, where codification has been adopted as a tool of juridical predominance aimed at containing the influence of the Islamic traditional ways of delivering justice and controlling the territory. On this, see Hallaq, *Can Shariʿa Be Restored?*, *cit.*, pp. 22–23.

[110] The idea of *taqlīd* refers to the act of accepting rules of *fiqh* "based on understanding texts as interpreted by early members of a chosen guild" and "accepting the view of a recognized leading jurist without scriptural proof of its correctness" (Russell Powell, *Shariʿa in the Secular State. Evolving Meanings of Islamic Jurisprudence in Turkey*, Routledge, London-New York 2016, p. 27). From this point of view, it can be considered as the "opposite of ijtihād" (Joseph Schacht [1955], "The Schools of Law and Later Developments of Jurisprudence", in *Law in the Middle East*, vol. I, *cit.*, p. 74). As evident, the tension between *taqlīd* and *ijtihād* is closely related to the asserted closure of the gates of *ijtihād* and to the conditions at which it is possible to propose new legal interpretations.

nineteenth century, following the so-called Edict of Gülhane (*Gülhane Hatt-ı Şerif*) of 1839 and the subsequent Imperial Reform Edict (*Islâhat Hatt-ı Hümâyûnu*) of 1856, in the context of the Tanẓīmāt reforms of the Ottoman empire.[111] From a political point of view, this period represented a major era of modernization and innovation of the overall structure of the sultanate, but from a juridical point of view it is nevertheless necessary to point out that it coincided with the importation of Western-derived legal conceptions,[112] such as the organizations of manmade laws in codes.[113] It is in this period that the use of *qānūn* was pushed to the point of equating Western legislation, for its form and substance, however without formally questioning the *sharīʿa*-based legal system. The empire, which would have guided the Muslim community as a formal caliphate until 1924, had already started that process of progressive assimilation to the Western legal models that would have led, later on, to the creation of a *de facto* State-based system in the Ottoman territories.

[111] For the reforms and the Edicts, see Coşkun Çakır, "Tanzimat" (voice), in *Encyclopedia of the Ottoman Empire*, eds. Gábor Ágoston, Bruce Masters, Facts on File, New York 2009, pp. 553–555; in the same volume, Cemil Aydin, "Reform" (voice), pp. 484–486. Cf. Stanford J. Shaw, Ezel Kural Shaw [1977], *History of the Ottoman Empire and Modern Turkey*, vol. II, *Reform, Revolution and Republic. The Rise of Modern Turkey, 1808–1975*, Cambridge University Press, Cambridge 2002, pp. 55 ff.

[112] As Stanford and Ezel Shaw observe, during "the nineteenth century the Ottoman empire witnessed a sustained effort of reform that saw the long-preserved and honored institutions of the classical Ottoman state replaced by new ones, inspired by an increasing knowledge of European thought, society, and government and modified to satisfy Ottoman needs and conditions. In the process the scope of government was extended far beyond the limits imposed by the traditional Ottoman way into every aspect of life, overwhelming the autonomous religious, economic, and social groups that had survived for so long as the substrata of Ottoman society. A new, modern, westernized ruling bureaucracy replaced the old Ruling Class, extended its power throughout the empire, and created a highly complex system of government that ruled with an autocracy unmatched in traditional times" (S. Shaw, E. Shaw, *History of the Ottoman Empire and Modern Turkey, cit.*, p. vii). With regard to the process of Westernization of the Ottoman empire, see Selcuk Aksin Somel, "Westernization" (voice), in *Historical Dictionary of the Ottoman Empire*, The Scarecrow Press, Lanham-Oxford 2003, pp. 322–323. Cf. the already mentioned work of An-Na'im, *Islam and the Secular State. cit.*, p. 191–196.

[113] Regarding Ottoman codification, which according to Rubin leads to the so-called Ottoman legalism, see Avi Rubin, *Ottoman Rule of Law and the Modern Political Trial. The Yildiz Case*, Syracuse University Press, Syracuse 2018, pp. 23–58. Mallat observes that the process of legal codification "was also tied closely to the phenomenon of 'reception' of European laws. It was a process directly associated with colonization, and the Middle East was no different from other parts of the non-Western world in this respect" (Mallat, *Introduction to Middle Eastern Law, cit.*, p. 121).

Before this period, while the compilation of *fiqh* could be rather frequent in scholarly and doctrinal works,[114] the idea of a real codification can be considered substantially alien to Muslim thought. Once again, the legal practice of ancient times, in its concrete and actual manifestation, offers the chance to investigate the most intimate and significant philosophical and juridical perspectives of a given civilization. Therefore, as codification represents the apex of Western juridical attempts to regulate reality by force of human rationality, the absence of it in the Muslim world until relatively recent times clearly indicates the actual impossibility of developing a juridical discourse around form and procedure of law, if not by adopting Western legal standards and principles. On the contrary, the presence of collections of *fiqh* in Islam, and the importance attached to this activity by the various legal schools, suggests that the main field of juridical reasoning is the investigation of a preexistent normative reality, whose objectiveness and whose extraneity to the human dimension do not require any formal or procedural requisite for its being in force, apart from the rational effort of the interpreter.

4.5 *Sources of Law and Roots of* Fiqh

In the previous paragraphs, I examined the relationship between law and human reason, intended as an instrument to produce or derive legal provisions from an origin. At this point, it is necessary to investigate what is to be considered the primary origin of law in the two systems of thought. Once again, the analysis of this latter point appears to be intimately tied to the aforementioned nexus law-reason.

[114] With the progressive establishment of legal schools, the corpus of *fiqh* grew considerably, and its organization in collections and compilations was something acquired to the traditions of the *madhāhib*. However, the essential difference between the concept of *fiqh* and the Western idea of law prevents us from equalizing *fiqh* compilations and Western legal codification. Therefore, it is not possible to agree on the definition of *fiqh* as "codification of *sharīʿa*" (as in Ahmad, *The Nature of Islamic Political Theory*, *cit.*, pp. xv, 183, 192). Regarding the activity of collecting *fiqh*, see Muhammad Amanullah, Habibur Rahman, "The Origin and Evolution of Fiqh Codification. A Preliminary Analysis", in *Journal of Islam in Asia*, vol. XIII, n. 1, June 2016, pp. 194–219. This last article offers a historical survey on the process of systematic organization of *fiqh* compilations and collections. However, it is not possible to agree with the authors when stating that codification "simply means the process of forming a legal code" (ibid., p. 192): codification, on the contrary, is not to be regarded as a neutral process but a way of understanding legal systematization from a precise philosophical and juridical perspective, which is not superimposable to the one typical of *fiqh*.

With the term *origin*, I mean the wellspring from which law is perceived to first stem and develop, that is to say what a given civilization or culture believes to be the original beginning of the juridical phenomenon. Origin, in this perspective, has a fundamentally neutral significance, while other terminologies, which will be later explained, show the intimate meaning that a certain tradition attaches to them in reasoning of a specific and coherent vision of law.[115]

The Western world, in the centuries of its history, gave different answers to the question of the origin of law, from the classical Greek and Roman societies to the present day. The most complete theorization of the origin of law can be considered the conception of *source*. Dating back to Cicero[116] and Livy,[117] the metaphor of the *fons* appears to be particularly eloquent in highlighting some structural elements that characterize the idea of the origin of law in the Occidental view. Despite the initial Latin use of the terminology, this idea represented a common feature throughout all Western juridical history. However, in its stable and final conceptualization it can be mainly considered as a product of modernity and one of the outcomes of the overall theorization of a State-based model, in which law

[115] For the distinction between origin and source, and for the concept of source as a juridical category of comprehension and interpretation, see Giovanni Bombelli, "Momenti di una normatività giuridica complessa. Da Esiodo ai presocratici", in *Il Diritto tra Testo e Immagine*, eds. Carla Faralli, Valerio Gigliotti, Paolo Heritier, M. Paola Mittica, Mimesis, Milan-Udine 2014, pp. 125–128.

[116] "His enim explicatis, fons legum et iuris inueniri potest". ("Once we have explained these things, we can find the source of laws and of justice") Cicero, *De Legibus*, I, 16 (English excerpt from *On the Commonwealth and On the Laws*, *cit.*, p. 110).

[117] Referring to the XII Tables, Livy stated: "Eas leges habiturum populum Romanum quas consensus omnium non iussisse latas magis quam tulisse videri posset. Cum ad rumores hominum de unoquoque legum capite editos satis correctae viderentur, centuriatis comitiis decem tabularum leges perlatae sunt, qui nunc quoque, in hoc immenso aliarum super alias acervatarum legum cumulo, fons omnis publici privatique est iuris" ("The Roman people would have the kind of laws that their unanimity might seem not only to have passed but also to have proposed. When the laws seemed to have been sufficiently amended in accordance with the comments made about each section, the Laws of the Ten Tables were passed in the *Comitia Centuriata*. Even now, amid the great pile of statutes heaped one on top of another, they are the fountainhead of all public and private law") (Livy [27 BCE-14 AD], *Ab Urbe Condita*, III, 34, English excerpt from *The History of Rome*, books 1–5, trans. Valerie M. Warrior, Hackett Publishing, Indianapolis-Cambridge 2006, pp. 204–205).

in general and legislation in particular are thought to be produced according to a hierarchically ordained system of sources.[118]

In the Islamic view, it is once again necessary to distinguish between *sharīʿa* and *fiqh*. While the origin of *sharīʿa* is undisputedly to be identified with the divinity, with regard to *fiqh* the question is more complex. In this case, a concept that can be referred to the idea of origin is *uṣūl al-fiqh*, which addresses the fundamental issue of the instruments by which *sharīʿa* provisions can be derived and interpreted, thus forming the corpus of *fiqh*. This conception constitutes an essential point in analyzing the Muslim juridical perspective, representing the very way in which the human intellect acts in order to grasp the transcendent will of the divinity and to translate it into concrete rules of conduct. Again, it shows the moment in which the inscrutable lawmaking activity of Allāh finds a knowable and visible outcome by virtue of an act of rational comprehension. The actual ways in which the Islamic jurists deduce legal opinions and provisions from *sharīʿa* are the *uṣūl al-fiqh*, the origin of the Islamic rulings, whose foundations and practice are to be regarded as one the most important fields of juridical research and activity.[119] The term can be properly

[118] It is difficult to provide a univocal definition of source of law. In this book, I will focus on the eligibility of the source to the material production of legal provisions. From this perspective, various authors can be recalled to stress this peculiar and fundamental conception. According to Boer, for instance, a source of law "is anything that can be conceived of as the originator of legal norms" (Alexander Boer, *Legal Theory, Sources of Law and the Semantic Web*, Ios Press, Amsterdam 2009, p. 80). According to Guastini, in "a material sense every act that *produces* norms constitutes a source of law: whatever be its name, its process of formation, and the organ from which it descends" (Riccardo Guastini, *Le fonti del diritto. Fondamenti teorici*, Giuffrè, Milan 2010, p. 46). The most interesting definition is however provided by Kelsen, who underlines the ties between the idea of source and the creation of law. According to the jurist, the metaphor "is used not only to designate the different methods of creating law but also to characterize the reason for the validity of law, and especially the ultimate reason. But, in a wider sense, every legal norm is a source of that other norm the creation of which it regulates. It is a characteristic element of law in general, and hence also of international law, that it regulates its own creation" (Hans Kelsen [1952], *Principles of International Law*, The Lawbook Exchange, Clark 2003, p. 303).

[119] With regard to this, Weiss states that "there can be no denying that it constitutes, or came over time to constitute, the mainstream of legal-theoretical thought in Islam" (Bernard G. Weiss, "Editor's Introduction" to *Studies in Islamic Legal Theory*, ed. Bernard G. Weiss, Brill, Leiden-Boston-Köln 2002, p. xvii).

translated as *roots* of *comprehension*.[120] As mentioned, Sunnī Islam usually recognizes four roots: *Qur'ān*, *sunnah*, *ijmāʿ*, *qiyas*, notwithstanding the differences between the various legal schools for the acceptance of all the four roots and other instruments of interpretation.[121] The discourse about *uṣūl al-fiqh* is not to be considered univocal and differs according to the teachings of the different schools and jurists. It is primarily carried out in dependence of the thought of eminent scholars and by doctrinal works, among which the principal and most important text is undoubtedly the *Kitab ar-risāla fī uṣūl al-fiqh* by al-Shāfiʿī (767–820), commonly known as *Risāla*, which systematizes the roots as foundations of the juridical comprehension of Islam.[122]

In literature, source of law and *uṣūl al-fiqh* are usually juxtaposed and compared, drawing a substantial equation between these two essential concepts in their respective legal orders, to the point of defining *uṣūl*

[120] In literature, the translation of *Islamic jurisprudence* is common and recurring. However, in this book I will maintain the Arabic word *fiqh*, in order to preserve the original meaning without imposing on it a fundamentally Western concept such as *jurisprudence*, which implies a unique and own way of theorizing the role of man and reason in the process of lawmaking.

[121] For instance, the Ḥanbalī school generally looks cautiously to *qiyas*, because of its excessively subjective character, and restricts the use of *ijmāʿ*, admitting the normative dimension pf the consensus expressed by Muḥammad's companions (*ṣaḥābah*), while rejecting the one referred to the consensus expressed by later generations of Muslims.

[122] I already mentioned the edition translated and edited by Khadduri. For a commentary, see Joseph E. Lowry, *Early Islamic Legal Theory. The Risāla of Muhammad ibn Idrīs al-Shāfiʿī*, eds. Ruud Peters, Kevin Reinhart, Brill, Leiden-Boston 2007. The importance of the *Risāla*, to be considered as a milestone in the evolution of the Islamic legal theory and methodology, is highlighted by Khadduri himself: "During that time Islam expanded rapidly and absorbed new elements of culture and tradition. As a result, the Muslim world abounded in legal doctrines, the advocates of each vying for supremacy over the others. It was Shāfiʿī who provided in the ninth century of the Christian era a systematic legal method by which to synthesize the various legal doctrines into a coherent system" (Khadduri, *Preface* to *al-Risāla*, *cit.*, p. vi).

al-fiqh as "sources of Islamic law".[123] However, as already pointed out with regard to concepts such as State and law, imposing Western categories onto an Islamic context can result in a substantial misunderstanding in grasping the effective nature of fundamental juridical visions. The idea of source of law makes no exception, given that it differs from the Islamic view with regard to three essential points: firstly, regarding what originates from sources or roots; secondly, regarding the nature of what is to be intended by sources or roots; and lastly, regarding the dynamics and interactions between sources or roots.

Firstly, it is necessary to focus on *what* originates from the sources of law of the Western tradition and from the roots of *fiqh* in Islam. The idea of source refers to a comprehensive conception of law, in its broader meaning. In the Occidental view based on modern statehood, the overall conception of *jus* is examined through the lens of a hierarchical and ordained system of sources, from which every genre of legal provisions is generated, according to preexisting rules. What is produced, in this case, is substantially *law* as intended in the Western world, with all the aforementioned implications. In the case of the roots, as indicated by the original Arabic

[123] Without questioning the academic value of relevant studies, it is nevertheless necessary to point out the improper use of the terminology, which might lead to miscomprehension of some structural characteristics of the Islamic legal view. For instance, some authors use the definition "sources of Islamic law". In this paragraph, I will show the reasons why this terminological choice is not sharable. Correctly, Mallat speaks about "so-called 'sources' of Islamic law" (Mallat, *Introduction to Middle Eastern Law, cit.*, p. 108). For miscellaneous examples of the use of this terminology, see Daniel W. Brown, *A New Introduction to Islam*, Wiley-Blackwell, Chichester 2009, p. 158; Shahid Ashraf, *Judicial culture in Islam*, Anmol Publications, New Delhi 2006, p. 55; Mohammad Hashim Kamali, "Law and Society. The Interplay of Revelation and Reason in the Shariah", in *The Oxford History of Islam*, ed. John L. Esposito, Oxford University Press, Oxford 1999, p. 107; John Burton, *The Sources of Islamic Law. Islamic Theories of Abrogation*, Edinburgh University Press, Edinburgh 1990; Nighat Amin, *Some Salient Features of the Islamic Law and Constitution*, Pakistan Institute of Arts and Design, Karachi 1970, p. 5.

terminology, what originates is *fiqh*.[124] While the supreme Islamic normativity is *sharīʿa*, usually and simplistically associated with "law", *fiqh* is the comprehension of it and its translation in concrete opinions and rules (*furūʿ al-fiqh*).[125] Therefore, it is possible to state that the origin of *sharīʿa* does not rely in the four roots, which on the contrary refer to the derivation of *fiqh*, but stems directly from the unknowable divine will of Allāh. In substantially equalizing the roots and the sources, it is easy to fall into a first asymmetry: according to the Western view, all the branches of law in their internal and hierarchical articulations are ordained in a system of sources, while in the Islamic traditions the roots are the instruments of comprehension by which *fiqh*—and only *fiqh*—is derived. The sources are meant as a net comprehending and ordaining the various typologies of law, assuming as a parameter the moment of their production, while the roots are tools by which the interpreter comes to a closer understanding of a normativity whose creation has already been provided. Consequently, the association between roots and sources, again, misleads one to the consequent matching of law and *sharīʿa*, or of law and *fiqh*, with no actual perception of the divergences between an idea of normativity and its human comprehension.

Secondly, it should be noted that the very natures of the two concepts differ greatly. The idea of source evokes the image of a wellspring, from

[124] Despite the objective difficulty in defining *fiqh*, whose essential elements have already been mentioned in my introduction, it is necessary to recall at least two of them, which underline its essential character. A concise definition that is worth remembering is provided by Kamali, according to whom *fiqh* "is defined as knowledge of the practical rules of the Sharīʿa, which are derived from detailed evidence in the sources" (Mohammad Hashin Kamali, "The Sharīʿa: Law as the Way of God", in *Voices of Islam*, vol. I, *Voices of Tradition*, ed. Vincent J. Cornell, Praeger, Westport-London 2007, p. 150). Again, from this perspective, it can be termed as "a system that forms the basis for normative interpretation of the revelation, the application of its principles and commands to the field of human acts" (Muhammad-Basheer A. Ismail, *Islamic Law and Transnational Diplomatic Law. A Quest for Complementarity in Divergent Legal Theories*, Palgrave Macmillan, New York-Basingstoke 2016, p. 51).

[125] By this point, it is necessary to highlight the relationship between these two concepts: "From an historical perspective the relationship between *shariah* and *fiqh* can be summarized by saying that the *shariah* developed as the paradigm or model of the Islamic way of life, whereas *fiqh*, the application of the *shariah* to specific cases, developed as the paradigm of Islamic reasoning. In these two concepts, one normative and ideal and the other hermeneutical and practical, a true complementarity between theory and practice is achieved" (Vincent J. Cornell, "Fruit of the Three of Knowledge. The relationship between faith and practice in Islam", in *The Oxford History of Islam*, *cit*., p. 91).

which something flows, thus revealing a dynamic nature. Accordingly, law is *produced* from a certain source as water spurts from a fountain, in a relationship characterized by the production of an object—law—from an origin—source of law. Just as in the wellspring image, as new water continuously stems from its source, new laws and new norms can be produced and abrogated from legal sources, in an ordained system in whose framework every new normative act finds its organic collocation. The dynamic nature of the concept finds its core in the fact that from the same source new laws can be produced in a flow that can potentially be unbroken and continuous. Therefore, the idea of source is intimately tied to the Western vision according to which law can be an autonomous product of reason, meaning that it is continuously produced and replaced by will of human authority. On the contrary, the Arabic term indicating the roots of *fiqh* is *uṣūl*, which does not simply refer to the literal idea of root but to its metaphorical significance as origin or foundation.[126] The image summoned by this terminology is substantially different from the image of the wellspring, recalling the idea of fixity and stableness of the root. From this point of view, it is relevant to point out that from the same etymology the Arab word *aṣāla* descends, which means firmness, steadfastness, or purity of origin, which strengthens the idea of stableness and fixity.[127] The roots, as previously said, are not to be considered the origin of Islamic "law" but the origin of its human comprehension, which must refer to certain instruments to approach the divine path that Allāh revealed to humanity. Consequently, the *uṣūl* do not produce law but represent the means by which man can investigate the transcendent dimension of *sharīʿa*. Given the self-sufficient dimension of *sharīʿa*, whose collocation is beyond space and time and thus not subject to human revision, the means of its comprehension are oriented toward the understanding of an immutable object

[126] Cf. Hans Wehr [1952], "Uṣūl" (voice), in *A Dictionary of Modern Written Arabic*, ed. J. Milton Cowan, Harrassowitz Verlag, Wiesbaden 1979, p. 23.

[127] Ibid.

and cannot produce new norms and new rules,[128] but rather give a new and closer vision of the same reality.[129] In conclusion, while the source of law is a source of production,[130] the roots of *fiqh* are the roots of comprehension.

Lastly, the third divergence refers to the internal dynamics between the various sources or roots and their teleological perspective. The sources of law create a system that is both ordained and ordaining, given that it regulates the procedures according to which new laws and norms are produced, and at the same time is regulated by it.[131] Consequently, it can be considered as a self-sufficient and self-referential system in which all the

[128] As already mentioned, the concrete provisions derived by means of the roots may change in dependence of time and place, of the legal school, and of the comprehension of the jurist. However, while the understanding of Allāh's *sharīʿa* can change, *sharīʿa* itself cannot. Therefore, every change in *fiqh* is not to be considered as a new law or a new rule but as a new understanding of the same, immutable *sharīʿa*. To sum up, "jurists consider the *sharīʿa* as immutable" but "they acknowledge the diverse body of *fiqh* opinions as the product of human engagement with the textual sources of authority in Islam. In this dichotomy, God is infallible, but human effort to know God's Will with any degree of certainty is imperfect and fallible" (Tamir Moustafa, *Constituting Religion. Islam, Liberal Rights, and the Malaysian State*, Cambridge University Press, Cambridge 2018, p. 35). Cf. Faisal Kutty, "Blasphemy and apostasy laws in the Muslim world: a critical analysis", in *Research Handbook on Islamic Law and Society*, ed. Nadirsyah Hosen, Edward Elgar Publishing, Cheltenham-Northampton 2018, pp. 244.245; Louay Fatoohi, *Abrogation in the Qur'an and Islamic Law. A Critical Study of the Concept of "Naskh" and its Impact*, Routledge, London-New York 2013, p. 236.

[129] As Bhala points out, the etymology of the word *fiqh* is eloquent as for its nature of knowledge, comprehension, understanding. According to the author, the term "literally means 'understanding'. It is derived from the verb '*faqaha*', which means 'to understand'. Used in the context of the *Sharīʿa*, *fiqh* refers to the totality of human comprehension of the perfect, immutable, and Divine law as revealed in the *Qur'ān* and *Sunnah*, and as explained, elaborated, and interpreted by Islamic legal scholars" (Raj Bhala, *Understanding Islamic Law. Sharīʿa*, Matthew Bender & Co., Newark 2011, p. 289).

[130] The terminology in use in certain European countries is eloquent in indicating the productive and dynamic nature of the idea of *source* of law, such as in the Italian case, where the terminology *fonte di produzione* has been acquired to the juridical lexicon. In Spanish, the same concept is expressed through the equivalent periphrasis *fuentes de producciòn*, and in German through *Rechtsgeltungsquellen*.

[131] Once again, and as already explained, Kelsen argues that law regulates its own creation. See Kelsen, *Principles of International Law*, *cit.*, p. 303.

dynamics of interactions are mainly internal.[132] A source-based legal model is essentially conventional, meaning that it can change and be modified through its own instruments and on the basis of its own rules. For its renewal or modification, it does not feel the necessity of referring to external elements and outer dimensions,[133] having all the necessary instruments already within its perimeter of action. As for the teleological perspective, it can easily be argued that, especially in the modern era, the idea of a source of law is functional to the fulfillment of a double exigency. On the one hand, it responds to the need of the consociates to know what is to be considered law, and the rules and procedures by which law is produced. On the other hand, it serves the necessity of establishing an order in producing and enforcing law, that is to say establishing an order between the sources, regardless of it being hierarchical, chronological, or other forms of conventional order.

The system of the roots of *fiqh*, on the contrary and in spite of their scholarly nature, cannot be considered properly conventional, given that it investigates an eternal and immutable reality that is to be termed essentially objective, external, and preexisting to man. On this basis, the roots fulfill another and distinct kind of necessity, which is not comparable in nature to the need of establishing an order in the Western sources. The roots try to determine a closer comprehension of something whose reality relies on a transcendent and divine will, and whose collocation is therefore external to the *uṣūl* system itself, eminently human in its systematization. Therefore, the dynamics of interactions of the roots are not limited to the

[132] For an interesting reflection about the self-sufficiency and self-referentiality of law in the Western view, it is possible to analyze Teubner's theory of autopoietic law, which explains in detail the aforementioned characters. See Gunther Teubner [1987], "Introduction to Autopoietic Law", in *Autopoietic Law. A New Approach to Law and Society*, ed. Gunther Teubner, De Gruyter, Berlin-New York 1988, pp. 1–11. Also, on the same issue cf. Niklas Luhmann, "The Self-Reproduction of Law and its Limits", in *Dilemmas of Law in the Welfare State*, ed. Gunther Teubner, De Gruyter, Berlin-New York 1988, pp. 111–127.

[133] This is true with the exception of the extreme case of the complete abolishing of a legal order and its replacement by another order, as in the case of a revolution, where the formal rules and procedures by which law is produced are repelled and replaced by the pure constituent will of creating *ex novo* a new order. It is the case in which a ruling power is ousted and in which a constituent power emerges, which will later on create its own authorities and its own procedures and sources of law.

internal spectrum of the roots themselves: apart from the interactions between them, usually complex and debated, there is another interaction that is to be regarded as the preeminent one, which is the relationship between the roots—the *instruments* of comprehension—and *sharīʿa*—the ultimate *object* of comprehension. While in the Western view the system of sources is usually closed in their own internal dynamics, the roots of *fiqh* cannot avoid the constant reference to an external reality, that is to say the supreme normativity of Islam. As a consequence, the teleological perspective implied in this vision is necessarily tied to the objectivity and eternity of the normative dimension of *sharīʿa*, toward which the roots tend in their hermeneutical effort of understanding. The ultimate aim of the roots, therefore, is not simply regulating and prioritizing the modalities by which legal provision might be derived but assuring the fidelity of actual legal practice to divine command, although with a considerable degree of flexibility and adaptability to concrete circumstances. While the sources of law in the West may be changed of modified within the framework of their own system, the roots of *fiqh* are not freely disposable to man, because of their constant reference to an eternal dimension, outside of the concrete perception of the interpreter by virtue of other means.

In conclusion, the ideas of source of law and root of *fiqh* present important divergences for their structural elements and cannot be considered superimposable without relevant conceptual biases. In particular, the source is part of a self-sufficient system whose aim is to regulate the production of law and to establish an order in the legislative production, regulating the interactions between different normative acts. The nature of the idea of source is thus dynamic and conventional. On the contrary, the *uṣūl al-fiqh* constitute a system of comprehension of an objective and external normative reality, whose characteristics of fixity and objectivity, in spite of the possible evolution of the opinions thence derived, are necessarily mirrored in the roots themselves and in the legal order of which they are foundational elements.

CHAPTER 5

Spiritual Command and Temporal Rule

5.1 The Terms of the Question

One of the most debated topics regarding Islam in a broader sense, and *sharīʿa* in particular, refers to the separation between the religious and political dimensions. This issue is addressed in the most numerous and various manners and according to the most different of approaches. It is common to speak about a possible separation between "State" and "church" in order to establish the principle of secularity.[1] According to other commentators, Islam lacks a separation between "sin" and "crime", due to the missing philosophical phase of the Enlightenment.[2] Some other times, referring to a different but equally misleading terminology, it is common to refer to the necessity of differentiating "religion" from

[1] This terminology is rather common among commentators, although usually outside of the academic world, for its evident misleading juxtapositions of concepts belonging to different contexts. Cf. however Ann K. S. Lambton, *State and Government in Medieval Islam. An Introduction to the Study of Islamic Political Theory – The Jurists*, Routledge, London-New York 1981, p. xv.

[2] Cf. Oliver Leaman, *Islamic Philosophy. An Introduction*, Polity Press, Cambridge 2009, pp. 192 ff.

F. L. Ramaioli, *Juridical Perspectives between Islam and the West*, Global Issues, https://doi.org/10.1007/978-3-031-37844-7_5

"politics" or "morality" from "law".[3] However, all these notions reflect a specific and distinctive way of conceiving of man and God, society and justice, which cannot be imposed upon the Muslim context without its unavoidable denaturation. Once again, all these visions tend to universalize the Western way of shaping and understanding reality, and do not manage to properly grasp the effective terms of the question.

Concepts such as State and church are to be referred to a specific philosophical framework, and in spite of their progressive spread throughout the world, they cannot be held as universal notions. While the structural elements of the State have already been examined, the idea of church is shaped by the Christian *ecclesia*, and neither it is conceptually separable from the Christian view nor can it come to mean in a broader sense "religious community". As for the Enlightenment, it is clearly a specific phase that occurred not by chance in Western history, and once again it is not a sort of universal endpoint in a progressive global history, whose occurrence is to be believed by faith and regardless of a proper historical and philosophical contextualization.[4] Regarding the separation between religion and politics, the question is more complex; however once again it usually mirrors a Western vision of State and community. The logical premise of this position, as a matter of fact, is that concepts such as religion and politics be univocally and universally defined in order to examine their theoretical or practical separation in a given context. On the contrary, what is expressed as religion or politics varies greatly according to the system of thought from which we move, thus showing conceptual

[3] The question of the separation between "religion" and "politics" is a recurring topic in literature. Rosenthal, for instance, uses this terminology in his interesting reflection on secularism in modern Islam: Erwin I. J. Rosenthal, "Some reflections on the separation of religion and politics in modern Islam", in *Islamic Studies*, vol. III, n. 3, September 1964, pp. 249–284.

[4] This approach, still influencing the present debate at least in its terminology, first rose in the Enlightenment era, characterized by a fatalistic optimism in a homogeneous and universal notion of progress. Mah, for instance, underlines two essential conceptions of this perspective: progressivism and universalism (Harold Mah [2003], *Enlightenment Phantasies. Cultural Identity in France and Germany, 1750–1914*, Cornell University Press, Ithaca-London 2004, p. 157).

boundaries that are far from finding a stable definition.[5] For instance, the Western view on religion, from the Latin *religio*, is not superimposable on the Islamic *dīn*, which may be translated with religion or faith—and also with law, in the past—however with evident differences as to its theorization and historical outcomes. As Lewis notes, for Muslims the term *religion* "does not have the same connotation as [it] has for Christians or even had for medieval Christians", provided that to Muslims "it means both more and less than the equivalent term for Christians".[6] Most importantly, aside from its non-coincidence with its Christian counterpart, the idea of religion referred to in Islam does not coincide with the post-Enlightenment conception of religion reduced to a private belief, thus influencing our very possibility to understand the nature of Islam, as well as of other religious creeds.[7] Given the inexistence of a global phenomenon called "religion,"[8] in spite of its concrete "incarnations" in time and space, the discourse about the separation between religion and politics as carried out in the Western world is not necessarily applicable to *dīn* and *dawla* in Islam. This plan of reasoning is biased by the lack of a simple observation:

[5] Dubuisson suggests that the Western categories shaping the academic science of history of religions should not be used outside the perimeter of the Western world, given the lack of proper historical and philosophical contextualization that would result from such an analysis. Once again, it is important to underline that the concept of "religion", as created and debated in the Western discourse, is not to be considered as a void and neutral category with which to examine heterogeneous phenomena, which take roots in completely different contexts. Cf. Daniel Dubuisson [1998], *The Western Construction of Religion. Myths, Knowledge, and Ideology*, trans. William Sayers, The Johns Hopkins University Press, Baltimore-London 2003.

[6] Bernard Lewis, *Islam and the West*, Oxford University Press, Oxford 1993, p. 3. For a comparative analysis, see Ammeke Kateman, *Muḥammad ʿAbduh and His Interlocutors. Conceptualizing Religion in a Globalizing World*, Koninklijke Brill, Leiden 2019, pp. 46–68. Once again, the philological reflection of Glei and Reichmuth, according to whom the two concepts are nevertheless comparable to a certain extent, is interesting (Reinhold Glei, Stefan Reichmuth, "Religion between Last Judgement, law and faith: Koranic dīn and its rendering in Latin translations of the Koran", in *Religion*, vol. XLII, n. 2, April 2012, pp. 247–271).

[7] According to Esposito, this "tendency to define religion as a system of belief restricted to personal or private life, rather than as a way of life, has seriously hampered our ability to understand the nature of Islam and many of the world's religions. It has artificially compartmentalized religion, doing violence to its nature, and has reinforced a static, reified conception of religious traditions rather than revealed their inner dynamic nature" (John L. Esposito [1992], *The Islamic Threat. Myth or Reality?*, Oxford University Press, Oxford 1999, p. 260).

[8] On this point, see William James [1902], *The Varieties of Religious Experience. A Study in Human Nature*, Routledge, London-New York 2002, p. 26; Ugo Bianchi [1970], *The History of Religions*, Brill, Leiden 1975, pp. 201–212.

the actual extent of the ideas of religion and politics in Islam does not coincide with the boundaries of the respective conceptions in the West, with a consequent divergence in the basic categories of comprehension. Therefore, this position ends up being actually based on the separation between religion and politics in the Western view, with a substantial attempt to replicate it in different contexts.

The real terms of the question should focus on two issues: first, whether it is possible to term *sharīʿa* as "religious law", using a common terminology; second, whether there is a functional separation of religious and secular authority in the Muslim context. The analysis of these two points will help in grasping the real significance of the question, especially with regard to the normative dimension of Islam.

5.2 Sharīʿa *as Religious Law*

As already explained, it seems to be impossible to define *sharīʿa* as "law" as is commonly intended in the West, although its ideal represents the capstone of the Muslim legal order. In order to discuss another recurring definition of *sharīʿa*, it is necessary at this point to examine the possibility of defining it as "religious". Preliminarily, it is necessary to clarify what is to be intended by "religious", with two possible meanings: firstly, something whose origin is religious; secondly, something regulating a religious matter.

Regarding the first point, *sharīʿa* can definitely be termed religious, provided that its normativity stems from divinity. In the contemporary scenario, the perception of the divine origin of law is something rather unique to the Islamic tradition, while the majority of the other perspectives assume the human authorship of law, even in the case of religiously inspired or oriented regulations. Nowadays, *sharīʿa* represents a sort of *unicum* in the spectrum of compared legal conceptions, and one of its peculiarities is represented by its divine origin, which in principle does not need any mediation except that of jurist hermeneutics. However, it is necessary to specify that while the wellspring of *sharīʿa* is religious, the understanding and knowledge of it are eminently human. In this case, it is possible to summarize by stating that the Islamic legal order is religious with regard to the authority whose will and command give existence to juridical provisions and human with regard to the capability of man to translate it into concrete norms and rules through a work of constant research and ultimately to give them proper enforcement and application.

Regarding the second point, the question is undoubtedly more complex and articulated. In order to give an answer to the question whether *sharīʿa* regulates a religious object, it is necessary to determine to which extent the Islamic supreme normativity permeates the lives of the Muslim believers. Notwithstanding the divergences between schools and traditions, authors agree in defining *sharīʿa* as a way of life whose regulations and principles encompass the entire existence of man in all of its aspects.[9] The field of regulation provided by *sharīʿa* is not thus limited to what, in Western thought, has been considered as "legal" or "juridical", meaning with these definitions *what* can actually be regulated by substantive law. It transcends the conceptual boundaries the West developed in order to delimit the juridical sphere from other aspects of human life, whose discipline necessarily falls out of the spectrum of what it is to be considered as "law". On the contrary, *sharīʿa* is a "complete scheme of life and an all-embracing social order",[10] whose principles are not enclosed in a specific field. Being "the path" provided by the divinity to mankind, the supreme aim of *sharīʿa* is to lead men to eternal salvation, thus regulating what is ideally the overall existence of the believer.[11] Therefore, religious practice and rituals represent *one* of the various aspects of human life in its aspiration toward salvation, and not the only field in which, consequently, *sharīʿa* has a preeminent role to play in leading humanity to its ultimate goal. While analyzing the religious dimension of *sharīʿa* it is necessary to have regard for its scope and aim: being eternal salvation as a

[9] In my introduction I recalled the concise but exhaustive definitions of *sharīʿa* given by Weiss and Khadduri, according to whom the concept should be defined exactly as a comprehensive way of life which gives shape and form to the existence of the believers. Katz correctly speaks about "comprehensiveness of the law" while referring to *sharīʿa*, in order to highlight this very point (Marion Holmes Katz. *Body of Text. The Emergence of the Sunni Law of Ritual Purity*, State University of New York Press, Albany 2002, p. 1). Roberts focuses on this topic stating that *sharīʿa* "is not a legal code in the Western sense and should not be confused with Western notions of limited government. Islam is intended to be comprehensive, and Sharia, in theory, regulates all aspects of a Muslim's life, including both rights and duties, not only as regards Allah, and other Muslims, but also as regards non-Muslims" (Glenn L. Roberts, *Islamic Human Rights and International Law*, Dissertation.com, Boca Raton 2007, p. 13). See also Diane Morgan, *Essential Islam. A Comprehensive Guide to Belief and Practice*, Praeger, Santa Barbara 2010, p. 165.

[10] Syed Abul'Ala Maududi, *Islamic Law and Constitution*, Jamaat-e-Islami Publications, Lahore 1955, p. 27.

[11] This is true in principle and regardless of the fields in which the sciences of *fiqh* do not provide answers, like public administration, to which historically supplied the use of *qānūn*.

comprehensive concept for the believer, in the pursuit of which all the dimensions of existence are involved, the path followed to obtain it must necessarily show the same degree of comprehensiveness. It reflects the all-encompassing nature of Islam itself, which is not "a compartment of life, so to speak, distinct from other compartments which are the concerns of nonreligious authorities administering nonreligious laws. Rather, it is the entirety of life, and its rules include civil, criminal, and even what we would call constitutional law".[12] It is *also* possible to conclude that *sharīʿa* regulates religious matters, such as rituals and worship, having also developed internal distinctions between religious and secular aspects,[13] but its theoretical perspective is not limited to religion, since it reaches the multitude of various dimensions of life, including family relations, economics, prevention and repression of crime, and so on.[14] The recurrent definition of *sharīʿa* as "religious" law can be misleading, since it points out what is just one facet of a complex and far-reaching conception, whose boundaries fall beyond the mere religious practice.

Another common distinction refers to the dichotomy *sharīʿa-qānūn*, with the former assertively being a "religious" law and the latter being a

[12] Lewis, *Islam and the West*, *cit.*, p. 4.

[13] In the Islamic legal discourse, the part of *sharīʿa* dedicated to divine worship goes under the name of *ibādah*, while the term *muʿāmalāt* designates other legal matters such as commercial transactions and family law. It is not to be believed, however, that this distinction be between religious rules and non-religious rules, given that the category of what is "religious" clearly transcends worship and rituals. Moreover, as Hughes observes with reference to the Islamic classification of human actions, it is evident an "intersection of the legal, the ritualistic (i.e. the religious) and the moral" (Aaron W. Hughes, *Muslim Identities. An Introduction to Islam*, Columbia University Press, New York 2013, p. 137).

[14] Peters and Bearman underline the far-reaching nature of the concept, whose eligibility to regulate and discipline both heavenly and earthly matters shows a fundamentally comprehensive nature, which falls beyond what can be properly termed as religious law (Rudolph Peters, Peri Bearman, "The Nature of the Sharia", introduction to *The Ashgate Research Companion to Islamic Law*, eds. Rudolph Peters, Peri Bearman, Ashgate, Farnham-Burlington 2014, pp. 1–7). Noor Mohammed stresses the comprehensive dimension of *sharīʿa*, which constitutes "the main guidelines for spiritual as well as temporal Muslim conduct in this life as preparation for the hereafter [...] The umbrella of *Sharia* in Islamic society covers the entire spectrum of Islamic life and ethical values in both temporal and spiritual activity" (Noor Mohammed, "Principles of Islamic Contract Law", in *Understanding Islamic Law. From Classical to Contemporary*, eds. Hisham M. Ramadan, Altamira Press, Lanham-New York-Toronto-Oxford 2006, pp. 95–96).

"secular" one.[15] According to Weber, for instance, the distinction between *sharīʿa* as sacred law and *qānūn* as secular law mirrors a sort of universal conception, which could be considered in some way similar to the Western perspective, inherent to the separation between the religious and political spheres.[16] These positions are not sharable because of the erroneous basis from which they—more or less implicitly—move. Those who address *sharīʿa* as religious law in contraposition with *qānūn* as secular legislation base their opinion on the substantive matter regulated by the law itself that, from this perspective, should be exclusively referred to in religious practice as *sharīʿa* and in secular administration as *qānūn*. While this latter was effectively used in order to provide legal coverage to unsolved questions concerning public institutions, taxation, and administrative activities, *sharīʿa* transcended the conceptual boundaries of religious rites and morality, ideally applying to matters we would today define as secular. The dichotomy *sharīʿa-qānūn* based on the religious-secular distinction is further put into question if we consider that *sharīʿa* prevailed over *qānūn*, establishing an unequal legal dualism, with the theoretical impossibility of inscribing this dynamic within the idea of division of competences.

When discussing the complex relationship between *sharīʿa* and *qānūn*, which however changed and evolved over time, An-Naʿim hints at a more effective way to draw a distinction between the two concepts. According to the author, the substantial and crucial dissimilarity relies not on the

[15] In this sense, see Siraj Sait, Hilary Lim, *Land, law and Islam. Property and human rights in the Muslim world*, vol. I, Zed Books, London 2006, p. 47; Dina Rizk Khoury, "Administrative Practice Between Religious Law (Sharīʿa) and State Law (Kanun) on the Eastern Frontiers of the Ottoman Empire", in *Journal of Early Modern History*, vol. V, n. 4, 2001, p. 305; Pier Francesco Zarcone, "Turchia, minoranze e laicità", in *Studi Interculturali*, eds. Mario Faraone, Gianni Ferracuti, n. 3, Mediterrànea-Centro di Studi Interculturali, Trieste 2013, p. 10.

[16] The most important author endorsing this theory is Weber in his interesting analysis of *sharīʿa* and the Islamic way of administering justice. See Max Weber [1921–1922], *Economy and Society. An Outline of Interpretive Sociology*, eds. Guenther Roth, Klaus Wittich, University of California Press, Berkeley-Los Angeles-London 1978, pp. 818–822.

object of the regulation but on the enforcing authority.[17] This opinion is sharable with an essential *caveat*: rather than speaking about the authority enforcing a certain regulation, we should speak about the authority who authors that regulation. It is correct to identify the distinguishing element between secular and religious rules and laws in the authorities from which they find origin and not with reference to the sole moment of enforcement.[18] On the contrary, the moment of the origination of a rule—and consequently, its authorship—appears to be a more appropriate distinguishing element. In Muslim discourse, it is the authority who authors the rule that effectively marks the distinction between a "secular" and a "religious" law. From this perspective, *sharīʿa* is to be held as a religiously derived way of conceiving normativity, which nevertheless comprehends the most various aspects of social, political, and moral life. On the contrary, *qānūn* is not necessarily secular as the object of its regulation, but it is a corpus of administrative rules issued by an earthly authority. This distinction is relevant because it identifies what, in my opinion, is the only objective way to deal with a possible distinction between religious and secular dimensions in the Islamic legal tradition. From this point of view, the analysis should not be based on norms and juristic opinions, but rather on authorities and rulers; not on the nature of law, but on its origin and authorship.

In light of what has been said, the terms of the question become clearer, and the fundamental question arises: does the Islamic legal tradition theorize a possible separation between religious and secular authorities?

[17] "From my perspective, all law or legislation that is enforced through state institutions is secular, even when drawn from or based on *Sharīʿa* principles. Since it is not possible to enforce all the various interpretations of *Sharīʿa* by different scholars because of strong disagreements among and within the schools, enforcement through state institutions will necessarily have to be selective among competing views. Moreover, whatever principles of *Sharīʿa* are enforced, the actual enforcement happens through the political will of the state and not by virtue of their being *Sharīʿa* principles as such". Abdullahi Ahmed An-Naʿim, *Islam and the Secular State. Negotiating the Future of Sharīʿa*, Harvard University Press, Cambridge 2008, p. 191.

[18] A dedicated paragraph of Chap. 5 will deal with the concept of enforceability.

5.3 Authority and Authorities: Between Secular Command and Spiritual Guidance

Secularism in the Islamic legal order has been analyzed from many varied perspectives. As previously pointed out, one possible approach relies on the separation between religion and politics based on the matter regulated by the law, which could be alternatively religious or secular. Another approach addresses the bindingness of the law, which in *sharīʿa* is graduated along different degrees of imperativeness. Drawing a distinction between secularism and laicism, Mazrui suggests that the former "is not a domain of God *in absentia*, but the domain of God's indulgent permissiveness".[19] However, while *sharīʿa* undoubtedly also possesses a non-compulsory dimension of religious guidance of the believers,[20] it should not be forgotten that this represents just one aspect of a more complex phenomenon, which cannot be reduced to one of its components. Permissiveness as non-bindingness is not to be considered a basis from which to examine the possibility of legal secularism in Islam, provided that God's mercifulness as a legal principle refers to a dimension which may be considered as religious in nature as *sharīʿa*'s imperativeness with regard to other fundamental aspects. This position moves from the possibility granted to believers not to conform their behavior to a religious legal principle, which is not termed as mandatory. However, it is hard to define this perspective as secular, given that it is nevertheless inscribed within a religious narrative.

As mentioned above, the most objective way of dealing with this issue—and in order to draw an effective comparison with the Western way of conceiving the relationship between law and religion—is by referring to the authorities from which the law originates and is enforced. Coming back to the question of the previous paragraph, it is necessary to analyze whether a separation of religious and secular authorities in Islam and in the West is alternatively possible or necessary.

[19] Ali A. Mazrui, *Resurgent Islam and the Politics of Identity*, eds. Ramzi Badran, Thomas Uthup, Cambridge Scholar Publishing, Newcastle upon Tyne 2014, p. 1.

[20] The issue of the bindingness of *sharīʿa* will be dealt with in Chap. 5.

5.3.1 *Spiritual and Temporal Authorities in the West*

In the Western world, the separation between religious and secular powers was first introduced with the advent of Christianity and with the Christianization of the Roman Empire.[21] In classical thinking, a separation between authorities could be regarded as accidental, and pragmatically induced by the circumstances, but in no way as theoretically conceptualized. It should not to be forgotten, with regard to this, that the Roman emperor exercised both secular and religious functions, being addressed by the title of *pontifex maximus*, that is to say, the supreme authority who builds a bridge between humanity and the gods.[22] Moreover, the foundation's narrative of Rome, from which the Roman rituality of political legitimacy derives, refers to the mythical priest-kings of ancient ages, among whom Numa Pompilius represents the primary archetype.[23] It is not by chance that Augustus, while establishing his ideally peaceful and heavenly inspired rule, presented himself as a successor to Numa, more than as a successor to Romulus.[24]

Christianity, on the contrary, proposed a new separation between spiritual and temporal authorities, whose representatives should have upheld a concord but never been confused for one another. The primary source of the Christian teaching on this separation relies on a passage of the synoptic Gospels, in which Jesus commands to "repay to Caesar what belongs to

[21] In a broader reflection on the separation of politics and religion in an Islamic modern society, the point is well underlined by Anwar M. Barkat, "Church-State relationships in an ideological Islamic State", in *The Ecumenical Review*, vol. XXIX, n. 1, January 1977, pp. 39–40.

[22] Cf. Matthew Bunson [1994], "Pontifex Maximus" (voice), in *Encyclopedia of the Roman Empire*, ed. Matthew Bunson, Facts on File, New York 2002, p. 443. In the framework of Roman religiosity, it is possible to agree with Gradel, according to whom we "instinctively see Jupiter as a religious figure, a Roman emperor as a political one. This distinction between religion and politics is christianizing, as is basically the very concept of 'religion' itself" (Ittai Gradel, *Emperor Worship and Roman Religion*, Clarendon Press, Oxford 2002, pp. 27–28).

[23] Cf. the classic text of Howard Hayes Scullard [1935], *A History of the Roman World, 753 to 146 BC*, Routledge, London-New York 2013, p. 47.

[24] With regard to Augustus as a new Numa, as for the religious devotion in his political narrative, see Trevor S. Luke [2014], *Ushering in a New Republic. Theologies of Arrival at Rome in the First Century BCE*, University of Michigan Press, Ann Arbor 2017, pp. 242–260; Angeline Chiu, *Ovid's Women of the Year. Narratives of Roman Identity in the Fasti*, University of Michigan Press, Ann Arbor 2016, p. 102.

Caesar and to God what belongs to God", [25] thus establishing a manner of distinguishing between the obedience to earthly laws and to God's rule, and legitimizing both of them. Accordingly, saint Paul in the letter to Romans asks the *ecclesia* to obey secular authorities, once again legitimizing the separation between a religious and a temporal dimension of power. [26] Besides being part of the doctrinal background of early Christianity, this position also reflects the historical contingencies of the time, in which Christians were a minoritarian group willing to establish peaceful relationships with the established authorities and to avoid conflict.

Following the Christianization of the Roman Empire, the spiritual dimension of power was inscribed within the Roman institutional architecture, providing a differentiation the empire had never fully theorized before. The Roman pontiff, from this perspective, gradually inherited some of the symbolic attributions of the Caesars, such as the title of *pontifex maximus*[27] and the use of red shoes, which later came to symbolize the blood of the martyrs.[28] With this fundamental passage, the conception of power of the classic pre-Christian age underwent a major change, that is, its division into two parallel and yet separated branches, spiritual and temporal, represented respectively by the pontiff and by Caesar—then later, by the Byzantine βασιλεύς (*basileús*). The partial attribution of royal garments to the pope clearly symbolizes what is not to be considered as the introduction of a new dimension of religious power in a secular empire, but instead as the division of a unique and comprehensive idea of rule in two functional—and equally supreme—authorities, each one responsible for its own sphere of competence. This conception was not only practiced as derived from the Gospels and from Paul's teaching, but was properly theorized by pope Gelasius in the letter to emperor Anastasius I, *Famuli*

[25] *Gospel according to St. Matthew*, 22, 21. Cf. *Mark*, 12, 13–17; *Luke*, 20, 20–26 (trans. *New American Bible*).

[26] Cf. *Rom.* 13, 1–2.

[27] Dijkstra and Van Espelo analyzed the usage of the title and its passage from the emperors to the popes, not without ambiguities and contradictions. The official acquisition of the title of *pontifex maximus* to the pontifical titulature, as well as its abandonment by the Caesars, could be posterior to what had been priory theorized in literature. However, the symbolic character of this fundamental passage remains as a sign of the inheritance by the pope of Rome of imperial garments. Cf. Roald Dijkstra, Dorine Van Espelo, "Anchoring Pontifical Authority: A Reconsideration of the Papal Employment of the Title Pontifex Maximus", in *Journal of Religious History*, vol. XLI, n. 3, September 2017, pp. 312–325.

[28] Cf. Arthur Penrhyn Stanley, *Christian Institutions. Essays on Ecclesiastical Subjects*, Charles Scribner's Sons, New York 1881, p. 229.

vestrae pietatis, of 494 AD.[29] Emperor Justinian I, in his *Corpus Juris Civilis*, expressed this principle clearly as well, in his notable position on the συμφωνία (*symphōniā*) between the two authorities,[30] entitled to respectively spiritual and temporal powers, on whose concord the peace of Christendom was laid.

In the framework of the medieval *Respublica Christiana*, this bipartition becomes much clearer with the reaffirmation of the separation of the functions of *imperium* and *sacerdotium*, with the former entitled to temporal rule and the latter to spiritual guidance.[31] These two powers should

[29] Gelasius spoke about two powers governing the world, respectively the *auctoritas sacrata pontificum* and the *regalis potestas*. Denzinger defines the letter as "the most known document of the ancient Church regarding the two powers on earth" (Heinrich Denzinger [1854], *Enchiridion symbolorum, definitionum et declarationum de rebus fidei et morum*, ed. Peter Hünermann, Edizioni Dehoniane, Bologna 1996, p. 191). For an explanation of the Gelasian doctrine as for the duality of powers, see Walter Ullmann [1955], *The Growth of Papal Government in the Middle Ages. A Study in the Ideological Relation of Clerical to Lay Power*, Routledge, London-New York 2010, pp. 24–26. For an in-depth analysis of the letter, with a proper historical contextualization, see Rocco Ronzani, o.s.a., "La lettera "Famuli uestrae pietatis" di Gelasio di Roma all'Imperatore Anastasio I", in *Augustinianum*, vol. LI, n. 2, Istituto Patristico Augustinianum, 2011, pp. 501–549.

[30] The reference is to *Corpus juris civilis*, *Novellae*, VI, *Praefatio*, where it is stated "Maxima quidem in hominibus sunt dona dei a superna collata clementia sacerdotium et imperium, illud quidem divinis ministrans, hoc autem humanis praesidens ac diligentiam exhibens; ex uno eodemque principio utraque procedentia humanam exornant vitam. Ideoque nihil sic erit studiosum imperatoribus, sicut sacerdotum honestas, cum utique et pro illis ipsis semper deo supplicent. Nam si hoc quidem inculpabile sit undique et apud deum fiducia plenum, imperium autem recte et competenter exornet traditam sibi rempublicam, erit consonantia quaedam bona, omne quicquid utile est humano conferens generi". (*Corpus Juris Civilis*, vol. III, eds. Rudolf Schöll, Wilhelm Kroll, Weidmannsche Buchhandlung, Berlin 1895, pp. 35–36). For an analysis, see Michael Azkoul, "Sacerdotium et Imperium: the Constantinian Renovatio According to the Greek Fathers", in *Theological Studies*, vol. XXXII, n. 3, September 1971, pp. 431 ff.

[31] Regarding the relationship between spiritual and temporal powers in the Middle Ages, see J. A. Watt [1988], "Spiritual and Temporal Powers", in *The Cambridge History of Medieval Political Thought, c. 350-c. 1450*, ed. J. H. Burns, Cambridge University Press, Cambridge 2007, pp. 367–423. For an in-depth analysis of the relationship between pope and emperor in the Middle Ages, with interesting considerations about the separation of competences in the ideal framework of the *monarchia mundi*, see Othmar Hageneder [1985], "Il dominio del mondo nel medioevo", in *Il Sole e la Luna. Papato, Impero e regni nella teoria e nella prassi dei secoli XII e XIII*, trans. Gabriele Ingegneri, ed. Maria Pia Alberzoni, Vita e Pensiero, Milan 2000, pp. 11–31.

have been exercised in harmony,[32] and yet in order to pursue the supreme aim of the *salus animarum*, to remain separate. With the metaphorical figure of the "two swords", they were to be considered theoretically autonomous and equal; practically, one of the two could gain more political influence, but they could never be confused in a single ruler, be he the pope or the emperor. Therefore, medieval Christianity conceived its overall theorization of social and political rule fundamentally as a duality: it was a world whose destiny should have been guided by two supreme institutions, each one charged with its own and unique attributions and prerogatives. This bipartition is thus to be considered not simply as typical of the Western world as a consequence of its Christian heritage; on the contrary, it is to be considered as structural and necessary, due to the indispensable separation of authorities and powers which characterized it from the beginning of the Christian era. Again, it is not simply that this bipartition occurred for historical or social reasons; it could not but have occurred, due to its proper theorization in a given philosophical context.

In the course of the history of Christendom, it happened more than once that one of the two authorities prevailed over the other, and the struggles between the two were frequent in order to achieve more influence over the overall *Respublica*. It is sufficient to recall the Byzantine experience of caesaropapism, in which the imperial power assumed the protection of the ecclesiastic authority, thus acquiring a *de facto* supremacy over it. Again, it is possible to recall the period of the investiture controversy, when papacy and empire underwent a deep conflictual phase as to the appointment of high ecclesiastic officials. However, the conflicts that periodically took place between the two powers underline a fundamental aspect and reveal the structural nature of the bipartition of authority in medieval Europe: all the controversies and crisis that fractured the harmony of *imperium* and *sacerdotium* regarded the extension of the boundaries of the respective competences, thus assuming the very idea of the separation between the two as necessary and unavoidable. Even in the most acute phase of the controversy, it never acquired the extent of a confrontation in which one of the two powers aimed at the annihilation of the other, which continued to be perceived as necessary to the comprehensive

[32] Cf. Timothy Samuel Shah, Daniel Philpott, "The Fall and Rise of Religion in International Relations: History and Theory", in *Religion and International Relations Theory*, ed. Jack Snyder, Columbia University Press, New York 2011, p. 30.

life of the heavenly ordained *Respublica Christiana*.[33] The political and juridical order of medieval Christendom, in conclusion, theorized not just the separation of secular and religious authorities, but conceptualized its necessity, politically embodied in the functional boundaries that separated the two powers, from which so many controversies arose between clergy and laity, and between papal and imperial supporters.

After the rupture of the medieval unity, and with the progressive fall of the idea of a *monarchia mundi*, this vision based on two authorities was however safeguarded. The spiritual power was maintained in the hand of the clergy, while the temporal authority underwent significant changes, being concentrated in the apparatus of the modern State, divided into multiple sovereignties. The transformations faced by the Western world after the Middle Ages, however, only serve to confirm the uninterrupted existence of two separate powers, notwithstanding the various shapes of their concrete incarnations throughout the centuries of European history.

In comparing the Western and Muslim approaches to this topic, the real distinguishing point lies in the *necessity* of this bipartition. Hence, the real structural feature of the Western view on politics and law is to be identified in the unavoidable requisite of the existence of two separate authorities, based on a shared and non-questionable philosophical and religious narrative.[34] As Lewis correctly observes while drawing a comparison

[33] With regard to this, it is interesting to notice that even in the bull *Unam Sanctam* issued in 1302 by pope Boniface VIII, who dogmatically affirmed the subordination of the temporal power to the guidance of the spiritual one, the necessity of both authorities is never put in question. On the contrary, the pontiff stressed the necessity of the known "two swords" in the Catholic church, stating that "[i]n hac eiusque duos esse gladios, spiritualem videlicet et temporalem, evangelicis dictis instruimur. Nam dicentibus Apostolis, ecce gladii duo hic, in ecclesia scilicet cum Apostoli loquerentur, non respondit [D]ominus nimis esse, sed satis". (Text from *Revue des Questions Historiques*, year XXIV, n. 46, Bureaux de la Revue, Paris July 1889, p. 255.)

[34] It is not possible to agree with Shireen Hunter, who argues that during the Holy Roman Empire the two authorities were actually fused into one. In my opinion, Hunter incurs in two kinds of errors. First, she mistakes the theoretical bipartition of powers with the actual extent of the competences of each one of them, which could of course be questioned and challenged. Second, she argues that the emperor in the Middle Ages could be considered as a religious leader, mistaking once again the dimension of his religious and heavenly derived legitimacy with its role and attribution as a political figure. Cf. Shireen T. Hunter, *The Future of Islam and the West. Clash of Civilizations or Peaceful Coexistence?*, Praeger, Westport-London 1998, p. 34.

between Islam and the West regarding this, "[i]n the long and varied history of Christendom, the two have always been there – sometimes in association, sometimes in conflict; sometimes one predominant, sometimes the other—but always two and not one."[35]

5.3.2 *Spiritual and Temporal Authorities in Islam*

In Sunnī Islam, on the contrary, a separation of roles and attributions has never been theorized in a univocal and absolute way.[36] However, this does not mean that such a separation never occurred in a factual sense in the course of Muslim history. According to the pragmatic and flexible nature of Islamic political theory in which theoretical conceptualizations are subordinated to the concrete needs of the *ummah* and of the *sharīʿa*, the eventuality of a separation between spiritual and temporal authorities is to be regarded as the consequence of historical and political contingencies

[35] Bernard Lewis, *Faith and Power. Religion and Politics in the Middle East*, Oxford University Press, Oxford-New York 2010, p. xi.

[36] Ibid., pp. 45 ff. Among classic Islamic scholars, Ibn Khaldūn recognizes the uniqueness of Islam in its all-encompassing nature, being at the same time "a message, a system of legislation and the implementation of this legislation. Amongst all the religions, Islam is unique in encompassing both spiritual and temporal power" (Ali Abdel Razek [1925], *Islam and the Foundations of Political Power*, trans. Maryam Loutfi, ed. Abdou Filali-Ansary, Edinburgh University Press, Edinburgh 2012, p. 74). It is to be noted, however, that Razek does not share the opinion of Ibn Khaldūn with regard to this point. In my opinion, Ibn Khaldūn's position simply mirrors the comprehensiveness of *sharīʿa* as guidance for the believer in every matter of life, and it is therefore worth consideration. Lambton remarkably observes that in Islam "there is no doctrine of the temporal end which alone belongs to the state and the eternal end which belongs to, and in the prerogatives of, the church; no balance between the two; each equal to the other when acting in its own sphere; each equally dependent on the other when acting in the sphere of the other and no tension between the historic community and the church as custodian of the universal common elements in human existence" (Lambton, *State and Government in Medieval Islam, cit.*, p. xv). Crone shares this position as well, observing that due to the environment "in which it originated, Islam was thus embodied in a political organization almost from the start: the *umma* was a congregation and a state rolled together. Christians originated with dual membership. As believers they belonged to the church and were administered by the clergy; as citizens they belonged to the Roman empire and were ruled by Caesar. Islam originated without this bifurcation. As believers *and* as citizens they were members of the *umma* and ruled by the Prophet, thereafter by his successors" (Patricia Crone, *God's Rule. Government and Islam*, Columbia University Press, New York 2004, p. 13).

rather than part of a comprehensive political and philosophical theory.[37] Similarly, *sharīʿa* itself developed internal distinctions between properly religious and non-religious rules, however without questioning its comprehensiveness from a theoretical point of view.

During the period of the *rāshidūn* caliphs, the supreme Islamic magistrate held both the spiritual and secular authority over the community of the believers. Following the establishment of this new kind of a-national society by Muḥammad, and given the exigency of consolidating it through its initial expansion, the caliph mirrored the absolute authority of the Prophet, in order to fulfill his obligations as his vicar. The caliph is referred to as the supreme *imām* of the community, but he is the political and military commander of the believers as well. He is the substitute of the Messenger of Allāh, thus exercising all the necessary powers in order to guide the *ummah* toward salvation, being both spiritual and temporal.[38] With the Umayyad and Abbasid caliphates, the political organizations of the Muslim community underwent significant changes. Starting with the transformation of the caliphate from an elective charge to a hereditary one, it came to be organized in a more sophisticated and articulated way, resembling, in some aspects, a kingdom. Even in the Ottoman sultanate, which can be considered as the earthlier among the caliphal experiences, the sultan retained the title of caliph for himself as a symbol of the religious unity of the Muslims. The title survived as far as the collapse of the empire, until 1924 when it was definitely abolished and represented a fundamentally religious charge, although deprived of actual political

[37] An-Na'im himself, who postulates the presence of a sort of separation between spiritual and temporal authorities in classical Islam, admits its factual and occasional nature, speaking of "pragmatic functions" of the political power in ensuring an effective control of the territory (An-Na'im, *Islam and the Secular State, cit.*, p. 49).

[38] In my opinion, with regard to the power of the early caliphs in both secular and spiritual matters, the definitory study of Crone and Hinds overcomes every possible objection from other scholars. See C Patricia Crone, Martin Hinds [1986], *God's Caliph. Religious Authority in the First Centuries of Islam*, Cambridge University Press, Cambridge 2003, especially pp. 1–23. As Swenson suggests, at least until the fall of the Abbasids the title of caliph "was applied to the head of Islam as well as to the head of the Muslim Empire", in order to "celebrate the main rituals of Islam, to defend it, and to administer the religion" (Donald S. Swenson [2005], *Society, Spirituality, and the Sacred. A Social Scientific Introduction*, University of Toronto Press, Toronto 2009, p. 110). Consider also Nurullah Ardıç, *Islam and the Politics of Secularism. The Caliphate and Middle Eastern modernization in the early 20th century*, Routledge, London-New York 2012, p. 176.

power.[39] Having regard for the history of the Sunnī caliphates, it is possible to state that this supreme office could be considered as both political and religious, without a clear distinction between the boundaries of these two concepts.

During the various caliphal phases, a factual separation between religious experts and political officials had already been created. For instance, the term *sulṭān* came to indicate a ruler vested with political authority,[40] *vizir* a minister or an administrative high-ranking official,[41] and *ʾamīr* a military commander or a governor.[42] On the contrary, the doctors in Islam are commonly known as *ʿulamāʾ*[43] or, in different contexts, as *mullah*.[44] Nevertheless, this *de facto* separation never evolved in the establishment of a hierarchical clerical order,[45] in charge of proper and predetermined attributions, and separated from secular power. On the other hand, it served the cause of the pragmatical organization of the community, in which everyone had to play their role according to their own competences. The jurists themselves, in turn, exercised a scholarly function by which they had to properly detect the will of the divinity and apply it to earthly cases, with an ill-defined boundary between its secular and religious nature.

[39] Cf. the already mentioned works by Azmi Özcan, *Pan-Islamism. Indian Muslims, the Ottomans and Britain, 1877-1924*, Brill, Leiden 1997, pp. 48–54, and Caroline Finkel, *Osman's Dream. The Story of the Ottoman Empire, 1300-1923*, John Murray Publishers, London 2005, ch. 15.

[40] Hüseyin Yılmaz explains that the term simply meant a political ruler without any univocal conceptualization of the title and its attributions. According to the author, it refers "to executive power through which sovereign authority is exercised" (Hüseyin Yılmaz, *Caliphate Redefined. The Mystical Turn in Ottoman Political Thought*, Princeton University Press, Princeton 2018, p. 145).

[41] See Louis Gardet, *Les hommes de l'Islam. Approche de mentalités*, Hachette, Paris 1977, p. 118.

[42] See the relative voices in Ludwig W. Adamec, *Historical Dictionary of Islam*, Scarecrow Press, Lanham-Toronto-Plymouth 2009, p. 35; John L. Esposito (ed.), *The Oxford Dictionary of Islam*, Oxford University Press, Oxford 2003, p. 19.

[43] Cf. Adamec, *Historical Dictionary of Islam, cit.*, p. 313.

[44] The term is used in a non-univocal way, and it is commonly used to refer to religious functionaries and clerics. See "Mullah" (voice) in Esposito, *The Oxford Dictionary of Islam, cit.*, p. 214.

[45] From this point of view, the case of Shīʿa Islam appears to be different, with an established and institutionalized clerical order, whose hierarchy is still not comparable with, for instance, the one of Catholicism. On this, see Mohammed Ayoob, Danielle Nicole Lussier, *The Many Faces of Political Islam. Religion and Politics in Muslim Societies*, University of Michigan Press, Ann Arbor 2020, pp. 27–29.

Therefore, in Sunnī Islam the bipartition of authorities has never been univocal and, most of all, has never been theorized as necessary. Aside from factual and contingent specializations in various competences, from an ideal point of view Islamic authorities are united at the point of being considered a single entity, and it is not by chance that a renowned scholar such as al-Ghazālī in defining the archetype of political authority refers to the biblical prophet-kings David and Salomon, thus ideally returning to a monotheistic pre-Christian context.[46] In Islam, the ideal continues to be represented by the non-institutionalized and fluidly theorized figure of the *imām*, whose title etymologically refers to the idea of "standing in front of others", thus denoting a community leader, without any univocal specification as to its religious or political role.[47]

Following what has been said regarding the absence of the concept of *persona ficta* in classical Islam, we can once again argue that the West could develop a separation between secular and spiritual powers because of its capability of theorizing abstract juridical and political figures, such as, in this case, *imperium* and *sacerdotium*. These latter two are to be regarded as pieces of abstraction, whose coincidence with the *persona actualis* of a particular ruler is to be termed as transient, and not necessary. On the contrary, Islam never conceptualized *in abstracto* the idea of political powers and their possible declinations in spiritual and temporal spheres. Here, as already observed, the idea of power closely adheres to the physical ruler who exercises it, thus innervating itself in the various needs of the *ummah*, without pre-conceptual and dogmatic schemes. Politics and statecraft—and in a broader sense the idea of political governance—were usually

[46] "Political authority and religious morality are blended into a single prism in al-Ghazali's thought, with the monotheistic Prophet-Kings David and Solomon cited. A methodology based on the juristic account of the Shari'ah dominates al-Ghazali's renewal in the recovery and continuation of the past of the monotheistic prophets. The Qur'an is the foremost authority and source in the interpretation of a state based on Islamic precepts. As a universal principle, ethical conduct is the only worthy means to acquire political authority for al-Ghazali in his citation of the Qur'anic verses about the Prophet David who was also the King of the Israelites. The monotheistic past supplies many appropriate examples about the purposes of politics – protection of religion and freedom" (Mohammed Moussa, *Politics of the Islamic Tradition. The Thought of Muhammad al-Ghazali*, Routledge, London-New York 2016, p. 102).

[47] Once again, with regard to the meaning of the term, see G. Hussein Rassool, *Islamic Counselling. An Introduction to Theory and Practice*, Routledge, London-New York 2016, p. 253.

referred to with the term *siyāsa*,[48] but this concept is intended as the concrete recognition of a branch of human activity,[49] and not, like it may be in the Western world, as an abstract figure in opposition to other categories such as religion or law. On the contrary, the intimate union of politics and the multifaceted *sharīʿa* is exhaustively expressed by the phrase *al-siyāsa sharʿiyya*, which can be freely translated as "governance according to *sharīʿa*",[50] and considered as a structural and essential requisite for the exercise of power.

5.3.3 Conclusive Remarks

In conclusion, the Western and Islamic views differ on a fundamental point, which is not related to ruling intended in a concrete and practical way but rather to its theoretical conception. In the West, the separation between spiritual and temporal authorities is to be termed as necessary and unavoidable, despite the fact that these two powers had sometime come into conflict, trying to prevail over the other with alternate fortunes. This

[48] Regarding this, see Hamilton Alexander Rosskeen Gibb [1954 –], *The Encyclopaedia of Islam, SAN-SZE*, Brill, Leiden 1997, pp. 693 ff. Briefly, it can be argued that "*siyāsa* is, on the one hand, the formulation of an active behaviour in a way that considers appropriately its consequences. On the other hand, it implies a certain pragmatic rationalism in overseeing affairs that is, above all, present in *siyāsa* as political management. In regard to this latter meaning, *siyāsa* was used interchangeably in early Islam to denote statecraft, government, the manner of governing or the ability to govern" (Abdessamad Belhaj, "Law and order according to Ibn Taymiyya and Ibn Qayyim al-Jawziyya: a re-examination of siyāsa sharʿiyya", in *Islamic Theology, Philosophy and Law. Debating Ibn Taymiyya and Ibn Qayyim al-Jawziyya*, eds. Birgit Krawietz, Georges Tamer, De Gruyter, Berlin-Boston 2013, p. 402.

[49] With regard to this, Lewis observes that *siyāsa* denotes "a skill or a craft rather than a doctrine or a philosophy" (Bernard Lewis, *Political Words and Ideas in Islam*, Markus Wiener Publishers, Princeton 2008, pp. 32–33). As I argue in my work, the Western world would on the contrary conceive politics mainly as a doctrine or philosophy, in abstract separated by other fields of human action and comprehension. Lewis, in this passage, emphasizes the concreteness of the Islamic perspective in approaching politics, conceived above all as the pragmatic human activity of governing.

[50] According to the doctrine of *siyāsa sharʿiyya*, the political authority was enabled to enact regulations and administrative orders (*qānūn*), insofar as this activity was compliant with *sharīʿa*. Cf. Leonard Wood, "Legislation as an instrument of Islamic law", in *The Oxford Handbook of Islamic Law*, eds. Anver M. Emon, Rumee Ahmed, Oxford University Press, Oxford 2018, pp. 556–557. The term *siyāsa sharʿiyya* was firstly used by Ibn ʿArabī (1165–1240), although "later sources on *siyāsa sharʿiyya* relies heavily on Ibn Taymiyya" (Belhaj, *Law and order according to Ibn Taymiyya*, *cit.*, p. 402).

happened fundamentally for two reasons. First, because of the Christian thoughts about Caesar and God, which later on came to shape the overall conception of Western power with the Christianization of the Roman Empire. Second, because of the capability of Western jurists to create abstract juridical figures of power and authority, whose conceptualization could come to life in theory aside from taking shape in concrete praxis. On the contrary, in the Sunnī perspective a certain bipartition between temporal and spiritual powers may occur, but it is regarded as an occasional occurrence, justified by the pragmatical needs of the Islamic community and by the flexibility of its political governance. However, it is once again the ruler, and not the abstract conception of his power to be at the center of the Muslim reflection, whose supreme aim is to achieve salvation for believers by following "the straight path". This latter goal being a unitary one, in which there is no place for a univocally theorized difference of roles, the non-necessary nature of the separation between temporal and spiritual powers follows as a natural consequence. Therefore, while the Christian world elaborated a theoretically refined vision of power and authority, Islam shaped its view on the basis of the concrete necessities of a community whose purpose was to survive and flourish. Again, while the Occidental thought proceeded to the creation of a sophisticated but rather fixed system of authority based on a dual-track, the Islamic world developed a flexible and adaptive system, capable of undergoing the necessary changes in order to respond to the various needs of the *ummah*.

It is for this very reason that, even today, we refer to the Christian religion and to the corpus of its spiritual teachings with the term Christianity, while we refer to the political body of the Christian lands with the term Christendom. The term Islam, on the contrary, addresses a comprehensive reality, the separation of whose single parts happens to be difficult even from a terminological point of view.[51]

5.4 Reasons to Punish: A Teleological Analysis

In order to carry out a deeper analysis of the divergence between the Islamic and Western perspectives on the separation between temporal and spiritual power, it is necessary to examine the criminal systems of these two worlds. As a premise, I will start by stating that it is improper to speak about a "criminal system" in Islam, since it would once again reflect an

[51] Cf. Lewis, *Faith and Power, cit.*, p. 41.

eminently Western conception that, as already said, does not find an analogous equivalent in the Muslim world. However, every legal order feels the need to punish and prevent some kinds of actions, thus elaborating its own method of administering justice. The repression of crime does not simply represent a way by which a given community prevent and compensate the commission of acts in some way perceived as harmful or illicit; on the contrary, it is first of all a mirror by which to investigate how a civilization understands essential and constitutive elements of society itself, such as justice and retribution, compensation, and rehabilitation. The philosophy of punishment and its complex rituality,[52] which of course can greatly change depending on the cultural and historical contexts, not only represents a unique source of information about the pragmatic necessities of a community but suggests elements on its way of understanding law and authority as well. Hence, a teleological reflection on the ultimate aim of the idea of punishment appears to be of particular interest, especially with specific regard to the West and Islam.[53]

5.4.1 Reasons to Punish in the West

In the West, the criminal sanction carried out by the use of force has been thought of mainly as a pragmatic response to the necessity of maintaining social order. This is true regardless of the various approaches to the issue and regardless of the ways in which, along the course of history, Western civilization has shaped the features of its idea of justice. Therefore, in the West the structural element of the concept of punishment is found in its

[52] Regarding the rituality of punishment, it is worth remembering what Foucault stated with regard to the so-called liturgy of *supplice*, in which framework the spectacularism of torture represents a constitutive element. According to Foucault, "torture forms part of a ritual. It is an element in the liturgy of punishment and meets two demands. It must mark the victim. It is intended, either by the scar it leaves on the body, or by the spectacle that accompanies it, to brand the victim with infamy; even if its function is to 'purge' the crime, torture does not reconcile; it traces around or, rather, on the very body of the condemned man signs that must not be effaced: in any case, men will remember public exhibition, the pillory, torture and pain duly observed. And, from the point of view of the law that imposes it, public torture and execution must be spectacular, it must be seen by all almost as its triumph" (Michel Foucault [1975], *Discipline & Punish. The Birth of the Prison*, trans. Alan Sheridan, Vintage Books, New York 1995, p. 34).

[53] I briefly deal with this fundamental issue in my article "La funzione della pena tra Occidente e mondo islamico: una prospettiva teleologica", in *Dignitas. Percorsi di carcere e giustizia*, May 2016, www.rivistadignitas.it.

being pragmatically functional for the maintenance of a given idea of social order.[54]

In a context characterized by its Christian heritage, this is easily understandable, given the separation of spiritual and secular authorities that has already been analyzed in the previous paragraph. Coercive measures were indeed a prerogative of the temporal authorities on the basis of the principle by which *Ecclesia non sitit sanguinem*. The religious and moral aim of purging the offender from sin was on the other hand demanded of the spiritual power, which, however, could not exercise any repressive and coercive power without the intervention of the secular authority. Even in complex and articulated criminal systems like the Holy Inquisition, whose mechanisms of internal functioning were based on the close cooperation of ecclesiastic and lay branches of law, the theoretical separation of competences was always maintained: the competence in matters of sanctions and punishment was indeed an exclusive prerogative of the so-called secular arm, which was not to be arbitrarily used by the church.[55] While the aim of the ecclesiastic inquisitorial authorities was thus the extirpation of heresy from society, pursuing the supreme goal of the *salus animarum*, the temporal power was mainly concerned with granting social order through the means of coerciveness.

With regard to this, Aquinas is quite clear in stating that the ultimate aim of capital punishment is the prevention of criminal acts.[56] Saint Thomas suggests that any rebellion against a given order is naturally followed by an act of punishment by the guarantor of that order, aimed at reestablishing and ultimately safeguarding it from any further subversion.[57] Following this premise, he states that the sinner is to be considered

[54] Cf. S. M. Shahidullah, *Comparative Criminal Justice Systems. Global and Local Perspectives*, Jones & Bartlett Learning, Burlington 2014, pp. 148 ff.

[55] Regarding the cooperation between inquisitorial authorities and secular ones, see Gretchen Starr-LeBeau, Kimberly Lynn, "Inquisitions", in *Judging Faith, Punishing Sin. Inquisitions and Consistories in the Early Modern World*, eds. Charles H. Parker, Gretchen Starr-LeBeau, Cambridge University Press, Cambridge 2017, pp. 52–65.

[56] Thomas Aquinas, *Summa Theologiae*, I-II, q. 87, art. 1–3.

[57] Thomas suggests that "we find that the natural inclination of man is to repress those who rise up against him. Now it is evident that all things contained in an order, are, in a manner, one, in relation to the principle of that order. Consequently, whatever rises up against an order, is put down by that order or by the principle thereof". *Summa Theologiae*, I-II, q. 87, art. 1, translation by the Fathers of the English Dominican Province [1912], *Summa Theologica, Volume II - Part II, First Section*, Cosimo Classics, New York 2007, p. 973.

a disrupter of multiple levels of order, that is to say, the order of God, of man, and of reason.[58] Hence, the punishment inflicted by the temporal authorities represents the response to the subversion of the order imposed by man in the framework of the *lex humana*. This point implies two relevant consequences. First, it is logically implied as a theoretical possibility that the offense against God is not simultaneously considered an offense against human law and *vice versa*. Due to the different levels of order, and the respective levels of laws, here it seems a primary form of separation between sin and crime was theorized,[59] whose definitive theorization would be provided centuries later, in a completely different context. Second, the aim of the punishment inflicted by man according to his law may not coincide with the aim of the punishment inflicted by God. With regard to this latter point, Saint Thomas is explicitly clear in stating that human laws punish an evildoer in order to prevent others from committing further illicit acts, thus maintaining social order in the community.[60]

With the emergence of modern statehood, the dimension of criminal justice as a functional response by public authorities aiming at maintaining social order is even more evident. In the modern State, criminal sanctions

[58] According to the Aquinas, "the sinner acts against his reason, and against human and Divine law. Wherefore he incurs a threefold punishment; one, inflicted by himself, viz. remorse of conscience; another, inflicted by man; and a third, inflicted by God". *Summa Theologiae*, I-II, q. 87, art. 1 (ibid., p. 973).

[59] As Biondi observes, even "the preaching of Jesus admits a separation between the divine and human order, and therefore the possibility that, in the non-essential points, the two orders may not coincide. The divine law ranges in the field of the spirit and the supernatural, and therefore proclaims certain truths that would be inconceivable to translate into juridical norms, aimed at regulating human relationships and rendering externally coercible the claims deriving from it" (Biondo Biondi, *Il diritto romano cristiano*, vol. I, Giuffré, Milan 1952, p. 66). Regarding the same point, and about the separation between sin and crime due to the progressive elaboration of the distinction between spiritual and temporal powers in Catholic canon law, see Andrew Skotnicki, "History of Religion and Crime", in *The Social History of Crime and Punishment in America. An Encyclopedia*, ed. Wilbur R. Miller, SAGE Publications, Thousand Oaks 2012, p. 1530.

[60] "Even the punishment that is inflicted according to human laws, is not always intended as a medicine for the one who is punished, but sometimes only for others: thus when a thief is hanged, this is not for his own amendment, but for the sake of others, that at least they may be deterred from crime through fear of the punishment". Thomas Aquinas, *Summa Theologiae*, I-II, q. 87, art. 3 (trans. by the Fathers of the English Dominican Province [1912], *Summa Theologica, Volume II - Part II, First Section*, Cosimo Classics, New York 2007, p. 975).

belong to the Leviathan-State as one of the most relevant expressions of its sovereign power. Whether all the laws come from the State, as the unique source of law, the instrument of criminal punishment comes as the most direct and explicit manifestation of the monopoly of public power,[61] in societies in which there is no more place for intermediate bodies and *jura propria*. The mechanistic nature of the criminal sanction in this context only serve to highlight its eminently concrete and pragmatic nature, once again aimed at granting prevention by the means of repression. As for law in general, the instrument of punishment does not have any moral implication, being the manifestation of an absolute power whose primary legitimacy comes from the Hobbesian dialectic of imposing one's own rule by force.[62] In order to establish a social and political order, the State exercises the use of force according to the exorcizing and cathartic rituality of punishment, considered as the most functional to its long-term preservation. In this perspective, the only order is the order of the State, and there are no crimes and sanctions if not the ones created by the State. With regard to the teleological perspective of punishment in this context, the thought of Catholic diplomat Joseph De Maistre appears to be particularly significant. According to De Maistre, the maintenance of social order must be based on a triad composed of the figures of the pope, king, and executioner. Especially this latter, as the physical and iconic incarnation of criminal sanction and supreme punishment, is qualified as the true

[61] This teleological perspective on crime and punishment is valid even in the case of a Hegelian society based on the idea on an ethical State. Regarding punishment, Hegel shows a basically retributivist position, according to which punishment is to be considered as the nullification of an evil and as the restoration of a right, marking the transition from *Unrecht* to *Recht* (see Allen W. Wood [1990], *Hegel's Ethical Thought*, Cambridge University Press, Cambridge 1995, pp. 108 ff.). In this context, the individual lives in function of the State, and therefore the idea of punishment cannot be seen but as a mean to safeguard the State, and not necessarily the morality of the individual. This is particularly evident regarding Hegel's consideration of punishment as the denial of the crime as a universal law (cf., for a critical position, Philip J. Kain, *Hegel and Right. A Study of the Philosophy of Right*, State University of New York Press, Albany 2018, p. 44).

[62] Once again, the "earthly" nature of the criminal sanction in this context is clearly underlined by Hobbes' distinction between sin and crime, with all the aforementioned implications. See Laurie M. Johnson Bagby, *Hobbes's Leviathan. A Reader's Guide*, Continuum, London 2007, p. 56.

guarantor of peace and stability in a given society, without which "order gives way to chaos".[63]

With the advent of the Enlightenment, new visions on criminal repression, social prevention, and legal sanctions emerged in the juridical and political debates.[64] Notwithstanding the philosophical fracture that characterized this period with respect to previous times, the nature of criminal sanctions as responses to social disvalues of illicit acts, to safeguard internal peace and social order, is never really put into question. With a further and deeper separation between legality and morality, fostered by intellectuals such as Samuel von Pufendorf and Christian Thomasius,[65] the instrument of punishment could only be reduced to its functional nature in preventing criminal acts in society. In the new juridical discourse on crime and retribution, and especially in the thought of authors such as Voltaire and Rousseau, the punitive and repressive methods of public authority could be rethought in light of the principles of the Enlightenment, but not the very aim of punishment, which could be considered constant. In this context, sanction continues to be considered the concrete response not a moral disvalue, but to social danger. The rather eloquent example is of Cesare Beccaria, who advocated the abolition of the death penalty, but mainly because of its being nonfunctional and ineffective in preventing crime and maintaining order. Beccaria's reflection, one the most important of this period concerning this fundamental issue, does not approach the matter from a moral perspective, but on a functional and sociological one.[66] According to the author, indeed, the sanction should aim at "preventing the offender from causing new damages to his citizens, and diverting others from doing the same".[67]

[63] "Every greatness, every power, every subjection is based on the executioner: he constitutes the horror and the bond of the human association. Take this incomprehensible agent out of the world, and at the same time order gives way to chaos, thrones sink and society disappears". Joseph De Maistre [1821], "Les Soirées de Saint-Pétersbourg", in *Oeuvres complètes*, Slatkine, Geneva 1979, pp. 32–33.

[64] See Georg Rusche, Otto Kirchheimer [1939], *Punishment and Social Structure*, Transaction Publishers, New Brunswick-London 2009, pp. 72 ff.

[65] See Adriano Cavanna, *Storia del diritto moderno in Europa. Le fonti e il pensiero giuridico*, vol. I, Giuffré, Milan 1982, pp. 339–340.

[66] In the words of Beccaria: "Is death a really *useful* and *necessary* punishment for the security and the good order of society? Are tortures and penances *just*, and do they achieve the *end* laws pursue? What is the best manner in preventing crimes?" (Cesare Beccaria [1764], *Dei delitti e delle pene*, Lackington, Allen, and co., London 1801, p. 4).

[67] Ibid., p. 45.

Even the principle of the rehabilitation of the offender,[68] which came to be a fundamental part of criminal models in contemporary Western systems,[69] does not change perspective as to the aim punishment pursues. The rehabilitation principle cannot be qualified as a form of moral re-education, but on the contrary comes to be a new form by which authority prevents further crime in a way alternative to repression.[70] As for Beccaria, the idea of purging the crime by annihilating the offender—principle of retribution—up to his physical removal from society, is seen as a

[68] Rehabilitation can be defined as "modification of an offender's criminal behavior", which seeks to "terminate or reduce criminal activity through counseling, group therapy, job training, or similar programs" (Alfred Blumstein, Jaqueline Cohen, Jeffrey A. Roth, Christy A. Visher (eds.), *Criminal Careers and "Career Criminals"*, vol. I, National Academy Press, Washington 1986, pp. 15–16). For an overview on rehabilitation and crime prevention, see David Weisburd, David P. Farrington, Charlotte Gill, "What Works in Crime Prevention?", introduction to *What Works in Crime Prevention and Rehabilitation. Lessons from Systematic Reviews*, eds. David Weisburd, David P. Farrington, Charlotte Gill, Springer, New York 2016, pp. 1–15.

[69] For a historical perspective of treatment and rehabilitation, see Iain Crow, *The Treatment and Rehabilitation of Offenders*, SAGE, London-Thousand Oaks-New Delhi 2001, pp. 3–20. For a comprehensive history of the principle of rehabilitation in the English system, see Anthony H. Goodman, *Rehabilitating and Resettling Offenders in the Community*, Wiley-Blackwell, Chichester 2012, especially pp. 33 ff.

[70] Two aims may be reconducted to the idea of rehabilitation. First, the prevention of crime. Second, avoiding "immunizing" the offender by the means of mere repression and isolation. Given that the offender is part of the society whose order is necessary to protect, the principle of rehabilitation provides a combination of crime prevention and re-education and resettlement of the offenders themselves. This seems to be a unique teleological perspective, which considers the offender an active part of the community, thus deserving to be re-inserted in it. However, in literature the question is debated, with special attention to the principal beneficiary of the rehabilitation—the offender or society as a whole. Bennet speaks about a twofold aim of rehabilitation, not without concerns: "Fundamentally, the distinction here is between interventions that are aimed at the offender's own good, and those that are aimed at the general social good. On the former branch, we might think of rehabilitation as aiming to enable the offender to live a good, worthwhile, productive or at least law-abiding life as an expression of individual concern for him as a human being. On the latter, we can think of rehabilitation as aiming to enable the offender to live a good, worthwhile, productive or at least law-abiding life because treating offenders in that way is the most cost-effective way to reduce crime or reduce risks of harm" (Christopher Bennet, "Punishment and Rehabilitation", in *Punishment and Ethics. New Perspectives*, eds. Jesper Ryberg, J. Angelo Corlett, Palgrave Macmillan, New York-Basingstoke 2010, p. 61). In my opinion, a focus only on the principle of rehabilitation as an instrument to be used on the offender, with no implication or with minor implications on society, risks to become the imposition of a moral conversion, as it will be explained in the following footnote.

non-effective method and is considered to be ultimately non-useful to its goal. Through rehabilitation the authority pursues the same aim that secular authorities of previous ages had pursued, that is to say, shaping a criminal model that proves itself functional in preventing crime and maintaining order. In spite of a recurrent and questionable view in the juridical debate that would effectively interpret rehabilitation as moral conversion,[71] it is possible to conclude that even today, when the idea of punishment is usually mitigated by humanitarian principles, the criminal sanction represents a way of pragmatically and concretely safeguarding social order.

To summarize, we can state that the Western world has experimented with different criminal models and methodologies each one with distinctive rationales, ranging from retribution to rehabilitation, however maintaining a structural point in the teleological orientation of criminal sanction: in the West the criminal sanction has an eminently social nature and is aimed at preventing crime and maintaining order, without any relevant moral implication.

5.4.2 Reasons to Punish in Islam

In the Islamic world, the aforementioned aim is on the contrary complemented by an intrinsic moral dimension deeply inherent to the elements of crime and punishment. As preliminarily observed, the very definition of "criminal law" mirrors a Western-based classification, and it is therefore appropriate to note two further points, which are to be understood in the comprehension of Islamic crimes and punishments.

First, the discipline of illicit activities is an inseparable part of the "straight path" of the *sharīʿa*, thus organically placed in this comprehensive perspective that aims at leading the believer toward salvation. Consequently, crimes and sanctions are to be analyzed not as a separated

[71] For instance, Carrara argued that society "has the duty of trying to achieve in every way the emendation of the offender" and that "as an instrument to such effect, it must take advantage of the time of the atonement of the punishment in order to act effectively on the soul of the condemned" (Francesco Carrara, "Emenda del reo assunta come unico fondamento e fine della pena", in *Opuscoli di diritto criminale*, ed. Francesco Carrara, vol. I, Giachetti, Prato 1878, p. 189). More recently, Francesco Palazzo [2003], *Corso di diritto penale. Parte generale*, Giappichelli, Turin 2013, p. 36. This view is to be rejected because of the various philosophical problematics it poses, among which the most important is, in my opinion, the non-univocal legitimacy of the moral imposition actuated by the State on the offender's morality, especially in secular and pluralist contexts.

branch of law but as part of a *unicum*, in strict connection with the philosophical and juridical mechanisms of a *sharīʿa*-based order. A teleological reflection on Islamic punishment should necessarily be carried out in the broader framework of the purposes of *sharīʿa* (*maqāṣid al-sharīʿa*), which involves the protection of religion, life, intellect, procreation, and property.[72] What in literature is sometimes addressed as "Islamic criminal law",[73] with the previously mentioned interpretative and categorial clarifications, is thus to be referred to those conducts that are considered forbidden by *sharīʿa*, according to the roots of *fiqh*.[74]

Second, the Islamic legal order recognizes three levels of forbidden actions and relative ways of punishment and compensation: *ḥadd* (pl. *ḥudūd*), *qiṣāṣ*, and *taʿzīr*.

The *ḥudūd* crimes[75] refer to actions that are explicitly forbidden by Allāh because they are illicit and immoral, whose punishment is

[72] Traditionally, the majority of authors agree in recognizing the aforementioned five goals of *sharīʿa*, that is to say, the protection of religion, life, intellect, procreation, and property. Other authors recognized as *sharīʿa's* purposes justice and happiness as well, while in modern times the doctrine of *maqāṣid* is sometimes used for fostering innovative interpretations of *sharīʿa*-derived provisions. About the *maqāṣid*, regarding which authors are not always concord and whose theorization is debated, see briefly Jasser Auda, *Maqāṣid Al-Sharīʿa. A Beginner's Guide*, The International Institute of Islamic Thought, London-Washington 2008, especially pp. 1–16.

[73] Just to cite a few monographs in which the term recurs from the titles: Tahir Wasti, *The Application of Islamic Criminal Law in Pakistan. Sharia in Practice*, Brill, Leiden-Boston 2009; Luqman Zakariyah, *Legal Maxims in Islamic Criminal Law. Theory and Applications*, Brill, Leiden-Boston 2015; Olaf Köndgen, *The Codification of Islamic Criminal Law in the Sudan. Penal Codes and Supreme Court Case Law under Numayrī and al-Bashīr*, Brill, Leiden-Boston 2018.

[74] It is worth considering that a "distinguishing feature of Islamic ideology concerning crime is its view that crime is a violation of God's law and thus is directed against God before the immediate victim" (Abdullah H. M. Al-Khalifah, "Religiosity in Islam as a Protective Mechanism against Criminal Temptation", in *American Journal of Islamic Social Sciences*, vol. XI, n. 1, Spring 1994, p. 6).

[75] For a comprehensive and detailed analysis, see Mohammad Hashim Kamali, *Crime and Punishment in Islamic Law. A Fresh Interpretation*, Oxford University Press, New York 2019, pp. 21–185. See also Gamil Muhammed Hussein, "Basic Guarantees in the Islamic Criminal Justice System", in *Criminal Justice in Islam. Judicial Procedure in the Sharīʿa*, eds. Muhammad Abdel Haleem, Omar Sherif, Kate Daniels, I.B. Tauris, London-New York 2003, pp. 37–43; Rudolph Peters, *Crime and Punishment in Islamic Law. Theory and Practice from the Sixteenth to the Twenty-First Century*, Cambridge University Press, Cambridge 2005, pp. 53–65; Ali Akram Khan Sherwani, *Impact of Islamic Penal Laws on the Traditional Arab Society*, M.D. Publications, New Delhi 1993, pp. 54–57.

predetermined by *sharīʿa* and must be carried out in public without any possible modification by judicial discretion. They comprehend actions such as drinking alcohol, committing apostasy, unlawful sexual intercourse (*zināʾ*), false accusation of *zināʾ* (*qadhf*), and highway robbery and theft.[76] The recurrence of *ḥudūd* sanctions was however less frequent than the sanctions carried out on the basis of the other groups because of the high judicial requirements in terms of proofs and evidences,[77] and represents therefore a marginal manifestation of this phenomenon as to its frequency.

Qiṣāṣ[78] refers to the retributive idea of retaliation, and more than designating a criminal action, it designates a system of justice and compensation. By *qiṣāṣ* it is intended that the possibility exists for the victim or their heirs to take compensation by inflicting on the offender a punishment equal to the offense. It is applied in the case of voluntary injuries or homicide, and its usage recalls pre-Islamic Arabia, to the Mosaic law of the Old Covenant, and to the Code of Hammurabi with its principle of "an eye for an eye".[79] Moreover, in this case the punishment may be converted into the obligation of granting to the victim or the family a sum of money (*diya*, commonly known as "blood money"), according to a principle of financial compensation or extinguished by pardon.

In the case of offenses that are not specified according to the Islamic revelation, the judgment is left to the discretion of the *qāḍī* (judge). This latter case is the case of *ta'zīr*,[80] which represents a residual form of sanction in cases not covered by the previous two groups. As a further

[76] Cf. Cliff Roberson, Dilip K. Das, *An Introduction to Comparative Legal Models of Criminal Justice*, CRC Press, Boca Raton-London-New York 2008, p. 145.

[77] Cf. Rudolph Peters, "The Islamization of Criminal Law: A Comparative Analysis", in *Die Welt des Islams*, New Series, vol. XXXIV, n. 2, November 1994, pp. 250–252.

[78] See Hussein, *Basic Guarantees in the Islamic Criminal Justice System*, *cit.*, pp. 43–44; Peters, *Crime and Punishment*, *cit.*, pp. 38–53; Sherwani, *Impact of Islamic Penal Laws*, *cit.*, pp. 48–54.

[79] Cf. Ann Black, Hossein Esmaeili, Nadirsyah Hosen, *Modern Perspectives on Islamic Law*, Edward Elgar Publishing, Cheltenham-Northampton 2013, p. 221.

[80] See Hussein, *Basic Guarantees in the Islamic Criminal Justice System*, *cit.*, pp. 44–45; Peters, *Crime and Punishment*, *cit.*, pp. 65–68; Sherwani, *Impact of Islamic Penal Laws*, *cit.*, pp. 57–60. It is relevant to notice that a *ta'zīr* penalty may be applied even for *hadd* or *qiṣāṣ* conducts, for instance, in cases when the legal requirements for other kinds of punishments are not met. Therefore, *ta'zīr* has not just a residual and subsidiary nature as for the prosecuted action, but for the punishment as well. In light of this, it is correct to say that *ta'zīr* mainly reflects the perspective of retribution and deterrence, wherever it is not possible to adopt different instruments of compensation. Regarding this latter point, see M. H. Kamali, *Crime and Punishment in Islamic Law*, *cit.*, pp. 188–189.

classification, the crime represents an offense that can be committed against Allāh, man, or both of them.[81]

Evidently, these classifications are self-sufficient and based on autonomous categories, which do not find analogies in the Western models. While analyzing the Islamic legal perspective concerning crime, it is necessary to autonomously consider this vision without imposing other sorts of classification that are conceptually alien to the Muslim context. The way of structuring the legal system with respect to the idea of repressing and preventing illicit conducts, with particular attention to the relationship between crime and punishment, shows some important philosophical and juridical implications and outcomes, which are worth a deeper look.

The idea of *qiṣāṣ* highlights the actual inexistence in Islam of the dichotomy of public-private, which represents a typical feature of Western modernity.[82] While a differentiation in terms of gravity of the offenses between *qiṣāṣ* and *ḥadd* exists, it is not an analogous form of separation between the public sphere, inherent to the common interest of society, and the private one, inherent to the interest of the individual. As is evident, in the case of *qiṣāṣ*, conducts such as homicide and voluntary injury are perceived to be offenses against individuals, and in some way judged with the involvement of the victim or by the heirs, who can require retaliation, accept monetary compensation, or pardon the offender.[83] In the case of an *ḥadd* conduct, the offense is not simply perceived as a harmful conduct against an individual or the community but directly involves the

[81] See Adel Omar Sherif, "Generalities on Criminal Procedure under Islamic Sharīʿa", in *Criminal Justice in Islam*, *cit.*, p. 5.

[82] I speak here of Western modernity because before the modern period there were indeed cases in which, with regard to homicide and criminal prevention, the public and private elements were inextricably confused in one, as in the case of the early Medieval barbarian law of Europe. In these cases, for instance, we can draw some parallelisms with the Islamic system of *qiṣāṣ*, with specific regard to the monetary compensations of violent crimes like homicides and to the consideration of homicide as an offense prevalently conceived against individuals. On these last points, see Michel Rouche [1982], "Break-up and metamorphosis of the West: fifth to seventh centuries", in *The Cambridge Illustrated History of the Middle Ages, 350-950*, vol. I, ed. Robert Fossier, trans. Janet Sondheimer, Cambridge University Press, Cambridge 2003, pp. 80–81.

[83] Peters highlights the private dimension of retaliation, stating that it belongs to "the domain of private prosecutions, in the sense that the culprit can only be sentenced and punished if the victim or his heirs demand punishment" (Peters, *The Islamization of Criminal Law*, *cit.*, p. 247). Crone puts in light the private dimension of this kind of criminal offenses as well (Crone, *God's rule*, *cit.*, p. 281).

divinity. The very term *ḥudūd* can be translated as "boundaries",[84] that is to say, the boundaries in terms of conduct and behavior that have been settled for men by Allāh for eternity, which found its decisive and definitive form of settlement in the Qur'ānic revelation. This distinction, however, is not superimposable on the Western concept of public or private interest[85] because of an inextricable nexus between the social and moral dimensions of a crime, which is usually found in the Western view.

This latter point represents one of the most interesting and relevant focuses in the debate about criminal actions according to the Islamic perspective and could only greatly influence the interactions between Islamic *sharīʿa* and Wester legal systems. As has already been mentioned, in the Islamic legal tradition the sanction can be intended as retribution for an illicit conduct in order to prevent further criminal conducts and maintain social order. This is actually a common feature between the Islamic and Western views, which both feel the exigency of punishing offenders to order society. However, while in Western history this conception has not been characterized by a moral dimension—if not marginally and occasionally—in Islam, on the contrary, it is a structural and essential element of the discipline of crime and punishment with "no clear-cut boundary between morality and legality".[86]

The conception of crime as the violation of a divine command, as prescribed by *sharīʿa*, brings about relevant and necessary religious implications, as well as juridical ones. While in the West the crime may represent the breaking of a human rule, in Islam it is often associated with the breaking of a divine prescription, as in the case of an *ḥadd* action. Therefore, and given the absence of a structured differentiation between secular and spiritual powers, in the Islamic context the separation between the ideas of

[84] It is interesting to notice that Catafago literally translates in his dictionary the term with "boundaries, confines", however adding the definition of "penal laws", with the evident adoption of a Western perspective. Cf. Joseph Catafago, *An English and Arabic Dictionary in Two Parts*, part I, Bernard Quaritch publisher, London 1856, p. 91.

[85] Kamali suggests that the case of *qiṣāṣ* cannot be simply defined as a "private" offense because of the religious and moral disvalue of the conduct of homicide, which calls in cause the divinity as well. Nevertheless, it is possible to argue that the criminal methodology of *qiṣāṣ* is based on a privatistic approach, in the sense that the crime is to be prosecuted mainly by the victim or the heirs. Cf. Kamali, *Crime and Punishment in Islamic Law, cit.*, p. 209.

[86] Lambton, *State and Government in Medieval Islam, cit.*, pp. xv-xvi. Niazi similarly argues that one "of the distinguishing features of Islamic law is that there is no divergence between the law and morality. Every crime is a sin as well" (Liaquat Ali Khan Niazi, *Islamic Law of Tort*, Research Cell, Cayal Singh Trust Library, Lahore 1988, p. 13).

sin and crime comes to be much less defined. The real differentiation to be drawn is whether a certain sin should be criminally prosecuted or not, and the answer is strictly associated with the aforementioned moral dimension of the crime.

In Islam, every action considered as a "crime" according to the aforementioned classification is to be considered as a sin as well. However, a sin is not to be criminally prosecuted in every circumstance. For instance, it should not be prosecuted when, as a private action, its exposure in a trial would cause the immorality of the action to spread across the community. As for sins that can be considered as secret and merely private, the opportunity should be examined to prosecute them according to a preventive analysis of the possibility for other believers to emulate their immorality. As a consequence, it is evident that the ultimate aim of prosecuting crime is to prevent the *ummah* from the pervasive nature of sin.[87]

The moral dimension of crime and punishment in Islam can be deduced from other elements. For instance, the institute of the *kaffarah* can be considered as a particular penalty that can be inflicted on an offender for the atonement of his fault, which has been traditionally applied for non-intentional or semi-intentional murder. In this case, the offender must perform religious acts such as worshipping or fasting in order for the sin to be forgiven.[88] As is evident, the objective that *kaffarah* penalties pursue is not related to the prevention of crime such as in the case of retaliation, nor that they pursue a human level of justice. On the contrary, *kaffarah* penalties refer to a moral dimension of the illicit action, with the direct involvement of the divinity, from whom the offender must ask for forgiveness, with a consequent superhuman element that comes to be incorporated into the legal system. *Kaffarah*, representing an additional or alternative sanction, is however considered to be part of the overall structure that has to enforce *sharīʿa* and is conceptually ascribed to the juridical phenomenon which the Western world refers to with the term "criminal law".

[87] See Deborah Scolart, *L'Islam, il reato, la pena. Dal fiqh alla codificazione del diritto penale*, Istituto per l'Oriente C.A. Nallino, Rome 2013, p. 16. According to the author "every crime is indeed a sin as well, because the offender violates with his conduct an explicit command of God", but not necessarily *vice versa* (ibid., pp. 21–22).

[88] Cf. Muhammad al-Madni Busaq, *Perspectives on Modern Criminal Policy & Islamic Sharia*, trans. Zubair Ahmad, Naif Arab University for Security Sciences, Riyadh 2005, p. 163–164, 166.

The moral dimension of the criminal sanction is highlighted with regard to another two elements, mainly inherent to the *qiṣāṣ* and *ḥudūd* penalties. In the case of *qiṣāṣ*, the crime is considered to be a private offense to an individual, with the consequent adoption of a semi-contractual scheme for the retaliation prescribed for the crime. As already mentioned, the victim or their family may alternatively accept a monetary compensation, ask for the retaliation, or pardon the offender. This latter case is particularly significant in underlining that the crime is not to be considered just as a private offense inflicted on an individual, but is to be regarded as a *moral* offense as well. Therefore, the crime may be extinguished not just by the retaliation—the perfect image of the idea of criminal retribution from ancestral ages—but also by the moral conciliation between victim and offender.[89] Again, in cases involving public interests, where pardon of the victim is not permitted, the repentance of the offender may be accepted by a judge or by an adjudicating authority to remit the crime, evidently with a preeminent moral conception of criminal justice.[90] If in the Western perspective the pardon of the victim and the repentance of the offender might be taken into account as single elements in the comprehensive procedure of determining the criminal sanction, they can almost never constitute the dividing line between acquittal and condemnation. Given the preeminent nature of the Western criminal sanction as aimed at preventing social conflict and giving order to society, a moral judgment on the offender or the victim is destined to be considered marginal or irrelevant. Mainly in the case of *qiṣāṣ*, but not limitedly to it,[91] on the contrary, the moral dimension of judgment prevails on the idea of prevention and retribution, and the pardon granted by the victim to the offender may lead to the absolution of the crime.

[89] For an analysis of pardon in the Islamic legal view, see Hanifah Haydar Ali Tajuddin, Nasimah Hussin, Majdah Zawawi, "Restorative justice in Islamic law: application in Malaysian legal history and the criminal justice system", in *Research Handbook on Islamic Law and Society*, ed. Nadirsyah Hosen, Edward Elgar Publishing, Cheltenham-Northampton 2018, pp. 256–257. Cf. Scolart, *L'Islam, il reato, la pena*, *cit.*, p. 26.

[90] See Tajuddin, Hussin, Zawawi, *Restorative justice in Islamic law*, *cit.*, p. 259.

[91] In this section I refer mainly to *qiṣāṣ* for its being conceived as a private offense, but it is to be noted that the institute of pardon could be granted even in the case of *ḥudūd* actions and *taʿzīr* penalties, but only in case of conducts involving offenses to individuals and not to Allāh. Given the complexity of the matter and the divergences of opinions, I refer to retaliation cases in order to better explain my point of view on this subject.

In the case of *ḥudūd* actions, and as the Arabic terminology evidently shows, the offender breaks the moral boundaries established by the divinity and is to be punished without any possible judicial discretion, if the strict requirements for sanctioning are met. The sanction, in this context, must be public in nature, and all the community must take part in it. The most relevant example is punishment by stoning or lapidation, in which the sanction is not inflicted by the rather impersonal instrument of the executioner, organically inserted into a judicial procedure, but by the members of a community themselves. This peculiar participation of the social body in the punishment of the offender represents the most vivid example of the moral relevance of the relationship between crime and sanction in Islam.[92] The community, by taking part in the process of punishing an evildoer, undergoes a sort of moral purification, not just by creating distance between the sin and the sinner, but at the same time operating as an instrument of a divinely inspired justice. It is the *ummah*, which recognizes the offender and the guilt of the sin inside of the community, that feels the need to expel the sin from it by establishing a form of direct and immediate criminal justice. Once again, the aim is not simply the repression of crime intended as social danger, but the prevention of moral disvalue from spreading inside the community, pushing this latter to seek purification through an active form of punitive justice.

On the basis of what has been observed, it is possible to conclude that in Islam criminal justice is exercised when the original equilibrium between the *ummah* and Allāh is compromised by the spread of sin. In this context, the instrument of the sanction represents a remedy for restoring a lost equilibrium, on the one hand preventing other illicit actions and on the other hand purifying at the same time the offender and the community. Punishment, from this point of view, is not to be regarded just as instrumental in pursuing a form of social justice, but it is itself an end when conceived as a means of atonement, both for the individual and for the community. According to Hisham Ramadan, "one of the rationales of the

[92] Cf. Scolart, *L'Islam, il reato, la pena*, *cit.*, p. 29. In the context of a broader reflection that involves not just Islam but even the Jewish tradition, Jany notes the correlation between the participation of the community in execution by stoning and the lack of a central authority in charge of enforcing law and inflicting sanctions. Cf. Janos Jany [2012], *Judging in the Islamic, Jewish and Zoroastrian Legal Traditions. A Comparison of Theory and Practice*, Routledge, London-New York 2016, p. 85.

punishment in Islamic law is to cleanse the Muslim offender by imposing the appropriate punishment", to such an extent that it can be considered "a spiritual salvation method".[93]

5.4.3 *Conclusive Remarks on Punishment*

In conclusion, a teleological analysis of crime and sanction in the West and in Islam helps to grasp the divergence in the philosophical perspectives implied in the punitive instance. Once again, the different theorizations of the existence of a temporal and a spiritual power greatly influence the answer to the fundamental question regarding the reasons to punish. In the Western context, based on a bipartition of authorities, the secular power and its legal systems could develop a repressive mechanism whose aim was basically autonomous from—although sometimes complementary to—the spiritual aim of the ecclesiastic power. In Islam, on the contrary, *sharīʿa* has to be regarded as an all-encompassing phenomenon, whose aim is not just ordering society and protecting the community and its social life, but leading the believer to eternal salvation as well. The goal of *sharīʿa* cannot be accomplished exclusively in this earthly life but mirrors a conception on the basis of which the path settled by the divinity necessarily implies a superhuman goal, with evident juridical consequences in terms of punishment and atonement.[94] Therefore, every possible comparison between the two perspectives, especially concerning criminal repression, must take into due account this necessary premise, in order to avoid conceptual biases and improper categorial superimpositions.[95]

[93] Hisham M. Ramadan, "On Islamic Punishment", in *Understanding Islamic Law. From Classical to Contemporary*, ed. Hisham M. Ramadan, AltaMira Press, Lanham-New York-Toronto-Oxford 2006, p. 43. Cf. Scolart, *L'Islam, il reato, la pena*, *cit.*, 31–32.

[94] Peters suggests that some penalties in *sharīʿa* have a "vertical dimension", "in that they relate to reward and punishment in the Hereafter" (Peters, *Crime and Punishment*, *cit.*, p. 30).

[95] Regardless of his well-documented exposition, in my opinion Gamil Hussein improperly speaks about "principle of legality" and "non-retroactivity of criminal law" with regard to Islam (Hussein, *Basic Guarantees in the Islamic Criminal Justice System*, *cit.*, p. 45). As evident, it is to be considered a conceptual and categorial bias, given that the aforementioned principles imply a human authorship of law, with the consequent possibility of the replacement of existing provisions with new ones, thus with a completely different relationship between law and time, and between normativity and mankind.

CHAPTER 6

Entering into a Dialogue: From Theory to Practice

6.1 Legal Orders Between Imitation and Colonization

The previous chapters have focused on the comparison between two juridical and philosophical perspectives with particular regard to specific subjects such as territoriality, authority, legitimation, and so on. With few exceptions, this analysis has been conducted in the abstract, that is to say: having regard for the two legal orders independently and autonomously considered. However, this analysis could not be complete, and this matter would not have been exhaustively examined, without a concrete comparison between the two juridical views in specific historical circumstances.

Before describing the various possible fields where the Islamic and Western legal orders come across nowadays, it is appropriate to examine the historical context in which these two worlds first encountered one another in terms of legal philosophy and legal practice.

Needless to say, Islam and the West interlaced close contact immediately from the Hegira and the creation of the Muslim *ummah*. The relationship between Christian Europe and the Islamic world has always been characterized by enriching cultural exchanges and violent conflicts, by florid commercial trades and religious confrontation, often at the same

F. L. Ramaioli, *Juridical Perspectives between Islam and the West*, Global Issues, https://doi.org/10.1007/978-3-031-37844-7_6

time and without interruption. It cannot be denied that each one exercised a certain fascination with the other, thus leading eminent scholars of their respective worlds to deepen their knowledge of their counterparts,[1] separated by natural or conventional boundaries.

The Muslim attempts at militarily expanding the community of believers into Europe, and the Islamic conquest of territories such as Southern Italy and Spain, for the first time saw the grounding of Islamic political and legal models unto a European context. Especially in Spain, where the influences of various cultures resulted in a particularly florid artistic and philosophical activity, the political idea of the caliphate was autonomously reestablished after the fall of the Umayyads of Damascus and Harran. Here, the Greek philosophy was transmitted to the most important European centers of research and learning, with mutual benefits both for Islamic culture, which loaned the word for philosophy (*falsafa*) from the Greek φιλοσοφία (*philosophía*), and for Europe, which could rediscover treasures of knowledge through the Arabic mediation.[2] The short-lived *Khilāfat Qurṭuba*,[3] as it came to be known, can be considered one of the most successful examples of exportation of the Islamic way of ruling and administering justice in a Western territory fundamentally alien to those conceptions.[4] However, after the process of the *Reconquista* and with the fall of Granada in 1492, the territory of Spain was rendered back to Europe—not intended as a geographical space but as a cultural tradition. As a consequence, the Islamic juridical and political perspective was

[1] On the Islamic side, it is worth remembering the famous traveler Ibn Jubayr (1145–1217), who described the court of Sicily of Roger II, as well as its usages and customs. Also, Ibn Khaldūn, in his already mentioned historical work *Muqaddimah*, gave a description of European kingdoms and realms. On the European side, it is interesting to recall the *Cribratio Alkorani* of the aforementioned cardinal Nicholas of Cusa, which represents one of the most important attempts to investigate the Islamic holy text from a Catholic and Western point of view.

[2] On this subject examined in the wider perspective of the evolution of Western philosophy and of the circulation of philosophical ideas, see Trevor Curnow, *Wisdom. A History*, Reaktion Books, London 2015, pp. 125–152.

[3] Caliphate of Córdoba. On this subject, see Janina M. Safran, *The Second Umayyad Caliphate. The Articulation of Caliphal Legitimacy in al-Andalus*, Harvard University Press, Cambridge-London 2000, especially pp. 111 ff.

[4] In this chapter, I will discuss only the encounter between the Islamic world and the Western nations, thus without mentioning the Islamic conquest of the Middle East, of some parts of Asia, and of Norther Africa, where the process of Islamization, even in juridical terms, was clearly more penetrative and long-lasting.

progressively abandoned in favor of a European one, notwithstanding the residual traces of the ancient Muslim dominance.

Again, the case of the Islamic conquest of Constantinople of 1453 is emblematic. This year marks not just the fall of the Oriental Roman empire but the transition of one of the historical territories of Christendom to the Islamic world. Constantinople did not only represent an urban center of the Sunnī empire but became the capital city of the last caliphate of Muslim history, whose supreme ruler acquired the title of Caesar of Rome as well. In this context and in the multicultural framework of the Ottoman sultanate, more than a juridical contamination between legal models, it is appropriate to speak about the replacement of the ancient Roman legal order with the new Islamic one, in its peculiar Ottoman declination and with residual elements of roman law (*qānūn*).

Undoubtedly, the aforementioned experiences can be considered as a first relevant encounter between these two legal views, whose circumstances and contingencies are of great interest from a historical point of view as well. However, these cases show the tendency of a determined legal order to seek an exclusive affirmation in a given territory, by progressively replacing existing ones. The cases of Córdoba and Constantinople witnessed the replacement of preexisting juridical models and the consequent implantation of a traditional Muslim legal system, nevertheless leaving spaces of autonomy to alien communities through personal status law.[5]

Given the characters of exclusiveness and self-sufficiency that are structurally inherent to the idea of legal order, it is possible however to state that a certain degree of juridical contamination between the two perspectives did not take place before the nineteenth century.[6] The real and most relevant encounter proceeded along two different lines: on the one hand,

[5] An example is represented by the Ottoman *millet* system, a historical conception granting a certain degree of autonomy to non-Muslim communities in Muslim territories. On this, see Fatih Öztürk, *Ottoman and Turkish Law*, iUniverse LLC, Bloomington 2014, pp. 1–22. As for the influence of the *millet* in the post-Ottoman context, Castellino and Kavanaugh describe it as "possibly the first manifestation of what could be deemed 'minority rights law'" (Joshua Castellino, Kathleen A. Kavanaugh, *Minority Rights in the Middle East*, Oxford University Press, Oxford 2013, p. 268).

[6] Weiss describes this passage with a certain efficacy: "In past days, Islamic law – the law articulated in volumes of fiqh and in collections of fatwās – enjoyed a pride of place in Muslim societies that in the modern world it no longer has. By 'past days' I mean the days before the Muslim world came under the political and cultural ascendancy of the West, days preceding the onset of a modernity fashioned by the West" (Bernard G. Weiss, *The Spirit of Islamic Law*, University of Georgia Press, Athens-London 1998, p. 186).

by imitation, and on the other hand, by colonization. The first one represents the voluntary introduction into a certain legal structure of elements and conceptions which are to be considered as fundamentally alien to it. The second one represents the external and forced imposition of such elements and conceptions following a military, political, or even cultural domination.

With regard to the process of imitation, the most relevant cases are undoubtedly the French invasion of Egypt of 1798[7] and the Tanẓīmāt period of the Ottoman empire, started in 1839, which represented the response of the Ottoman administration to inevitable political and economic necessities of modernization and innovation.[8] In this case, a Muslim political entity—the sultanate—deepens the knowledge of administrative, military, and juridical Western institutions in order to import them and insert them in its own legal and political framework. This process is usually carried out by a given community when facing contingent challenges, the majority of which is responding to the exigency of emulating foreign models and systems that somehow proved themselves to be more successful on the stage of history. During the period of the reforms, the slowly declining Ottoman empire felt the powerful counterpart of Europe and experienced diplomatic disadvantages with Western States, which could be considered as innovative and modern in terms of technology, political and legal sciences, and military innovation. Therefore, the need for importing and adapting Western structures, along with juridical notions and conceptions, came to be considered an absolute necessity in order to transform Muslim communities into modern States, which could eventually be considered as more dignified members of the international community and not as declining powers whose reminiscences brought back to mind ancestral applications perceived in modern times as barbaric and

[7] After Napoleon invaded Egypt, the Egyptian Muslim community started to feel the European superiority in terms of technological power and political administration, and as a reaction many Muslim intellectuals supported the idea of Westernization intended as modernization. The resulting intellectual movement is known as al-Nahḍah, invoking a "renaissance" for the Muslim world. Cf. Roger M. Savory, "The religious environment in the Middle East", in *Business and the Middle East. Threats and Prospects*, eds. Robert A. Kilmarx, Yonah Alexander, Pergamon Press, New York-Oxford-Toronto-Sydney-Paris-Frankfurt 1982, p. 17.

[8] See the dedicated notes in Chap. 3, paragraph 4.

anachronistic.[9] This process of imitation comes with undeniable difficulties. Firstly, it presupposes a deep knowledge of the institutions that is necessary to emulate and can only be carried out after a long period of observation and analysis. Secondly, and most importantly, it is extremely difficult to grant an overall coherence to a legal system in which a substantial part comes from a completely different cultural context and is subsequently adapted to fit within a preexisting framework. On the other hand, the advantage of such an approach is that it is voluntarily carried out by the administrators of the entity to innovate and modernize, without any external imposition.

The process of colonization fundamentally followed the reversal and opposite path. In this case, the assimilation of extensive legal and institutional reforms was brought about by external powers and resulted in an imposition aiming at replacing part of the preexisting political structures with colonial institutions.[10] In the case of colonization, Muslim societies were not necessarily willing to create Western-derived political and juridical structures as in the abovementioned scenario but faced the unavoidable destiny of witnessing the contamination of ancient and traditional conceptions with newly established constructs, such as in the case of modern nationality and statehood. This could take place not only in the case of political colonization but also with pervasive forms of cultural penetration, whose outcomes in terms of juridical Westernization were basically similar.[11] Westernization through colonization was carried out by European

[9] This is not true only for the Ottoman empire but represents a constant in similar cases, which can take place all around the world. For instance, it is worth remembering the case of Tokugawa Japan, which after the visit of the "black ships" of commodore Matthew Perry in 1853 entered a period of decline that eventually led to the fall of the military *bakufu*. The new Meiji government started a never-seen before process of modernization and innovation whose outcome was the adoption of a Prussian-like constitutional system.

[10] European colonialism resulted in a process of Westernization of Islamic societies, which necessarily extended to the juridical aspect. On the idea of Westernization in the Islamic world, see Behrooz Ghamari-Tabrizi, "Westernization" (voice), in *The Princeton Encyclopedia of Islamic Political Thought*, eds. Gerhard Bowering et al., Princeton University Press, Woodstock 2013, pp. 594–595. For a critical discussion on the same concept, see Ibrahim M. Abu-Rabiʿ, *Intellectual Origins of Islamic Resurgence in the Modern Arab World*, State University of New York Press, Albany 1996, pp. 12–26.

[11] An-Na'im observes that this process took place not only in territories which were formally colonized but also in other countries, thus with a different form of colonization, whose imposition of models and systems prescinded from the political conquest. See Abdullahi Ahmed An-Naʿim, *Islam and the Secular State. Negotiating the Future of Sharīʿa*, Harvard University Press, Cambridge 2008, p. 86.

powers, which mastered the founding theories of the institutions of the West, whose basis they wanted to implant in colonized lands. However, this process was meant to be pragmatically functional to its aim of control and domination, without particular care for the overall coherence of the resulting legal systems.

These two processes, which took place sometimes alternatively and sometimes jointly, marked a major shift in the juridical history of the Muslim world, to such an extent that the return to a pre-colonial era, juridically speaking, is still considered to be anachronistic and fundamentally a utopia, even decades after decolonization.[12] However, a further point needs to be properly taken into account. Colonization and imitation were not just the means by which Western-derived institutions replaced the Islamic traditional way of ruling and administering justice, in its various declinations across the Muslim world. As already observed, this would have basically been the re-proposal of what the world had already witnessed in the ages of reciprocal conquests, in which the conquerors imposed their own legal order unto the conquered land. On the contrary, in this case it is possible to notice a certain degree of juridical and political contamination that had never been experimented with before in the various exchanges between the West and the Islamic world. With juridical contamination I do not simply mean the mixture of substantive contents of legal provisions, but for the most part the circulation of conceptions and conceptual categories independently from the historical and cultural context in which they gradually came to maturation.

For instance, with the colonization process it was gradually inserted into the Muslim context the abstract conception of the modern State, whose sovereign institutions were intended as supreme sources of law. With regard to this, the most relevant point is that every notion contained in the abovementioned affirmation was not simply to be theoretically imposed but shaped and constructed from the beginning in a context in which it had been practically inexistent. Therefore, both colonizers and colonized faced the challenge of creating the basis for the comprehension

[12] Hallaq analyzes this possibility, concluding that *sharīʿa* cannot be actually restored as in the pre-colonial era (Wael B. Hallaq, "Can Shariʿa Be Restored?", in *Islamic Law and the Challenges of Modernity*, eds. Yvonne Yazbeck Haddad, Barbara Freyer Stowasser, AltaMira Press, Walnut Creek 2004, pp. 21–53). The restoration of *sharīʿa* in its allegedly purest and uncorrupted form, rejecting Western and non-Islamic legal constructs, is however fostered by fundamentalist and radical Muslim groups and organizations, such as ISIS, as it will be mentioned in the course of this chapter.

of ideas such as law, statehood, sovereignty, institution, which did not necessarily find counterparts in the traditional Muslim view. For instance, the very concept of "Islamic law", whose theoretical contradictions have already been explained, was developed in this period, as a reaction to the imposition of the Western concept of "law" unto an Islamic society.[13]

However, given the ancestral and deeply rooted nature of the basic ideas of the Islamic legal order in the cultural background of Muslim civilization, the newly established institutions and laws did not replace *in toto* the preexisting traditions and legal models. Indeed, the two systems coexisted together: they were variously legitimated—by the State or by custom, by the divinity or by the colonial governors—and met each other in a non-defined space between legality and factuality.[14] The penetration of modern and Western conceptions was highly incisive and transformed the appearance of Muslim societies, but at the same time it is undisputed that the vision of the *sharīʿa* has never been erased totally from the colonized countries.

The interactions between the two legal orders have been various and differentiated, and it is not possible to discuss them without dedicating the proper space to every different approach. However, it is necessary to highlight two common aspects of the Westernization process that affected Muslim legal systems for either imitation or colonization: the outcomes of this process can be considered as irreversible and partially contradictory.

[13] As already mentioned, the imputability of the vision of *sharīʿa* to the Western conception of law is not to be taken for granted as a universal assumption but represents the outcome of a historically contextualized superimposition of Western categories and Islamic juridical phenomena. The notion of an "Islamic law" is therefore relatively recent and constitutes an evidence of this process of progressive Westernization of the Islamic legal order. As Baamir observes, the "concept of Islamic law was not in use at the time of classical Muslim scholars; it started to develop as a reaction to the Western influence on Muslim scholars and philosophers, especially after the French occupation of Egypt" (Abdulrahman Yahya Baamir [2010], *Sharīʿa Law in Commercial and Banking Arbitration. Law and Practice in Saudi Arabia*, Routledge, London-New York 2016, p. 6).

[14] With regard to this, Hallaq speaks about a crisis taking place in modern Islam, with a dislocation on the perception on legal authority: the State-established manmade authority as imported by the Western world, and the traditional *sharīʿa*-based idea of normativity remained as it survived the various processes of colonization and decolonization. Cf. Wael B. Hallaq, "Juristic Authority vs. State Power: the Legal Crises of Modern Islam", in *Journal of Law and Religion*, vol. XIX, n. 2, 2003–2004, pp. 243–244.

As An-Naʿim points out,[15] the process of juridical penetration of Western conceptions and visions is to be considered irreversible. The categories of comprehension of the juridical reality that have been imposed by, or learnt from, the Western world transformed not just the daily social and legal praxis but the very understanding of basic ideas of the political and legal dialectic. Moreover, the international system progressively developed a customary legal order that was—and evidently still is—largely based on the Western approach to law and authority, with special regard to the notions of territoriality and sovereignty. Being the actual field in which various visions and conceptions interact, the features characterizing the international juridical space as conceptually shaped over the course of centuries are something from which the Muslim countries cannot prescind. The Westphalian system, with its foundational rules, represents a philosophical counterpart with which every other legal perspective must necessarily relate. In order to be part of the international community, post-colonial Islamic countries indeed needed to share common narratives about fundamental legal issues, thus accepting the colonial legacy with its new way of understanding the juridical phenomenon. In a world where political relations are structurally based on communication and cooperation, the refusal of such basic rules and views which had been largely taken for granted would result in isolation and therefore marginalization. On this basis, a future return to a pre-colonial *sharīʿa*-based system, deprived of any Western influence, is indeed anachronistic and improbable, although longed for in some fundamentalist contexts.

In this scenario, the West and Islam, and modernity and tradition, are strictly interlaced in a new system in which it is hard to state which soul seems to prevail over the other. This necessarily leads to some forms of conceptual contradictions and incoherence that cannot be avoided and that have to be termed as basically structural to post-colonial Islamic legal

[15] According to the author, and not limitedly to the juridical field, the transformation brought about by "European colonialism and its aftermath [...] is so profound and deeply entrenched, permeating all aspects of economic activities, political processes, social life, and communal relations, including the provision of education, health care, and other services, that a return to precolonial political philosophies and systems is practically impossible. Any change and adaptation of the present system can be sought or realized only through the concepts and institutions of this domestic and global postcolonial reality" (An-Na'im, *Islam and the Secular State, cit.*, p. 125).

models.[16] Two worlds and two visions of reality coexisting on the same ground, and usually inserted in a single and comprehensive framework, can result in a balance of interests whose equilibrium is sometimes hard to maintain and preserve. In this case, we witness a more or less forced coexistence of two perspectives, which sometimes are opposite and sometimes are deeply divergent from one another. Therefore, the real question is whether a similar legal system could elaborate a common and organic vision in order to place such different views and notions in a single and coherent horizon, embracing two worlds without denaturing any one of them.

6.2 *Law and* Sharīʿa *Between Space and Time*

Space and time are two general categories whose univocal theorization tends to be erroneously taken for granted in every context. They are general categories in that they prescind from the juridical discourse and can be applied over a variety of fields.[17] However, their conception can greatly change depending on the philosophical perspective orienting and shaping a given legal order. In the context of the encounter between the Western and the Islamic legal views, space and time are far from being intended as according to a single and analogous outlook. On the contrary, the ways in

[16] As it has been observed, "Throughout this long and eventful period of time, the processes of legal modernization in the Arab world have been caught up in a spiraling dynamic of largely contradictory political and ideological impulses that have ranged from partial or wholesale adoption of Western codes of law to mass-based efforts in support of renewed Islamification of laws and legal institutions and that have variously legitimized their activities in the name of 'modernity' and 'progress', 'morality' and 'authenticity', or a mixture thereof" (Yvonne Yazbeck Haddad, Barbara Freyer Stowasser, "Introduction" to *Islamic Law and the Challenges of Modernity*, *cit.*, p. 2).

[17] "As basic philosophical categories, time and space are particularly suitable as a framework for a general cultural history, because they are comprehensive, universal and essential. [...] All people, everywhere, in all ages, have a distinctive experience of time and space and, however unconscious, some conception of it. It is possible to interpret how class structures, modes of production, patterns of diplomacy, or means of waging war were manifested historically in terms of changing experiences of time and space". Stephen Kern [1983], *The Culture of Time and Space, 1880-1918*, Harvard University Press, Cambridge-London 2003, pp. 2–4

which these two worlds perceive them bring about relevant implications in terms of juridical theory and concrete legal praxis.[18]

With regard to space, the view according to which a determined legal system produces its effects limited to a spatial partition is considered once again as a product of Western modernity. This perspective moves from the assumption that the supreme source of law is identified with a centralized sovereign power and represents the core of the political and juridical theory of the modern State. Moreover, it mirrors the tendency of Western stationary populations to appropriate the space around them, inscribing their life into a defined spatiality, thus creating a rather stable and static social and juridical order.[19] The structural dimension of spatiality is also highlighted by Schmitt, who conceptually links the term νόμος (*nómos*) to the significance of border, thus assigning it an intrinsic geographical connotation.[20] Notwithstanding the progressive transition from the idea of State to a fluid and non-determined vision concerning a global space with multiple actors, the international community is still largely influenced in its overall conception by the characterizing factors of independent and territorial sovereignties engaged in nominally equal relationships. Therefore, in the modern international order, the dimension of space acquires a specific and non-neutral character, which serves as a boundary between various existing legal systems. When normativity is perceived as taking its origin mainly from the State, the confrontation between law and space becomes unavoidable: space becomes a structural element in analyzing the theorization of law because it is on the basis of a geographical delimitation that a certain regulation is considered to be in force or not.

It is evident that this vision appears to be greatly divergent from the traditional Islamic one, and its gradually taking roots in Muslim territories—by force of colonization or imitation—could only bring about irreversible changes in the ways in which Islamic communities thought about the administration of justice. From a merely cultural point of view, Islamic society was born from nomadic Arab populations, that developed a

[18] On the different understandings of space and time according to the cultural perspectives from which we examine them, see John Hooker, *Working Across Cultures*, Stanford University Press, Stanford 2003, pp. 21–37. According to the author, in a concise but exhaustive way, space and time "are objective properties of the physical world that have nothing much to do with culture. At any rate, this is the Western view" (ibid., p. 21).

[19] Ibid., p. 24.

[20] On this, see Carl Schmitt [1950], *Der Nomos der Erde im Völkerrecht des Jus Publicum Europaeum*, Duncker & Humblot, Berlin 1974, pp. 36–48.

radically different idea of spatiality, tending to organizing spaces in a dynamical way when moving along their routes.[21] It is not by chance, again, that in Muslim architecture an open emptiness is usually prevalent over a close fullness, in a context in which the dimension of travel is always present. This is mirrored in the conception of *sharīʿa* as a borderless form of normativity, which follows the believers wherever they might be. Given the unique origin of the Islamic idea of *sharīʿa* intended as a divine revelation, the rational effort of the jurist is considered as continuous research, which cannot be limited by territorial boundaries, being aimed at detecting a universal and superior reality that does not change depending on geographical delimitations. From this perspective, if the universality of the ideas of *ummah* and *sharīʿa* could be considered as a utopia that was never effectively achieved and maintained, their theorization as universal elements in the lives of Muslim believers was something that had never been really questioned. With the Westernization of the Muslim lands, for the first time the principle of universality had to face the challenge of meeting the rivalry of modern statehood. The progressive transformation of Islamic territories into modern States did not represent uniquely the abandonment of the universality of the *ummah* in practice—as it happened many times in the centuries of Islamic history—but it is considered as a challenge from a theoretical point of view as well, that is to say questioning its validity as a principle that had shaped Islamic political and juridical life for ages.

In the colonial and post-colonial era, the conception of *sharīʿa* as a universal rule of conduct lived along with a Western kind of law that, on the contrary, found its limits of application in the boundaries of the State. *Sharīʿa*, being basically unanchored to the idea of geographical space as a constitutive dimension of legal efficacy, could hardly find an organic collocation in the framework of the State, and at the same time it could not be simply replaced by a newly established and space-dependent legal conception like the Western one. The ambiguity of the relationship between *sharīʿa* and the modern State does not rely on substantive principles but in the relationship between law and spatiality. If the West elaborated a conception of law in which spatiality acts as a constitutive element, in Islam geographical boundaries are to be considered as conceptually alien to the domain of *sharīʿa*, and in some way preclusive of its ideal aspiration to universality.

[21] Cf. Hooker, *Working Across Cultures, cit.*, p. 24.

The encounter between these two visions even significantly affected the conception of the relationship between law and time. Following Christian eschatology, the West conceived time as being basically linear,[22] and its idea of law participates in a specific relationship with the dimension of temporality, which along with geographical space can be considered as constitutive of its essence. The human level of law, whatever its theorization, is a product of human reason, thus object of an act of creation. The implication that logically follows is that in the Western view the law comes into existence not only in a specific geographical spatiality but in a specific temporality as well, which can affect its efficacy and dominate its various declinations in a given system.[23] The Western thought has always dealt with the idea of regulating the effects of its normative acts with regard to their efficacy with respect to time, elaborating various criteria like the chronological one, which represents a milestone of Western legal theory even nowadays. Again, the discussion over the idea of non-retroactivity of criminal law, just to mention a topical issue in modern legal theory, is nothing but a reflection about the close and necessary relationship between law and time. The very idea of the "source" of law, as already mentioned, shows a particular dynamicity as to the continued creation and replacement of existing normative acts, and from Roman times it suggests that law is a time-dependent phenomenon. In the Western view, the human authorship of law determines its collocation in a precise chronological horizon and its organic insertion in a timeline whose coordinates come to

[22] Cf. Mariana Valverde, ""Time Thickens, Takes on Flesh": Spatiotemporal Dynamics in Law", in *The Expanding Spaces of Law. A Timely Legal Geography*, eds. Irus Braverman, Nicholas Blomley, David Delaney, Alexandre Kedar, Stanford University Press, Stanford 2014, p. 61; Brent D. Slife, *Time and Psychological Explanation*, State University of New York Press, Albany 1993, pp. 14–16. This general assumption does not prevent, however, some Western thinkers, such as Niccolò Machiavelli, from developing a peculiar vision of time, neither linear nor circular, but grounded in the idea of catching the occasion (cfr. Giovanni Fiaschi, "La differenza di Machiavelli. Realtà e prassi politica", in *La filosofia politica di Machiavelli*, eds. Giulio M. Chiodi, Roberto Gatti, Franco Angeli, Milan 2015, p. 25), with potential influences on the present time.

[23] This point is made particularly clear by Grotius, according to whom "for the Nature of a human Law is such, that it depends upon the Will of the Legislator, not only in its Institution, but also in its Duration. But the Law-Maker ought not to take away the Law, without a reasonable Cause for it, which if he does, he transgresses the Rules of political Justice. But as he can take away the Whole Law, so he may suspend the Obligation of any Part of it, as to this or that Person, or this or that particular Fact, the same Law in all other Respects remaining in Force" (Grotius, *De jure belli ac pacis libri tres*, II, 20, XXIV; English excerpt from *The Rights of War and Peace*, trans. Jean Barbeyrac, ed. Richard Tuck, Liberty Fund, Indianapolis 2005, p. 999).

vest a fundamental importance. Therefore, determining *when* a certain provision has been sanctioned as "law" by an act of authority results decisively in determining its efficacy and validity.

However, if what has been said so far could be considered obvious in the Western tradition, it is not to be taken for granted in other cultural contexts. From the Muslim point of view, *sharīʿa* originates from a transcendent divinity and thus refers to the dimension of eternity, beyond the earthly categories of space and time. It has been revealed to mankind from a timeless perspective,[24] from a dimension beyond human events. The originative moment of *sharīʿa* is not inside history but beyond it. The human activity that comes to relevance, in this case, is not a creative activity but a deductive and declaratory one. If *sharīʿa* belongs to Allāh, what belongs to man is *fiqh*, that is to say the comprehension and the knowledge of "the path" revealed by the divinity.[25] Given these premises, as is evident, the relationship between *sharīʿa* and time is extremely different from what has been observed with regard to the Western view.[26]

[24] Qaraḍāwī suggests that *sharīʿa* can easily be applied in every place and in every time due to its adaptability and speaks of "universal and timeless relevance" of this peculiar idea of normativity. Cf. Yūsuf Qaraḍāwī, *Islamic Law in the Modern World*, Wamyh House International for Printing, Publishing and Distribution, Riyadh 2000, p. 63.

[25] If a comparison between Islam and the West must be made, it should be the one between *fiqh*, as deductive activity investigating a preexisting reality, and the judicial function of common law tribunals according to the declaratory theory, "which posits that judges do not make law but rather declare what it always has been" (Ben Juratowitch, *Retroactivity and the Common Law*, Hart Publishing, Oxford-Portland 2008, p. 1). Both systems witness the prevalence of a deductive and substantially interpretative reasoning which points at a reality external to it, whose premises have already been laid. However, the difference relies in the fact that *fiqh* refers to *sharīʿa*, which is an eternal and immutable reality, while the common law judicial reasoning refers to positive law, which is static as far as the lawmaker does not change it.

[26] The anecdote related by Fikentscher regarding the relationship between *sharīʿa* and time is particularly interesting. In the late 1970s, colonel Muʿammar al-Qadhdhāfī of Libya was interviewed by a representative of Amnesty International, who "gave him a list of persons in jail having been arrested without due process of law, and consequently kept in jail without any basis in legality, whether under the 'existing' *shari'a* or modern law. Colonel Gaddafi answered that this would pose no problem. He would give order right away to enact statutes which declared unlawful the acts those persons in jail had done. The representative of Amnesty International tried to explain the concept of expostfacto law, which under any modern legal system is regarded as a violation of the rule of law. To this Colonel Gaddafi answered that Libya does not live under modern Western law, but under the shari'a, and since the *shari'a* is *forever* valid, retroactive statutory interpretations of the *shari'a* are a matter of logic" (Wolfgang Fikentscher [1995], *Modes of Thought: A Study in the Anthropology of Law and Religion*, Mohor Siebeck, Tübingen 2004, p. 423).

In light of this, comparisons between the two views regarding principles such as non-retroactivity of law and *nulla poena sine lege* appear to be senseless,[27] in that a common ground from which to move is lacking. All the principles and notions inherent to the chronological extension of the effects of normative acts move from a certain conception of the relationship between time and law. Therefore, forcing comparisons on typically Western principles and mechanisms would result in ignoring the different premises from which a legal vision develops and flourishes, while universalizing and imposing a single way of understanding the interactions between normativity and temporality. Asking ourselves whether a *sharīʿa*-based legal system would be compatible with the basic (Western) guarantees of criminal law,[28] such as the aforementioned principles, may represent a tempting political reflection; however, from a juridical point of view, it would result in a biased question *ab origine*, and it would result in a misleading understanding of a delicate and sensitive issue.

In Islam, the jurist puts every effort in understanding a preexisting normative reality, which prescinds from him, and goes necessarily beyond him. It overcomes space and time, in that it belongs to an eternal dimension, whose effects on human life are exercised from *outside*. From *within*, the Islamic society must try to investigate it. In order to do so, it refers to the roots of *fiqh*, which are necessarily developing into a historical framework but ideally point to an immutable dimension that will never be fully

[27] In addition to the example already mentioned in the previous chapter (Gamil Muhammed Hussein, "Basic Guarantees in the Islamic Criminal Justice System", in *Criminal Justice in Islam. Judicial Procedure in the Sharīʿa*, eds. Muhammad Abdel Haleem, Omar Sherif, Kate Daniels, I.B. Tauris, London-New York 2003, p. 45), see, for such a comparison whose methodological approach is in my opinion not sharable, M. Cherif Bassiouni, *The Sharīʿa and Islamic Criminal Justice in Time of War and Peace*, Cambridge University Press, Cambridge 2014, pp. 126 ff. Some modern scholars highlight the traces of a conception of non-retroactivity in *Qur'ān* and *sunnah*, but even in this case the terms of the question are not comparable, due to the different theorization of structural elements such as time, normativity, and legal legitimacy.

[28] The case of criminal law is particularly significant, representing one of the most discussed and recurring comparison between the two perspectives. However, it is possible to examine other cases belonging to the field of civil law, such as the disciplines for the protections of the legitimate expectations in contracts (i.e., the German notion of *Vertrauensschutz*), grounded as they are in completely different cultural contexts, and dependent as they are from determined philosophical conceptions.

understandable to mankind.[29] On the contrary, the West acknowledges and fully recognizes the possibility that the law is a human phenomenon which originates from *within* human history and from *within* human history spreads its effects. Therefore, in the Western conception, due to its earthly nature, law is "incarnated" in a spatiotemporal dimension and cannot but live as a time- and space-dependent phenomenon. As Christ is born inside history and lives in the dimensions of space and time, being at the same time at their origin and being affected by them, Western law speculates about the abstract dimensions of space and time, while being incardinated in the spatiotemporal web. While the Islamic view investigates eternity, where man is a researcher and not an author, according to the Western conception, law is primarily a human fact, and as a human fact it is organically inscribed in the general categories of space and time.

The West developed juridical principles based on the understanding of the relationship between the law and the general categories of spatiality and temporality, because insofar as law lives, it is inextricably linked to these categories.[30] Both the creation of law and its comprehension are firmly inscribed in this framework, from which they can intellectually abstract, but from which they cannot prescind. On the contrary, in Islam there is always a gap between *sharīʿa* and *fiqh*, which mirrors the conceptually necessary gap between the spatiotemporal dimension and eternity. From this point of view, *sharīʿa* autonomously lives outside of these categories, which become relevant only when man needs to transfer it to concrete norms and rules. The culminant moment is however beyond space and time, which in this context cannot be considered as proper legal categories, but accidental dimensions in which the *sharīʿa* is not living and taking shape but a transient and fallible understanding of it.

[29] "*Sharīʿa* embodies the sublime principles of the faith that transcend time and place. *Fiqh*, in contrast, is the imperfect effort of humans to apply these broad principles to specific conditions. It is a product of incomplete human understanding of the divine text, as well as flawed human judgement". Bruce K. Rutherford, *Egypt after Mubarak. Liberalism, Islam, and Democracy in the Arab World*, Princeton University press, Princeton-Woodstock 2008, p. 104.

[30] It is worth mentioning the reflections of Goldman, who addresses law as "a normative practice dependent upon time" (David B. Goldman, *Globalisation and the Western Legal Tradition. Recurring Patterns of Law and Authority*, Cambridge University Press, Cambridge 2008, pp. 69–70).

6.3 *Law and* Sharīʿa *Between Morality and Coerciveness*

As already mentioned, *sharīʿa's* translation as "Islamic law" is misleading for several reasons, mainly inherent in the different philosophical perspectives implied in the concept of *sharīʿa* and in the concept of *law*. The concrete encounter between these two normative visions, during the progressive Westernization of Muslim legal systems in the course of the nineteenth and twentieth centuries, highlighted various practical differences between *sharīʿa* and Western law that are worthy of deeper analysis. In this paragraph I will focus on some pragmatically different views, which were brought to confrontation in this specific historical context. As Esmaeili, Marboe, and Rehman suggest,[31] we can focus here on three practical features: the substantive extent of what can be termed as law, the idea of bindingness, and the idea of enforceability.

6.3.1 The Conceptual Extensions of Law and *Sharīʿa*

Firstly, the boundaries the Western conception drew in order to delimitate the proper domain of law do not coincide with the conceptual boundaries of the *sharīʿa*. From this point of view, it is again necessary to reject the simplistic and erroneous vision according to which both Western law and Islamic *sharīʿa* are differentiated, mainly because of a different substantive content. On the contrary, it must be observed that the perimeter of the domain of "law" and its actual extension, resulting from centuries of development and consolidation, are the consequence of a determined and

[31] According to the authors, "it is necessary to clarify that 'law', at least in the Western understanding, means norms of general application which are binding and enforceable. They have to be distinguished from other norms, such as moral or religious norms. This is often the first misunderstanding, when 'Sharia' is translated with 'Islamic law'. Not all norms in the Sharia are meant to be binding in a legal sense and be enforceable by state authorities. Rather the Sharia represents an all-encompassing normative system addressed to the believers in Islam. As such it also includes moral and religious norms. By contrast, in the Western understanding, moral and religious may serve as sources of inspiration or politically influence the 'law' of the state, but they differ from the notion of law" (Hossein Esmaeili, Irmgard Marboe, Javaid Rehman, *The Rule of Law, Freedom of Expression and Islamic Law*, Hart Publishing, Oxford-Portland 2017, p. 39). The ideas of enforceability and bindingness are analyzed by Rohe as well, in the author's attempt to correctly highlight the biases implied in equating *sharīʿa* and Western law (see Mathias Rohe, *Islamic Law in Past and Present*, trans. Gwendolin Goldbloom, Brill, Leiden-Boston 2015, pp. 10 ff.).

precise philosophical perspective and are by no means a void and neutral space, to be simply filled by normative contents. In this way, the Western thought gradually came to delimit a normative space, separating it from other equally important but substantially different fields.[32] The previously mentioned separation between law and morality—however not without points of contact and interlacement—is nothing but evidence of the progressive delineation of a conceptual space, with which the West shaped the perimetral extension of its field of "law". If it is undoubtedly true that in the West law exercises a great influence on social relations and habits, as well as on institutional dynamics, it is also true that not everything attaining to these domains can be termed as legal in nature. From ancient ages, Western law has elaborated a unique and characteristic language, institutional behavior, and ways of reasoning and understanding reality, thus distinguishing the legal sphere from other domains of human activity. Within the domain of law, Western thought has progressively divided various subcategories, each one characterized once again by proper linguistic and technical features. In the Middle Ages, for instance, the major sub-division regarded the separation between civil law and canon law, designated as ***utrumque jus***, that is to say two differentiations of the same phenomenon (***jus commune***). In the modern era, the sub-qualifications of law acquired a more extensive importance, with the differentiation between criminal law and civil law, and again with the subsequent creation of procedural law and administrative law.[33] It is also in this context that State law came to be considered as a sub-system of a wider international legal order, anchored in shared paradigms. It is possible to read this juridical differentiation in systems and conceptual spheres according to the *Systemtheorie* of

[32] The questions concerning the delimitation of the domain of law are deeply interlaced with the necessity of giving a universal and univocal definition of law, definition that as well-known does not actually exist. Therefore, and following the virtual impossibility of univocally defining what is law in general, it is not possible to delimit a "domain of law" universally valid in every time and place. As Opałek observes, "one can only try to find solutions within the range of particular systems, or group of systems […] When leaving out the peculiarities of legal systems (group of systems) one can only find some answers formal in their characters, running the danger of tautologies which can hardly be avoided" (Kazimierz Opałek, "The concept of "positive law"", in *Kazimierz Opałek Selected Papers in Legal Philosophy*, ed. Jan Wolenski, Springer, Berlin-Heidelberg 1999, p. 165).

[33] The conception of ***droit administratif*** was firstly introduced after the French Revolution and represented a pillar of the Napoleonic institutional reorganization, which created a professional and functional bureaucracy as a basis for the functioning of the State architecture.

Luhmann,[34] whose theoretical model is, not by chance, particularly fit to describe the dynamics of Western social and institutional sciences.

Islamic *sharīʿa* shows a conceptual extension and a grade of comprehensiveness that is by no means coincident with the Western perimeter of law.[35] As previously said, *sharīʿa* encompasses the whole existence of the believer, with morality and religious practice playing a relevant role in the supreme form of Muslim normativity. While the West witnessed a progressive separation between law and morality, elaborating two different

[34] The fundamental text about the *Systemtheorie* is clearly Niklas Luhmann [1984], "Social Systems", trans John Bednarz jr., Dirk Baecker, eds. Timothy Lenoir, Hans Ulrich Gumbrecht, Stanford University Press, Stanford 1995. According to Luhmann, these systems "are oriented by their environment not just occasionally and adaptively, but structurally, and they cannot exist without an environment. They constitute and maintain themselves by creating and maintaining a difference from their environment, and they use their boundaries to regulate this difference" (ibid., pp. 16–17). The boundaries, that is to say the actual extension of the system, represent a fundamental character of the system itself. With regard to law, I refer to the conceptual boundaries defining the different domains of "law" and "*sharīʿa*" like Luhmann refers to the boundaries of a given system. A further point of particular interest relies in the self-reproducing function characterizing the systems, which Luhmann addresses to with the term *autopoiesis*. According to the author, a system "can operate only with structures that it has built itself. It cannot import structures. [...] The system generates itself. Not only does it produce its own structures, like certain computers that are able to develop programs for themselves, but it is also autonomous at the level of operations. It cannot import any operations from its environment" (Niklas Luhmann [2002], *Introduction to Systems Theory*, trans. Peter Gilgen, ed. Dirk Baecker, Polity Press, Cambridge-Malden 2013, pp. 73–74, 77). From this perspective, the emergence of a given system cannot be an artificial act of creation, but rather the spontaneous outcome of a gradual process of accrual. This point is particularly relevant for the present analysis insofar it suggests that Western law, considered as system articulated in sub-systems, functions on the basis of categories and structures that are not to be considered neutral but that on the contrary represent the precise result of the autopoietic power of the system of producing its own and unique structures of functioning. For a specific and detailed analysis of law as a social system, see again Niklas Luhmann [1993], *Law as a Social System*, trans. Klaus A. Ziegert, eds. Fatima Kastner, Richard Nobles, David Schiff, Rosamund Ziegert, Oxford University Press, Oxford 2004, pp. 53 ff.

[35] It is worth remembering the words of Crone regarding this point: "What medieval Muslims regarded as law included much that modern students have trouble recognizing as such", because "the law extended into areas such as filial piety, the proprieties of clothing, behaviour at funerals, how to greet non-Muslims, and other matters that a modern Westerner would treat as purely moral, or as mere etiquette" (Patricia Crone, *God's Rule. Government and Islam*, Columbia University Press, New York 2004, pp. 8–9).

conceptual spheres, in Islam it would be inconceivable to theoretically separate a moral aspect from a legal aspect of *sharīʿa*, given that this latter concept comprehends the two former ones, being at the same time moral *and* normative in nature. The Western legal view, from the Muslim perspective and as imposed in the colonial and post-colonial era, could only create a legal vacuum for the absence of specific previsions on morality and religious practice, whose outcome is far more uncertain than a simple and more direct replacement of preexisting norms.[36] In this case, *sharīʿa* provisions are by no means repelled and abrogated by new Western-based normative rules, but on the contrary tend to fill the gaps created by a new regulatory system whose boundaries are not coincident with the traditional Muslim ones. In a specular way, other fields that the West felt as belonging to the domain of law are completely alien to *sharīʿa*. The regulation of the public powers and the discipline of the prerogatives of the political authorities constitute the factual basis upon which the West shaped its conception of administrative law, which extensively permeates the life of the administrative structures of most countries up to the present day. Here, political theory feels the unavoidable exigency to express its dynamics in juridical norms, thus setting forth determined rules that can guarantee the overall functioning of the institutional structure. The very intuition of putting the exercise of power under legal restraints, at the birth of modern constitutionalism, is an expression of this aspect of Western law. On the contrary, the Islamic view does not regard this matter as part of the domain of its supreme and traditional normativity. In the Muslim view, according to which the personal dimension of the ruler prevails over the institutional element, the administrative actions undertaken by the rulers and the officials are not perceived as part of the complex

[36] For the interactions between *sharīʿa* and Western law during the colonial period, see Léon Buskens, "Sharia and the Colonial State", in *The Ashgate Research Companion to Islamic Law*, eds. Rudolph Peters, Peri Bearman, Ashgate, Farnham-Burlington 2014, pp. 209–222. Regarding this period, Buskens speaks of "legal pluralism", in that colonial law was shaped as to incorporate parts of *sharīʿa*-derived provisions, mainly in family law matters. As previously stated, the colonial period did not simply repel the traditional Islamic legal order but implanted a new one on the same ground. In my opinion, the non-coincidence of Western and Islamic normative spaces from a conceptual point of view was decisive in order to determine the survival of *sharīʿa*, or at least of traces of it, in the framework of the successive and posterior legal systems.

system of a divinely revealed normative order but as the contingent and pragmatical instrument by which it is possible to provide answers to practical problems.[37] While the West in some way dignified the administrative action by inscribing it within its legal tradition, Islam relegated it to the domain of the more functional and fast-changing ideas of *siyāsa* and *qānūn*, not depriving it of political dignity but stressing its extraneity to the conception of *sharīʿa*. Therefore, such expressions as "caliphal law"[38] are to be considered as potentially misleading, because they do not take into due account the different extension between the ideas of *sharīʿa* (and *qānūn*) and the idea of Western law. On the contrary, it would be correct to state that while such matters as the discipline of power and its functioning are perceived as belonging to the domain of law by the West, in Islam they are perceived as belonging to different spheres of human knowledge and action. To sum up, it is possible to observe that while *qānūn* is

[37] I already dealt with this issue while discussing the dichotomy *sharīʿa-qānūn* in Chap. 3, par. 3. While *qānūn* could be considered as part of a legal system from a Western perspective, it is necessary to remember here that it cannot be regarded as part of the Islamic legal order but a functional method of regulating political matters. Therefore, it can be said that fields such as the ones abovementioned are to be considered as conceptually alien to the normative space of Islam.

[38] This terminology is used by Crone and Hinds in their already mentioned text about the figure of the caliph (Patricia Crone, Martin Hinds [1986], *God's Caliph. Religious Authority in the First Centuries of Islam*, Cambridge University Press, Cambridge 2003, pp. 43–57). While the analysis of the two authors appears to be properly detailed and historically contextualized, it would need a clarification as for this point, furtherly taking into account the different extent of the domain of law and the conceptual boundaries of its Islamic counterpart. In an Islamic context, speaking about caliphal law would be inappropriate, while it would make sense only with a theoretical premise: what is intended in the West by "law" does not coincide with the normative field gradually shaped by the Muslim societies. Therefore, it would be necessary to point out that the so-called caliphal law would be considered as law only in a Western context, that is to say extrapolating it from its original cultural framework. It is however to be noted that this process of definition of an Islamic legal space, in which caliphal rule was not contemplated as a source (or root) of law, took a certain amount of time to be properly defined and systematized. Gradually, *sharīʿa* and *fiqh* came to form part of a "law of the jurists" or "law of the scholars", excluding the political rulers as active parts of the legal system. In this sense, see Sami Zubaida, *Law and Power in the Islamic World*, I.B. Tauris, New York 2003, p. 78; Wael B. Hallaq, *The Origins and Evolution of Islamic Law*, Cambridge University Press, Cambridge 2005, p. 68.

conceptually not dissimilar to the Western *lex*, it falls however outside of the perceived domain of the Islamic *jus* (legal order).[39]

These gaps between these two conceptions, involving a different perception about the actual extension of the normative phenomenon, bring about relevant consequences. The complete replacement of a normative system with another one, perfectly coincident as for the conceptual boundaries delimiting its extension, appears to be quite simple in its dynamic, that is to say the total abrogation of preexisting norms and rules and their replacement with new ones. In this context, the possible consequences are the acceptance of the new legal course or its conflictual rejection. In the case of *sharīʿa* in the colonial and post-colonial era, due to the non-coincidence of the perimeter of the two orders, a third possibility emerges, that is to say a more or less conflictual interpenetration and a more or less peaceful coexistence, which live not necessarily in the official mechanism of legislative production and enforcement, but as a common and ancestral practice, and in a factual and non-official way.[40]

[39] In my opinion, this last point is particularly interesting. In the Western world, the Roman concept of *jus* is intended as a comprehensive idea of legal order, while *lex* represents a particular category inherent to the comprehension of a determined normative act. In this way, the conceptually broader idea of *jus* comprehends the particular idea of *lex*, which alone is not exhaustive to understand the juridical phenomenon. On the contrary, the Muslim legal tradition does not follow this categorization, and a phenomenon like the ductile *qānūn* can be in some ways similar to *lex* but excluded from what in Islam is perceived as the overall domain of *jus*.

[40] Here I refer to two different cases, as for the survival of *sharīʿa*. On the one hand, *sharīʿa* continues to be followed independently of the new colonial rule, as a common practice and in spite of the new legal course. As a self-sufficient concept and given the deep differences with Western law in terms of theorization and conceptual extension, it cannot be simply abrogated by a Western-derived positive law. On the other hand, the colonial legal system incorporates part of *sharīʿa*-based provisions in its mechanisms of functioning. This model, regardless of the substantive content of positive laws, gives origin to a legislation that is fundamentally Western in nature, however with an official role given to *sharīʿa*. This is actually what happens in some contemporary constitutional system, as it will be explained in this chapter. In this context, it is significant to understand the permeability of the traditional Islamic legal conceptions to the new colonial rule, in terms of resistance to change and at the same time capability of adaptation.

6.3.2 Bindingness Between Law and *Sharīʿa*

Secondly, a major divergence between the Western idea of law imposed in the nineteenth century upon Muslim contexts is that law is generally considered as a *binding* normative act. While the dimension of bindingness appears to a Western audience as inextricably linked to the idea of law, at the point that every emphasis on this point could result in an apparent tautology, in the Islamic view it is not to be taken for granted. In the West, the Roman concept of *lex* appears to be linked to the idea of bindingness from its very etymology, which involves the action of *ligare* (to tie, to link).[41] Obligation comes from the same root, implying the idea of *ob-ligare*,[42] once again describing a binding act, which in some way constrains the will of the obliged subjects to its normative content. Moreover, the human authorship of law, intended as an instrument of authority, can only bring about the logical consequence of its coerciveness, its power to bind, in order to be functional to the objective it pursues. If in the Western view the political authority rules by virtue of normative and legislative acts, thus vesting its commands with a preeminently juridical dimension, the law must be obeyed by the subjects of the authority. Its imperativeness, therefore, is not considered as an accidental element but as a constitutive feature of what can be regarded as the principal juridical category of the

[41] According to the Aquinas "dicitur enim lex a ligando, quia obligat ad agendum" (Thomas Aquinas, *Summa Theologiae*, I, II, q. 90, art. 1). A second etymology, according to St. Augustine and St. Isidore of Seville, as mentioned by saint Thomas as well, links *lex* to *legere*, emphasizing its dimension of publicity (cf. Jean-Robert Armogathe, "Deus legislator", in *Natural Law and Laws of Nature in Early Modern Europe. Jurisprudence, Theology, Moral and Natural Philosophy*, eds. Lorraine Daston, Michael Stolleis, Ashgate, Farnham-Burlington 1988, pp. 276–277; Anton-Hermann Chroust [1973], "The Fundamental Ideas of St. Augustine's Philosophy of Law", in *Augustine and Modern Law*, eds. Richard O. Brooks, James Bernard Murphy, Routledge, London-New York 2016, p. 173), in that it binds the consociates to its public provisions. As evident, the first etymology appears to be more relevant for the present analysis.

[42] It is interesting to notice that in the case of *ob-ligare*, the etymology suggests not just a binding act but a binding act involved in a mutual relationship of rights and duties. Cf. Pierpaolo Donati, Margaret S. Archer, *The Relational Subject*, Cambridge University Press, Cambridge 2015, p. 47.

Occidental world.[43] Therefore, the law substantiates itself in a binding command given by a legitimate authority that can regard a positive obligation (*facere*) or a negative one (*non facere*).[44] Traditionally, this latter category is prevalent, especially in the field of criminal law, with norms binding the subject to abstain from committing certain actions. This conception of bindingness must not be confused with the idea of coercion, which is undoubtedly a predominant element in the Western legal tradition, but not as constitutive of the idea of law. As Schauer observes, this dimension of bindingness is more linked to the idea that, at least according to the Western view and for a number of reasons, law "makes us do things we do not want to do. It has other functions as well, but perhaps the most visible aspect of law is its frequent insistence that we act in accordance with its wishes, our own personal interests or best judgment notwithstanding".[45] Therefore, this dimension of law does not necessarily rely on the presence of a sanction in case of violation of the command, given that a sanction, however recurrent, is not always present in case of violations. On the contrary, the idea of bindingness relies on the philosophical perspective that links the imperative nature of law to the ideal impossibility for the subject to escape its obligations. Therefore, and from ancestral times, the West has

[43] Kelsen, for instance, links the dimension of bindingness to the validity of law and describes law as "coercive order". According to Kelsen, the first characteristic "common to all social orders designated by the word 'law' is that they are orders of human behavior. The second characteristic is that they are coercive orders" (Hans Kelsen [1960], *Pure Theory of Law*, trans. Max Knight, The Lawbook Exchange, Clark 2008, p. 33). As van Roermund concisely states, following Kelsen's *Pure Theory*, bindingness "relates to law *qua* authoritative practice geared towards ending or precluding social conflict" (Bert van Roermund, *Legal Thought and Philosophy. What Legal Scholarship is About*, Edward Elgar, Cheltenham-Northampton 2013, p. 235). While the aforementioned literature considers law as a coercive order in a universal perspective, as evident this view in particularly fit to describe Western law, given that other kinds of legal orders adopt different categorial schemes, as explained in my introduction. Notwithstanding a certain claim for universality, these positions are relevant in order to understand the unavoidable link between law and bindingness in the Western legal thought.

[44] To these two groups it is possible to add a third category, the one of tolerances (*pati*). However, at a deeper analysis, this latter category can be easily reduced to the group of *non facere*, as it imposes to the subject not to rebel to a certain behavior carried out by someone else. About this tripartition, see briefly Leon Petrazycki [1905–1907], *Law and Morality*, Routledge, London-New York 2017, p. 162. An example of the false dichotomy between *non facere* and *pati* is related to servitudes, which are sometimes labelled as *non facere* obligations, sometimes as *pati*, and sometimes as both.

[45] Frederick Schauer, *The Force of Law*, Harvard University Press, Cambridge 2015, p. 1.

regarded law as a qualified command in front of which it is theoretically not possible to rebel,[46] based on the fundamental dichotomy of lawful-unlawful and licit-illicit.[47] If in medieval Europe the link between law and bindingness was present but more flexible and adaptive, with the creation of the modern State the dimension of law as authoritative command becomes absolute, with the definitive consolidation of a trend whose traces were already visible in pre-modern history. With the progressive evolution of the conception of law in an increasingly globalized context, the idea of law as implicitly binding has never been challenged, with exceptions made for the acts of the so-called soft law.[48] However, even in this case specialized literature has explained how, despite its actual denomination, soft law

[46] Regarding law as coercion but not implying necessarily a sanction, it is worth remembering again Kelsen's position: "The coercion that is implied in the motivation is a psychic coercion, which is a possible effect of the idea an individual has of the law, and which takes place within this individual. And this psychic coercion must not be confused with the prescription of the coercive act, which takes place within the legal order" (Kelsen, *Pure Theory of Law*, *cit.*, p. 35).

[47] The reference is again to Luhmann, according to whom "law achieves this function by coding events in its environment using a binary code that is unique to itself: legal/illegal", and "normative closure is the context for ongoing self-observations by the system within the scheme of lawful/unlawful" (Luhmann, *Law as a Social System*, *cit.*, pp. 9, 109). Borrowing Luhmann's terminology, King and Thornill explain that "the recognition of a communication as a specifically legal communication depends upon the legal system's deployment of the lawful/unlawful code in the interpretation of this environment" (Michael King, Chris Thornhill, *Niklas Luhmann's Theory of Politics and Law*, Palgrave Macmillan, New York-Basingstoke 2003, p. 56). As it has been observed on King's writings, "in Western legal systems, law depends for its ontology on a binary code of lawful/unlawful, legal/illegal, and the like. To carry this a step further, law is a prime way of classifying everyday acts with exclusivist taxonomies ..." (Don Handelman, "Bureaucratic Logic, Bureaucratic Aesthetics: The Open Event of Holocaust Martyrs and Heroes Remembrance Day in Israel", in *Aesthetics in Performance. Formations of Symbolic Construction and Experience*, eds. Angela Hobart, Bruce Kapferer, Berghahn Books, New York-Oxford 2005, p. 212).

[48] Among the various definitions that could be given of this peculiar kind of acts, it is worth remembering the words of Snyder, according to whom they are "rules of conduct which, in principle, have no legally binding force but which nevertheless may have practical effects" (Francis Snyder, "The Effectiveness of European Community Law: Institutions, Processes, Tools and Techniques", in *The Modern Law Review*, vol. LVI, n. 1, January 1993, p. 32).

does not present the basic and structural elements in order to be properly defined as "law",[49] mostly for its non-binding nature.[50]

In the Islamic legal order, the question is radically different. The relationship between the idea of bindingness and *sharīʿa* is commonly regarded from two opposite and equally misleading extremes, whose positions are easily and correctly rejected in academic analysis. Firstly, it is commonly believed that *sharīʿa* is always a coercive and imperative set of rules, which must be mandatorily followed so as not to incur sanctions. Secondly, it is sometimes believed that *sharīʿa*, given its moral and religious inspiration, is only a suggestion for the believer, with no trace of imperativeness in any of its derived provisions. Both opinions are not sharable, although each one correctly grasps a single facet of a more complex phenomenon.

Sharīʿa, due to its comprehensiveness in terms of ideally embracing every aspect of the life of the believer, represents a guidance in various matters of life, part of which can be addressed with mandatory and binding commands, and part of which can be addressed with moral suggestions. Therefore, *sharīʿa*-derived provisions can be binding for prohibiting or commanding certain actions, and non-binding for suggesting doing or not doing other actions. The science of *fiqh* describes the liceity of the personal conduct of the believer according to a unique form of categorization, commonly referred to as *al-aḥkām al-ḫamsa* (the five

[49] Cf. Roberto Bin, "Soft law, no law", in *Soft law e hard law nelle società postmoderne*, ed. Alessandro Somma, Giappichelli, Turin 2009, pp. 31–40. For an analysis concerning the problematic of soft law within a legal system, see Bart van Klink, Oliver W. Lembcke, "A Fuller Understanding of Legal Validity and Soft Law", in *Legal Validity and Soft Law*, eds. Pauline Westerman, Jaap Hage, Stephan Kirste, Anne Ruth Mackor, Springer, Berlin-Heidelberg 2018, pp. 145–164.

[50] According to Ferrarese, "perhaps nothing makes the distance from the concept of 'norm' as visible as the existence of a wide typology of so-called *soft law* rules, which renounce to the binding force, and try to find application by focusing on other motivations different from the obedience that one owes to a 'command'. This particularly 'mild' form of legal commitments therefore renounces precisely to that sanctioning message that was at the heart of the 'norm'" (Maria Rosaria Ferrarese, "Globalizzazione giuridica" (voice), in *Enciclopedia del diritto. Annali dal 2007*, vol. IV, Giuffrè, Milan 2007, pp. 564).

decisions).[51] Human actions are indeed categorized into five groups, based on their degree of permissibility: obligatory (*wājib* or *farḍ*), recommended (*mustaḥabb*), neutral or permitted (*mubāḥ*), disliked (*makrūh*), and forbidden (*ḥarām*).[52] As is evident, the relationship between the supreme Islamic normativity and the idea of bindingness appears to be much more complex and multifaceted, due to the various degrees of imperatives distinguishing the classification of human actions.

With regard to this, a few points are worth mentioning.

Firstly, it is necessary to note that *sharīʿa*-derived rules are not always mandatory, given that some conducts of human behavior are encouraged or discouraged without a proper element of imperativeness, thus overcoming the dichotomy liceity-illicitly. However, there are categories of actions, such as *wājib* and *ḥarām*, which undoubtedly involve an element on bindingness, being it positive (*to perform* obligations) or negative (*not to perform* obligations). With regard to this, the Islamic conception appears to be much more variegated in the graduation of the judgment of permissibility of human actions, not limiting itself to command or to prohibit.[53]

[51] These five categories were systematized about two centuries after Muḥammad's death, as Schacht observes (Joseph Schacht [1950], *The Origins of Muhammadan Jurisprudence*, Clarendon Press, Oxford 1959, p. 133), and since then have become a fundamental part of the Islamic legal discourse. A major role in the systematization of the five categories has undoubtedly been played by al-Ghazālī. For al-Ghazālī's position about their importance, see Harvey J. Sindima, *Major Issues in Islam. The Challenges Within and Without*, Hamilton Books, Lanham-Boulder-New York-Toronto-Plymouth 2018, p. 398. To be noted that the Ḥanafī school adds two more categories, conceptually dividing *wājib* from *fard*, and adding *makrūh taḥrīman* as a category distinct from *makrūh* and *ḥarām*. However, being this categorization typical of just one legal school, in my work I will refer to the classic "five decisions". About the Ḥanafite categorization, see Ahmad Zaki Ḥammad, "Ghazālī's Juristic Treatment of the Sharīah Rules in al-Mustasfā", in *American Journal of Islamic Social Sciences*, vol. IV. n. 2, 1987, pp. 173.

[52] About the five decisions in general, see Seymour Gonne Vesey-Fitzgerald, "Nature and Sources of the Sharīʿa", in *Law in the Middle East*, vol. I, *Origin and Development of Islamic Law*, eds. Majid Khadduri, Herbert J. Liebesny, The Lawbook Exchange, Clark 2009, pp. 98–100; Aaron W. Hughes, *Muslim Identities. An Introduction to Islam*, Columbia University Press, New York 2013, p. 137; Frederick Mathewson Denny [1994], *An Introduction to Islam*, Routledge, London-New York 2016, pp. 194 ff.

[53] The dichotomy that sometimes recurs in the Islamic discourse between *halal*, as licit, and *ḥarām*, as illicit, has progressively been graduated along the lines expressed in the aforementioned five categories, with all their grades of liceity.

While Western law usually limits itself to bind the subject to its disposition, *sharīʿa* shows various levels of bindingness, ranging from what must be performed to what must be avoided, passing through what is neutral and can either be done or ignored without any consequences. If Western law commands, *sharīʿa* can command, encourage, suggest, forbid, and so on, in a grade of articulation basically unknown to Occidental standards.

Secondly, the category of neutral actions is rather a *unicum* if we have regard for the Western tradition, in which neutral actions, as for their lawfulness, are generally not contemplated by the law. In the West, following the Latin periphrasis *ubi lex voluit dixit, ubi noluit tacuit*, neutral actions are demanded not by the law, which on the contrary deals with prohibited or mandatory actions, but by the law's silence. The Islamic legal tradition, on the contrary, creates a dedicated and specific category for neutral actions, whose commission does not involve a judgment on moral liceity. However, notwithstanding their extraneity to a judgment of such a kind, it would not be correct to speak about their extraneity to the domain of *sharīʿa*, given that—in opposition to the Western idea of law—they are explicitly contemplated by the Islamic juridical science.

Lastly, while the Western legal view shaped its vision of liceity and bindingness preeminently focusing on the idea of prohibition, thus imposing abstention from committing certain actions, the Islamic view enshrines in its classification actions whose commissive and affirmative practice is compulsory or at least encouraged. It is sufficient here to recall the five pillars of Islam (*arkān al-Islām*),[54] whose performance is to be considered binding for all Muslim believers. This can be considered as a consequence of the moral dimension of *sharīʿa* which, as previously said, is inseparable from its normative nature. On the contrary, this helps considering the teleological nature of Western law, whose τέλος (*telos*) is not necessarily linked to the imposition or encouragement of a certain morality but to the fulfillment of a fundamentally social function. *Sharīʿa*'s all-encompassing nature, in a context characterized by the absence of a univocal separation of secular and spiritual authorities, brings about the necessity of shaping categories functional to all the aims it pursues, including moral and religious ones.

[54] As well known, the five pillars are the profession of faith (*shahāda*), prayer (*ṣalah*), almsgiving and charity (*zakāh*), fasting (*sawm*), and the pilgrimage to Mecca (*ḥajj*). As mentioned, the pillars are to be considered as *wājib*.

6.3.3 Enforceability, Law, *Sharīʿa*

The procedures according to which law is enforced, as well as the sanctions for its violation, represent core elements of the administration of justice in a given system. However, this aspect appears sometimes as secondary and less relevant than the preceptive dimension of legislative constructs. It is usually believed that the enforcement of law defines a procedural aspect which is not only logically subsequent to the substantive content of the normative provision but somehow alien to it as well.

On the contrary, the aspect of the enforceability of law can be regarded as relevant as the substantive dimension of the juridical phenomenon, in that it reveals a precise philosophical orientation. The way in which law is enforced represents the passage from a static moment to a dynamic one,[55] and brings to visible life what, in the act of lawmaking or lawgiving, had been conceived as an intellectual conception. The concrete administration of justice makes tangible the principles of law through the meticulous observance of a rituality, which changes in dependence to several variables, intimately linked to the way of conceiving the legal order. Therefore, the procedural aspects of law's enforceability are not to be considered as a neutral category, somehow common to every idea of law, but once again a distinguishing and culturally oriented dimension of it.[56]

[55] Moving from the Latin terminology (*jus quod ad actiones pertinent*), it is possible to say that procedural law represents the proceedings according to which the law is seen in action, thus in its dynamic moment.

[56] Hence, the importance of analyzing this topic from a philosophical point of view and in a broader sense of creating the awareness around what could be termed as philosophy of procedural law. This latter is a subject to which not enough space has been dedicated in literature so far, given the relevant consequences it could bring about in the juridical discourse. Among the few authors to have dedicated a study to this subject, Garbellini Carnio correctly states that "procedural law is not simply a 'branch' of law, but a dimension. This suggests the possibility of locating processual philosophy in an intersectional point of a great division of legal philosophy between philosophy of private law and philosophy of public law (and of the State) and therefore of showing that these dualisms such as processual/material and private/public need to be overcome together with the traditional views usually based on them" (Henrique Garbellini Carnio, "Filosofia do direito processual e procedimentalização do direito", in *Revista de Processo*, vol. CCXXXI, May 2014, p. 370).

The West shaped its way of enforcing law in a predominantly procedural way, that is to say by the elaboration of precise procedures according to which justice should be administered. The Western legal world structured itself along a path moving from the arbitrary will of the sovereign to the mediation of a procedural and impersonal element, thus providing a guarantee for a more or less homogeneous application of law. The emblematic and iconic figure of this proceduralism in enforcing law is represented by the image of the judge, not intended as an individual but intended as an organ inscribed in an elaborated circuit of courts and tribunals.[57] The first distinguishing element of the Western conception of legal enforceability is thus represented by the mediation of an impersonal procedure, a mediation that becomes relevant in the relationship between the individual and the law. Generally speaking, and with minor exceptions, law cannot be enforced directly by the individual, given that the administration of it is institutionally monopolized by legitimated authorities. From this point of view, the individual is involved in the legal phenomenon—that is, as titular of rights and duties—but is alien to the phase of its enforceability, conceived as the apex of the system of judicial administration. Law, in general, and procedural law, in particular, come to be established *ne cives ad arma ruant*, that is to say in order to prevent an arbitrary application of law that would derive from individuals taking justice into their own hands. Thus, legal procedures embody the idea of neutrality as a guarantee against abuse of power, by regulating not only the substantive content of law in order to *quisque suum tribuere* but the formalities through which such provisions are concretely applied. As a traditional and chivalrous

[57] As one of the preeminent voices of legal realism, Leon Green grasps the vital importance of this point. According to the author, "the judge is the most responsible unit in our social structure", and therefore "his judgment is the most vital factor in law administration" (Leon Green, *The litigation process in tort law. No place to stop in the development of tort law*, Bobbs-Merrill Company, Indianapolis 1977, p. 158).

duel,[58] the judicial activity is conceived by the West as the performance of a ritual whose rules ensure the correct and neutral—impersonal—"vivification" of substantive law as an abstract and general rule of conduct. The mediation of an impersonal and procedural element appears therefore to be necessary to ordain the administration of justice and to avoid arbitrary rule.[59]

The second distinguishing element characterizing the Western position involves the idea that law is always enforceable and consequently that

[58] I do not adopt the metaphor of the duel by chance. Until rather recent times, the figure of the duel was present in almost every civilization, and its origins date back to ancestral ages. However, in the Western world the duel enriches itself of a juridical dimension, constitutive and connatural to its aim of pursuing a form of (private) justice. From the Western point of view, it is the law what distinguishes a duel from a mere fight and consequently justice from violence. It is the procedural element of law, with its rituality and its rules of conducts, that ensures the necessary neutrality and detachment that can inscribe the intrinsic violence of the duel into the circuit of the administration of justice. In this sense, the duel "was supported by binding rules that steered, controlled, and limited the use of force. Without these rules a duel was no longer a duel, a fact which state legislation also took into account by only regarding those fights carried out in accordance with the regulations as legally privileged duels. Fights without strict rules fell under the regular laws for physical injury, manslaughter, or murder" (Ute Frevert, "The Taming of the Noble Ruffian: Male Violence and Dueling in Early Modern and Modern Germany", in *Men and Violence. Gender, Honor, and Rituals in Modern Europe and America*, ed. Pieter Spierenburg, Ohio State University Press, Columbus 1998, p. 49). Once again, the normative dimension of the duel is not to be found only in the legitimation given to it by State law. In the Western perspective the duel, as the claim for direct enforceability following an unjust tort, *needs* to be structurally ascribed to the juridical phenomenon, notwithstanding its possible being unlawful in regard of a certain legal system. As one of the major theorists of the duel writes, "if the duel Code lies outside of the law, if it is not possible to have other codes than the ones sanctioned by the law, let's do not hesitate, however, to give this name to the rules imposed by honor, because honor is not something less sacred than the governmental laws" (Comte de Chatauvillard, *Essai sur le Duel*, Imprimerie d'Edouard Proux et comp., Paris 1836, p. 5). In this excerpt, it is evident that even when the duel appears to be outlawed, the Western though felt the exigency of regulating it, whether referring to customary uses or creating as in this case an *ad hoc* legal system for the duels. The ancient duel codes, like the mentioned *Essai* of Chatauvillard or the *Codice Cavalleresco* by Jacopo Gelli of 1879, represent an iconic example of how the Western thought inextricably linked the duel to a normative dimension, being it recognized or not by State law.

[59] As Feibleman writes, a formal procedure "is a standing protection against the abuse of power on the parts of individuals, who must perforce follow the rules even when undertaking to right a wrong. Legal procedures exercise some control over coercion by submitting litigants to formalities which operates in the name of reason" (James K. Feibleman, *Justice, Law and Culture*, Martinus Nijhoff, Dordrecht-Boston-Lancaster 1985, p. 131).

enforceability is a structural element of law.[60] Even in Roman times, the Roman citizen had the right to be brought in front of the emperor to be properly judged,[61] and so to witness the mechanism of law's enforcement properly applied. The very idea of the Roman process (*processus per formulas*), long before the imperial era, had been conceived upon the basis of *actiones*,[62] so to provide a practical way to have the law enforced. In medieval times, the complex legal system was articulated in multiple jurisdictions, according to various regulations, each one with its own circuits of judges.[63] Moreover, the figure of the medieval monarch was also considered as a supreme *iudex*, that is to say someone entitled with *jurisdictio*—the power of *jus-dicere*, with a central judicial function.[64] Again, from the time of the *habeas corpus*,[65] which still constitutes one of the basic principles of most Western criminal justice systems, the right to be translated in front of a court to be judged according to the law shows how the idea of enforceability can be regarded as inherent to the very idea of law as elaborated by Western legal thought.

[60] In a dedicated study Reiff elaborates a comprehensive theory of enforceability, which once again is better fit to describe the Western legal reality. In his analysis, Reiff notes that "enforceability and social cooperation are inextricably intertwined. Enforceability is not something we can simply add or remove from a system of rights at will, for the means of enforcement arise out of the very social structures that makes rights possible. It is impossible for these social structures to be present and for all means of enforcement to be absent" (Mark R. Reiff, *Punishment, Compensation, and Law. A Theory of Enforceability*. Cambridge University Press, Cambridge 2005, p. 48). The author links the idea of enforceability to the idea of rights, with the implicit premise regarding the contextualization of the evolutionary development of a theory of rights in the (Western) legal thought. As a logic consequence, we may deduce that enforceability be a structural element in that legal orders in which the conception of rights arose, thus with particular reference to the Western world.

[61] The most famous episode is undoubtedly St. Paul's case, as related in *Acts*, XXV, 1.

[62] See *ex mult.*, Danilo Ceccarelli Morolli, *A Brief Outline of Roman Law*, Gangemi, Rome 2012, pp. 75 ff.

[63] From this point of view, particularly relevant is the phenomenon of the wandering justices, iconic embodiment of a justice which was not based on a territorial dimension but on multiple levels of laws, according to various criteria—religion, race, profession, etc.—and in which every jurisdiction exercised its authority through enforcement of its specific regulations

[64] As Grossi observes, "the prince is celebrated by the medieval mindset for his capacities as a judge – as the great bringer of justice to his people. […] The power of the prince is, and will be for all the duration of medieval jurisprudence, made up of a complex system of powers amongst which judicial authority is central. This system also includes, secondarily, the authority of *ius dicere* ('declaring the law') – the role of making the law manifest to the prince's subjects" (Paolo Grossi [2007], *A History of European Law*, trans. Laurence Hooper, Wiley-Blackwell, Chichester 2010, p. 13).

[65] The *habeas corpus* was firstly introduced by the Magna Charta of 1215, which I will discuss in par. 4 of this chapter.

From the Islamic perspective, on the contrary, the idea of enforceability is not to be considered as structural to *sharīʿa*, whose derived provisions, on the contrary, may or may not be enforced. Not all the rules elaborated by the system of *fiqh* are in fact suitable to be enforced, due to the comprehensiveness of the spectrum of *sharīʿa*. Indeed, this latter comes to comprehend rules of moral conduct and religious practice, as well as spiritual duties with respect to the divinity, whose enforcement cannot always be carried out by human authorities. While other provisions may be decided according to judicial procedures and coercively enforced, not any rule derived from *sharīʿa* shows as a constitutive element the possibility of it being enforced.[66] As previously explained, another reason in dependence of which an Islamic rule of *fiqh* may or may not be enforced refers to the moral opportunity to expose the factual case, in order to prevent sin from spreading through the community.[67] Once again, the question cannot be resolved in a univocal way and is strictly inherent to the teleological perspective of *sharīʿa* and is thus to be resolved according to a number of relevant variables. This very fluidity, as to the relationship between law and enforceability, represents one of the major divergences between the West and Islam about this point.

As for the procedural element, the enforcement of *sharīʿa*-derived provisions prescinds from the impersonal dimension that characterizes the Western approach. While the West progressively founded a sort of legal

[66] The provisions concerning morality are often remitted to the individual conscience and are not always complied with by the use of coerciveness. Cf. Rudolph Peters, Peri Bearman, "The Nature of the Sharia", introduction to *The Ashgate Research Companion to Islamic Law*, *cit.*, p. 4. Hallaq argues that the unity of normative and moral aspects in *sharīʿa* "did not less than equip it with efficient, communally based, socially embedded, bottom-top methods of control that earned it remarkably willing obedience and – as another consequence – made it less coercive than any church or imperial law Europe introduced since the fall of the Roman Empire" (Wael B. Hallaq, "What is Sharīʿa?", in *Yearbook of Islamic and Middle Eastern Law*, vol. XII [2005–2006], eds. Eugene Cotran, Martin Lau, Brill, Boston-Leiden 2007, p. 152). Hallaq's view is particularly interesting in that the author underlines the "bottom-top" methods of enforcement and control which indeed distinguish *sharīʿa* from Western law, and that qualifies the enforcement of *sharīʿa* as non-necessarily mediate by a circuit of judges and courts, but as an expression of the community of the believers in following the "straight path". Moreover, by defining it "less coercive", Hallaq stresses the idea that *sharīʿa* is not to be considered always enforceable, highlighting that enforceability be not a structural element in the Islamic legal order.

[67] Cf. Deborah Scolart, *L'Islam, il reato, la pena. Dal fiqh alla codificazione del diritto penale*, Istituto per l'Oriente C.A. Nallino, Rome 2013, p. 16.

liturgy, intended as a preordained ritual,[68] in order to grant a detached and non-arbitrary application of law, Islam shaped its legal order along a different path. From this point of view, the figure of the Islamic *qāḍī*[69] is not exactly comparable to the figure of the Western judge. The Western judge exercises indeed a monopoly of the enforcement of law that finds in him its necessary embodiment and its physical personification.[70] The intervention of private individuals in the administration of justice, for example in the case of the jury, in any case needs to be legitimated by the judicial power, that is to say to be inscribed in a framework whose legitimacy comes from the legal authority and not from the individuals themselves. Without the figure of the Western judge, the idea of Western law exists in the abstract but cannot find a way to innervate itself properly in the social and political context. Without the judge, in conclusion, the law loses its visibility and becomes a product of the pure intellect.[71] On the contrary, the *qāḍī* does not represent the embodiment of the *sharīʿa*, nor does he

[68] When speaking of the administration of justice as a rituality and a liturgy, I borrow once again the terminology used by Michel Foucault [1975], *Discipline & Punish. The Birth of the Prison*, trans. Alan Sheridan, Vintage Books, New York 1995, p. 34.

[69] In this section I do not refer to the modern *qāḍī*, who sometimes operates in contemporary hybrid Islamic legal systems, whose office is more comparable to that of a Western judge because of later post-colonial influences. Here, I refer to the *qāḍī* as a classical figure in the administration of justice of the Islamic legal tradition. With regard to this, see Anver M. Emon, "Sharīʿa and the Modern State", in *Islamic Law and International Human Rights Law. Searching for Common Ground?*, eds. Anver M. Emon, Mark Ellis, Benjamin Glahn, Oxford University Press, Oxford 2012, pp. 61–62.

[70] In a State-based system this is particularly evident. However, here I do not necessarily refer to State law: in the Western legal perspective, the judge represents the referential point of the administration of justice *in a given system*. Therefore, even in legal orders characterized by a plurality of interconnected systems (i.e., the medieval legal order), the judge exercises the monopoly of the administration of the specific law he is called to enforce, be it religious, secular, corporative, and so on.

[71] Once again, it is worth remembering Green's words: "There can be no power without machinery; there can be no law without judges and courts and rules. But machinery without power is impotent. Hence 'law' as here conceived is the power of passing judgment" (Green, *The litigation process in tort law, cit.*, p. 154).

gain his legal authority from the political ruler by whom he is appointed.[72] His actual presence does not constitute an essential condition for *sharīʿa* to exist and to be enforced. The *qāḍī*, appointed by the political power, derives his authority from an earthly source, which is not necessarily the same source legitimizing the eternal *sharīʿa*, which is not at the disposal of man. Moreover, the *qāḍī* can be considered an important but accidental element of a *sharīʿa*-based system, given that even without the *qāḍī sharīʿa* it would continue to exist and deploy its effects, especially in issues directly involving the morality of the believers. In the case of *sharīʿa*, an impersonal mediation between the idea of normativity and the individual, expressed by a series of prefixed procedures of enforcement, is not strictly necessary.[73] Strict requirements are, for instance, necessary for the *ḥudūd* penalties but not for obligations referring to religious worship. The preceptive power of the *sharīʿa* directly involves the believer in soul and flesh, and thus can be considered as a non-mediate form of normativity, with which man can benefit from direct contact, through the means of juristic hermeneutics, and does not necessary need official organs to enforce it.

In addition, it is worth mentioning that the administration of justice through the *qāḍī* does not see in the *qāḍī* himself the preeminent organ of the system as in the Western case, where the judge rules over a specific case according to a certain form of regulation. The process in front of a *qāḍī* is developed according to a dialogical form and involves the research of the rightest solution through the investigation of *sharīʿa*. In order to do

[72] Although appointed by the ruler, the judicial authority of the *qāḍī* does not come from the ruler by whom he is appointed, as the Western judge who is vested with public authority by virtue of his appointment. As distinguished twelfth-century Ḥanafī jurist al-Kāsānī observed, "the *qāḍī* does not become a *qāḍī* by virtue of the appointing power of the ruler, nor does he work for him. Rather, he becomes a *qāḍī* by virtue of the appointing power of the Muslims, for whom he works" (al-Kāsānī, *Badā'i'aṣ-ṣanā'i' fī tartīb aš-šarā'i*, vol. XI, cit. in Wael B. Hallaq, *The Impossible State. Islam, Politics, and Modernity's Moral Predicament*, Columbia University Press, New York 2013, pp. 188–189, note 131). The *qāḍī*, therefore, does not follow the conceptual path of legitimation typical of the Western view but on the contrary is here considered as an instrument working for the community of the believers, with a consequent direct participation of the individuals in the administration of justice. On this, cf. Ulrich Rebstock, "A Qāḍī's Errors", in *Islamic Law and Society*, vol. VI, n. 1, 1999, p. 8.

[73] The *qāḍī* used to follow procedures while judging, but as previously explained the procedures he followed do not constitute the essential element in enforcing law. Moreover, as Hallaq notes, from a procedural point of view "the work of the court appealed to pre-capitalist and non-bureaucratic social constructions of moral integrity that sprang directly from the local site of social practice" (Wael B. Hallaq, *An introduction to Islamic Law*, Cambridge University Press, Cambridge 2009, p. 164).

so, it is not only the figure of the *qāḍī* who comes to relevance but the figure of the jurist (*faqīh*) as well.[74] The *faqīh*, as a private expert in the practice of *fiqh* as the very terminology suggests, may represent even a more important figure than the *qāḍī*, given that the Islamic legal order is fundamentally an order of the jurists. It is the *faqīh*, in this context, that may be considered the protagonist of this activity of juridical research and deduction, and it is the *faqīh* that, through the emission of a *fatwā*, whenever asked to do so, presents to the *qāḍī* the solution of the case. Although a *fatwā* can be considered as a non-binding response to a judicial question, it may orient the *qāḍī*'s judgment based on its authoritative nature. Therefore, in addition to the implications deriving from the aforementioned philosophical divergences, even the practical form of the process is usually incomparable. It can be said, on the contrary, that it reflects the different perspective in understanding not only justice but the relationship between law and man as well.

In conclusion, the Western world shaped its legal order around the emblematic figures of the legislator and the judge, while in Islam the most relevant figure involved in legal affairs is represented by the jurist, and the overall legal conception in Islam can be described as a "law" of jurists.[75] From this apparently simple starting point, the aforementioned implications about enforceability and concrete administration of justice must necessarily follow.

6.4 Sharīʿa, *Law, and Constitution*

One of the most important challenges the encounter between the Islamic and the Western legal views brought about was the confrontation between *sharīʿa* and the idea of modern constitutionalism. A constitution is not

[74] About the relationship between *qāḍī* and jurists, see John L. Esposito, Natana J. DeLong-Bas, *Shariah. What Everyone Needs to Know*, Oxford University Press, Oxford 2018, pp. 66–69. See also Brinkley Messick, "The Judge and the Mufti", in *The Ashgate Research Companion to Islamic Law*, *cit.*, pp. 73–92.

[75] The suggestive definition of "law of the jurists", or "jurist's law", comes from Weiss, *The Spirit of Islamic Law*, *cit.*, p. 186, and from Joseph Schacht, *An Introduction to Islamic Law*, Oxford University Press, Oxford 1964, pp. 209–210. Weber, while analyzing *sharīʿa*, defines it as a jurist's law as well (Max Weber [1921–1922], *Economy and Society. An Outline of Interpretive Sociology*, eds. Guenther Roth, Klaus Wittich, University of California Press, Berkeley-Los Angeles-London 1978, pp. 820–821). For an analysis of his position on this subject, see Bryan S. Turner [1974], *Max Weber Classic Monographs*, vol. III, *Weber and Islam*, Routledge, New York-London 2006, p. 111.

simply a high-ranking normative act belonging to the Western category of "law", with all the aforementioned implications. On the contrary, it mirrors a precise way of understanding the dynamics of power and authority.[76]

[76] A clarification about this point is necessary. I do not share the view according to which a constitution necessarily embodies a substantive idea or principle of law, such as the equality in front of the law or the democratic principle. In particular, I do not share the opinion that democracy be in some way structurally inherent to the idea of constitutionalism, because this vision would result in an improper ideologization of a juridical construct, in whose framework democracy represents a possibility albeit not the only one. A constitution is rather to be considered a legal category, whose declinations in specific contexts can greatly vary according to ideological, historical, and cultural contingencies, as the empirical evidence clearly shows. Therefore, when speaking of the non-neutral nature of the idea of constitution, I do not refer to the substantive content that can be attached to a specific charter but to the precise philosophical vision behind its categorial form. As a comprehensive category, a constitution reflects the way in which a State conceives the relationships between its institutions, its people, and its political power. Various definitions of constitution fail, in my opinion, to grasp the idea that a constitution be fundamentally a way of considering this relationship, instead of a set of more or less homogeneous substantive principles. On the contrary, among the various sharable definitions, I recall here the one according to which a constitution "is the politico-legal document of documents to which a state gives a special name or attaches particular qualities in order to distinguish it from all other state documents of a politico-legal nature" (Henc van Maarseveen, Ger van der Tang, *Written Constitutions. A Computerized Comparative Study*, Oceana Publications-Sijthoff & Nordhoff, Dobbs Ferry-Alphen aan den Rijn 1978, p. 234). Van Maarseveen and van der Tang correctly underline the necessary link between the constitution and the idea of State, two legal-philosophical categories that shared a common path of evolution. This definition helps highlighting the formal (but non-neutral) nature of the idea of constitution. Another definition that is worth remembering is the one according to which a constitution "is the supreme and fundamental law, by which the sovereign constituent power (ultimately, the people, or, in a federation, the constituent States) established the constituted powers (the Parliament, Government and other institutions). A Constitution establishes, rather than merely describes, the rights and duties of the people, the powers and functions of the various institutions of government, and the relationships between them" (W. Elliot Bulmer, *A Model Constitution for Scotland. Making Democracy Work in an Independent State*, Luath Press, Edinburgh 2011, p. 32). This last definition helps understanding the fact that a constitution shares in part the same philosophical features of Western law. According to these definitions, it is possible to derive from the category of constitution various implications: firstly, the existence of a State vested with sovereign power, the existence of institutions, and the human authorship of law. As I will furtherly explain, these three main implications constitute the points to which I will refer in dealing with the idea of a constitution intended as a legal category.

Although the idea of constitutionalism should be properly regarded as a product of Western modernity,[77] as a consequence of the French Revolution and of the theorization of the separation of powers, its historical premises are far more ancient. Ancient Greece, with the idea of πολιτεία (*polītetā*), had already developed legal systems based on forms of government described in modern times as "constitutions", as in the case of Athens and Sparta.[78] Moreover, by the time of the *Magna Charta Libertatum* of 1215, the authority of the king acknowledged limitations to its ideally absolute power, taking into consideration rights and liberties of the barons, and assuring guarantees such as a first affirmation of the *habeas corpus* principle.[79] With the *Magna Charta,* political authority provides itself with self-limiting boundaries by means of a normative act, aiming at regulating the exercise of power. Notwithstanding all the differences due to the historical context, it is possible to consider this fundamental document as a primeval origin of the characteristics that, subsequently, would have been enshrined in the idea of modern constitutionalism.[80]

Friedrich proposed a concise and yet exhaustive explanation of the purpose of constitutionalism, which at its core responds to "the need for

[77] Although fundamental juridical documents such as the *Magna Charta* represent an essential shift in considering the relationship between law and power, thus marking the premises for the following evolution of the idea of constitutionalism, they cannot be considered constitutional acts themselves. Properly said constitutionalism is indeed a product of modernity, with a more specific differentiation between private and public spheres, as a consequence of the emergence of the modern State and its monopoly of law. As La Torre argues, the step "from pre-modern to modern constitutionalism is made possible thanks to a deep change in the prevailing political paradigm. 'Constitution' or 'fundamental' would now be a law only if it dealt with the public, not private, sphere; only if it was directed to shape and regulate expressions and acts of political power" (Massimo La Torre, *Constitutionalism and Legal Reasoning. A New Paradigm for the Concept of Law*, Springer, Dordrecht 2007, p. 4).

[78] On this, see Scott Gordon, *Controlling the State. Constitutionalism from Ancient Athens to Today*, Harvard University Press, Cambridge 1999, pp. 60–85.

[79] "Nullus liber homo capiatur, vel imprisonetur, aut disseisiatur, aut utlagetur, aut exuletur, aut aliquo modo destruatur, nec super eum ibimus, nec super eum mittemus, nisi per legale judicium parium suorum vel per legem terre". *Magna Charta Libertatum*, 39.

[80] Cf. Gottfried Dietze, *Magna Carta and Property*, University of Virginia Press, Charlottesville 1965, p. 48. For an in-depth analysis of the influence of the principles of the Magna Charta on English and American constitutionalism, see A. E. Dick Howard, *The road from Runnymede. Magna Carta and constitutionalism in America*, University of Virginia Press, Charlottesville 1968, especially pp. 203 ff.

subjecting all authority to legal restraints".[81] From this point of view, the enactment of a constitution regulates the legitimate exercise of power, giving shape to a determined form of government, and by doing so prevents the rise of arbitrary rule.[82] A constitution, from a philosophical perspective, inscribed the political authorities within a legal framework, setting forth rules and norms to regulate the functioning of power.[83] It is worth precising that constitutionalism is not a synonym of democracy, given that the idea of constitutionalism does not necessarily refer to a specific form of government or to predetermined contents. On the contrary, the instrument of a constitution, considered once again as a scheme of qualification and as a legal category, aims at regulating the procedures and the principles according to which power is exercised, whatever decisions are made in this context. Again, a constitution can be considered as the maximum expression of legislative power, in that it comes as an emanation of juridical sovereignty. Following Kelsen's view about the *Grundnorm*,[84] it is possible to state that a constitution does not need to be legitimated by virtue of procedures *within* the constitutional framework, but on the contrary, it legally legitimates itself or, in broader sense, is politically legitimated by the sovereign authority by an act of pure will. If constitutionalism, once applied through its philosophical premises and through the legal enactment of a constitution, prevents arbitrary uses of power, its first

[81] Carl Joachim Friedrich, *Constitutional government and democracy. Theory and practice in Europe and America*, Blaisdell Publishing Company, Waltham 1968, p. 9.

[82] Cf. Michael Carlton Tolley, *State Constitutionalism in Maryland*, Garland Publishing, New York-London 1992, p. 19.

[83] With regard to this, it is necessary to observe that the goal of a constitutional State "is not only to bind the organization and exercise of state power to some kind of internal rules that create an orderly structure in a technical sense. Rather, state power is to be bound to a fixed, bilateral obligatory law, one that limits powers, creates responsibility, and secures freedom" (Ernst-Wolfgang Böckenförde [1997], "The Concept and Problems of the Constitutional State", in *Constitutional and Political Theory. Selected Writings*, vol. I, trans. Thomas Dunlap, eds. Mirjam Künkler, Tine Stein, Oxford University Press, Oxford 2017, p. 141).

[84] Cf. Hans Kelsen [1945], *General Theory of Law and State*, trans Anders Wedberg, Harvard University Press, Cambridge 1949, pp. 115–117.

establishment must necessarily pass through an arbitrary and self-legitimating act, giving birth to a new juridical course.[85]

Considering what has been said, it is possible to state that the idea of constitutionalism refers to a concept that cannot but be totally alien to the Islamic legal tradition.[86] A constitution, as the highest-ranking legislative act in a given system, distinguishes itself through three main features. Firstly, it shares the conceptual premises of Western law in general, as for its human authorship, its relationship with space and time, and its being functional to the aim pursued by public powers. Regardless of the specific contents of constitutional provisions, constitutionalism appears to be closely inherent to political authority, in that it originates from it and at the same time it regulates it. On the contrary, *sharīʿa* neither originates from political authority nor regulates its functioning. As previously said, the Islamic tradition does not consider the regulation of public powers as properly belonging to the domain of "law" but ascribes it to the more fluid sphere of politics. Secondly, a constitution is historically linked to the ideas of State and sovereign power, which express themselves in *constituent* power, by virtue of which a constitution eventually comes into existence. From this point of view, there cannot be a constitution, properly intended, in absence of the philosophical premises inherent in the idea of

[85] Despite the apparently paradoxical nature of this affirmation, Ross correctly argues that even the most democratic form of government is born by virtue of a (theoretically and conceptually) violent act. With regard to this, see Daniel Ross, *Violent Democracy*, Cambridge University Press, Cambridge 2004, especially p. 8. Although I do not discuss here the establishment of democratic institutions, the opinion of Ross is however sharable in that it grasps the necessarily arbitrary nature of the constituent power, intended as the necessary non-legitimated and self-legitimating cornerstone of a comprehensive architecture whose various parts need to be legitimated by it.

[86] The so-called constitution of Medina (commonly known in Arabic as *dustūr al-Madīnah* or *saḥīfat al-Madīnah*) of 622 AD cannot be recognized as a proper constitution, in spite of the denomination with which is usually referred to in literature. In fact, and regardless of the completely different historical and philosophical context in which the idea of constitutionalism was born, the document does not present the necessary and structural features of a constitution. Referring to international legal categories, it would be more appropriate to define it a treaty, stipulated in order to grant social and political peace between various religious and ethnic groups. As for the terminology, instead of a constitution it would be more correct to speak about a covenant, in order to avoid conceptual misunderstandings. Cf. Rainer Grote, Tillman J. Röder, "Constitutionalism in Islamic Countries", introduction to *Constitutionalism in Islamic Countries. Between Upheaval and Continuity*, eds. Rainer Grote, Tillman J. Röder, Oxford University Press, Oxford 2012, pp. 3–4.

modern statehood.[87] Thirdly, a constitution is functional to the regulation of the established powers, which are embodied in institutions. As a necessary implication, a constitution can exist only in presence of institutions, with all the implications that have already been observed regarding the idea of *persona ficta*. If a constitution is indeed an act ideally characterized by a stable temporal projection, it can only refer to impersonal institutions, and not to transient and punctual phenomena.

While these kinds of features are clearly alien to the domain of *sharīʿa*, a parallelism—with all due differentiations—can more easily be drawn with the concept of *qānūn*, in that it originates from an earthly authority. However, the historical usage of *qānūn* was never pushed conceptually so forward so as to constitute a proper constitutional charter, up to the encounter between the Islamic countries and Western constitutional models.[88] The first major attempts to adopt a constitution in a Muslim context,

[87] In more recent times, a certain debate arose about the possible constitutionalization of international law, based on a possible and factual constitutionalizing power of non-State actors in a globalized world (cfr. Jan Klabbers, Anne Peters, Geir Ulfstein, *The Constitutionalization of International Law*, Oxford University Press, Oxford 2009; Jürgen Habermas, "The Constitutionalization of International Law and the Legitimation Problems of a Constitution for World", trans. Ciaran Cronin, in *Constellations*, vol XV, n. 4, 2008, pp. 444–455). Although undoubtedly interesting, in my opinion this phenomenon takes the moves from the original idea of constitutionalism but actually evolves following completely different lines at the point of being considered a conceptually different phenomenon. On the main differences between these two ideas, see Christian Walter, "Progress in International Organization: A Constitutionalist Reading", in *Progress in International Law*, eds. Russell A. Miller, Rebecca M. Bratspies, Martinus Nijhoff Publishers, Leiden-Boston 2008, pp. 138–142.

[88] Grote and Röder point out that not only the idea of constitutionalism "first came to the Islamic world as an essentially European concept" but also that the constitutional discourse in the Muslim world is based upon "recent attempts to reinterpret the Islamic tradition in light of the requirements of constitutionalism" (Grote, Röder, *Constitutionalism in Islamic Countries, cit.*, p. 3).

following the Western example, were the constitution of Tunisia of 1861[89] and the constitution of the Ottoman empire of 1876. This latter can be regarded as one of the prominent juridical reforms carried out following the Tanzimât renovation.[90] These two charters were drafted under direct European influence and do not simply represent the enactment of a constitution, but the actual adoption of a philosophical vision that had been alien to Islam for all the centuries of its history. The Arab name of the Tunisian charter of 1861, *qānūn al-dawla al-tūnisiyya*, and the Turkish name of the Ottoman one, ***kanûn-u esâsî***, explicitly recall the idea of *qānūn*, conceived as an earthly and pre-Islamic form of regulation, and by no means the idea of *sharīʿa*, which belongs to another level of juridical comprehension. Constitutionalism can be thus considered as a foreign product, incorporated in the Ottoman *qānūn* and later on accepted by almost all the Muslim countries.

Evidence is provided through the variety of the terms initially used to translate the term "constitution", which ranged from *qānūn* to *nizām* (order, command, decree) to *dustūr*. In particular, this last term progressively gained major consent and became the most used in referring to the Western idea of constitution, even nowadays. However, from an etymological point of view and in spite of its modern and contemporary usage,

[89] In spite of its being in force for only three year, the Tunisian constitution of 1861 represents a relevant juridical experiment, being the first written constitution of the Muslim world. It was enacted in a time in which Tunisia formed a factually independent province of the Ottoman sultanate and aspired to modernize its political structure under European influence. The Western cultural inspiration for the constitution is also proved by the fact that prior to its enactment it was submitted to Napoleon III in Algiers. Regarding the charter, see Nathan J. Brown, *Constitutions in a Nonconstitutional World. Arab Basic Laws and the Prospects for Accountable Government*, State University of New York Press, Albany 2002, pp. 16–20; Hedia Khadhar, "La Révolution française, le Pacte fondamental et la première Constitution tunisienne de 1861", in *Revue des mondes musulmans et de la Méditerranée*, ns. 52–53, *Les Arabes, les Turcs et la Révolution française*, 1989, pp. 132–137.

[90] Regarding the constitutional period of the Ottoman empire from a historical point of view, see Selçuk Akşin Somel, "Constitution/Constitutional Periods" (voice), in *Encyclopedia of the Ottoman Empire*, eds. Gábor Ágoston, Bruce Masters, Facts on File, New York 2009, pp. 144–145. For an in-depth analysis, see Robert Devereux, *The First Ottoman Constitutional Period. A Study of the Midhat Constitution and Parliament*, The Johns Hopkins Press, Baltimore 1963; Roderic H. Davison, *Reform in the Ottoman Empire, 1856-1876*, Princeton University Press, Princeton 1963, pp. 358–408. From a linguistic point of view, consider also Johann Strauss, "A Constitution for a Multilingual Empire: Translation of the Kanun-i Esasi and Other Official Texts into Minority Languages", in *The First Ottoman Experiment in Democracy*, eds. Christoph Herzog, Malek Sharif, Ergon Verlag, Würzburg 2016, pp. 21–52.

the term *dustūr*, coming from the Persian *dastur*, reflects a completely different reality. Indeed, it was originally used to refer to an individual exercising power and later on generally to rules, regulations, and standards of conduct.[91] Therefore, a constitution being a normative act that is by no means conceptually superimposable to *sharīʿa* or to autochthonous Muslim conceptions of authority and power, the real question to examine is how the philosophical and juridical relationship between *sharīʿa* and constitution actually developed and progressed.

In the framework of so-called Islamic constitutionalism—which would be more appropriate to call "constitutionalism of Muslim countries"[92]—I categorize the relationship between *sharīʿa* and constitution based on four major groups, notwithstanding possible minor divergences inside of each classification. Each one represents a different approach to the contingent necessity of reconciling these two visions and inscribing them in a single legal framework, and therefore each one presents a unique—and sometime implicit—philosophical solution to an apparently unanswerable question. Given the high interest on this latest point, also in light of the contemporary constitutional scenario, it would be appropriate to dedicate the proper space to each one of these models. Falling however outside of

[91] On this point, see Ami Ayalon, *Language and Change in the Arab Middle East. The Evolution of Modern Arabic Political Discourse*, Oxford University Press, Oxford 1987, pp. 94–96.

[92] The term "Islamic constitutionalism" is rather popular in academic writings and is commonly used to address the constitutional corpus of the Muslim world, with its charters, basic laws, and recurrent principles. Quraishi-Lander, with regard to this, defines Islamic constitutionalism as "a sharia-mindful way of thinking about the nature and allocation of power – political, religious, legislative, judicial and so on" (Aisfa Quraishi-Landes, "Legislating Morality and Other Illusions about Islamic Government", in *Locating the Sharīʿa. Legal Fluidity in Theory, History and Practice*, ed. Sohaira Z. M. Siddiqui, Brill, Leiden-Boston 2019, p. 178, note 9). Khan and Ramadan conceive Islamic constitutionalism as a modern development of the concept of *ijtihād*, thus seeing compatibility between constitutionalism and Islam (L. Ali Khan, Hisham M. Ramadan, *Contemporary Ijtihad. Limits and Controversies*, Edinburgh University Press, Edinburgh 2011, pp. 113–145). I prefer to avoid this terminology that could be misleading. Speaking about an Islamic constitutionalism implicitly suggests that the idea of constitutionalism, as briefly analyzed above, could in some way be properly Islamic, that is to say an expression of the Islamic legal tradition, or at least an outcome of its evolution. Not sharing this view, I prefer speaking about a form of constitutionalism applied to Islamic countries, which gradually developed their own legal principles and, most of all, their own ways of reconciling the Western idea of constitutionalism with their Islamic cultural heritage. In light of this, the terminology used by Grote and Röder for the title of the aforementioned work appears to be particularly appropriate.

the aim of this book, I will list here four approaches in which constitutional systems may be classified according to the interactions between *sharīʿa* and Western law.

A first approach consists of adopting a Western-like constitutional model and at the same time expunging the *sharīʿa* from the legal system of the country. Evidently, it can be considered as one of the most radical and invasive methods, provided that it tries to replace a traditional legal vision, deeply inherent to the philosophical conceptions of Muslim countries, with a non-superimposable foreign legislation, with all the foreseeable problems of adaptability. The most famous case is the forced secularization imposed by the Young Turks to the Republic of Turkey, after the fall of the Ottoman empire and the abolition of the caliphate.[93] Another less obvious example is the kingdom of Morocco, where some *sharīʿa*-inspired principles may influence national legislation in its substantive content but are not directly considered as sources of law.[94] In this last case, the Muslim elements are considered to be a cultural legacy capable of inspiring the legislative activity, which however is developed according to Western procedures, thus based on a determined philosophical perspective. Islam is here deprived of its intrinsic normative dimension and becomes an object of national law and not its origin. This approach, with all its possible diversifications and subcategorizations, is the most open to the idea of Westernization of the legal systems of Muslim countries, following the influence of the process of European colonization.[95]

A second approach consists of establishing a hybrid double-track system, in which the national charter enshrines *sharīʿa* as part of the

[93] On this issue, see Niyazi Berkes, *The Development of Secularism in Turkey*, Routledge, New York-London 1998, especially pp. 461 ff.

[94] As for the Moroccan constitution of 2011, it is the case of the attribution of the caliphal title of *amīr al-muʾminīn* to the king (art. 41, par. 1), who is however a sovereign of a national State. Again, it is possible to mention the constitutional role of the *fatāwā* (art. 41, par. 3), which are however deprived of their normative role. Substantive Islamic content transposed into national legislation can be mainly found in the *mudawwana*, the Moroccan family code.

[95] Other examples of countries sharing this approach are Tunisia, Algeria, Brunei, Djibouti, and Bangladesh. It is possible to add to this list also Indonesia, the country with the largest Muslim population in the world. However, in the Indonesian autonomous region of Aceh the influence of *sharīʿa* is more accentuated and follows different lines of interactions.

constitutional system. This is the case of Egypt[96] and of the majority of Sunnī countries, such as Qatar, the United Arab Emirates, Pakistan, and so on. With regard to Shīʿa Islam, it is worth mentioning that a similar system is presented by the constitution of Iran, which was the first country to ever introduce this model in the constitutional history of the Muslim world.[97] Usually, the constitutional charters of these countries define *sharīʿa* as "main source of legislation",[98] or prescribe that no law inconsistent with *sharīʿa* shall be enacted by State organs.[99] Here, *sharīʿa* acquires an indirect normative nature, in that it comes to be part of the constitutional model, however hardly finding a way to be directly applied without the mediation of national legislation. In this approach, the main point of interest is inherent to how to ensure an overall coherence of the legal system and providing a univocal mechanism of coordination between the different sources of law. In particular, if *sharīʿa* is a "source of legislation", it is necessary to find a way to harmonize these two visions and to locate them within a single conceptual framework, as in the case of the process of

[96] In the constitutional history of Egypt, since 1971 the *sharīʿa*-clause has always been at art. 2 and underwent various evolution. Among the extensive literature existing on this issue, see Cornelis Hulsman (ed.) *The Sharia as the Main Source of Legislation? The Egyptian Debate on Article II of the Egyptian Constitution*, Tectum Verlag, Marburg 2012. On the hermeneutical aspects involving the Supreme Constitutional Court, which acquires here a preeminent importance, see Nathan J. Brown, Adel Omar Sherif, "Inscribing the Islamic Shari'a in Arab Constitutional Law", in *Islamic Law and the Challenges of Modernity*, *cit.*, p. 67–75. For the latest evolutions, see Cornelius Hulsman (ed.), *The 2014 Egyptian Constitution. Perspectives from Egypt*, Tectum Verlag, Baden-Baden 2017.

[97] The reference is to the constitution of the Sublime State of Persia of 1906, as amended by supplementary fundamental laws on October 7th, 1907. On this, see Shaheen Sardar Ali, *Modern Challenges to Islamic Law*, Cambridge University Press, Cambridge 2016, p. 60.

[98] The *sharīʿa* clauses can be in turn divided into two groups. The first group comprehends constitutions defining *sharīʿa* as "a main source of legislation" or analogous formulations. This is the case of Syria, Qatar, Kuwait, Bahrain the United Arab Emirates, the self-proclaimed Sahrawi Arab Democratic Republic, and the national authority of Palestine. A second group comprehends the constitutions defining *sharīʿa* as "the main source of legislation" or analogous formulations. This is the case of Libya, Oman, Somaliland, Yemen, the Maldives, Mauritania, as well as the previous constitution of Sudan. The case of Egypt is emblematic, in that its 1971 constitution defined *sharīʿa* as "a main source of legislation" (art. 2), only to be amended in 1980 to define it as "the main source of legislation". Therefore, the evolution of the Egyptian constitutional discipline, with special reference to the phraseology used in this clause, is particularly useful to analyze the various implications of this model.

[99] This approach is shared by Afghanistan, Iraq, Pakistan, and Somalia.

constitutional review.[100] In this approach, this is undoubtedly the richest in terms of juridical and philosophical implications, two worlds effectively meet, sharing the same juridical space and being rooted in the same ground.

A third approach consists in recognizing *sharīʿa* as the primary form of national normativity, considering it a sort of constitution[101] and the same time adopting Western-like norms as a second-ranking regulation. This model is typical of the legal system of the kingdom of Saudi Arabia and presents some interesting features.[102] The most important and yet problematic one is that it attempts to theoretically preserve a preeminent role for *sharīʿa* but at the same pragmatically adopting Western instruments and standards. In this model, *sharīʿa* does not enter into the constitutional framework by virtue of a specific clause, thus acquiring legitimacy and deriving its validity from it. On the contrary, this model is specifically characterized by the original applicability of *sharīʿa* regardless of any constitutional clause. The Saudi Basic Law of 1992 simply acknowledges the direct applicability of *sharīʿa*, thus acknowledging a different and extraconstitutional source of legal legitimacy, which necessarily goes beyond Western constructs and notions. Nevertheless, national legislation is currently enacted by the kingdom, which tries to restore the ancient dichotomy *sharīʿa-qānūn*, in a system trying to preserve an equilibrium between the Islamic nature of its theoretical conception and the practical mechanisms of State functioning, which are undoubtedly influenced by the West.

The last model embodies by far the most radical approach and can be considered as a specular form of the first. This approach involves the total

[100] On this, see Tamir Moustafa, "The Political Role of the Supreme Constitutional Court: Between Principles and Practice", in *Judges and Political Reform in Egypt*, ed. Nathalie Bernard-Maugiron, The American University in Cairo Press, Cairo-New York 2008, pp. 92–95.

[101] The Saudi Basic Law define *Qurʾān* and *sunnah* as its constitution (art. 1), however with the theoretical problem inherent to the transposition of the role and the conceptual scope of constitutionalism into an Islamic context. To be noted that the definition of the holy book of Islam as constitution was already used by the Libyan Declaration on the Establishment of the Authority of the People of 1977 (art. 2).

[102] On the Saudi case, see the comprehensive work of Frank E. Vogel, *Islamic Law and Legal System. Studies of Saudi Arabia*, Brill, Leiden-Boston-Köln 2000; of the same author, see also "Saudi Arabia. Public, Civil, and Individual Shariʿa in Law and Politics", in *Shariʿa Politics. Islamic Law and Society in the Modern World*, ed. Robert W. Hefner, Indiana University Press, Bloomington-Indianapolis 2011, pp. 55–93. Consider also Dorthe Bramnsen, "Divine Law and Human Understanding – The Idea of Shariʿa in Saudi Arabia", in *Shariʿa As Discourse. Legal Traditions and the Encounter with Europe*, eds. Jørgen S. Nielsen, Lisbet Christoffersen, Ashgate, Lanham-Burlington 2010, pp. 157–178.

rejection of Western-derived legal instruments and constructs, including the idea of constitutionalism and the restoration of an exclusively Islamic legal order, with the exclusive enforcement of *sharīʿa*. This method is not typical of States, which present a form of Westernization *ab origine*, due to their acceptance of the ideas of territoriality and sovereignty. On the contrary, it is a vision usually proposed by fundamentalist groups, such as ISIS, in whose juridical view every Western and non-Muslim contamination is to be rejected, in order to provide an allegedly genuine restoration of *sharīʿa*, that would be in some way precluded by the adoption of Western legal models.[103] ISIS, in particular, represents an interesting case, assuming the form of a self-proclaimed caliphate, who does not simply pretend to reject the Western idea of law but enters into competition with it. If, for instance, the Muslim *ummah* is originally and necessarily a-national, ISIS' *ummah* is anti-national.[104] The hybridization with the West is theoretically denied but is factually present in ISIS' antagonism and exclusivism, whose idea of legal order presents unique and interesting features that would be worthy of dedicated analysis.

In this chapter, I focused on theoretical and practical aspects of two comprehensive juridical visions and of two ways based on which to understand the juridical phenomenon. However, it is not believed that such reflections are purely speculative. On the contrary, through a philosophically oriented legal comparison it would actually be possible to show how an apparently historical and cultural reflection can greatly influence the concrete legal practice of contemporary States as well. Moreover, it is usually a common opinion that the history of *sharīʿa* be concluded in the post-colonial era, while in reality some juridical questions that arise from the analysis of the legal systems of contemporary Muslim countries, with special reference to the relationship between Western law and *sharīʿa*, are by no means less relevant than the ones of the past.

[103] Legal literature on ISIS' juridical views is actually lacking. Among authors who have written about this topic, with special reference to ISIS' relationship with the post-Westphalian international order, see Robert J. Delahunty, "An Epitaph for ISIS? The Idea of a Caliphate and the Westphalian Order", in *Arizona Journal of International & Comparative Law*, vol. XXXV, n. 1, 2018, pp. 1–70; Tal Mimran, "In A Broken Dream: Lessons from The Rise and Demise of the Self-Declared Caliphate of the Islamic State in Syria and Iraq", in *Journal of Transnational Law & Policy*, vol. XXIX, 2019–2020 (July 2020), research paper n. 08–20, pp. 1–53. Consider also my volume, Federico Lorenzo Ramaioli, *Islamic State as a Legal Order. To Have No Law but Islam Between Shari'a and Globalization*, Routledge, London-New York 2022.

[104] On ISIS' conception of *ummah*, see James Piscatori, Amin Saikal, *Islam Beyond Borders. The Umma in World Politics*, Cambridge University Press, Cambridge 2019, pp. 134–159.

CHAPTER 7

Conclusion: New Juridical Instruments for a New World

The present book was not meant to be the point of arrival of a self-sufficient and complete analysis of the Islamic legal tradition, a field far too wide to ever be considered exhausted or somehow sufficiently explored. On the contrary, it was meant to represent a starting point for new reflections, according to different methodologies. Again, it was not intended to provide definitive conclusions on issues subject to constant transformations, especially in the contemporary scenario, but on the contrary to offer a different point of view on matters usually examined according to other perspectives. Needless to say, as the title of this book suggests, this is only *a* tale of these two worlds, one among various possible analyses, as carried out through my personal point of view, without any pretense of exhaustivity or completeness.

The point of view I intended to provide is evidently the point of view of a Western jurist, who nevertheless tries not to consider ideas and conceptions shaped in different cultural and religious environments without taking a number of essential variables into due consideration. Among these variables, I attach the highest importance to the way in which the triangular relationship between man as a rational being, God as a creator, and the legal order as a comprehensive vision is conceived and developed. Therefore, I attempted to highlight the legal implications following a certain conception of space and time in relation to law, as well as different

F. L. Ramaioli, *Juridical Perspectives between Islam and the West*, Global Issues, https://doi.org/10.1007/978-3-031-37844-7_7

approaches to questions relating to political power and legal authority. From my point of view, only by considering all these points as variables, instead of constants, will it be possible to assume a correct perspective to *start* examining the question and drawing eventual parallelisms and comparisons.

On the contrary, considering the philosophical premises from which a juridical conception is derived and the foundations on which it is based as constants would inevitably lead to universalize the observer's way of conceiving reality, systematically—and often unconsciously—projecting it onto contexts completely alien. As specified in my premises and as explained in the previous chapters, this process of universalization of the Western juridical conception is often associated with the implicit assumption that other legal orders may somehow share the same categorial outlook on fundamental legal issues and, in a broader sense, on reality, justice, and life. Therefore, my approach based on juridical categories intended to provide a philosophical instrument, considered as a variable in every legal order, to preliminarily analyze the structural elements of a determined juridical conception, on the basis of which it shall eventually be possible to build a comprehensive and comparative reflection.

This approach requires first of all a rational effort in order to circumvent the consolidated schemes in which law is often considered. The first effort, as far as concretely possible, is to pay a particular attention to the terminology we use to describe Islamic legal notions, especially in a comparative analysis, because of the relatively easiness with which a precise term, imposed onto a different cultural context, can substantially alter the very way in which a phenomenon in perceived in its overall conceptualization and in its location within a wider framework. This is not a secondary consequence, provided that the means by which we carry out juridical reasonings necessarily pass through the use of language, and naming figures, constructs, and ideas in certain ways means at the same time defining their conceptual boundaries and giving forms and shapes to their essence. Regarding this, earlier in my book I recalled the biblical account of the creation of Adam, where the naming of a thing somehow hides the power of controlling them in their essence.

In light of this and from a Western point of view, it will be possible to consider specific issues of the Islamic legal tradition, in all its variety and complexity, avoiding the risk of oversimplifying questions belonging to a peculiar and specific cultural, social, and religious context, and at the same time examining them according to their own categorial outlook. This approach will prevent us from falling into a first stereotype, according to which the Islamic and the Western legal perspectives would in some way be comparable in their methodological approach, in their functional dimension, and, most of all, in their constitutive premises, thus minimizing the structural divergences of understanding and conceiving the juridical reality. Besides being a process of oversimplification, this stereotype leads to the aforementioned risk of biasing any subsequent analysis imposing conceptual schemes of comprehension that are supposed to be shared and common, but that are far from being so. I speak of a stereotype, because, with a prior analysis of the context in which determined ideals come to life and of the functional aim they serve, every juridical comparison is reduced to a comparison between substantive contents of "laws"—this last concept understood as positivistic normative acts typical of the Western modernity. Needless to say, this attitude appears superficial and inappropriate while dealing with a topical and multifaceted issue as the relationship between two great juridical traditions, each one of them progressively shaping its respective world; each one creating a world of knowledge and of debate, of dispute and of wisdom, of governance and of speculation, and ultimately of peace and war.

Avoiding this stereotype does not mean, at the same time, precluding every possible way to a dialogue based on similitudes and comparable concepts. On the contrary, every dialogue, just like every comparison, needs to take moves from a shared understanding of the world or at least from the common ground of sharing common premises and common definitions. In my introductory lines, and following the tradition of Scholasticism, I highlighted the importance of starting a reflection, especially in the juridical field, with an adequate *explicatio terminorum*. Similarly, every dialogue cannot prescind from the preliminary investigation on the actual common ground from which a reflection may indeed rise and develop. The minimization of this passage in the laudable intent of drawing easy parallelisms in substantive issues, such as the compatibility of Islamic legal notions with human right principles or with liberal democracy, would inevitably lead to recurring cultural misappropriations or to inappropriate conclusions. From this point of view, the acquired awareness of the differences inherent to these two visions would already represent a starting point to develop a juridical dialogue and to carve new instruments with which to face the challenges of the contemporary world.[1] Only in this way will it eventually be possible to conceive legal multiculturalism as "a dialog among different areas of globalizing civilization",[2] with all its interconnections and exchanges.

Equally important is to reject the opposite stereotype, however grounded in the same process of universalization of Western legal categories and notions. This stereotype, sometimes recurring while comparing these two perspectives, is the one according to which the Islamic legal tradition would not be as sophisticated or as advanced as the Western one, being somehow at a different and underdeveloped phase of evolution. From a substantive point of view, this position recurs when speaking about human rights, gender equality, and rule of law, while historically speaking it represents a common premise of the argument concerning the lack in Islamic history of phases like the Enlightenment or the French Revolution. As already explained, these argumentations are to be rejected because of their lack of proper historical and cultural contextualization. Moreover, and most importantly, this stereotype is grounded in a sort of "legal evolutionism",[3] that is to say the belief that the juridical phenomena shall be understood and conceived in a univocal way, with progressive and linear steps toward a final awareness. Needless to say, besides sharing the recurring bias of universalizing particular categories and considering mutable variables as eternal constants, this approach lacks proper scientific

[1] In the field of multicultural dialogue, which is something relevant in a juridical analysis as well, it is necessary to recall the tension between affirming one's identity and opening to otherness. In particular, assuming the category of cultural difference as logically preceding identity would ultimately put into question every form of conceptual universalization. Similarly, in our case, the awareness of the structural differences in two juridical perspectives can not only question an undiscriminated Westernization of juridical notions but also lead to a more contextualized dialogue between legal orders. On this, cf. Randi Gressgård [2010], *Multicultural Dialogue. Dilemmas, Paradoxes, Conflicts*, Berghahn Books, New York-Oxford 2012, pp. 87–88.

[2] Krzysztof Abriszewski, "Inner/intercultural dialog and long-range ethics", in *Cultures. Conflict-Analysis-Dialog*, proceedings of the 29th International Ludwig Wittgenstein Symposium, Kirchberg am Wechsel, Austria 2006, eds. Christian Kanzian, Edmund Runggaldier, Ontos Verlag, Heusenstamm 2007, p. 336.

[3] Here, I borrow the terminology of Peter Stein, *Legal Evolution. The Story of an Idea*, Cambridge University Press, Cambridge 1980, in this sense especially at p. 19. The concept was later reinterpreted by Fitzpatrick in rejecting the erroneous position according to which customary law represented an underdeveloped stage on the path of the evolution of a legal system, before a natural separation between law and society (Fitzpatrick, *The Mythology of Modern Law*, *cit.*, pp. 87–91).

basis, as well as conscious premises defining its foundations. Far from being neither monolithically conceived nor underdeveloped with respect to other juridical visions, the Islamic legal tradition flourished in variety, flexibility, and richness, greatly influencing the society it came to shape and contributed to create. It had "multiple voices",[4] each one of them contributed to create a multifaceted and complex reality. In particular, the class of the jurists, even belonging to various schools, engaged in a constant dialogue and in perpetual research, performing those hermeneutical efforts that made their activity essential not just for the development of the juridical sciences in the Muslim world but for the conceptualization of a way of conceiving justice and social life. This complex and multifaceted view, to which also Shīʿa Islam greatly contributed, simply followed a different—and sometimes opposite—path of development with respect to other legal conceptions, like the Western one. On the contrary, assuming a linear and ultimately coinciding evolutionary track for every legal order would result in an act of ideology, to be believed by faith.[5]

In light of what has been said in the previous chapters, it is possible to draw some general conclusions, however with the necessary premise that these conclusions represent once again the starting point for developing and stimulating further reflections. Although defining the conclusions for a starting point may sound paradoxical, I believe that in this way it would be ultimately possible to progressively define a new approach not just for the analysis of the juridical relationship between Islam and the West but for the methodological definition of a philosophically oriented legal comparativism.

A first conclusion to be drawn from this analysis is inherent in the ideas of territoriality, which characterized the way in which Western modernity

[4] Aycob, Lussier, *The Many Faces of Political Islam*, *cit.*, p. 26.

[5] Particularly interesting is the metaphorical concept of legal transplant, which "suggests a teleological development toward a fixed endpoint—legal systems will mature into liberal democratic rule of law just as Aristotle's tiny acorn will one day become a sturdy oak tree" (Randall Peerenboom [2006], "What have we learned about law and development? Describing, predicting and assessing legal reforms in China", in *Law and Society in East Asia*, eds. Christoph Antons, Roman Tomasic, Routledge, London-New York 2016, p. 162). This process of legal transplantation may indeed be led intentionally for political purposes, like in the case of colonialism, or, as I intend here, it may be understood as a sort of natural process guiding all the legal orders toward a final endpoint—being it represented by human rights law, liberal democracy, or other principles. This last notion is evidently linked to the idea of legal evolution, already mentioned in these conclusive remarks. The image of legal transplant is also used by Chiba, *Legal Pluralism*, *cit.*, p. 151.

built up the features of the State, and universalism, as the inspiring juridical and political ideal of the Muslim world. Although a never-realized and never-achieved chimera, Islamic universalism represented an essential aspiration that, in abstract, theorized the existence of a single and a-national *ummah* of the believers, in spite of the frequent and constant fractures that affected Muslim political history. Most importantly, the idea of universalism reveals some essential and structural characteristics of the Islamic legal conception, whose concrete experiences cannot prescind from this ideal. This point is even more important with regard to two essential moments: the creation of the Westphalian international system and its progressive extension all over the world, and, in recent years, the continuous and slow-proceeding erosion of the same system in favor of the emergence of non-State actors and entities. In this context, every conceptual analysis between the Islamic and Western perspectives, with particular attention to legal reasoning, must take into due account the dichotomy of territoriality-universalism, especially in an international scenario in which this binomial undergoes unexpected transformations. This reflection must however be located in the broader discourse of the future of the Nation-State and of the (re)thinking of the international order, in whose framework it is necessary to investigate what the relationship between Islam and the future international models will be like.

Another fundamental point to be taken into due account is the essentiality of the juridical dimension in Islam, which comes to represent a constitutive characteristic of its vision of the world. From this point of view, Islamic nomocentrism is undoubtedly interesting from a sociological and religious point of view, but is certainly more important in a juridical analysis, especially in the contemporary context, where it can bring about relevant implications in terms of strategies of integration and intercultural dialogue. Ignoring the structural nature and the teleological perspective of the legal dimension of Islam leads necessarily to the miscomprehension of the very foundations of the Islamic civilization and consequently of the actual role Muslim countries and Islamic religious affiliations will play in global geopolitics. At the same time, it is necessary to properly contextualize the concept of religion in the Islamic world, with its *own* ideal perimeter and conceptual boundaries, avoiding the risk of projecting the role Christianity played and plays in the Western world onto a Muslim context, where the interactions between religion and politics—admitting the usability of this terminology—follow completely different schemes. In particular, it is necessary to properly address the issue regarding the (non) conceptualization of a systematic separation between secular and religious authorities in the Muslim world, once again avoiding the error of considering this an underdevelopment along the road to national secularization—with this last concept representing once again the outcome of a particular philosophical and historical path, and by no means a universal endpoint.[6] In light of this, a topic of major interest is certainly represented by the common areas that both legal orders—Western and Islamic—consider to belong to the juridical field, thus leading to a potential overlapping between the two conceptions in territories in which both visions are rooted, historically or recently. Indeed, this last point cannot be ignored when analyzing legal systems characterized by an attempted integration between Western categories and Islamic principles, or *vice versa*, as well as when examining the issue of legal pluralism in Western countries characterized by a stable presence of Muslim diasporas.

What is perhaps the most important point of my reflection is however related, in my opinion, to the divergences in the role human reason plays in the legal order, with Islam adopting a fundamentally contemplative and deductive perspective, and the West an eminently creative one. In both views, human reason plays a fundamental role and is an extremely vibrant and flexible element in building and shaping the juridical architecture of the respective civilizations. However, the difference in the theorization of its role comes from divergent philosophical premises in conceiving the nature of man, the nature of the divinity, and their relationship with the idea of normativity, premises that, even in the case of complete equality in terms of substantive legal contents, can completely change the way in which such contents are located within the wider spectrum of juridical comprehension and practice. This analysis can only imply fundamental—and extremely practical and concrete—consequences to the way in which man deals with the idea of normativity, deeply affecting social and political life in a given system. Some examples are the relationship between law, space, and time in the West, a relationship that is completely different in the Muslim tradition, and that, far from being a conceptual and theoretical exercise, marks a demarcation line between concepts we deem as essential, such as the rule of law, the preclusion of *ex post facto* laws, and most of all the role of the jurist and of the interpreter in the legal order.

[6] On this misconception, see Abdullahi Ahmed An-Naʿim, "The individual and collective self-liberation model of Ustadh Mahmoud Mohamed Taha", in *Beyond the Secular West*, ed. Akeel Bilgrami, Columbia University Press, New York 2016, pp. 62–67.

However, it would be a mistake to think that these two visions of the world can live detached from one another and, most importantly, from the concreteness of the real world. These are models of thought and methods of comprehension that, although usually theorized in the abstract, keep on living in concrete life, influencing social behaviors and political notions, periodically undergoing physiological changes and engaging in a mutual and constant dialogue. In other words, every legal order in the course of history lives a life of interactions, exchanges, conflicts, and relations, hardly remaining in a state of perennial immutability. From this point of view, the Islamic and the Western legal orders make no exception, as the history of the respective civilizations exhaustively shows. As I argued in my introduction, in the last century this dialogue became closer and closer, to the point of representing a new and previously unknown stage of this relationship. Both because of self-organized Westernization process of the legal system, like in the late-Ottoman empire, and because of the colonization processes of African and Middle Eastern territories, for the first time these two different visions and these two different perspectives came to coexist on the same ground, sharing not only a physical spatiality but also the same field of implementation. Even in this framework, and to the present day, the different methods of coordination between Western law and Islamic *sharīʿa*, as well as the various attitudes toward their interactions, show the extreme variety that characterized the juridical dialogue between the West and Islam. As is clearly visible when analyzing the various constitutional systems of the Muslim world, the possible approaches greatly varied depending on historical, cultural, and juridical variables. Hybrid approaches are undoubtedly the most interesting ones from a scholarly point of view, both for the internal variety characterizing the legal systems sharing this attitude and for the legal questions they pose. Generally speaking, and having regard for all the possible models involved in this dialogue between Western law and Islamic *sharīʿa*, particular attention is to be paid to the overall coherence of the legal system, having regard for all its elements and to their ultimate harmonization. Contrarily to the case of substantive antinomies in a legal corpus of norms, rather easy to target and possibly to solve, in these cases the antinomy is neither visible nor it is explicitly shown in positivistic regulations. On the contrary, in these cases the potential antinomy derives from the forced reconciliation of two different perspectives, each one considered to be self-sufficient and shaped according to particular philosophical premises, into a single comprehensive framework, which is often trapped into the unsolved tension between the two. It is a hidden antinomy, but especially because of its aethereal nature more insidious, particularly nowadays when the dimension of the "law" is sometimes simplistically reduced to positivistic norms and where the idea of *jus* is often confused with the dimension of *lex*. Here, precisely in this tension toward an overall coherence of a legal system,[7], aimed at regulating a multifaceted and complex reality, the juridical challenge of this dialogue is met and faced by our contemporaneity.

All the abovementioned reflections do not belong to our past but instead to our future. Issues such as the ones analyzed in this book are not to be considered relegated in an ancestral age, like the traditions in whose context they have originated, but on the contrary represent topical subjects that will be able to greatly influence not just our contemporaneity but the future legal debate for years to come. The postmodern world, as described by Lyotard, Derrida, and others, is already behind us,[8] and the future is delineating ahead new and previously unseen dimensions that, in terms of juridical challenges and problematics, we would never have thought of in the past. As in every historical age, it is particularly difficult to be aware of the deep changes that are affecting our own time, while living inside of its temporality. Nevertheless, our contemporaneity is seemingly experimenting with a new phase, that is to say a radical and progressive transition from once consolidated legal models to an apparently

[7] The idea of an overall coherence of the legal system is explored by Neil MacCormick, *Rhetoric and The Rule of Law: A Theory of Legal Reasoning*, Oxford University Press, Oxford 2005, especially pp. 121–142. Interpreting and discussing MacCormick's position, Carbonell points out that it is only within a "systemic context that the legal material acquires its significance. Therefore, the ideal of overall coherence governs the view of the legal system as a system, and helps to make sense, to bring together and to order the multiplicity of the different kinds of norms that comprise the whole legal system" (Flavia Carbonell, "Coherence and Post-sovereign Legal Argumentation", in *Law and Democracy in Neil MacCormick's Legal and Political Theory. The Post-Sovereign Constellation*, eds. Agustín José Menéndez, John Erik Fossum, Springer, Dordrecht-Heidelberg-London-New York 2011, p. 162).

[8] In different fields of knowledge, some authors already suggest that the present time cannot be termed postmodernism anymore, trying to investigate what may lie beyond this curtain of uncertainty. Among these authors, consider the reflections of Ihab Hassan, "Beyond Postmodernism", in *Angelaki: Journal of the Theoretical Humanities*, vol. VIII, n. 1, 2003, pp. 3–11. Consider also Garry Potter, José López, "After Postmodernism: The Millennium", in *After Postmodernism. An Introduction to Critical Realism*, eds. Garry Potter, José López, The Athlone Press, London-New York 2001, pp. 1–18. Alternatively, Augé speaks of supermodernity, whose spatiality is represented by non-spaces (Marc Augé [1992], *Non-places. Introduction to an Anthropology of Supermodernity*, trans. John Howe, Verso, London-New York 1995, especially pp. 110 ff).

a-systemic reality, where a coherent and organic juridical vision finds it hard to emerge. It should not be excluded that this conceptual turmoil, where powers *de jure condendo* and *de jure condito* merge in attempting to shape visions and craving images of the future, may already represent a new fluid model characterized precisely by its a-systemic nature and by the absence of a proper theorization,[9] in contrast to what the world had witnessed before.

In this new world, whose juridical characteristics are far from being properly understood and defined, more than ever it is necessary to crave new conceptual instruments not just to comprehend our contemporaneity but to systematize its necessary juridical dimension, somehow inherent to every civilization, although changing in shapes and forms. It is therefore necessary to define "a newly invigorated legal methodology to make sense of old and new legal pluralities",[10] and to face the challenges of a post-modern reality whose level of complexity is far more advanced than we could have expected only a few years ago. In light of this, this book aims to be a humble contribution in offering a different point of view on a subject that is far from being exhaustively explored, especially in the present day.

[9] As Suter points out in describing globalization, it is to be seen "more as chaos than conspiracy, with no overall guiding hand. It is a matter of 'disorder' rather than 'order'" (Keith Suter, *Global Order and Global Disorder. Globalization and the Nation-State*, Praeger, Westport-London 2003, p. 2). Similarly, the new international model for a globalized world could be a non-order, that is to say the negation of the idea of order.

[10] Werner F. Menski, "Cherrypicking Customs: on What Happens When Custom is not Taught", in *The Shade of New Leaves. Governance in Traditional Authority. A Southern African Perspective*, eds. Manfred O. Hinz, Helgard K. Patemann, Lit Verlag, Berlin 2006, p. 402.

Bibliography

Abiad N.: *Sharia, Muslim States and International Human Rights Treaty Obligations. A Comparative Study*, British Institute of International and Comparative Law, London 2008

Abizadeh A.: "The Representation of Hobbesian Sovereignty: Leviathan as Mythology", in *Hobbes Today. Insights for the 21st Century*, ed. S. A. Lloyd, Cambridge University Press, Cambridge 2013

Abriszewski K.: "Inner/intercultural dialog and long-range ethics", in *Cultures. Conflict-Analysis-Dialog*, proceedings of the 29th International Ludwig Wittgenstein Symposium, Kirchberg am Wechsel, Austria 2006, eds. Christian Kanzian, Edmund Runggaldier, Ontos Verlag, Heusenstamm 2007

Abu-Rabiʿ I. M.: *Intellectual Origins of Islamic Resurgence in the Modern Arab World*, State University of New York Press, Albany 1996

Adamec L. W.: *Historical Dictionary of Islam*, Scarecrow Press, Lanham-Toronto-Plymouth 2009

Agamben G. [2003]: *State of Exception*, trans. Kevin Attell, The University of Chicago Press, Chicago-London 2005

Agamben G.: *Il Regno e la Gloria. Per una Genealogia Teologica dell'Economia e del Governo*, Neri Pozza, Milan 2007

Agamben G. [2011]: *The Highest Poverty. Monastic Rules and Form-of-Life*, trans. Adam Kotsko, Stanford University Press, Stanford 2013

Aḥmad M. ʻA.: *The Nature of Islamic Political Theory*, Maʻaref, Karachi 1975

Akbarzadeh S., MacQueen B.: "Framing the debate on Islam and human rights", in *Islam and Human Rights in Practice*, eds. Shahram Akbarzadeh, Benjamin MacQueen, Routledge, London-New York 2008

F. L. Ramaioli, *Juridical Perspectives between Islam and the West*, Global Issues, https://doi.org/10.1007/978-3-031-37844-7

Akgunduz A.: *Introduction to Islamic Law. Islamic Law in Theory and Practice*, Iur Press, Rotterdam 2010

Al-Alwani T. J.: *Issues in Contemporary Islamic Thought*, The International Institute of Islamic Thought, London-Washington 2005

Albrecht S.: *Dār al-Islām Revisited. Territoriality in Contemporary Islamic Legal Discourse on Muslims in the West*, Brill, Leiden-Boston 2008

al-Faruqi I. R.: *Islam and Other Faiths*, ed. Ataullah Siddiqui, The Islamic Foundation and the International Institute for Islamic Thought, Herndon 1998

al-Ghunaimi M. T.: *The Muslim Conception of International Law and the Western Approach*, Martinus Nijhoff, The Hague 1968

Ali A. Y. [1934]: *The Meaning of the Holy Qur'ān*, Amana Publications, Beltsville 2004

Ali S. S.: *Modern Challenges to Islamic Law*, Cambridge University Press, Cambridge 2016

Al Jerrahi T. B.: *The Name and the Named. The Divine Attributes of God*, Fons Vitae, Louisville 2000

al-Jibouri Y. T.: *Allah. The Concept of God in Islam*, vol. I, AuthorHouse, Bloomington 2012

Al-Khalifah A. H. M.: "Religiosity in Islam as a Protective Mechanism against Criminal Temptation", in *American Journal of Islamic Social Sciences*, vol. XI, n. 1, Spring 1994

Alleau R. [1976]: *La scienza dei simboli. Contributo allo studio dei principi e dei metodi della simbolica*, Sansoni, Florence 1983

al-Māwardī A. H. [972–1058]: *Al-Aḥkām as-Sulṭaniyyah. The laws of Islamic governance*, trans. Asadullah Yate, Ta-Ha Publishers, London 1996

al-Qaradawi Y.: *Approaching the Sunnah. Comprehension & Controversy*, International Institute of Islamic Thought, London-Washington 2006

al-Shāfiʿī M. [767–820]: *al-Risāla fī Uṣūl al-Fiqh (Treatise on the Foundations of Islamic Jurisprudence)*, trans. Majid Khadduri, Islamic Texts Society, Cambridge 1997

Amanullah M., Rahman H.: "The Origin and Evolution of Fiqh Codification. A Preliminary Analysis", in *Journal of Islam in Asia*, vol. XIII, n. 1, June 2016

Amin N.: *Some Salient Features of the Islamic Law and Constitution*, Pakistan Institute of Arts and Design, Karachi 1970

Amirmokri V.: *L'Islam et les droits de l'homme: l'islamisme, le droit international et le modernism islamique*, Les Presses de l'Université Laval, Saint-Nicolas (Québec) 2004

Angell N.: *The Great Illusion*, G. P. Putnamn's Sons, New York-London 1913

Anjum O.: *Politics, Law, and Community in Islamic Thought. The Taymiyyan Moment*, Cambridge University Press, Cambridge 2012

An-Naʿim A. A.: *Islam and the Secular State. Negotiating the Future of Sharīʿa*, Harvard University Press, Cambridge 2008

An-Naʿim A. A.: "The individual and collective self-liberation model of Ustadh Mahmoud Mohamed Taha", in *Beyond the Secular West*, ed. Akeel Bilgrami, Columbia University Press, New York 2016

Ardıç N.: *Islam and the Politics of Secularism. The Caliphate and Middle Eastern modernization in the early 20th century*, Routledge, London-New York 2012

Aristotle [IV c. BCE]: *Rhetoric*, trans. John Henry Freese, William Heineman publisher, London 1926

Aristotle [IV c. BCE]: *Politics*, trans. C. D. C. Reeve, Hackett Publishing Company, Indianapolis-Cambridge 1998

Armogathe J. R.: "Deus legislator", in *Natural Law and Laws of Nature in Early Modern Europe. Jurisprudence, Theology, Moral and Natural Philosophy*, eds. Lorraine Daston, Michael Stolleis, Ashgate, Farnham-Burlington 1988

Ashraf S.: *Judicial culture in Islam*, Anmol Publications, New Delhi 2006

Askari H.: "Economic Development in Islam", in *Economic Development and Islamic Finance*, eds. Zamir Iqbal, Abbas Mirakhor, The World Bank, Washington 2013

Atilgan A.: *Global Constitutionalism. A Socio-legal Perspective*, Springer, New York 2017

Auda J.: *Maqāṣid Al-Sharīʿa. A Beginner's Guide*, The International Institute of Islamic Thought, London-Washington 2008

Auda J.: "Realizing the Maqasid in the Sharīʿah", in *The Objectives of Islamic Law. The Promises and Challenges of the Maqasid al-Sharīʿah*, eds. Idris Nassery, Rumee Ahmed, Muna Tatari, Rowman & Littlefield, Lanham-London 2018

Augé M. [1992]: *Non-places. Introduction to an Anthropology of Supermodernity*, trans. John Howe, Verso, London-New York 1995

Ayalon A.: *Language and Change in the Arab Middle East. The Evolution of Modern Arabic Political Discourse*, Oxford University Press, Oxford 1987

Aydin C., "Reform" (voice), in *Encyclopedia of the Ottoman Empire*, eds. Gábor Ágoston, Bruce Masters, Facts on File, New York 2009

Ayoob M., Lussier D. N.: *The Many Faces of Political Islam. Religion and Politics in Muslim Societies*, University of Michigan Press, Ann Arbor 2020

Ayoub M. (ed.): *Contemporary Approaches to the Qur'ān and Sunnah*, International Institute of Islamic Thought, London-Washington 2012

Ayubi N. N. [1991]: *Political Islam. Religion and Politics in the Arab World*, Routledge, London-New York 2005

Azkoul M.: "Sacerdotium et Imperium: the Constantinian Renovatio According to the Greek Fathers", in *Theological Studies*, vol. XXXII, n. 3, September 1971

Baamir A. Y. [2010]: *Sharīʿa Law in Commercial and Banking Arbitration. Law and Practice in Saudi Arabia*, Routledge, London-New York 2016

Baderin M. A. [2006]: "Effective legal representation in "Sharīʿah" courts as a means of addressing human rights concerns in the Islamic criminal justice system of Muslim States", in *Issues in Islamic Law*, vol. II, ed. Mashood A. Baderin, Routledge, London-New York 2016

Badry R.: "Consultation" (voice), in *The Princeton Encyclopedia of Islamic Political Thought*, ed. Gerhard Bowering, Princeton University Press, Princeton 2016

Barkat A. M.: "Church-State relationships in an ideological Islamic State", in *The Ecumenical Review*, vol. XXIX, n. 1, January 1977

Barzilai G. [2003]: *Communities and Law. Politics and Cultures of Legal Identities*, University of Michigan Press, Ann Arbor 2006

Bassiouni M. C.: *The Sharīʿa and Islamic Criminal Justice in Time of War and Peace*, Cambridge University Press, Cambridge 2014

Bauman Z.: "On glocalization: or globalization for some, localization for some others", in *Thesis Eleven. Critical Theory and Historical Sociology*, vol. LIV, n. 1, August 1998

Beaulac S.: *The power of language in the making of international law. The word sovereignty in Bodin and Vattel and the myth of Westphalia*, Martinus Nijhoff Publishers, Leiden-Boston 2004

Beccaria C. [1764]: *Dei delitti e delle pene*, Lackington, Allen, and co., London 1801

Beck U.: *Was ist Globalisierung? Irrtümer des Globalismus — Antworten auf Globalisierung*, Suhrkamp Verlag, Frankfurt am Main 1997

Beetham D.: *The Legitimation of Power*, Macmillan, London 1991

Belhaj A.: "Law and order according to Ibn Taymiyya and Ibn Qayyim al-Jawziyya: a re-examination of siyāsa sharʿiyya", in *Islamic Theology, Philosophy and Law. Debating Ibn Taymiyya and Ibn Qayyim al-Jawziyya*, eds. Birgit Krawietz, Georges Tamer, De Gruyter, Berlin-Boston 2013

Bennet C.: "Punishment and Rehabilitation", in *Punishment and Ethics. New Perspectives*, eds. Jesper Ryberg, J. Angelo Corlett, Palgrave Macmillan, New York-Basingstoke 2010

Bennison A. K.: *The Great Caliphs. The Golden Age of the ʿAbbasid Empire*, I.B. Tauris, London-New York 2009

Bercé Y. M.: "Succession et Vacance", in *Les Monarchies*, ed. Yves-Marie Bercé, Presses Universitaires de France, Paris 2015

Bergmann G., Zerby L.: "The Formalism in Kelsen's Pure Theory of Law", in *Ethics*, vol. LV, n. 2, January 1945

Berkes N.: *The Development of Secularism in Turkey*, Routledge, New York-London 1998

Berkey J. P.: *The Formation of Islam. Religion and Society in the Near East, 600-1800*, Cambridge University Press, Cambridge 2003

Berkowitz R.: *The Gift of Science. Leibniz and the modern legal tradition*, Harvard University Press, Cambridge 2005

Bertocci P. A. [1970]: *The Person God Is*, Routledge, London 2002

Bhala R.: *Understanding Islamic Law. Sharīʿa*, Matthew Bender & Co., Newark 2011

Bianchi U. [1970]: *The History of Religions*, Brill, Leiden 1975

Biehler G.: *Procedures in International Law*, Springer, Berlin-Heidelberg 2008

Bielefeldt H:, "“Western” versus “Islamic” Human Rights Conceptions?: A Critique of Cultural Essentialism in the Discussion on Human Rights", in *Political Theory*, vol. XXVIII, n. 1, February 2000

Bilal Philips A. A.: *The Fundamentals of Tawheed (Islamic Monotheism)*, International Islamic Publishing House, Riyadh 2005

Bin R.: "Soft law, no law", in *Soft law e hard law nelle società postmoderne*, ed. Alessandro Somma, Giappichelli, Turin 2009

Binder L.: "Al-Ghazâlî's Theory of Islamic Government", in *The Muslim World*, vol. XLV, n. 3, 1955

Biondi B.: *Il diritto romano cristiano*, vol. I, Giuffré, Milan 1952

Bix B. [1993]: "The Application (and Mis-Application) of Wittgenstein's Rule-Following Considerations to Legal Theory", in *Wittgenstein and Law*, ed. Dennis Michael Patterson, Ashgate Publishing, Farnham 2004

Black A. [2001]: *The History of Islamic Political Thought. From the Prophet to the Present*, Edinburgh University Press, Edinburgh 2011

Black A., Esmaeili H., Hosen N.: *Modern Perspectives on Islamic Law*, Edward Elgar Publishing, Cheltenham-Northampton 2013

Blei K.: *Freedom of Religion and Belief. Europe's Story*, Van Gorcum, Assen 2002

Blumstein A., Cohen J., Roth J. A., Visher C. A. (eds.): *Criminal Careers and "Career Criminals"*, vol. I, National Academy Press, Washington 1986

Bodin J. [1576]: *The Six Bookes of a Commonweale*, I, trans. Richard Knolles, Harvard University Press, Cambridge 1962

Böckenförde E. W. [1978]: "The State as an Ethical State", in *Constitutional and Political Theory. Selected Writings*, vol. I, trans. Thomas Dunlap, eds. Mirjam Künkler, Tine Stein, Oxford University Press, Oxford 2017a

Böckenförde E. W. [1997]: "The Concept and Problems of the Constitutional State", in *Constitutional and Political Theory. Selected Writings*, vol. I, trans. Thomas Dunlap, eds. Mirjam Künkler, Tine Stein, Oxford University Press, Oxford 2017b

Boer A.: *Legal Theory, Sources of Law and the Semantic Web*, Ios Press, Amsterdam 2009

Bombelli G.: "Momenti di una normatività giuridica complessa. Da Esiodo ai presocratici", in *Il Diritto tra Testo e Immagine*, eds. Carla Faralli, Valerio Gigliotti, Paolo Heritier, M. Paola Mittica, Mimesis, Milan-Udine 2014

Bork J.: *Zum Konstrukt von dār al-islām und dār al-ḥarb. Die zeitgenössische Rezeption eines Konzepts des klassischen islamischen Rechts*, De Gruyter, Berlin-Boston 2020

Bosworth C. E.: "Laḳab" (voice), in *The Encyclopaedia of Islam*, eds. Clifford Edmund Bosworth, Emeri Johannes van Donzel, Charles Pellat, vol. V, ns. 87–88, Brill, Leiden 1982

Boulaabi A.: *Islam et pouvoir. Les finalités de la Charia et la légitimité du pouvoir*, L'Harmattan, Paris 2005

Bouzenita A. I.: "The Siyar – An Islamic Law of Nations?", in *Asian Journal of Social Science*, vol. XXXV, n. 1, March 2007

Bramsen D.: "Divine Law and Human Understanding – The Idea of Shariʿa in Saudi Arabia", in *Shariʿa As Discourse. Legal Traditions and the Encounter with Europe*, eds. Jørgen S. Nielsen, Lisbet Christoffersen, Ashgate, Farnham-Burlington 2010

Branca P.: "Pouvoir de iure et pouvoir de facto dans la pensée polique islamique classique", in *Authority, Privacy and Public Order in Islam*, proceedings of the 22nd Congress of the Union Européen des Arabisants et Islamisants, Peeters Publishers & Department of Oriental Studies Bondgenotenlaan, Leuven 2006

Brown B. F.: "The Influence of St. Thomas Aquinas on Jurisprudence", in *The Catholic Lawyer*, vol. III, n. 4, art. 11, Queens, Autumn 1957

Brown D. W.: *A New Introduction to Islam*, Wiley-Blackwell, Chichester 2009

Brown N. J.: *Constitutions in a Nonconstitutional World. Arab Basic Laws and the Prospects for Accountable Government*, State University of New York Press, Albany 2002

Brown N. J., Sherif A. O.: "Inscribing the Islamic Shari'a in Arab Constitutional Law", in *Islamic Law and the Challenges of Modernity*, eds. Yvonne Yazbeck Haddad, Barbara Freyer Stowasser, AltaMira Press, Walnut Creek 2004

Buchanan A.: *Justice, Legitimacy, and Self-Determination. Moral Foundations for International Law*, Oxford University Press, Oxford-New York 2004

Bull H. [1977]: *The Anarchical Society. A Study of Order in World Politics*, Palgrave, Basingstoke-New York 2002

Bulmer W. E.: *A Model Constitution for Scotland. Making Democracy Work in an Independent State*, Luath Press, Edinburgh 2011

Bunson M. [1994]: "Pontifex Maximus" (voice), in *Encyclopedia of the Roman Empire*, ed. Matthew Bunson, Facts on File, New York 2002

Burckhardt T.: *L'art de l'Islam. Langage et Signification*, Sindbad, Paris 1985

Burns J. H.: *The True Law of Kingship. Concepts of Monarchy in Early-modern Scotland*, Clarendon Press, Oxford 1996

Burton J.: *The Sources of Islamic Law. Islamic Theories of Abrogation*, Edinburgh University Press, Edinburgh 1990

Busaq M. M.: *Perspectives on Modern Criminal Policy & Islamic Sharia*, trans. Zubair Ahmad, Naif Arab University for Security Sciences, Riyadh 2005

Buskens L.: "Sharia and the Colonial State", in *The Ashgate Research Companion to Islamic Law* n.d.

Çakır C.: "Tanzimat" (voice), in *Encyclopedia of the Ottoman Empire*, eds. Gábor Ágoston, Bruce Masters, Facts on File, New York 2009

Calasso G., Lancioni G. (eds.): *Dār al-islām / dār al-ḥarb. Territories, People, Identities*, Brill, Leiden-Boston 2017

Campanini M. [2004]: *The Qur'ān. The Basics*, trans. Oliver Leaman, Routledge, London-New York 2007

Carbonell F.: "Coherence and Post-sovereign Legal Argumentation", in *Law and Democracy in Neil MacCormick's Legal and Political Theory. The Post-Sovereign Constellation*, eds. Agustín José Menéndez, John Erik Fossum, Springer, Dordrecht-Heidelberg-London-New York 2011

Cardini F. [2007]: *Europa e Islam. Storia di un Malinteso*, Laterza, Rome-Bari 2015

Carrara F.: "Emenda del reo assunta come unico fondamento e fine della pena", in *Opuscoli di diritto criminale*, ed. Francesco Carrara, vol. I, Giachetti, Prato 1878

Cartledge P.: *Ancient Greek Political Thought in Practice*, Cambridge University Press, Cambridge 2009

Casanova J.: "Religion Challenging the Myth of Secular Democracy", in *Religion in the 21st Century. Challenges and Transformations*, eds. Lisbet Christoffersen, Hans Raun Iversen, Hanne Petersen, Margit Warburg, Ashgate, Farnham-Burlington 2010

Caspar E.: *Geschichte des Papsttums von den Anfängen bis zur Höhe der Weltherrschaft*, vol. I, Mohr Verlag, Tübingen 1930–1933

Castellino J., Kavanaugh K. A.: *Minority Rights in the Middle East*, Oxford University Press, Oxford 2013

Catafago J.: *An English and Arabic Dictionary in Two Parts*, part I, Bernard Quaritch publisher, London 1856

Cavanna A.: *Storia del diritto moderno in Europa. Le fonti e il pensiero giuridico*, vol. I, Giuffré, Milan 1982

Ceccarelli Morolli D.: *A Brief Outline of Roman Law*, Gangemi, Rome 2012

Cerić M.: *Toward a Muslim Social Contract in Europe*, The Association of Muslim Social Scientists (UK)-The City Circle, Richmond 2008

Chakrabarty D.: "L'artificio della Storia", in *Parolechiave*, n. 31, *Occidentalismi*, June 2004

Chateaubriand F. R. [1824]: "Le roi est mort: vive le roi!", in *Oeuvres*, vol. IV, Dufour et Mulat, Paris 1852

Chatauvillard, *Essai sur le Duel*, Imprimerie d'Edouard Proux et comp., Paris 1836

Chaurasia R. S.: *History of Middle East*, Atlantic Publishers & Distributors, Delhi 2005

Cheng L., Sin K. K., Wagner A. (eds.): *The Ashgate Handbook of Legal Translation*, Ashgate, Farnhma-Burlington 2014

Chiba M.: *Legal Pluralism. Toward a General Theory Through Japanese Legal Culture*, Tokai University Press, Tōkyō 1989

Chiu A.: *Ovid's Women of the Year. Narratives of Roman Identity in the Fasti*, University of Michigan Press, Ann Arbor 2016

Chroust A. H. [1973]: "The Fundamental Ideas of St. Augustine's Philosophy of Law", in *Augustine and Modern Law*, eds. Richard O. Brooks, James Bernard Murphy, Routledge, London-New York 2016

Cicero M. T. [c. 52 BCE]: *De Legibus*, trans. *On the Commonwealth and On the Laws*, ed. James E. G. Zetzel, Cambridge University Press, Cambridge 1999

Clément F.: *Pouvoir et légitimité en Espagne musulmane à l'époque des Taifas (V-XI siècle)*, L'Harmattan, Paris 1997

Coke E. [1628]: *The First Part of the Institutes of the Laws of England*, vol. I, J. & W. T. Clarke *et al.*, London 1832

Cornell V. J.: "Fruit of the Three of Knowledge. The relationship between faith and practice in Islam", in *The Oxford History of Islam*, ed. John L. Esposito, Oxford University Press, Oxford 1999

Coughlin J. J.: *Law, Person, and Community. Philosophical, Theological, and Comparative Perspectives on Canon Law*, Oxford University Press, New York 2012

Coulson N. J.: *A History of Islamic Law*, Edinburgh University Press, Edinburgh 1964

Crone P., Hinds M. [1986]: *God's Caliph. Religious Authority in the First Centuries of Islam*, Cambridge University Press, Cambridge 2003

Crone P.: *God's Rule. Government and Islam*, Columbia University Press, New York 2004

Crow I.: *The Treatment and Rehabilitation of Offenders*, SAGE, London-Thousand Oaks-New Delhi 2001

Curnow T.: *Wisdom. A History*, Reaktion Books, London 2015

Daftary F., Jiwa S. (eds.): *The Fatimid Caliphate. Diversity of Traditions*, I.B. Tauris, London-New York 2018

Dahlén A. P.: *Islamic Law, Epistemology and Modernity. Legal Philosophy in Contemporary Iran*, Routledge, London-New York 2003

Dante [c. 1321]: *Paradiso*, trans. Henry Wadsworth Longfellow, Ticknor and Fields, Boston 1867

d'Aspremont J.: *Formalism and the Sources of International Law. A Theory of the Ascertainments of Legal Rules*, Oxford University Press, Oxford 2011

Davison R. H.: *Reform in the Ottoman Empire, 1856-1876*, Princeton University Press, Princeton 1963

De Bellefonds Y. L.: "The Formal Sources of Islamic Law", trans. M. Khalid Mas'ud, in *Islamic Studies*, vol. XV, n. 3, Autumn 1976

Debray R.: *Éloge des Frontières*, Gallimard, Paris 2010

Delahunty R. J.: "An Epitaph for ISIS? The Idea of a Caliphate and the Westphalian Order", in *Arizona Journal of International & Comparative Law*, vol. XXXV, n. 1, 2018

De Maistre J. [1821]: "Les Soirées de Saint-Pétersbourg", in *Oeuvres complètes*, Slatkine, Geneva 1979

Dennis G. W.: *The Encyclopedia of Jewish Myth, Magic and Mysticism*, Llewellyn Publications, Woodbury 2007

Denzinger H. [1854]: *Enchiridion symbolorum, definitionum et declarationum de rebus fidei et morum*, ed. Peter Hünermann, Edizioni Dehoniane, Bologna 1996

Devereux R.: *The First Ottoman Constitutional Period. A Study of the Midhat Constitution and Parliament*, The Johns Hopkins Press, Baltimore 1963

Dietze G.: *Magna Carta and Property*, University of Virginia Press, Charlottesville 1965

Dijkstra R., Van Espelo D.: "Anchoring Pontifical Authority: A Reconsideration of the Papal Employment of the Title Pontifex Maximus", in *Journal of Religious History*, vol. XLI, n. 3, September 2017

Domingo R.: *The New Global Law*, Cambridge University Press, Cambridge 2010

Donati P., Archer M. S.: *The Relational Subject*, Cambridge University Press, Cambridge 2015

Dubuisson D. [1998]: *The Western Construction of Religion. Myths, Knowledge, and Ideology*, trans. William Sayers, The Johns Hopkins University Press, Baltimore-London 2003

Dunn R. G.: *Identity Crises. A Social Critique of Postmodernity*, University of Minnesota Press, Minneapolis-London 1998

Duns Scotus J. [c. 1300–1308]: *Selected Writings on Ethics*, trans. Thomas Williams, Oxford University Press, Oxford 2017

du Plessis P. [1994]: *Borkowski's Textbook on Roman Law*, Oxford University Press, Oxford 2010

Dyzenhaus D.: "Why Carl Schmitt?", in *Law as Politics. Carl Schmitt's Critique of Liberalism*, ed. David Dyzenhaus, Duke University Press, Durham 1998

Eaton C. G.: *Islam and the Destiny of Man*, State University of New York Press, Albany 1985

El-Awa M. S.: "Confession and other methods of evidence in Islamic procedural jurisprudence", in *Criminal Justice in Islam. Judicial Procedure in the Sharīʿa*, eds. Muhammad Abdel Haleem, Adel Omar Sherif, Kate Daniels, I.B. Tauris, London-New York 2003

El Fadl K. A.: "Striking the Balance: Islamic Legal Discourses on Muslim Minorities", in *Muslims on the Americanization Path?*, eds. Yvonne Yazbeck Haddad, John L. Esposito, Oxford University Press, Oxford 2000

Emon A. M.: "Sharīʿa and the Modern State", in *Islamic Law and International Human Rights Law. Searching for Common Ground?*, eds. Anver M. Emon, Mark Ellis, Benjamin Glahn, Oxford University Press, Oxford 2012

Ercanbrack J. G.: *The Transformation of Islamic Law in Global Financial Markets*, Cambridge University Press, Cambridge 2015

Ergene B. A.: "Qanun and Sharia", in *The Ashgate Research Companion to Islamic Law*, eds. Rudolph Peters, Peri Bearman, Ashgate, Farnham-Burlington 2014

Ertman T.: *Birth of the Leviathan. Building States and Regimes in Medieval and Early Modern Europe*, Cambridge University Press, Cambridge 1997

Esmaeili H., Marboe I., Rehman J.: *The Rule of Law, Freedom of Expression and Islamic Law*, Hart Publishing, Oxford-Portland 2017

Esposito J. L. [1992]: *The Islamic Threat. Myth or Reality?*, Oxford University Press, Oxford 1999

Esposito J. L. (ed.): *The Oxford Dictionary of Islam*, Oxford University Press, Oxford 2003

Esposito J. L., DeLong-Bas N. J.: *Shariah. What Everyone Needs to Know*, Oxford University Press, Oxford 2018

Evans T.: "Power, hegemony and the universalization of human rights", in *Human Rights Fifty Years On. A Reappraisal*, ed. Tony Evans, Manchester University Press, Manchester-New York 1998

Ezzati A. F.: *The Spread of Islam. The Contributing Factors*, Islamic College for Advanced Studies Press, London 2002

Fabris C. M.: *La natura della persona giuridica nell'ordinamento canonico. Profili generali e particolari. Il caso della Caritas internationalis*, Giappichelli, Turin 2018

Fakhry M.: "Philosophy and Theology: from the Eighth Century C.E. to the present", in *The Oxford History of Islam*, ed. John L. Esposito, Oxford University Press, Oxford 1999

Falk R. A.: "The Interplay of Westphalia and Charter Conceptions of the International Legal Order", in *The Future of the International Legal Order*, vol. I, *Trends and Patterns*, eds. Richard A. Falk, Cyril E. Black, Princeton University Press, Princeton 1969

Fatoohi L.: *Abrogation in the Qur'an and Islamic Law. A Critical Study of the Concept of "Naskh" and its Impact*, Routledge, London-New York 2013

Feibleman J. K.: *Justice, Law and Culture*, Martinus Nijhoff Publishers, Dordrecht-Boston-Lancaster 1985

Ferrarese M. R.: "Globalizzazione giuridica" (voice), in *Enciclopedia del diritto. Annali dal 2007*, vol. IV, Giuffrè, Milan 2007

Fiaschi G.: "La differenza di Machiavelli. Realtà e prassi politica", in *La filosofia politica di Machiavelli*, eds. Giulio M. Chiodi, Roberto Gatti, Franco Angeli, Milan 2015

Fikentscher W. [1995]: *Modes of Thought: A Study in the Anthropology of Law and Religion*, Mohor Siebeck, Tübingen 2004

Finkel C.: *Osman's Dream. The Story of the Ottoman Empire, 1300-1923*, John Murray Publishers, London 2005

Fitzpatrick [1992] P.: *The Mythology of Modern Law*, Routledge, London-New York 2002

Foucault M. [1975]: *Discipline & Punish. The Birth of the Prison*, trans. Alan Sheridan, Vintage Books, New York 1995

Frändberg Å.: *The Legal Order. Studies in the Foundations of Juridical Thinking*, Springer, New York 2018

Frevert U.: "The Taming of the Noble Ruffian: Male Violence and Dueling in Early Modern and Modern Germany", in *Men and Violence. Gender, Honor, and Rituals in Modern Europe and America*, ed. Pieter Spierenburg, Ohio State University Press, Columbus 1998

Friedrich C. J. [1958]: *The Philosophy of Law in Historical Perspective*, The University of Chicago Press, Chicago-London 1963

Friedrich C. J.: *Constitutional government and democracy. Theory and practice in Europe and America*, Blaisdell Publishing Company, Waltham 1968

Friedrichs J.: "The Meaning of New Medievalism", in *European Journal of International Relations*, vol. VII, n. 4, December 2001

Fruchtman J. jr.: *The political philosophy of Thomas Paine*, The Johns Hopkins University Press, Baltimore 2009

Fukuyama F.: "The End of History?", in *The National Interest*, vol. XVI, Summer 1989

Fukuyama F.: *The End of History and the Last Man*, The Free Press, New York 1992

Gabriel R. A.: *Muhammad. Islam's First Great General*, University of Oklahoma Press, Norman 2007

Gardet L.: *Les hommes de l'Islam. Approche de mentalités*, Hachette, Paris 1977

Garbellini Carnio H.: "Filosofia do direito processual e procedimentalização do direito", in *Revista de Processo*, vol. CCXXXI, May 2014

Gerber H.: *Islamic Law and Culture, 1600-1840*, Brill, Leiden-Boston-Köln 1999

Ghamari-Tabrizi B.: "Westernization" (voice), in *The Princeton Encyclopedia of Islamic Political Thought*, eds. Gerhard Bowering *et al.*, Princeton University Press, Woodstock 2013

Gibb H. A. R. [1937]: "Al-Mâwardî's theory of the Khilâfah", in *Studies on the Civilization of Islam*, eds. Stanford J. Shaw, William R. Polk, Princeton University Press, Princeton 1982a

Gibb H. A. R. [1954 –]: *The Encyclopaedia of Islam, SAN-SZE*, Brill, Leiden 1997

Gibb H. A. R. [1962]: *Studies on the Civilization of Islam*, Princeton University Press, Princeton 1982b

Gilson E.: John Duns Scotus. *Introduction to His Fundamental Positions*, trans. James Colbert, T&T Clark, London-New York 2019

Glanert S. (ed.): *Comparative Law. Engaging Translation*, Routledge, London-New York 2014

Glassé C. [1989]: *The New Encyclopedia of Islam*, Altamira Press, Walnut Creek-London 2002

Glei R., Reichmuth S.: "Religion between Last Judgement, law and faith: Koranic dīn and its rendering in Latin translations of the Koran", in *Religion*, vol. XLII, n. 2, April 2012

Glenn H. P.: "Sustainable Diversity in Law", in *Legal Pluralism and Development. Scholars and Practitioners in Dialogue*, eds. Brian Z. Tamanaha, Caroline Sage, Michael Woolcock, Cambridge University Press, Cambridge 2012

Goldman D. B.: *Globalisation and the Western Legal Tradition. Recurring Patterns of Law and Authority*, Cambridge University Press, Cambridge 2008

Goldstein N.: *Religion and the State*, Facts on File, New York 2010

Gómez Dávila N. [1988]: *De Iure*, trans. Tomàs Molina, in *Revista Nova et Vetera*, Universidad del Rosario, Bogotà, September 2017

Goodman A. H.: *Rehabilitating and Resettling Offenders in the Community*, Wiley-Blackwell, Chichester 2012

Gordon S.: *"Controlling the State. Constitutionalism from Ancient Athens to Today"*, Harvard University Press, Cambridge 1999

Gradel I.: *Emperor Worship and Roman Religion*, Clarendon Press, Oxford 2002

Gragl P.: *Legal Monism. Law, Philosophy, and Politics*, Oxford University Press, Oxford 2018

Green L.: *The litigation process in tort law. No place to stop in the development of tort law*, Bobbs-Merrill Company, Indianapolis 1977

Greengrass M.: *Christendom Destroyed. Europe 1517-1648*, Penguin Books, London 2014

Gressgård R. [2010]: *Multicultural Dialogue. Dilemmas, Paradoxes, Conflicts*, Berghahn Books, New York-Oxford 2012

Grossi P. [1995]: *L'ordine giuridico medievale*, Laterza, Rome-Bari 2004

Grossi P. [2007]: *A History of European Law*, trans. Laurence Hooper, Wiley-Blackwell, Chichester 2010

Grote R., Röder T. J.: "Constitutionalism in Islamic Countries", in *Constitutionalism in Islamic Countries. Between Upheaval and Continuity*, eds. Rainer Grote, Tillman J. Röder, Oxford University Press, Oxford 2012

Grotius H. [1625]: *The Rights of War and Peace*, trans. Jean Barbeyrac, ed. Richard Tuck, Liberty Fund, Indianapolis 2005

Guastini R.: *Le fonti del diritto. Fondamenti teorici*, Giuffrè, Milan 2010

Guessoum N.: *Islam's Quantum Question. Reconciling Muslim Tradition and Modern Science*, I.B. Tauris, London-New York 2011

Habermas J.: "The Constitutionalization of International Law and the Legitimation Problems of a Constitution for World", trans. Ciaran Cronin, in *Constellations*, vol XV, n. 4, 2008

Haddad Y. Y., Stowasser B. F.: "Introduction" in *Islamic Law and the Challenges of Modernity*, eds. Yvonne Yazbeck Haddad, Barbara Freyer Stowasser, AltaMira Press, Walnut Creek 2004

Hageneder O. [1985]: "Il dominio del mondo nel medioevo", in *Il Sole e la Luna. Papato, Impero e regni nella teoria e nella prassi dei secoli XII e XIII*, trans. Gabriele Ingegneri, ed. Maria Pia Alberzoni, Vita e Pensiero, Milan 2000

Haley J. O.: *Law's Political Foundations. Rivers, Rifles, Rice, and Religion*, Edward Elgar, Cheltenham-Northampton 2016

Hallaq W. B.: "Was the Gate of Ijtihad Closed?", in *International Journal of Middle East Studies*, vol. XVI, n. 1, March 1984

Hallaq W. B.: "Juristic Authority vs. State Power: the Legal Crises of Modern Islam", in *Journal of Law and Religion*, vol. XIX, n. 2, 2003–2004

Hallaq W. B.: "Can Shariᶜa Be Restored?", in *Islamic Law and the Challenges of Modernity*, eds. Yvonne Yazbeck Haddad, Barbara Freyer Stowasser, AltaMira Press, Walnut Creek 2004

Hallaq W. B.: *The Origins and Evolution of Islamic Law*, Cambridge University Press, Cambridge 2005

Hallaq W. B.: "What is Sharīᶜa?", in *Yearbook of Islamic and Middle Eastern Law*, vol. XII [2005–2006], eds. Eugene Cotran, Martin Lau, Brill, Boston-Leiden 2007

Hallaq W. B.: *An introduction to Islamic Law*, Cambridge University Press, Cambridge 2009

Hallaq W. B.: *The Impossible State. Islam, Politics, and Modernity's Moral Predicament*, Columbia University Press, New York 2013

Hallaq W. B. [2009]: "Groundwork of the moral law: a new look at the Qurān and the genesis of sharīᶜa", in *Islamic Legal Theory*, vol. I, ed. Mashood A. Baderin, Routledge, London 2014

Halligan P. [1988]: "The Environmental Policy of Saint Thomas Aquinas", in *Aquinas and Modern Law*, eds. Richard O. Brooks, James Bernard Murphy, Routledge, London-New York 2016

Hamid E. A.: "Al-Mawardi's Theory of State: Some Ignored Dimensions", in *American Journal of Islamic Social Sciences*, vol. XVIII, n. 4, Fall 2001

Hammad A. Z.: "Ghazālī's Juristic Treatment of the Sharīah Rules in al-Mustasfā", in *American Journal of Islamic Social Sciences*, vol. IV. n. 2, 1987

Handelman D.: "Bureaucratic Logic, Bureaucratic Aesthetics: The Open Event of Holocaust Martyrs and Heroes Remembrance Day in Israel", in *Aesthetics in Performance. Formations of Symbolic Construction and Experience*, eds. Angela Hobart, Bruce Kapferer, Berghahn Books, New York-Oxford 2005

Harding A.: *Medieval Law and the Foundations of the State*, Oxford University Press, Oxford 2001

Hasan A.: *The doctrine of ijmā' in Islam*, Islamic Research Institute, Islamabad 1978

Hassan I., "Beyond Postmodernism", in *Angelaki: Journal of the Theoretical Humanities*, vol. VIII, n. 1, 2003

Hassan M.: Longing for the Lost Caliphate. A Transregional History, Princeton University Press, Princeton 2016

Hawting G. R. [1986]: *The First Dynasty of Islam. The Umayyad Caliphate, AD 661-750*, Routledge, London-New York 2000

Hegel G. W. F. [1821]: *Elements of the Philosophy of Right*, trans. H. B. Nisbet, ed. Allen W. Wood, Cambridge University Press, Cambridge 2003

Héran F.: "A few thoughts on the concept of social contract and equity between generations", in *Ages, Generations and the Social Contract. The Demographic Challenges Facing the Welfare State*, eds. Jacques Véron, Sophie Pennec, Jacques Légaré, Springer, Dordrecht 2007

Herder J. G.: *Another Philosophy of History and Selected Political Writings*, Hackett Publishing, Indianapolis 2004

Herzfeld M.: *Cultural Intimacy. Social Poetics in the Nation-State*, Routledge, New York-London 2005

Heyd U.: "Ḳānūn and Sharīʿa in old Ottoman criminal justice", in *Proceedings*, vol. III, n. 1, Israel Academy of Sciences and Humanities, Jerusalem 1967

Hill J. L.: *After the Natural Law. How the Classical Worldview Supports Our Modern Moral and Political Values*, Ignatius Press, San Francisco 2006

Hirst P.: "Carl Schmitt's Decisionism", in *Telos*, vol. VII, n. 72, July 1987

Hitti P. K.: *History of the Arabs*, MacMillan, New York 1949

Hobbes T.: *Leviathan, or the Matter, Form, & Power of a Common-wealth Ecclesiastical & Civil*, for Andrew Crooke, at the Green Dragonin St. Pauls Church-yard, London 1651

Hooker J.: *Working Across Cultures*, Stanford University Press, Stanford 2003

Horowitz M. C.: *Seeds of Virtue and Knowledge*, Princeton University Press, Princeton 1998

Howard A. E. D.: *The road from Runnymede. Magna Carta and constitutionalism in America*, University of Virginia Press, Charlottesville 1968

Howard-Hassmann R. E.: *In Defense of Universal Human Rights*, Polity, Cambridge 2018

Hughes A. W.: *Muslim Identities. An Introduction to Islam*, Columbia University Press, New York 2013

Hulsman C. (ed.): *The Sharia as the Main Source of Legislation? The Egyptian Debate on Article II of the Egyptian Constitution*, Tectum Verlag, Marburg 2012

Hulsman C. (ed.): *The 2014 Egyptian Constitution. Perspectives from Egypt*, Tectum Verlag, Baden-Baden 2017

Hunter S. T.: *The Future of Islam and the West. Clash of Civilizations or Peaceful Coexistence?*, Praeger, Westport-London 1998

Huntington S. P.: *The Clash of Civilizations and the Remaking of World Order*, Simon & Schuster, New York 1996

Hurvitz N.: "The contribution of early Islamic rulers to adjudication and legislation: the case of the mazalim tribunals", in *Law and Empire. Ideas, Practices, Actors*, eds. Jeroen Duindam, Jill Harries, Caroline Humfress, Nimrod Hurvitz, Koninklijke Brill, Leiden 2013

Hussein G. M.: "Basic Guarantees in the Islamic Criminal Justice System", in *Criminal Justice in Islam. Judicial Procedure in the Sharīʿa*, eds. Muhammad Abdel Haleem, Omar Sherif, Kate Daniels, I.B. Tauris, London-New York 2003

ibn ʿĀshūr M. Ṭ. [1946]: *Treatise on Maqasid al-Shariah*, trans. Mohamed el-Tahir el-Mesawi, The International Institute of Islamic Thought, London-Washington 2013

Ibn Khaldūn [1377], *The Muqaddimah. An Introduction to History*, trans. Franz Rosenthal, ed. N. J. Dawood, Princeton University Press, Princeton-Oxford 2005

Ismail M. B. A.: *Islamic Law and Transnational Diplomatic Law. A Quest for Complementarity in Divergent Legal Theories*, Palgrave Macmillan, New York-Basingstoke 2016

Jackson S. A.: *Islamic Law and the State. The Constitutional Jurisprudence of Shihāb al-Dīn al-Qarāfī*, Brill, Leiden-New York-Köln 1996

James W. [1902]: *The Varieties of Religious Experience. A Study in Human Nature*, Routledge, London-New York 2002

Janin H.: *The Pursuit of Learning in the Islamic World, 610-2003*, McFarland & Company, Jefferson-London 2006

Jany J. [2012]: *Judging in the Islamic, Jewish and Zoroastrian Legal Traditions. A Comparison of Theory and Practice*, Routledge, London-New York 2016

Jarmulak B.: "Theology of Beauty in Evdokimov", in *The Glory of Kings. A Festschrift in Honor of James B. Jordan*, eds. Peter J. Leithart, John Barach, Pickwick Publications, Eugene 2011

Jellinek G. [1900]: *Allgemeine Staatslehre*, Verlag von Julius Springer, Berlin 1929

Jelly F. M. o.p.: *Madonna. Mary in the Catholic Tradition*, Wipf and Stock Publishers, Eugene 1986

Johnson Bagby L. M.: *Hobbes's Leviathan. A Reader's Guide*, Continuum, London 2007

Juratowitch B.: *Retroactivity and the Common Law*, Hart Publishing, Oxford-Portland 2008

Kain P. J.: *Hegel and Right. A Study of the Philosophy of Right*, State University of New York Press, Albany 2018

Kamali M. H.: "Law and Society. The Interplay of Revelation and Reason in the Shariah", in *The Oxford History of Islam*, ed. John L. Esposito, Oxford University Press, Oxford 1999

Kamali M. H.: "The Sharīʿa: Law as the Way of God", in *Voices of Islam*, vol. I, *Voices of Tradition*, ed. Vincent J. Cornell, Praeger, Westport-London 2007

Kamali M. H.: *Crime and Punishment in Islamic Law. A Fresh Interpretation*, Oxford University Press, New York 2019

Kantorowicz E. H.: *The King's Two Bodies. A Study in Medieval Political Theology*, Princeton University Press, Princeton 1957

Kateman A.: *Muḥammad ʿAbduh and His Interlocutors. Conceptualizing Religion in a Globalizing World*, Koninklijke Brill, Leiden 2019

Katz M. H.: *Body of Text. The Emergence of the Sunni Law of Ritual Purity*, State University of New York Press, Albany 2002

Kayadibi S.: *Istiḥsan. The Doctrine of Juristic Preference in Islamic Law*, Islamic Book Trust, Kuala Lumpur 2010

Kelly D. R.: *The Human Measure. Social Thought in the Western Legal Tradition*, Harvard University Press, Cambridge-London 1990

Kelsen H. [1945]: *General Theory of Law and State*, trans Anders Wedberg, Harvard University Press, Cambridge 1949

Kelsen H. [1952]: *Principles of International Law*, The Lawbook Exchange, Clark 2003

Kelsen H. [1960]: *Pure Theory of Law*, trans. Max Knight, The Lawbook Exchange, Clark 2008

Keenan J. F. s.j.: *Goodness and Rightness in Thomas Aquinas's Summa Theologiae*, Georgetown University Press, Washington 1992

Kennedy H. [1981]: *The Early Abbasid Caliphate. A Political History*, Routledge, London-New York 2015

Kern S. [1983]: *The Culture of Time and Space, 1880-1918*, Harvard University Press, Cambridge-London 2003

Kersting W.: *Vertragstheorien. Kontraktualistische Theorien in der Politikwissenschaft*, Kohlhammer, Stuttgart 2016

Khadduri M. [1955]: "International Law", in *Law in the Middle East*, vol. I, *Origin and Development of Islamic Law*, eds. Majid Khadduri, Herbert J. Liebesny, The Lawbook Exchange, Clark 2009

Khadduri M. [1961], "Introduction" to al-Shāfiʿī, *al-Risāla fī Uṣūl al-Fiqh (Treatise on the Foundations of Islamic Jurisprudence)*, trans. Majid Khadduri, Islamic Texts Society, Cambridge 1997

Khadhar H.: "La Révolution française, le Pacte fondamental et la première Constitution tunisienne de 1861", in *Revue des mondes musulmans et de la Méditerranée*, ns. 52–53, *Les Arabes, les Turcs et la Révolution française*, 1989

Khan M. A. M.: "The Islamic State", in *Encyclopedia of Government and Politics*, eds. Mary Hawkesworth, Maurice Kogan, vol. I, Routledge, London-New York 1992

Khan L. A., Ramadan H. M.: *Contemporary Ijtihad. Limits and Controversies*, Edinburgh University Press, Edinburgh 2011

Khanam Y.: "Amir al-Mu'minin" (voice), in *Islam. A Worldwide Encyclopedia*, ed. Cenap Çakmak, Abc-Clio, Santa Barbara 2017

Khomeini R. [1970]: *Islamic Government. Governance of the Jurist*, trans. Hamid Algar, The Institute of Compilation and Publication of Imam Khomeini's Works, Tehran 2002

Khoury D. R.: "Administrative Practice Between Religious Law (Sharīʿa) and State Law (Kanun) on the Eastern Frontiers of the Ottoman Empire", in *Journal of Early Modern History*, vol. V, n. 4, 2001

Kibraev N.: "The Political and Legal Culture of Medieval Islam", in *Values in Islamic Culture and the Experience of History. Russian Philosophical Studies*, eds. Nur Kirabaev, Yuriy Pochta, vol. I, Council for Research in Values and Philosophy, Washington 2002

King M., Thornhill C.: *Niklas Luhmann's Theory of Politics and Law*, Palgrave Macmillan, New York-Basingstoke 2003

Klabbers J., Peters A., Ulfstein G.: "*The Constitutionalization of International Law*", Oxford University Press, Oxford 2009

Köndgen O.: *The Codification of Islamic Criminal Law in the Sudan. Penal Codes and Supreme Court Case Law under Numayrī and al-Bashīr*, Brill, Leiden-Boston 2018

Krabbe H.: *The Modern Idea of the State*, Martinus Nijhoff, The Hague 1922

Krisch N.: *Beyond Constitutionalism. The Pluralist Structure of Postnational Law*, Oxford University Press, Oxford 2010

Kurnaz S.: *Methoden zur Normderivation im islamischen Recht. Eine Rekonstruktion der Methoden zur Interpretation autoritativer textueller Quellen bei ausgewählten islamischen Rechtsschulen*, EB Verlag, Berlin 2016.

Kutty F.: "Blasphemy and apostasy laws in the Muslim world: a critical analysis", in *Research Handbook on Islamic Law and Society*, ed. Nadirsyah Hosen, Edward Elgar Publishing, Cheltenham-Northampton 2018

Lamalle S.: "Multilevel Translation Analysis of a Key Legal Concept: Persona Juris and Legal Pluralism", in *The Ashgate Handbook of Legal Translation*, eds. Le Cheng, King Kui Sin, Anne Wagner, Ashgate, Farnhma-Burlington 2014

Lambton A. K. S.: *State and Government in Medieval Islam. An Introduction to the Study of Islamic Political Theory – The Jurists*, Routledge, London-New York 1981

Laoust H.: *Essai sur les doctrines sociales et politiques de Takî-d-Dîn Ahmad b. Taimîya*, IFAO, Cairo 1939

Laoust H.: "La pensée et l'action politique d'al-Mâwardî", in *Revue des Etudes Islamiques*, n. XXXVI, Paris 1968

Lapidus I. M. [1988]: *A History of Islamic Societies*, Cambridge University Press, Cambridge 2014

Larkins J.: *From Hierarchy to Anarchy. Territory and Politics Before Westphalia*, Palgrave Macmillan, New York-Basingstoke 2010

La Torre M.: *Constitutionalism and Legal Reasoning. A New Paradigm for the Concept of Law*, Springer, Dordrecht 2007

Leaman O., Ali K.: *Islam. The Key Concepts*, Routledge, London-New York 2008

Leaman O.: *Islamic Philosophy. An Introduction*, Polity Press, Cambridge 2009

Lesaffer R. [2009]: *European Legal History. A Cultural and Political Perspective*, trans. Jan Arriens, Cambridge University Press, Cambridge 2012

Lev Y.: *State and Society in Fatimid Egypt*, Brill, Leiden 1991

Levi A.: "Ubi societas, ibi ius", in *Saggi di teoria del diritto*, Zanichelli, Bologna 1924

Lewis B.: *Islam and the West*, Oxford University Press, Oxford 1993

Lewis B.: *The Crisis of Islam. Holy War and Unholy Terror*, Modern Library, New York 2003

Lewis B.: *Political Words and Ideas in Islam*, Markus Wiener Publishers, Princeton 2008

Lewis B.: *Faith and Power. Religion and Politics in the Middle East*, Oxford University Press, Oxford-New York 2010

Linz J. J.: *Totalitarian and Authoritarian Regimes*, Lynne Rienner Publishers, Boulder-London 2000

Livy [27 BCE-14 AD]: *The History of Rome*, books 1–5, trans. Valerie M. Warrior, Hackett Publishing, Indianapolis-Cambridge 2006

Loughlin M.: "Politonomy", in *The Oxford Handbook of Carl Schmitt*, eds. Jens Meierhenrich, Oliver Simons, Oxford University Press, Oxford 2016

Lowry J. E.: *Early Islamic Legal Theory. The Risāla of Muhammad ibn Idrīs al-Shāfiʿī*, eds. Ruud Peters, Kevin Reinhart, Brill, Leiden-Boston 2007

Luhmann N. [1984]: "Social Systems", trans John Bednarz jr., Dirk Baecker, eds. Timothy Lenoir, Hans Ulrich Gumbrecht, Stanford University Press, Stanford 1995

Luhmann N.: "The Self-Reproduction of Law and its Limits", in *Dilemmas of Law in the Welfare State*, ed. Gunther Teubner, De Gruyter, Berlin-New York 1988

Luhmann N. [1993]: *Law as a Social System*, trans. Klaus A. Ziegert, eds. Fatima Kastner, Richard Nobles, David Schiff, Rosamund Ziegert, Oxford University Press, Oxford 2004

Luhmann N. [2002]: *Introduction to Systems Theory*, trans. Peter Gilgen, ed. Dirk Baecker, Polity Press, Cambridge-Malden 2013

Luke T. S. [2014]: *Ushering in a New Republic. Theologies of Arrival at Rome in the First Century BCE*, University of Michigan Press, Ann Arbor 2017

Lyotard J. F.: *La Condition postmoderne. Rapport sur le savoir*, éditions de Minuit, Paris 1979

MacCormick N.: *Rhetoric and The Rule of Law: A Theory of Legal Reasoning*, Oxford University Press, Oxford 2005

Madelung W. [1997]: *The Succession to Muḥammad. A Study of the Early Caliphate*, Cambridge University Press, Cambridge 2001

Magrì G.: "Giustizia", in *Luoghi della filosofia del diritto. Idee, strutture, mutamenti*, ed. Bruno Montanari, Giappichelli, Turin 2012

Mah H. [2003]: *Enlightenment Phantasies. Cultural Identity in France and Germany, 1750–1914*, Cornell University Press, Ithaca-London 2004

Makdisi G.: "Hanbali Islam", in *Studies on Islam*, ed. Merlin L. Swarz, Oxford University Press, Oxford 1981

Makdisi J.: "Legal Logic and Equity in Islamic Law", in *The American Journal of Comparative Law*, vol. XXXIII, n. 1, Winter 1985

Mallat C.: *Introduction to Middle Eastern Law*, Oxford University Press, Oxford-New York 2007

March A. F.: "Modern Islamic Conceptions of Sovereignty in Comparative Perspective", in *The Oxford Handbook of Comparative Political Theory*, eds. Leigh K. Jenco, Murad Idris, Megan C. Thomas, Oxford University Press, Oxford 2020

Masud M. K.: "The changing concepts of caliphate. Social construction of Sharīʿa and the question of ethics", in *New Directions in Islamic Thought. Exploring*

Reform and Muslim Tradition, eds. Kari Vogt, Lena Larsen, Christian Moe, I.B. Tauris, London-New York 2009

Masud M. K.: "Fatwā. Concepts of Fatwā", in *The Oxford Encyclopedia of the Modern Islamic World*, vol. II, ed. John L. Esposito, Oxford University Press, Oxford 1995

Mathewson Denny F. [1994]: *An Introduction to Islam*, Routledge, London-New York 2016

Maududi S. A. A.: *Islamic Law and Constitution*, Jamaat-e-Islami Publications, Lahore 1955

Maududi S. A. A. [1976]: "The Political Theory of Islam", in *Contemporary Debates in Islam. An Anthology of Modernist and Fundamentalist Thought*, eds. Mansoor Moaddel, Kamran Talattof, Palgrave Macmillan, New York-Basingstoke 2000

Mazrui A. A.: *Resurgent Islam and the Politics of Identity*, eds. Ramzi Badran, Thomas Uthup, Cambridge Scholar Publishing, Newcastle upon Tyne 2014

McGoldrick D.: "The compatibility of an Islamic/shari'a law system or shari'a rules with the European Convention on Human Rights", in *Islam and English Law. Responsibilities and the Place of Shari'a*, ed. Robin Griffith-Jones, Cambridge University Press, Cambridge 2013

Melchert C.: *The Formation of the Sunni Schools of Law. 9th-10th Centuries C.E.*, Brill, Leinde-New York-Köln 1997

Menski W. F.: *Comparative Law in a Global Context. The Legal Systems of Asia and Africa*, Cambridge University Press, Cambridge 2006a

Menski W. F.: "Cherrypicking Customs: on What Happens When Custom is not Taught", in *The Shade of New Leaves. Governance in Traditional Authority. A Southern African Perspective*, eds. Manfred O. Hinz, Helgard K. Patemann, Lit Verlag, Berlin 2006b

Merdjanova I.: *Rediscovering the Umma. Muslims in the Balkans between Nationalism and Transnationalism*, Oxford University Press, Oxford 2013

Messick B.: "The Judge and the Mufti", in *The Ashgate Research Companion to Islamic Law*, eds. Peri Bearman, Rudolph Peters, Ashgate, Farnham-Burlington 2014

Mettinger T. N. D.: *No Graven Image? Israelite Aniconism in Its Ancient Near Eastern Context*, Almqvist & Wiksell International, Stockholm 1995

Miller J.: *Rousseau. Dreamer of Democracy*, Yale University Press, New Haven-London 1984

Mimran T.: "In A Broken Dream: Lessons from The Rise and Demise of the Self-Declared Caliphate of the Islamic State in Syria and Iraq", in *Journal of Transnational Law & Policy*, vol. XXIX, 2019–2020 (July 2020), research paper n. 08–20

Mohammed N.: "Principles of Islamic Contract Law", in *Understanding Islamic Law. From Classical to Contemporary*, eds. Hisham M. Ramadan, Altamira Press, Lanham-New York-Toronto-Oxford 2006

Mohnhaupt H.: "The object of interpretation: legislation and competing normative sources of law in Europe during the 16th and 18th centuries", in *Interpretation of Law in the Age of Enlightenment. From the Rule of the King to the Rule of Law*, eds. Yasutomo Morigiwa, Michael Stolleis, Jean-Louis Halperin, Springer, Heidelberg-London-New York 2011

Moore P.: *The International Political Economy of Work and Employability*, Palgrave Macmillan, New York 2010

Morgan K. W. [1958]: *Islam, the Straight Path. Islam Interpreted by Muslims,* Motilal Banarsidass Publishing, Delhi 1993

Morgan D.: *Essential Islam. A Comprehensive Guide to Belief and Practice*, Praeger, Santa Barbara 2010

Mottahedeh R. P.: "The Foundation of State and Society", in *Islam. The Religious and Political Life of a World Community*, ed. Marjorie Kelly, Praeger, Westport-London 1984

Motzk H. (ed.): *Hadith. Origins and Developments*, Ashgate, Farnham 2004

Moussa M.: *Politics of the Islamic Tradition. The Thought of Muhammad al-Ghazali*, Routledge, London-New York 2016

Moustafa T.: "The Political Role of the Supreme Constitutional Court: Between Principles and Practice", in *Judges and Political Reform in Egypt*, ed. Nathalie Bernard-Maugiron, The American University in Cairo Press, Cairo-New York 2008

Moustafa T.: *Constituting Religion. Islam, Liberal Rights, and the Malaysian State*, Cambridge University Press, Cambridge 2018

Mutua M.: *Human Rights. A Political and Cultural Critique*, University of Pennsylvania Press, Philadelphia 2002

Nāṣirī 'A.: *An Introduction to Hadith. History and Sources*, trans. Mansoor Limba, Miu Press, London 2013

Niazi L. A. K.: *Islamic Law of Tort*, Research Cell, Cayal Singh Trust Library, Lahore 1988

Nicholas of Cusa [1461]: "Cribratio Alkorani", in *Nicolai de Cusa opera omnia* vol. VIII, *Cribratio Alkorani. Edidit commentariisque illustravit Ludovicus Hagemann*, Felix Meier Verlag, Hamburg 1986

Nielsen J. S.: "Transnational Islam and the Integration of Islam in Europe", in *Muslim Networks and Transnational Communities in and Across Europe*, eds. Stefano Allievi, Jorgen S. Nielsen, Brill, Leiden 2003

Norcliffe D.: *Islam. Faith and Practice*, Sussex Academic Press, Portland 1999

Oh I.: *The rights of God. Islam, human rights, and comparative ethics*, Georgetown University Press, Washington 2007

Opałek K.: "The concept of "positive law"", in *Kazimierz Opałek Selected Papers in Legal Philosophy*, ed. Jan Wolenski, Springer, Berlin-Heidelberg 1999

Opwis F.: *Maṣlaḥa and the Purpose of the Law. Islamic Discourse on Legal Change from the 4th/10th to 8th/14th Century*, Brill, Leiden 2010

Orsy L. M. s.j.: "Theology and Canon Law", in *New Commentary on the Code of Canon Law*, eds. John P. Beal, James A. Coriden, Thomas J. Green, Paulist Press, New York-Mahwah 2000

Ost F.: *Raconter la loi. Aux surces de l'imaginaire juridique*, Odile Jacob, Paris 2004

Otto J. M.: *Sharia and National Law in Muslim Countries*, Leiden University Press, Leiden 2008

Özcan A.: *Pan-Islamism. Indian Muslims, the Ottomans and Britain, 1877-1924*, Brill, Leiden 1997

Öztürk F.: *Ottoman and Turkish Law*, iUniverse LLC, Bloomington 2014

Palazzo F. [2003]: *Corso di diritto penale. Parte generale*, Giappichelli, Turin 2013

Peerenboom R. [2006]: "What have we learned about law and development? Describing, predicting and assessing legal reforms in China", in *Law and Society in East Asia*, eds. Christoph Antons, Roman Tomasic, Routledge, London-New York 2016

Peters F. E.: *The Monotheists. Jews, Christians, and Muslims in Conflict and Competition*, vol. II, *The Words and Will of God*, Princeton University Press, Princeton-Oxford 2003

Peters R.: "The Islamization of Criminal Law: A Comparative Analysis", in *Die Welt des Islams*, New Series, vol. XXXIV, n. 2, November 1994

Peters R.: *Crime and Punishment in Islamic Law. Theory and Practice from the Sixteenth to the Twenty-First Century*, Cambridge University Press, Cambridge 2005

Peters R., Bearman P.: "The Nature of the Sharia", in *The Ashgate Research Companion to Islamic Law*, eds. Rudolph Peters, Peri Bearman, Ashgate, Farnham-Burlington 2014

Petrazycki L. [1905–1907]: *Law and Morality*, Routledge, London-New York 2017

Pettit P.: "Corporate agency: the lesson of the discursive dilemma", in *The Routledge Handbook of Collective Intentionality*, eds. Marija Jankovic, Kirk Ludwig, Routledge, London-New York 2018

Pierson C. [1996]: *The Modern State*, Routledge, London-New York 2005

Piscatori J., Saikal A.: *Islam Beyond Borders. The Umma in World Politics*, Cambridge University Press, Cambridge 2019

Pizzorni R. M.: *La filosofia del diritto secondo S. Tommaso d'Aquino*, Edizioni Studio Domenicano, Bologna 2003

Poscher R.: "The ultimate force of the law: on the essence and precariousness of the monopoly on legitimate force", in *Ratio Juris*, vol. XXVII, n. 3, 2016

Potter G., López J.: "After Postmodernism: The Millennium", in *After Postmodernism. An Introduction to Critical Realism*, eds. Garry Potter, José López, The Athlone Press, London-New York 2001

Powell R.: *Shariʿa in the Secular State. Evolving Meanings of Islamic Jurisprudence in Turkey*, Routledge, London-New York 2016

Qaraḍāwī Y.: *Islamic Law in the Modern World*, Wamyh House International for Printing, Publishing and Distribution, Riyadh 2000

Quraishi-Landes A.: "Legislating Morality and Other Illusions about Islamic Government", in *Locating the Sharīʿa. Legal Fluidity in Theory, History and Practice*, ed. Sohaira Z. M. Siddiqui, Brill, Leiden-Boston 2019

Rabb I. A.: "Ijtihād" (voice), in *The Oxford Encyclopedia of the Modern Islamic World*, vol. II, ed. John L. Esposito, Oxford University Press, Oxford 1995

Rabīʿ M. M.: *The Political Theory of Ibn Khaldun*, Brill, Leiden 1967

Ramadan H. M.: "On Islamic Punishment", in *Understanding Islamic Law. From Classical to Contemporary*, ed. Hisham M. Ramadan, AltaMira Press, Lanham-New York-Toronto-Oxford 2006

Ramaioli F. L.: "La funzione della pena tra Occidente e mondo islamico: una prospettiva teleologica", in *Dignitas. Percorsi di carcere e giustizia*, May 2016, www.rivistadignitas.it

Ramaioli F. L.: *Islamic State as a Legal Order. To Have No Law but Islam Between Shari'a and Globalization*, Routledge, London-New York 2022.

Rassool G. H.: *Islamic Counselling. An Introduction to Theory and Practice*, Routledge, London-New York 2016

Ratzinger J. A. [H. H. Benedict XVI]: "Faith, Reason and the University. Memories and Reflections", in *Islamic Studies*, vol. XLV, n. 4, Islamic Research Institute, International Islamic University, Islamabad 2006

Razek A. A. [1925]: *Islam and the Foundations of Political Power*, trans. Maryam Loutfi, ed. Abdou Filali-Ansary, Edinburgh University Press, Edinburgh 2012

Rebstock U.: "A Qāḍī's Errors", in *Islamic Law and Society*, vol. VI, n. 1, 1999

Rebstock U.: "Abwägen als Entscheidungshilfe in den „uṣūl al-fiqh". Die Anfänge der „tarǧīḥ"-Methode bei al-Ǧaṣṣāṣ", in *Der Islam. Zeitschrift für Geschichte und Kultur des islamischen Orients*, vol. LXXX, n. 1, 2003

Rehman J.: *Islamic State Practices, International Law and the Threat from Terrorism. A Critique of the "Clash of Civilization in the New World Order*, Hart Publishing, Oxford-Portland 2005

Reiff M. R.: *Punishment, Compensation, and Law. A Theory of Enforceability*, Cambridge University Press, Cambridge 2005

Riles A., "Introduction" to *Rethinking the Masters of Comparative Law*, ed. Annelise Riles, Hart Publishing, Oxford-Portland 2001

Ringmar E. [1996]: *Identity, Interest and Action. A Cultural Explanation of Sweden's Intervention in the Thirty Years War*, Cambridge University Press, Cambridge 2007

Roberts G. L.: *Islamic Human Rights and International Law*, Dissertation.com, Boca Raton 2007

Roberson C., Das D. K.: *An Introduction to Comparative Legal Models of Criminal Justice*, CRC Press, Boca Raton-London-New York 2008

Robinson O. F. [1997]: *The Sources of Roman Law. Problems and Methods for Ancient Historians*, Routledge, London-New York 2006

Robleda O. s.j.: "La costante evoluzione dell'antico sistema giuridico romano: principi invocati per legittimare le diverse fasi evolutive", in *Ortodossia e revisionismo. Studio interdisciplinare su processi di legittimazione*, Università Gregoriana Editrice, Roma 1974

Rohe M.: *Islamic Law in Past and Present*, trans. Gwendolin Goldbloom, Brill, Leiden-Boston 2015

Romano S.: "Lo Stato moderno e la sua crisi. Discorso inaugurale per l'anno accademico 1909-1910", in *Annuario*, Università di Pisa, Tipografia Vannucchi, Pisa 1910

Romano S. [1918]: *L'ordinamento giuridico. Studi sul concetto, le fonti e i caratteri del diritto*, Sansoni, Firenze 1967

Ronzani R. o.s.a.: "La lettera "Famuli uestrae pietatis" di Gelasio di Roma all'Imperatore Anastasio I", in *Augustinianum*, vol. LI, n. 2, Istituto Patristico Augustinianum, 2011

Rosen L.: *Law as Culture. An Invitation*, Princeton University Press, Princeton 2006

Rosenthal E. I. J.: *Political Thought in Medieval Islam*, Cambridge University Press, Cambridge 1958

Rosenthal E. I. J.: "Some reflections on the separation of religion and politics in modern Islam", in *Islamic Studies*, vol. III, n. 3, September 1964

Rosenthal F.: "Dawla" (voice), in *The Encyclopaedia of Islam*, vol. II, eds. Bernard Lewis, Charles Pellat, Joseph Franz Schacht, Brill, Leiden 1965

Ross D.: *Violent Democracy*, Cambridge University Press, Cambridge 2004

Rouche M. [1982]: "Break-up and metamorphosis of the West: fifth to seventh centuries", in *The Cambridge Illustrated History of the Middle Ages, 350-950*, vol. I, ed. Robert Fossier, trans. Janet Sondheimer, Cambridge University Press, Cambridge 2003

Roy O. [2005]: *Secularism Confronts Islam*, trans. George Holoch, Columbia University Press, New York 2007

Rubin A.: *Ottoman Rule of Law and the Modern Political Trial. The Yildiz Case*, Syracuse University Press, Syracuse 2018

Rusche G., Kirchheimer O. [1939]: *Punishment and Social Structure*, Transaction Publishers, New Brunswick-London 2009

Rutherford B. K.: *Egypt after Mubarak. Liberalism, Islam, and Democracy in the Arab World*, Princeton University press, Princeton-Woodstock 2008

Ruthven M. [1984]: *Islam in the World*, Oxford University Press, Oxford 2006

Sachedina A.: *Islam and the Challenge of Human Rights*, Oxford University Press, New York 2009

Saeed A.: *Interpreting the Qur'ān. Towards a Contemporary Approach*, Routledge, London-New York 2006

Saeed A.: "The Nature and Purpose of the Community (Ummah) in the Qur'ān", in *The Community of Believers. Christian and Muslim Perspectives*, eds. Lucinda Mosher, David Marshall, Georgetown University Press, Washington 2015

Safran J. M.: *The Second Umayyad Caliphate. The Articulation of Caliphal Legitimacy in al-Andalus*, Harvard University Press, Cambridge-London 2000

Sait S., Lim H.: *Land, law and Islam. Property and human rights in the Muslim world*, vol. I, Zed Books, London 2006

Salim A.: *Challenging the Secular State. The Islamization of Law in Modern Indonesia*, University of Hawai'i Press, Honolulu 2008

Savory R. M.: "The religious environment in the Middle East", in *Business and the Middle East. Threats and Prospects*, eds. Robert A. Kilmarx, Yonah Alexander, Pergamon Press, New York-Oxford-Toronto-Sydney-Paris-Frankfurt 1982

Schacht J. [1950]: *The Origins of Muhammadan Jurisprudence*, Clarendon Press, Oxford 1959

Schacht J. [1955]: "The Schools of Law and Later Developments of Jurisprudence", in *Law in the Middle East*, vol. I, *Origin and Development of Islamic Law*, eds. Majid Khadduri, Herbert J. Liebesny, The Lawbook Exchange, Clark 2009

Schacht J.: *An Introduction to Islamic Law*, Oxford University Press, Oxford 1964

Schauer F.: *The Force of Law*, Harvard University Press, Cambridge 2015

Schepis M. F.: *Colui che ride. Per una ricreazione dello spazio politico*, Franco Angeli, Milan 2011

Schmitt C. [1922]: *Political Theology. Four Chapters on the Concept of Sovereignty*, trans. George Schwab, Massachusetts Institute of Technology, Cambridge 1985

Schmitt C.: *Der Leviathan in der Staatslehre des Thomas Hobbes. Sinn und Fehlschlag eines politischen Symbols*, Hanseatische Verlagsanstalt, Hamburg 1938

Schmitt C. [1950]: *Der Nomos der Erde im Völkerrecht des Jus Publicum Europaeum*, Duncker & Humblot, Berlin 1974

Schöll R., Kroll W. (eds.): *Corpus Juris Civilis*, vol. III, Weidmannsche Buchhandlung, Berlin 1895

Schuon F.: "Islamic art", in *Voices of Islam. Voices of art, beauty, and science*, vol. IV, ed. Vincent J. Cornell, Praeger, Westport-London 2007

Schwöbel C. E.J.: *Global Constitutionalism in International Legal Perspective*, Koninklijke, Leiden 2011

Scolart D.: *L'Islam, il reato, la pena. Dal fiqh alla codificazione del diritto penale*, Istituto per l'Oriente C.A. Nallino, Rome 2013

Scullard H. H. [1935]: *A History of the Roman World, 753 to 146 BC*, Routledge, London-New York 2013

Segovia J. F.: "Schmitt y Álvaro d'Ors. Una inspiración ad modum recipientis", in *Fuego y Raya*, n. 11, December 2016

Shabana A.: *Custom in Islamic Law and Legal Theory. The Development of the Concepts of 'Urf and 'Adah in the Islamic Legal Tradition*, Palgrave Macmillan, New York 2010

Shabbar S.: *Ijtihad and Renewal*, The International Institute of Islamic Thought, London-Washington 2008

Shah N. A.: *Islamic Law and the Law of Armed Conflict. The Conflict in Pakistan*, Routledge, London-New York 2011

Shah T. S., Philpott D.: "The Fall and Rise of Religion in International Relations: History and Theory", in *Religion and International Relations Theory*, ed. Jack Snyder, Columbia University Press, New York 2011

Shahidullah S. M.: *Comparative Criminal Justice Systems. Global and Local Perspectives*, Jones & Bartlett Learning, Burlington 2014

Shaw M.: *Theory of the Global State*, Cambridge University Press, Cambridge 2000

Shaw S. J.; Shaw E. K. [1977]: *History of the Ottoman Empire and Modern Turkey*, vol. II, *Reform, Revolution and Republic. The Rise of Modern Turkey, 1808-1975*, Cambridge University Press, Cambridge 2002

Sherif A. O.: "Generalities on Criminal Procedure under Islamic Sharīʿa", in *Criminal Justice in Islam. Judicial Procedure in the Sharīʿa*, eds. Muhammad Abdel Haleem, Adel Omar Sherif, Kate Daniels, I.B. Tauris, London-New York 2003

Sherwani A. A. K.: *Impact of Islamic Penal Laws on the Traditional Arab Society*, M.D. Publications, New Delhi 1993

Shiner W.: *Proclaiming the Gospel. First-Century Performance of Mark*, Trinity Press International, Harrisburg 2003

Siegman H.: "The state and the individual in Sunni Islam", in *The Muslim World*, vol. LIV, n. 1, 1964

Sindima H. J.: *Major Issues in Islam. The Challenges Within and Without*, Hamilton Books, Lanham-Boulder-New York-Toronto-Plymouth 2018

Singh R. K.: *Textbook on Muslim Law*, Universal Law Publishing, New Delhi 2011

Skotnicki A.: "History of Religion and Crime", in *The Social History of Crime and Punishment in America. An Encyclopedia*, ed. Wilbur R. Miller, SAGE Publications, Thousand Oaks 2012

Slife B. D.: *Time and Psychological Explanation*, State University of New York Press, Albany 1993

Snyder F.: "The Effectiveness of European Community Law: Institutions, Processes, Tools and Techniques", in *The Modern Law Review*, vol. LVI, n. 1, January 1993

Somel S. A.: "Constitution/Constitutional Periods" (voice), in *Encyclopedia of the Ottoman Empire*, The Scarecrow Press, Lanham-Oxford 2003a

Somel S. A.: "Westernization" (voice), in *Historical Dictionary of the Ottoman Empire*, The Scarecrow Press, Lanham-Oxford 2003b

Soper P.: "On the Relation between Form and Substance in Law", in *Ratio Juris*, vol. XX, n. 1, March 2007

Stanley A. P.: *Christian Institutions. Essays on Ecclesiastical Subjects*, Charles Scribner's Sons, New York 1881

Starr-LeBeau G., Lynn K.: "Inquisitions", in *Judging Faith, Punishing Sin. Inquisitions and Consistories in the Early Modern World*, eds. Charles H. Parker, Gretchen Starr-LeBeau, Cambridge University Press, Cambridge 2017

Stein P.: *Legal Evolution. The Story of an Idea*, Cambridge University Press, Cambridge 1980

Stern C. A.: "Justinian: Lieutenant for Christ, Legislator for Christendom", in *Regent University Law Review*, vol. XI, n. 1, 1998–1999

Stone M. [1995]: "Focusing the Law: What Legal Interpretation is Not", in *Wittgenstein and Law*, ed. Dennis Michael Patterson, Ashgate Publishing, Farnham 2004

Strauss J.: "A Constitution for a Multilingual Empire: Translation of the Kanun-i Esasi and Other Official Texts into Minority Languages", in *The First Ottoman Experiment in Democracy*, eds. Christoph Herzog, Malek Sharif, Ergon Verlag, Würzburg 2016

Summers R. S.: "On Giving Legal Form its Due. A Study in Legal Theory", in *Proceedings of the 21st IVR World Congress*, Lund (Sweden), August 12th-17th, 2003, part 2, *Law and Practice*, eds. Svein Eng, Franz Steiner Verlag, Stuttgart 2005

Summers R. S.: *Form and Function in a Legal System. A General Study*, Cambridge University Press, Cambridge 2006

Suter K.: *Global Order and Global Disorder. Globalization and the Nation-State*, Praeger, Westport-London 2003

Swenson D. S. [2005]: *Society, Spirituality, and the Sacred. A Social Scientific Introduction*, University of Toronto Press, Toronto 2009

Tagliapietra A.: "Lo Stato come narrazione", in *Giornale Critico della Storia delle Idee*, year III, n. 5, Mimesis, Milan 2011

Tajuddin H. H. A., Hussin N., Zawawi M., "Restorative justice in Islamic law: application in Malaysian legal history and the criminal justice system", in *Research Handbook on Islamic Law and Society*, ed. Nadirsyah Hosen, Edward Elgar Publishing, Cheltenham-Northampton 2018

Tamanaha B. Z.: "Understanding Legal Pluralism: Past to Present, Local to Global", in *Sydney Law Review*, vol. XXX, Law Book Co. And Sydney Law School, Sydney 2008

Tamanaha B. Z.: *Legal Pluralism Explained. History, Theory, Consequences*, Oxford University Press, Oxford 2021

Teubner G. [1987]: "Introduction to Autopoietic Law", in *Autopoietic Law. A New Approach to Law and Society*, ed. Gunther Teubner, De Gruyter, Berlin-New York 1988

Thomas Aquinas [1265–1274]: *Summa Theologica, Volume II - Part II, First Section*, trans. Fathers of the English Dominican Province [1912], Cosimo Classics, New York 2007

Thomas Aquinas [1265–1274]: *Treatise on Law*, trans. Richard J. Regan, Hackett Publishing Company, Indianapolis-Cambridge 2000

Thompson A. C.: "After Westphalia: Remodeling a Religious Foreign Policy", in *War and religion after Westphalia, 1648–1713*, ed. David Onnekink, Ashgate Publishing, Farnham-Burlington 2009

Tibi B.: "The simultaneity of unsimultaneous: old tribes and imposed Nation-States in the modern Middle East", in *Tribes and States Formation in the Middle East*, eds. Philip Khoury, Joseph Kostiner, University of California Press, Berkeley 1990

Tolkien J. R. R. [1947]: "On Fairy-Stories", in *The Monsters and the Critics and Other Essays*, ed. Christopher Tolkien, Harper Collins, London 1997

Tolley M. C.: *State Constitutionalism in Maryland*, Garland Publishing, New York-London 1992

Torevell D.: *Liturgy and the Beauty of the Unknown. Another Place*, Routledge, London-New York 2007

Trier J.: "Zaun und Mannring", in *Beiträge zur Geschichte der deutschen Sprache und Literatur*, vol. LXVI, Halle 1942

Turner B. S. [1974]: *Max Weber Classic Monographs*, vol. III, *Weber and Islam*, Routledge, New York-London 2006

Tymieniecka A. T.: "Toward the Manifestation of Reason in the Edifice of Life", in *Manifestations of Reason. Life, Historicity, Culture*, part 2, *Phenomenology in the Adriatic Countries*, ed. Anna-Teresa Tymieniecka, Springer Science-Business Media, Dordrecht 1993

Ugilt R.: *Giorgio Agamben. Political Philosophy*, Humanities-Ebook, Penrith 2014

Ullmann W. [1955]: *The Growth of Papal Government in the Middle Ages. A Study in the Ideological Relation of Clerical to Lay Power*, Routledge, London-New York 2010

United States Conference of Catholic Bishops (ed.), *The New American Bible*, ed. United States Conference of Catholic Bishops, Washington 2002

Valkenberg P.: "Una Religio in Rituum Varietate: Religious Pluralism, the Qur'an, and Nicholas of Cusa", in *Nicholas of Cusa and Islam. Polemic and Dialogue in the Late Middle Ages*, eds. Christopher Levy, Rita George-Tvrtković, Donald Duclow, Brill, Leiden-Boston 2014

Valverde M.: ""Time Thickens, Takes on Flesh": Spatiotemporal Dynamics in Law", in *The Expanding Spaces of Law. A Timely Legal Geography*, eds. Irus Braverman, Nicholas Blomley, David Delaney, Alexandre Kedar, Stanford University Press, Stanford 2014

van Klink B., Lembcke O. W.: "A Fuller Understanding of Legal Validity and Soft Law", in *Legal Validity and Soft Law*, eds. Pauline Westerman, Jaap Hage, Stephan Kirste, Anne Ruth Mackor, Springer, Berlin-Heidelberg 2018

van Maarseveen H., van der Tang G.: *Written Constitutions. A Computerized Comparative Study*, Oceana Publications-Sijthoff & Nordhoff, Dobbs Ferry-Alphen aan den Rijn 1978

van Roermund B.: *Legal Thought and Philosophy. What Legal Scholarship is About*, Edward Elgar, Cheltenham-Northampton 2013

Ventura D.: *Giustizia e costituzione in Aristotele*, Franco Angeli, Milan 2009

Vesey-Fitzgerald S. G.: "Nature and Sources of the Sharīʿa", in *Law in the Middle East*, vol. I, *Origin and Development of Islamic Law*, eds. Majid Khadduri, Herbert J. Liebesny, The Lawbook Exchange, Clark 2009

Vikør K. S.: *Between God and the Sultan. A History of Islamic Law*, Oxford University Press, Oxford 2005

Vikør K. S.: "The origins of the sharia", in *The Ashgate Research Companion to Islamic Law*, eds. Rudolph Peters, Peri Bearman, Ashgate, Farnham-Burlington 2014

Vinx L.: *The Guardian of the Constitution. Hans Kelsen and Carl Schmitt on the Limits of Constitutional Law*, Cambridge University Press, Cambridge 2015

Vogel F. E.: *Islamic Law and Legal System. Studies of Saudi Arabia*, Brill, Leiden-Boston-Köln 2000

Vogel F. E.: "Saudi Arabia. Public, Civil, and Individual Shariʿa in Law and Politics", in *Shariʿa Politics. Islamic Law and Society in the Modern World*, ed. Robert W. Hefner, Indiana University Press, Bloomington-Indianapolis 2011

von Grunebaum G. E.: *Modern Islam. The Search for Cultural Identity*, University of California Press, Berkeley-Los Angeles 1962

von Jhering R. [1852–1865]: *Geist des römischen Rechts: auf den verschiedenen Stufen seiner Entwicklung*, Scienta Verlag, Aalen 1933

von Jhering R.: "Friedrich Karl von Savigny", in *Jherings Jahrbücher für die Dogmatik des bürgerlichen Rechts*, vol. V, G. Fischer, Jena 1861

von Savigny F. C., *Vom Beruf unserer Zeit für Gesetzgebung und Rechtswissenschaft*, Mohr und Zimmer, Heidelberg 1814

Walter C.: "Progress in International Organization: A Constitutionalist Reading", in *Progress in International Law*, eds. Russell A. Miller, Rebecca M. Bratspies, Martinus Nijhoff Publishers, Leiden-Boston 2008

Wasti T.: *The Application of Islamic Criminal Law in Pakistan. Sharia in Practice*, Brill, Leiden-Boston 2009

Watt J. A. [1988]: "Spiritual and Temporal Powers", in *The Cambridge History of Medieval Political Thought, c. 350-c. 1450*, ed. J. H. Burns, Cambridge University Press, Cambridge 2007

Watt W. M. [1965]: *A History of Islamic Spain*, Edinburgh University Press, Edinburgh 2001

Weber M. [1919], "Politics as vocation", in *From Max Weber. Essays in sociology*, Routledge London 1970

Weber M. [1921–1922]: *Economy and Society. An Outline of Interpretive Sociology*, eds. Guenther Roth, Klaus Wittich, University of California Press, Berkeley-Los Angeles-London 1978

Weber M. [1922]: *The Theory of Social and Economic Organization*, trans. A. M. Henderson, Talcott Parsons, ed. Talcott Parsons, The Free Press-The Falcon Wing's Press, Glencoe 1964

Weber M. [1922]: "Die drei reinen Typen der legitimen Herrschaft", in *Gesammelte Aufsätze zur Wissenchaftslehre*, Verlag von J. C. B. Mohr (Paul Siebeck), Tübingen 1988

Wehr H. [1952]: "Uṣūl" (voice), in *A Dictionary of Modern Written Arabic*, ed. J. Milton Cowan, Harrassowitz Verlag, Wiesbaden 1979

Weisburd D., Farrington D. P., Gill C.: "What Works in Crime Prevention?", in *What Works in Crime Prevention and Rehabilitation. Lessons from Systematic Reviews*, eds. David Weisburd, David P. Farrington, Charlotte Gill, Springer, New York 2016

Weiss B. G.: *The search for God's law. Islamic jurisprudence in the writings of Sayf al-Din al-Amidi*, University of Utah Press, Salt Lake City 1992

Weiss B. G., *The Spirit of Islamic Law*, University of Georgia Press, Athens-London 1998

Weiss B. G.: "Editor's Introduction" to *Studies in Islamic Legal Theory*, ed. Bernard G. Weiss, Brill, Leiden-Boston-Köln 2002

Wheatley S.: *The Democratic Legitimacy of International Law*, Hart Publishing, Oxford-Portland 2010

White M. J.: *Partisan or Neutral? The Futility of Public Political Theory*, Rowman & Littlefield, Lanham 1997

Whitman J. Q. [2006]: "Comparative Law and Religion", in *The Oxford Handbook of Comparative Law*, eds. Mathias Reimann, Reinhard Zimmermann, Oxford University Press, Oxford 2019

Wilks M. [1963]: *The Problem of Sovereignty in the Later Middle Ages. The Papal Monarchy with Augustinus Triumphus and the Publicists*, Cambridge University Press, Cambridge 2008

Wittgenstein L. [1922]: *Tractatus Logico-Philosophicus*, trans. D. F. Pears, B. F. McGuinness, Routledge, London-New York 2002

Wolff R. P. [1970]: *In Defense of Anarchism*, University of California Press, Berkeley-Los Angeles-London 1998

Wood A. W. [1990]: *Hegel's Ethical Thought*, Cambridge University Press, Cambridge 1995

Wood L.: *Islamic Legal Revival. Reception of European Law and Transformations in Islamic Legal Thought in Egypt, 1875-1952*, Oxford University Press, Oxford 2016

Wood L.: "Legislation as an instrument of Islamic law", in *The Oxford Handbook of Islamic Law*, eds. Anver M. Emon, Rumee Ahmed, Oxford University Press, Oxford 2018

Yılmaz H.: *Caliphate Redefined. The Mystical Turn in Ottoman Political Thought*, Princeton University Press, Princeton 2018

Zakaria R.: *Muhammad and the Quran*, Penguin Books, London 1991

Zakariyah L.: *Legal Maxims in Islamic Criminal Law. Theory and Applications*, Brill, Leiden-Boston 2015

Zarcone P. F.: "Turchia, minoranze e laicità", in *Studi Interculturali*, eds. Mario Faraone, Gianni Ferracuti, n. 3, Mediterrànea-Centro di Studi Interculturali, Trieste 2013

Ziccardi Capaldo G.: *The Pillars of Global Law*, Ashgate, Aldershot-Burlington 2008

Zifcak S.: "Western and Islamic Conceptions of the Rule of Law", in *Islam Beyond Conflict. Indonesian Islam and Western Political Theory*, eds. Azyumardi Azra, Wayne Hudson, Ashgate Publishing, Aldershot-Burlington 2008

Zubaida S.: *Law and Power in the Islamic World*, I.B. Tauris, New York 2003

Index[1]

[1] Note: Page numbers followed by 'n' refer to notes.

F. L. Ramaioli, *Juridical Perspectives between Islam and the West*, Global Issues, https://doi.org/10.1007/978-3-031-37844-7

V

W

Z

Printed by Printforce, the Netherlands